The Complete HOME HANDYWOMAN

The Complete HOME HANDYWOMAN

Edited by
Dawn Marsden
and Alan Morgan

cork wall + ceiling tiles

Book Club Associates
London

CREATIVE PROJECTS

DECORATING YOUR HOME

This edition
published 1977 by
Book Club Associates
by arrangement with
Octopus Books
59 Grosvenor Street
London W1
© 1977 Octopus Books Limited

ISBN 0 7064 0533 1

Printed in Great Britain

RESTORATION AND REPAIR

HOME MAINTENANCE

PLANNING YOUR LIGHTING

The organisation of your home lighting can be a satisfying and interesting project. Too many of us take lighting for granted and suffer endless frustration because its arrangement is badly thought out.

In general, lighting plays two important roles. Firstly, it is functional – that is, light is directed to where we want it when we want it – and secondly it is decorative, creating atmosphere and mood.

In order to achieve maximum flexibility in your lighting plan plenty of points are desirable, but even without these, modern methods of distribution can help you to compensate for this deficiency.

ASSESSING YOUR LIGHTING REQUIREMENTS

Start by drawing up a scale plan of your rooms (or even of the whole house) on squared paper. A scale of 1:50 (or ¼ in. to 1 ft) is large enough. Onto this plan, draw your furniture

and mark those areas where jobs which need close visual attention take place. Obviously it is to these places that maximum light must be directed. Mark, too, stairways, steps and other danger areas which require good, clear lighting in the interests of safety. It should become quickly apparent that in some rooms it will be desirable and necessary to change the position of the light source. Living rooms, for example, usually function as both sitting rooms and activity rooms, involving a whole range of activities from quiet chatting and watching television to reading,

sewing, playing games and cutting out dress patterns on the floor. In other rooms, like the kitchen, flexibility of function is less necessary. When you are working there, you probably need all the working surfaces brightly illuminated most of the time, so the need to change lighting is less vital. The same principle applies to bathrooms and lavatories.

Bedrooms serve all sorts of function so they, too, require careful lighting. When in bed, easily controlled bedside lights are probably all that is required, but when dressing or making up it is

1. Lighting should be angled
to avoid glare
2. Downlighters provide bright
direct lighting in the kitchen
3. Concealed lighting makes an
attractive feature of this
alcove
4. Subtle lighting creates a
restful effect
5. Well-positioned table lamps
give a soft, diffused light
6. A rise and fall fitting is
ideal for dual purpose areas

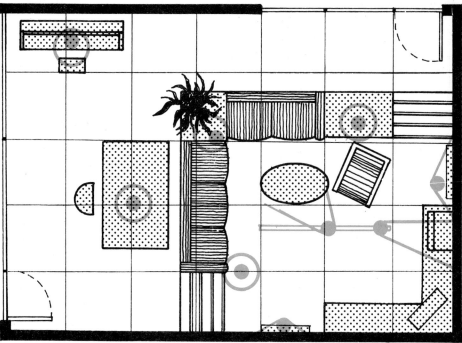

desirable – though not always flatter-ing – to see in brilliant detail every aspect of your clothes and make-up.

PLANNING YOUR LIGHTING

Glare is the enemy of comfortable lighting. With the best possible inten-tions you may arrange for a strong reading light or spotlight to shine directly on the book you are reading or the seam you are sewing and so create an extreme contrast between the gleam-ing page and the dark around the book. This will cause harmful glare and can be obviated by arranging for the light to fall not only on the page but also to spill onto the areas beyond the book (1). White paper is an efficient reflector and harsh contrast may need to be modified by lessening the strength of the source of light.

Terrible glare can be caused by having the source of light too near a work sur-face. If you raise the light so that it con-tinues to shine down on your work but is above your eye level, you will be much more comfortable than if the source is on a level with your eye.

Lighting from a single point is rarely satisfactory for most living rooms. The single light source in the centre of the ceiling really is not adequate in any but the smallest of rooms, except as a tem-porary measure. The extremities of a room of any size will not be adequately illuminated unless the bulb is so powerful that it causes glare and costs more to run than several smaller but strategically placed bulbs. So the case for multi-point, low-level lighting in sitting rooms, carefully placed and adjustable, is slowly building up. As too, will be your plan on squared paper, marked with areas of different func-tion, danger spots and other points which will require special solutions in each case.

Draw a plan of your room to scale, showing the position of each piece of furniture. You can then plan the distribution and type of lighting according to the different function it

must fulfil. Firstly decide where light is needed, then whether direct or indirect light is required and finally which fit-tings will best fulfil the different requirements.

SITING YOUR LIGHTS

Having made your plan, there is a simple way of testing your findings – simple and safe if you are careful. Fix a bulb-holder on a piece of lighting flex long enough to enable you to carry a bulb to any corner of any of your rooms at any height. On the other end, fix a plug. It is a good idea to fit the bulb-holder with a lampshade frame to pro-tect the bulb and to use as a handle when the bulb gets hot. Assemble a series of bulbs – 25 to 150 watts – and you are ready to carry out your pre-liminary lighting trials. You can simu-late the effects of shades by improvising with coloured papers (available from any art shop) and a small stapling machine. By using papers of different colours, you can roughly assess the colour of the shades that will eventually give the best effects. Remember to test the effect of completely opaque shades – ones which will not show light through them but merely direct it downwards or upwards. Armed with your little piece of apparatus you can take light into any corner of the room and test the effect of illumination on any group of furniture or in any posi-tion in which you require special concentration of light either for close work or else for decorative purposes. This will only allow you to assess the

effect of one bulb in one area at one time, but even so the method will open your eyes to the excitement of lights in positions you may not previously have considered. You can, of course, im-prove the efficacy of this simple system by connecting several wires and bulb holders to the plug, achieving more complex effects. But do be careful of improvised electrical apparatus. This survey will help you to identify any potential danger spots. Do not forget the outside of your house – there may be steps and paths which should be lit for safety reasons.

TYPES OF ELECTRIC LIGHT

Having marked on your plan where the light should come from and where it should be directed in each room and tested the positions as above, you can now work out what sort of light fittings you require. Basically there are two types of electric light in general domestic use – tungsten and fluor-escent. The first is the ordinary fila-ment light bulb, the second the familiar tubular light. (Filament lamps are made in tube form for situations in which a less powerful light than a fluorescent tube of the same size would provide.) The different effects of tungsten and fluorescent lighting on colours and textures make the planning of a light-

2

4

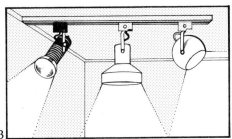

3

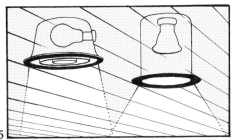

5

*Working areas should have
well controlled local lighting*

ing scheme an important part of colour scheming. You should always check paint and material colours in the light that is most frequently going to illuminate them. Most tungsten lighting simulates the warmth of day lighting, while fluorescent tubes tend to emphasise the blue end of the spectrum and debase warm colours, so that a room which looks warm and welcoming by day may appear cold and hostile when illuminated by fluorescent lighting. This characteristic can be compensated for by choosing tubes which are coloured to provide the best rendering of warm colours.

DISTRIBUTION OF LIGHT

Having decided where you want your sources of light and where you wish to direct light, you have to decide what sort of fittings are most suitable and how it is most practical to supply them with current. The distribution of your lighting is an important aspect. Basically a light fitting may cast light up, down, sideways or in a combination of directions. It may be used for direct lighting or for a more indirect effect such as a downward light direction creating soft pools of light.

If you decide to retain a central ceiling rose, there are many ways of using it. If the rose is above a dining table you can use a rise and fall fitting which allows you to lower the lamp below eye level while you are eating and raise it to provide more general lighting

when the table is not in use. You can make use of the rose to supply a light above a table not centrally placed by fixing a hook in the ceiling over the table and using an extended flex (2) to lower the lamp to the right level.

Surface-mounted tracks can be supplied from the ceiling rose (3). These enable you to use a collection of spots on the track to illuminate different areas of the room. Take care that the sum of the wattage of the bulbs you use does not exceed a safe maximum. Ask the advice of your electricity showroom or a competent electrician. The same track fitting can be used for a pendant light that is moveable – say from over a work or dining table to an easy chair.

Spots, whether mounted individually or on a track can be angled to cast a direct light, or to bounce off a wall, giving an indirect light. Take care to avoid beams from spots crossing at eye level, or causing glare in other positions. Permanent ceiling lights can be in the form of surface-mounted fittings with opal glass or similar diffused shades. These provide glare-free general lighting and are suitable for hallways, lavatories and bathrooms.

Uplighters are simple metal boxes decoratively finished and are excellent to provide illumination from below (4). They are particularly effective when deployed beneath groups of plants, which provide interesting shadow patterns on walls and ceilings. A low

wattage bulb is all that is required. Down-lighters recessed into the ceiling require professional fitting but do provide excellent general lighting (5). Standard lamps are extremely convenient allowing great flexibility of movement. Modern versions are elegant and unobtrusive.

The variety of table lamps is infinite and modern shades provide gentle diffused light that is easy on the eye and can be positioned exactly. They blend well with all furnishing styles.

Pictures can be lighted either by conventional shaded lights or by spots. The former really require wiring which provides an outlet above the picture, but can be used with round plastic flex neatly stapled to the wall and led to a skirting board mounted socket.

The advent of dimmers has done much for home lighting. Mounted in place of conventional switches, they allow an infinite range of lighting intensity which contributes to variety of lighting mood. They are inexpensive and easy to fit. Unfortunately they do not work with fluorescent tubes.

Basic principles of lighting are simple. Never site lights so that the beams cross your eye line; direct light at the object to be illuminated. Flat overall lighting tends to harden the edges of everything, showing up furnishings past their prime, while carefully arranged pools of light have the reverse effect. Fluorescent tubes and tungsten strip lights are excellent to illuminate curtains mounted behind pelmets or for low level kitchen lighting under wall mounted fitments. Good planning produces good lighting results. Safety first – take care always to check that the total wattage of the fittings you plan to use from one source of supply does not exceed the current supplied there.

HANGING PICTURES

Some lucky people appear to have the knack of being able to group the right pictures on the right wall with stupendous effect. In fact it is not *just* a knack; their effects reveal that they have persevered and worked things out properly.

Nor is it a matter of sheer taste – you need to plan before you start hanging. Too often we are prompted to hang a picture for the wrong reasons. It is really not a good idea to put a picture in a particular spot simply because there is already a hook there or to cover up a tear in the wallpaper, a damp mark or a dirty wall. Some people think that because they have a picture rail, they should hang things from it. This is usually guaranteed to give just the wrong effect. Picture rails are useful and will carry considerable weights, but pictures hung from them really do not look right if you are planning a modern scheme.

If you have picture rails they can be used as a decorative feature or they can be removed – they can rarely be used successfully nowadays for their original function.

If you want to be successful with pictures do not do anything without thought. Pictures are used to enhance your surroundings, to bring interest to dull walls and to make interesting focal points – even to split up one area from another.

Most people want to know how to mix pictures, to know what goes with what. The simple answer is that most pictures

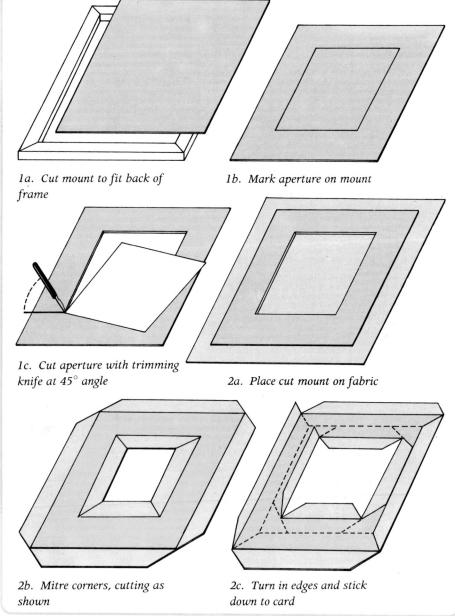

1a. Cut mount to fit back of frame

1b. Mark aperture on mount

1c. Cut aperture with trimming knife at 45° angle

2a. Place cut mount on fabric

2b. Mitre corners, cutting as shown

2c. Turn in edges and stick down to card

3

1. Coloured card mounts
2. Fabric covered mounts
3. Pictures grouped around a piece of furniture
4. A massed collection of pictures where similarity of subject, mount and frame lends unity
5. Pictures formally arranged on horizontal lines
6. A clever arrangement to complement a staircase
7. Perfect symmetry enhances a collection of pictures

5

6

4

7

can be made to go with one another, even when the style, shape and design are entirely different. Mixtures work well and can look most exciting. But if you have a few small pictures, try to introduce a kind of conformity. It is time and care that are needed, but remember that pictures hang for a long time, and care taken from the start is worth the effort.

UNIFORMITY

You can paint all the picture frames you intend to hang in one group in one matching colour, or use identical mounts. This is not a difficult job. It involves measuring coloured paper, cloth – plain, or with a small busy pattern – felt, wallpaper, etc., cutting it out to size and assembling as in the diagrams (1, 2). Alternatively consider hanging a group of pictures which all have identical frames. Another idea is to use the same subject or techniques as a theme; all the paintings could be in oils, water-colours or pastels, or could be pictures depicting only sailing or heads. There is no end to the variety of choice. Single pictures are best when they are large and imposing, or when you have a particular spot in which one looks right, such as a small return wall, or a position in which it relates to other objects and will not look incongruous.

A combination of grouped pictures and objects such as wall plaques, mounted butterflies, heads in relief, provides an interesting mixture in dimension as well as size to give eye-catching depth to your arrangement.

GROUPING PICTURES TOGETHER

When you have collected your pictures, how do you group them? It is actually simple. The easiest method is to lay your group on the floor below the wall on which you intend to hang them. If hanging a group above a piece of furniture, mark the position of the piece on the floor (with string) and on the wall with chalk and then move it away temporarily. Move your group of pictures around on the floor until you get a rough idea of how you think they look best. Then move away from them and look down at your arrangement from a distance, visualising how they will look on the wall. If your arrangement looks attractive, it is ready to hang. If it does not then move the pictures around until you are satisfied.

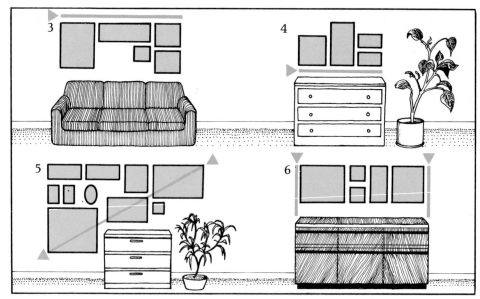

Another good idea is to draw your pictures on a piece of paper in your chosen order. If you use squared paper, you can be almost mathematically correct.

Look at the diagrams before you begin to hang your pictures. You will see that groups work best when they either hang from an imaginary top line (3), or move up from an imaginary bottom line (4). A third alternative is to draw a diagonal line from one side to the other as shown (5). This helps to achieve visual harmony. Total symmetry is rarely needed, though this can be effective.

WHERE TO HANG PICTURES?

The answer is anywhere, as long as they look right. There are simple pitfalls but it is worth stressing that pictures should always relate to something else – other decorative objects and furniture – so that your interior scheme blends well together. If, for example, you have a chest standing in the middle of one empty wall, then plan to hang your pictures above, around or beside it (6). The final decision is yours, but there are always places where pictures look best. Fireplaces, especially if you have an imposing one, always take kindly to a group hung around them. The fireplace is a focal point from the start, so why not emphasize it even more?

Hang pictures above a sofa, using its limits to encompass your arrangements. Do not hang them too low, otherwise people will bang their heads against your favourite Picasso.

On stairways, run pictures up one by one, following the rise of the stairs, or use the whole wall as a gallery. This

really brings a dreary stairway to life. Pictures always look good in groups, even if they are themselves not distinguished when hanging alone.

Learn by your mistakes – after all, everyone makes them – and do not become disheartened. A hole in the wall in the wrong place is not the end of the world. It can be easily rectified, even if it is rather large and flaky, caused by your lack of experience with an electric drill.

HANGING YOUR PICTURES

Draw your chosen line, whether at the top, bottom, or a diagonal, on the wall so that it can be easily rubbed out later. The next step is to measure up. Establish a centre point; not the centre of your entire wall, unless you are covering it with pictures, but the centre of your group of pictures. Mark this with a dot. If this sounds fussy to you, think of the irritation caused by seeing a wall of pictures hung askew, and persevere! Patience is of the utmost importance, as odd angles will later ruin the whole effect. Using your guide line on the wall, carefully transfer your arrangement from the floor in the formation in which you have decided to hang them. Use a spirit level to ensure the pictures are straight.

Choose the right tools, considering the type of wall you have to tackle. Make sure that you can bang nails or picture hooks into it with a hammer. You may have to use an electric drill for a solid cement wall, using Rawlplugs or filler to hold screws, or toggle bolts for a hollow wall. Avoid wires and pipes, check for uprights, and remember that for most walls all you need is a nail and a simple picture hook.

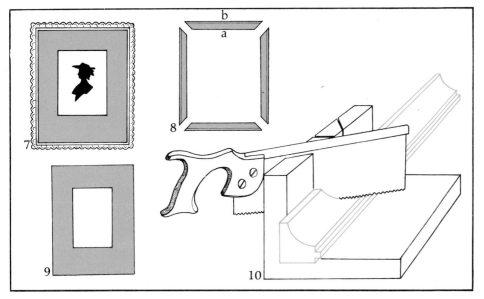

FRAMING PICTURES

If you have a collection of pictures it is very useful to be able to frame them yourself. Not only does this save money, but also, as you become practised in handling the materials, you will be able to achieve a more individual effect.

The main duty of a frame is to enhance its contents and generally this depends on two things: the colour and style of the subject matter and the colour scheme and decor of the room and background where your picture will hang. To frame a modern abstract poster with a costly Baroque moulding and to hang it against a background of wildly patterned wallpaper would be committing a framing sacrilege. Leave complicated mouldings to the experts.

Materials needed To make the small traditional frame shown here (7) you will need to stock up on the following equipment, most of which is available from art shops and do-it-yourself suppliers.

Frame moulding: this is still sold by the foot (30 cm.) and is available from specialist art shops and framers (some also provide a mitre cutting service for a small extra charge). A plain inexpensive moulding like a Hogarth is a good one to start with. Always buy slightly more than you need (8), determining the length of moulding by the required measurement of the *inside* rebate (a) although it is ordered by the length of the *outside* moulding (b) so allow for some wastage here.

Mitre block: pick one that is capable of cutting frames at least 5 cm. wide by 4·5 cm. deep ($2 \times 1\frac{3}{4}$ in.).

Glass: most glass merchants will cut this to size and polish the edges which makes it far easier to handle. Non-reflective picture glass is good on water-colours and prints but will blur the cross hatching and fine lines of an engraving.

You will also need: a corner clamp, a sharp plane, a picture saw (30·5 cm./ 12 in.), a bradawl for boring holes, a good supply of synthetic resin glue, picture pins, a small hammer, fine abrasive paper, backing card cut to same size as glass, gummed brown paper, screw eyes and picture wire to hang up.

Mounts These days a lot of frames do without mounts but for fine art postcards, small drawings and engravings, a coloured cover mount adds drama and improves proportions too. Cover mounts can be of fabrics like silk, hessian and velvet but a card mount is the easiest to start with. For this you will need a mount cutting knife, sharp blades and a metal rule. The trick here is to cut into the card making a bevelled edge of 45 degrees (see page 10, diagram 1); it takes some practice so try out on some odd pieces first of all. It works better, visually speaking, to have a broader base on your cover mount than the top and sides (9) especially if the picture is an 'upright' one. Normally the base is one third more than the top and sides. The choice of colour usually depends on the predominant colour in your picture; this can however tie you down decorwise. If you want a picture to go with everything pick a neutral colour: slate grey, chocolate brown and warm beige teamed with a narrow gold or silver moulding will always look elegant and blend anywhere. It is well worth experimenting with coloured paper

beforehand to test the effect.

Ready-made cover mounts can be bought from some art shops but these are usually the same width all the way round. Alternatively, if your photograph or print is slightly the worse for wear, professional dry-mounting on to coloured card will improve the condition. Look in the Yellow Pages for firms supplying this service; you will also have to supply your own card.

Marking the moulding With a pencil, mark off four lengths on the rebate side allowing 3 mm. ($\frac{1}{8}$ in.) on each length for trimming. (This allowance enables a picture to fit snugly into the completed frame. If the measurements were accurate at this stage the finished frame would be too small). Check that each of the four lengths is the correct shape and size.

Cutting the mitre Place the four lengths on the mitre block, rebate side positioned as shown in diagram. Saw carefully at 45 degrees (10) taking care to keep the cut as straight as possible. Plane over sawn cuts to the exact length. Try each length for fit, corner to corner, and finally try all four together.

Sticking For small frames a synthetic resin glue is adequate. Working in pairs, wrap a piece of tissue paper round each length to protect it before placing it in the corner clamp. Cover each end with glue and stick corner to corner, making two right angles. When the glue has set, stick the two remaining corners.

Assembly Working from the back of the frame, fit in the glass which should be clean and fingerprint free. Next, position your cover mount and then your print. If the print is valuable it should not be stuck down, otherwise use a blob of starch-based adhesive in each corner. Finally lay the backing card on top, lightly tap in picture pins and seal the gap all round with gummed paper.

To hang up Using a bradawl make holes, about one-third of the length from the top of the frame, on either side of frame (this prevents delicate wood from splitting). Fix the screw eyes and check these are level or the picture will not hang properly. Attach picture wire or nylon binding (*not* string, as this can rot away) to the screw eyes and hang. Fix wallplates if you want the picture to hang flush against the wall.

COLLECTIONS

One of the simplest ways of making your surroundings more beautiful, and amusing yourself at the same time, is by collecting things. Anyone can be a collector: you do not have to be rich and collections will fit just as happily into a bedsitter as into a stately home.

WHAT CAN YOU COLLECT?

It is all a question of what you want to give up, in terms of money, time and space. If your budget is limited, stick to something readily available at a low cost – and remember to tell all your friends what you are collecting! If time is limited, again you will want objects which come easily to hand. If it is space that is short, keep your collections to small-sized objects.

There is no need to justify the reasoning behind your collection to anybody and do not be put off by the very knowledgeable. A colour can provide the theme for a collection, but you could also start one around a certain area (everything you can find relating to the history of a particular town, for example) or around a certain time or event in your life, such as a holiday. Collections are for everybody, not just the connoisseurs of antiques.

DISPLAYING YOUR COLLECTIONS

You will want to put your collections on display: that is part of the fun of the game. And a collection certainly adds a uniquely personal note to any room.

Study your collection carefully. Are the objects rather difficult to clean? For example model galleons complete with rigging, or dolls dressed in minutely detailed costumes? Collections of this nature are best stored under cover. Model-making shops sell plastic domes, or you could hunt around junk shops for old glass domes. Alternatively you could house your collection in a small wall cabinet behind glass doors.

Some collections, for example those which combine various quite diverse items, are ideally displayed on open shelving units. There are no set rules for the best way to arrange your objects, you must just move them around until they look right – it is largely a question

of visual weight. Use your objects to break up a row of books, but make sure they all vary in shape and size. Do not start with a tall object and finish with the smallest causing your eye just to slope from one side to the other; mix up the different 'weights' for a good effect. Sometimes your objects will look better divided up into small groups, for example three items in one, four in another and so on. Try using one object to link a lot of smaller items together; stand a group of small bottles on a tile, for example.

Sometimes you can display your collections on a table top, grouping them together just as you would pictures. Beware if you have children or pets – even adults can accidentally sweep an object off a low table.

Some objects look best mounted on a board; heavier objects can be glued with an epoxy resin.

Many small objects need narrow shelving or display cases to look their best; they are lost in the average shelving system. Make your own wall-hung cases, for example hanging a divided wooden cutlery tray on the wall, with mirror plates.

It is worth remembering that many of the things we use everyday are in fact an attractive collection – providing they are displayed in a pleasing manner. A row of mugs, for example, can be stacked neatly along a shelf, or displayed on cup-hooks. Storage jars look lovely in an open box wall unit. Children can be encouraged to keep their toys tidy by making a collection.

6

7

1. A collection of souvenirs makes a colourful display
2. Unusual objects composed to form a striking feature
3. Formal grouping is appropriate for these souvenir mugs
4. Objects in everyday use may still be displayed to good effect
5. Small objects may be attractively arranged on a tabletop
6. An unusual background, tailor made to show off a collection
7. Everyday items may be effectively combined into a collection

15

STORAGE

'A place for everything and everything in its place' – this must be a maxim familiar to everyone. And although it sounds rather tediously tidy, it should at least be the aim of your storage strategy throughout the house. Whether you can get the family (and yourself) to conform to your carefully worked out systems is another matter! It is helpful first of all to consider the ways in which storage can be provided around the home for your family, for the solutions to storage problems are many and varied. The list below starts with the simplest ideas, which are usually the cheapest, and then goes on to list more expensive and sophisticated solutions.

FREE-STANDING BOXES

Systems based on a simple box unit can be surprisingly useful. You can use boxes on their ends as bins, where they will cope with general clutter, being particularly good for toys. Or you can turn boxes on their sides to make open storage compartments; these can be stacked to make fairly extensive storage system into which you can 'pigeon-hole' your belongings. At a most basic level, your boxes can be made of cardboard, and you can glean them from the supermarket. You will find that these are fairly strong, and you can smarten them up with oddments of paint left over from decorating projects, or you can face them with wallpaper. For a more durable finish, bind their vulnerable edges with cloth sticky tape. Alternatively, you can make your own more substantial boxes from 19 or

2   *Fit special joint into predrilled hole in panel of Cubebox*
2a   *Fix second panel at right angles*
2b   *Slide back panel into grooves in side panels*

25 mm. ($\frac{3}{4}$ or 1 in.) chipboard (which is the cheapest), 25 mm. (1 in.) timber, or 12 mm. ($\frac{1}{2}$ in.) plywood. Joints can be simply glued (use a woodworking p.v.a. adhesive) and nailed (1). You can add internal partitions if you wish. Size can be adapted according to what is going to be stored inside. Open boxes allow their contents to be easily seen and found but will look untidy if the contents are untidy! Those more proficient in woodworking can add doors or upward-opening flaps to their boxes with hinges.

HOOKS

Do not neglect the homely hook. A plentiful supply of hooks throughout the home enables you to keep the place tidier, as a lot of general clutter can be removed from the floor onto the wall. The simplest hooks to fix are screw-in cup-hooks which can be fixed to sides of cupboards, doors, undersides of shelves and so on. If you want to screw a cup-hook directly into a wall, you will have to drill a hole, and plug it first. In addition to kitchen utensils and crockery, large cup-hooks will cope with light-weight clothing, shoe bags and so on, being particularly useful for children's rooms. Sometimes it is easier to attach a row of hooks to a wooden batten, simply screwing them in, and then to attach the batten to the wall with screws and plugs. When screwing in a cup-hook, remember that you will have to make a starting hole with a gimlet or a bradawl.

Coat-hooks, single or double, attached with separate screws, are larger and sturdier than cup-hooks and will cope with heavy-duty hanging, providing they are firmly fixed into wood, or into a wall-plug.

For suspending a series of small objects such as kitchen utensils or tools, you could fix up a sheet of perforated hardboard and then use the special pegboard hooks which fit into the holes to provide hanging points wherever you want them.

In a garage, or attic, a rod with 'S' shaped meat hooks suspended on it can be useful for hanging up bulky items.

SHELVES

No home can seem to have too many shelves; they are useful in just about every room in the house. Their most obvious use is for books, but you can often store a wide variety of small items on them, at times when you cannot afford to install a cupboard. A set of sturdy shelves fitted with upright dividers at intervals will form open pigeon holes which can even be used for smaller articles of clothing – jumpers, socks and so on. Much cheaper than drawers!

Materials for shelving Shelves can be made of 19 mm. chipboard, with supports every 90 cm. (35 in.), or every 50 cm. (20 in.) if you are going to load your shelves with heavy books. Chipboard is the cheapest material you can buy for shelving (though some enterprising people have been able to salvage free old wood from skips – floorboards, for example – which, when sanded clean and smooth, has been perfectly serviceable). You will need to finish the edges of your chipboard with iron-on veneer strips; the board can be left its natural colour and varnished, or stained and varnished, or painted. You can also buy from d-i-y shops a wide range of veneered chipboards for shelving, including boards with a plain white melamine finish. These come in various standard widths, including 15 cm., 30·5 cm., and 46 cm. Alternative shelving materials include 12 mm. plywood, and 19 mm. blockboard. You can use natural timber 19 mm. thick for light items, and 25 mm. for heavy objects.

When making plans for shelving, always start by finding out the standard depths offered in the various materials at your local store; then you can tailor your design accordingly. Make a note of the price at the same time, so that you know what you are letting yourself in for! D-i-y shops will often cut your timber or board to size for you, but materials bought this way are more expensive than if you buy them uncut from a trade timber yard and cut them to size yourself.

4. Screw shelf bracket support firmly into wall ensuring that slats align horizontally
4a. Locate position for bracket in support
4b. Secure hooks in place by pressing bracket firmly in and down
(Harrison adjustable shelving)

Supporting and fixing shelves There are several different ways of supporting your shelves. The easiest and the quickest involves no wall fixing. You simply stack your shelves on suitable supports – you can use piled-up bricks, concrete blocks sold for screen-walling, breeze blocks, or solid blocks of timber (3). This type of shelving is informal and can easily be dismantled if you think you will be wanting to move the arrangement to another room, or another house or flat, in a short while. However, it is not recommended to a height of more than four shelves, as taller structures lack stability.

To fix shelving to the wall, you can use simple angle brackets; they do not look too ugly, if brackets and shelving are all painted to match the same colour as the wall. Alternatively, you can use one of the many systems available which have slotted uprights, into which you clip brackets in a choice of various sizes to suit your shelving. Your brackets should extend to within 12 mm. ($\frac{1}{2}$ in.) of the edge of your shelf. These brackets need not be unsightly if you paint shelf, wall and bracket the same colour when the job is finished. Decide on the position of your shelf, taking care to avoid places where people may bump their heads or walk into the shelf. Two brackets will support a shelf about 106 cm. (3 ft 6 in.) long; anything longer may need three brackets. You may also need extra brackets to support heavy loads. Your brackets should be positioned from 15–20 cm. (6–8 in.) in from each end of the shelf. Hold your shelf up to the wall and get it level using a spirit level. Draw a guiding line on the wall, underneath the shelf. Work out and mark the position of the first bracket. Put the shelf to one side and hold the bracket up to the wall to mark the position of the necessary fixings. Take down the bracket and using a No. 8 masonry bit in your drill, make the necessary holes in the wall. Plug with No. 8 plugs, then screw in your first bracket using No. 8 screws which should be long enough to penetrate through the plaster into the brickwork by about 20–25 mm. ($\frac{3}{4}$–1 in.).

Fix the other bracket in the same way (you can first replace the shelf if you wish just to check that it is perfectly level).

Rest your shelf on the two fixed brackets, and mark the position of the screw fixings to be made into the shelf.

Shelving for all situations
1. Low shelving under a
window provides useful storage
as well as an extra surface
2. Use shelves in a bathroom
for an improvised dressing
table
3. An alcove becomes an
attractive feature
4. Shelves in a bed-sitting
room give space for storage as
well as a working area
(Harrison adjustable shelving) 4

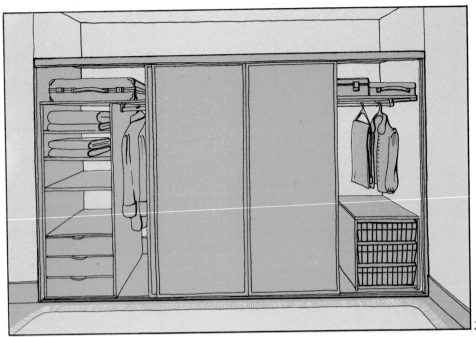

No. 6 screws should suffice, and these should penetrate 12 mm. ($\frac{1}{2}$ in.) into the shelf. Drill pilot holes, replace shelf and screw down firmly.

Alcoves Many people like to fix shelves into an alcove, and this looks particularly nice on either side of a chimney breast, making use of space which would be wasted otherwise. You can use one of the systems with slotted uprights and brackets, as described above; or you can simply attach wooden wall bearers to each side of your recess, making them the depth of your shelves. For long shelves, it is a good idea to fix a bearer along the back wall as well (1). Short wooden battens 25 mm. (1 in.) square are fine for small shelves; larger heavier shelves will need battens 50 by 25 mm. (2 by 1 in.). It is essential to get both bearers and shelves absolutely level.

For adjustable alcove shelving, you can screw vertical boards to either side of your recess, allowing them to rest on the skirting. To these, you can attach slotted metal 'bookcase' strip, which takes small metal brackets for your shelves.

Sizes and spacing for shelves What sizes should you make your shelves? Suitable thicknesses for structural strength have already been mentioned. The depth will be governed by the standard depths available, but it is worth noting that in rooms where space is very tight, even narrow shelving only 10 cm. (4 in.) deep can earn its keep – in a kitchen, for example, for single rows of mugs and jars, or in a bathroom, for bottles, jars and so on. A very wide shelf can often be incorporated into a system at table-top or work-top height, to provide a working surface (see two-way rooms, page 24). If your shelving is not adjustable you will need to work out your shelf spac-

ing very carefully: once fixed, it is very tedious to have to alter shelf positions. Measure carefully the things you will be wanting to store. If, for example, you are putting up shelves for books, you will make the best use of space if you place your shelves at differing distances apart, rather than deciding on one uniform distance. For example, a 19 cm. ($7\frac{1}{2}$ in.) gap will cope nicely with paperbacks, but you will also need shelves at intervals of say 23 cm. (9 in.) and 26 cm. (10 in.) for larger books, plus at least one very widely spaced shelf, say 31 cm. (12 in.) to take large illustrated volumes, etc. It is worth spending a bit of time on this initial basic planning. You should also remember that shelves higher than you can reach will only be useful for objects not in constant use.

BUILT-IN UNITS

Shelving, of course, constitutes the simplest form of built-in unit. Add a door, sliding or hinged, to a set of shelves in an alcove, and you have a built-in cupboard of the simplest kind, as the walls of your home form the cupboard back and sides. There are also many wardrobe systems which make use of this idea: the manufacturer merely provides the wardrobe fronts and internal fittings, including hanging rails, and you use your own wall as the cupboard back, thus saving on cost. End pieces are available for these systems, where they are not being built into a recess. Manufacturers also provide 'scribing' pieces with which you can fill the gap between the top of your system and the ceiling, and any

gaps at the sides, to give your arrangement a fully 'built-in' look. Many of these systems are designed specifically for do-it-yourself installation; clear instructions are provided and fixings are simple. However, it is usually helpful to have two people on the job, as it may be necessary to handle fairly large panels.

If you do not feel confident enough to fit doors to built-in units, it is worth remembering that roller blinds (very simple to fix) can often make an adequate and cheaper substitute.

Built-in units are not economical unless you plan to live in a home for some while – you will not be able to take them with you when you move, although you may be able to raise your selling price as a result of your built-in units.

Planning the insides of units Whether you build in your storage units yourself from scratch (for this you have to be a pretty experienced handywoman), or make use of one of the many kits for built-ins, commission or wheedle someone to do the whole job for you, one thing is vitally important: to arrange the dimensions of and the space inside the units in the best possible way for efficient storage (2). For hanging clothes, for example, you will need a minimum depth inside cupboards of about 55 cm. (22 in.); each adult person requires around 1 metre ($3\frac{1}{4}$ ft) of hanging rail, but you can save space here by providing some 'two tier' rails for storing shorter hanging items (e.g. shirts, folded trousers etc.) one above another. For a drawer, shelf or sliding tray, you should plan for a minimum depth of 30 cm. (12 in.) from front to back. One or two deep drawers, say 30 cm. (12 in.) deep (i.e. top to bottom) and over, are useful for thick bulky items and should be placed low down as they will be heavy when full. Shallower drawers and trays will be more useful for smaller, constantly used items such as cutlery in the kitchen, or underwear in the bedroom. Very often the space inside cupboard doors can be utilised (3) with racks for small packets and jars, or (in the kitchen) for saucepan lids. The above points are merely for general guidance. It is essential when planning, or adapting, all built-in systems to list and measure what you have to store, and then to proceed from there. Only in this way will you get the most out of storage systems which as they are being tailor-made, might just as well be tailor-made to your exact wishes!

FREE-STANDING STORAGE FURNITURE

Under this heading can be included all the conventional types of storage furniture available either new from furniture shops or second-hand from junk shops or auctions: wardrobes, chests of drawers, small cupboards, chests, dressers and so on. It is worth remembering that old-fashioned furniture is often built on more generous dimensions than modern counterparts, therefore you will be able to get more inside it. Of course, it will also take up more room and you should always take a note of your room dimensions with you when shopping second-hand to avoid lumbering yourself with something that will not fit the space available. A second-hand piece will often need a bit of handywork to make full use of its storage potential – a cavernous interior may be best divided up with shelves or racks, or sometimes it is possible to adapt furniture by splitting it into two, or taking off legs, or a similar piece of surgery.

One of the most attractive of modern storage furniture ideas is to provide a wall of storage in a living room, to include drop-down flaps for writing letters and serving drinks and meals, space for the television and record player, as well as storage for books, hobby gear, records, sewing materials and display space for precious possessions. These units are often sold in a choice of widths so that you can select a combination to fill one wall within a

few centimetres. This type of furniture, however, is not cheap. You can achieve an equally tailored look by combining whitewood base units, suitably painted or stained, with shelving or small wall cupboards.

Although the trend in recent years has been to knock down walls for an open-plan style of living, there are sometimes occasions when you would prefer in fact to divide a room: to make sleeping areas for two children, perhaps, or to divide off a dining section from a cooking area. Remember that a storage unit, whether free-standing or built-in will form an effective divider, at the same time earning the space it takes up by providing storage, which can be accessible from both sides of the unit, should this be convenient.

The manufacturers of several types of veneered chipboards offer leaflets containing furniture designs, including simple storage units, based on the standard sizes of their boards. They have developed simple fixing devices for joining the boards where necessary, thus enabling you to build your own storage at a reasonable cost with minimum professional know-how.

3

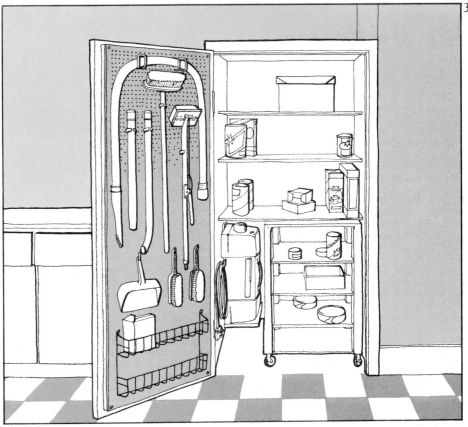

1

MAKING THE MOST OF EVERY SPACE

If the space seems to be running out in your home, it is worth considering some of the less obvious places to fit additional storage, which can sometimes be combined within another piece of furniture. *Coffee-tables*, for example, can also be cubes which will hold magazines and general livingroom clutter. A space in a bay could be used for a *window-seat* which also doubles up as a cupboard. A *chest* anywhere in the house (e.g. at the end of a bed) can be a useful seat and at the same offer storage under its lift-up lid. *Shelves and cupboards* can sometimes be fitted over doorways. The *space under the stairs* will hold far more of your possessions if you divide it up with shelves, hooks and so forth and fix up a light. *Headboards* can be combined with storage for books, etc. *Bed bases*, or the space underneath beds, can be pressed into service – use sliding trays or boxes under the beds you already have, or buy one of the many beds available with storage provided in the base.

And do not forget the farther-flung outposts of your home: as long as an area is clean and dry, it can perform a useful storage duty. You could put up shelves in the garage, for example, or equip your attic with handy hooks and racks, or build some cupboards in your outside loo! You will also find it helpful to read about two-way rooms and leisure centres.

2

1. An attractive arrangement
of shelving and storage units
2. A well-planned kitchen
utilizes every space
3. Specially constructed units
fit into the angle of a room
4. Simple boxes can serve
multiple purposes
5. Basic units can be built up
to fit individual requirements

TWO-WAY ROOMS

Today, in their homes, everybody is short of space. Large houses are expensive to buy, to maintain and to heat; and usually rate demands are exorbitant. So families are tending not to move as the children get bigger and more numerous. The spaces remain the same, but the demands on them are greater. Consequently the same spaces now have to do extra work; one way is to re-organise your rooms so that one room will cater for several different functions.

PLANNING
Careful planning is the basis of success for dual-purpose rooms. Analyse your requirements carefully. It is helpful to make a list of everything you expect your room to do; then try and arrange these functions in the order most important to you. You may well have to make some compromises and it is a good thing to have your priorities sorted out. Thus the list for a teenage bed-sitter might read: 1) sleeping, 2) studying, 3) reading, 4) playing records, 5) entertaining – although the occupier might put (2) further down the list than his or her parents would! Draw up a rough room plan and note on it all vital measurements; include the way doors open, the position and height of windows, position of lighting and power points, etc. Draw out your plan on squared paper using a scale of 1:20 (or $\frac{1}{2}$ in. to 1 ft). Then working to the same scale, cut out the shapes of all the bits of furniture which you hope to use in your two-way room. This enables you to move them around on your plan until you are satisfied that you have found the best position.

FURNITURE
The exact nature of your furniture will obviously be determined by the functions you expect your room to perform. However the need for plenty of storage is a common denominator in most two-way rooms. First thing to do is to make a list of all the things you will want to store, noting particularly large and bulky items that may need special provision

Whatever storage system you choose, make sure you utilise the inside of cupboards to maximum efficiency, with racks, hooks, adjustable shelves and so on. A cheaper alternative to a fully-fitted system is open shelving, or open box 'pigeon-hole' units.

You may well find that you need to provide a sturdy horizontal surface to be used for eating, studying, hobbies and so on. There are various ways of doing this. You can fix a wide shelf on a folding bracket to fold away when not in use; this is useful when space is tight. Or you can bridge the gap over two chests of drawers – cheapest way to do this is to use whitewood or second-hand chests and an inexpensive flush door. Or you can fix a wide shelf at a height of around 700–750 mm. (27–30 in.) . . . this can simply be fixed to the wall with cantilevered brackets, or could be part of a wall-shelving system. Make sure your fixings are really firm as your shelf will be doing the duty of a table, bearing considerable weight. Remember that low-level furniture and fitments make a room seem larger (always a primary consideration for two-way rooms). Moving about is easier too, because however thin you are, you take up less space at ankle/knee level than at hip/shoulder! Sometimes removing or cutting down the legs of furniture you have already can work wonders. Floor cushions, low-level tables and beds all add to the illusion of space. So do wall-mounted fitments; a wide shelf will seem to take up less room than a table or desk with bulky underframe (see suggestions above).

The way you arrange your furniture is important: the plan you made to start off with will be helpful here. You must have room to open doors and drawers; make sure that there is no possibility of two doors, or a door and a drawer, jamming together when they are both open. You will also need to leave room to move around.

The position of your window is important: it is pleasant to sit near a window for reading or working, but on the whole beds are best sited away from windows, because of the problems of downdraughts from cold glass.

DECORATION
Two-way rooms tend to be busy rooms, with a lot going on in a smallish space. Plan your colour schemes as a background to these activities. Restful schemes, built up from neutrals or tone-on-tone of the same basic colour, are ideal; you can always add bright touches of colour with small accessories at a later date. Avoid excessive use of pattern; it is likely that your floor and wall areas will be 'broken up' by furniture and fitments; a busy pattern will just add to the confusion. You can use mirrors to increase apparent space. If you place a mirror at right angles to a surface where it meets a wall or a cupboard, you will seem to double the surface; if you can position these mirrors so that you do not see your own reflection, the illusion will be complete. In the same way, if you place a mirror on the wall at right angles to a window, you can throw light into a darkish room.

FLOORS
Two-way rooms are hard-worked rooms: remember this when you select your floorings. Choose a flooring that wears well and is easy to clean, in a medium colour that will disguise dirt and staining. Suggested floorings: hard-wearing cords and carpet tiles, vinyl sheet or tiles, sealed cork tiles, or (more expensive) plain pile carpet (either Wilton or good-quality tufted).

LIGHTING AND HEATING
Preferably, a dual-purpose room should be able to be heated independently from the rest of the house when necessary, so that the room can be used when the central heating has been turned off (e.g. late at night). Plan therefore for a small heater of some kind, whether electric or gas. Oil heaters may create a problem as they give off considerable water vapour which may cause condensation.

Good lighting is important and you will need several different fittings to cope with multi-functions. All working surfaces, reading areas, etc., will need extra light: adjustable spotlights are probably the easiest fittings to install. As in all rooms, you will need one light that turns on at the door, but you may be able to find a more suitable position for this than the conventional middle-of-the-room. The flex can be lengthened and then the fitting hung from a hook in the ceiling at a convenient point . . . low over a table, for example, or beside a bed. A dimmer switch may be used for varying mood.

DUAL-PURPOSE IDEAS
Different families will need different

kinds of two-way rooms, but here are some dual-purpose ideas which you may find useful.

Bedroom/sitting room The 'bed-sitter' of course is the classic two-way room known to students the world over. But the idea is useful for homes too, for older children, elderly relatives, au-pair girls and so on. Lessons can be learned from the neatly planned bed-sitters in modern hostels; for example, simple sliding doors could conceal a whole wall, with space behind them for storage, washbasin/sink and even a cooking ring and grill. When planning these rooms, you should remember that the 'sitting' part may include sitting alone or sitting chatting with several people. Typical other activities may also include listening to the radio or records, reading, studying and so on. If you are including cooking facilities in your bed-sitter, you will also need to make provision for washing up; try and keep these facilities away from the main seating/sleeping area. Some sort of screen is ideal; this could be a set of open shelves which could be used to house the china or glass etc., when the washing up is finished. Alternatively, a simple bead screen, roller blind or curtain could be very easily fitted.

In tall rooms in old houses it may be possible to build a platform, which can be used with a ladder as a high level bed. Then the space underneath can be utilised for a storage or study area, or for eating. You will need to leave headroom of about 198 cm. (6 ft 6 in.). This idea is also useful for bedroom/workrooms and hall/home offices.

The bed is inevitably going to be used for sitting/lounging during the day. Make sure your bed is of a suitable type for sitting on – for example a firm-edge divan. If you can provide daytime storage for bedclothes, so much the better. Some beds now have 'built-in' storage in the base. Or it may be possible to provide boxes that slide underneath the bed (these could be old drawers fitted with castors). A continental quilt is easy to bundle away. Then the bed can be transformed with a tailored cover or gay spread and the pillows disguised as cushions with suitable covers (sew together two tea towels: they are just the right shape). If the bed is along the wall, its width will be too deep for comfortable sitting, and you should provide plenty of cushions: firm foam bolsters or wedges

are ideal. Alternatively, dispense with a conventional bed and use foam blocks of a suitable density for seating by day and sleeping by night.

Bedroom/workrooms Bedrooms are ideal places to catch up on reading, studying, model-making, or whatever needs peace and quiet away from the television. Good heating will be essential and you will see a need for some sort of working surface plus extra storage.

Hall/home office If you have a large hall, there is often a corner that can be comfortably equipped as an 'office', with telephone, storage space and writing surface. In small halls, it may even be possible to use the space under the stairs.

Dining room/hobby room or study Dining rooms used only at mealtimes are ideal for studying or pursuing a hobby. You must, however, provide a generous working surface with good lighting where books, papers, stamp collections, etc., can be left undisturbed, otherwise constant demands to clear up for the next meal are bound to provoke family tension.

Kitchen/second living room If you have a largish kitchen, you may have room for a couple of comfortable chairs and this makes a very pleasant place to

chat. Add a good light and you have a place to sew or read. Add a radio/cassette player and you have an extra place to listen to music, or radio talks/plays.

Spare bedroom/TV room If you are tired of the way the television dominates family life, you can banish it to a spare bedroom. Adequate heating is essential. A convertible sofa with extra floor cushions is ideal. When the room is needed as a bedroom, you can convert the sofa into a bed.

LEISURE CENTRES
Never have there been so many opportunities for relaxation and amusement within the home as there is today. How best then to arrange your home so that you and your family can not only go about your everyday life with maximum efficiency and minimum frustration, but can also relax and enjoy yourselves with maximum pleasure?

PLANNING YOUR ROOM
The first thing to do is to analyse your own particular requirements. It could be helpful to make a list of everything that each member of the family likes doing in his/her spare time and at the same time list the equipment plus facilities needed. Decide whether these

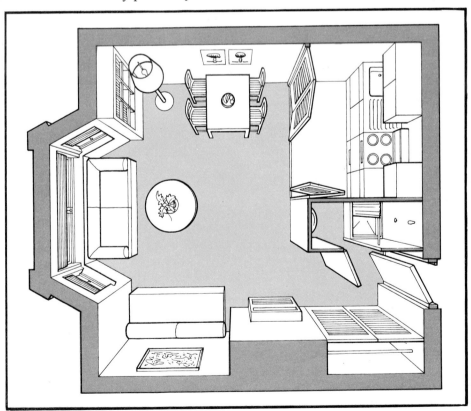

Suggested layout for a bed-sitting room. The kitchen area is screened off from the rest of the room with sliding doors,

and a shower unit is housed in the cupboard space. The bed converts into a second sofa.

activities are communal (watching television) or solitary (model-making). Some activities that only involve one person (e.g. sewing) nevertheless do not preclude the presence of other people in a room. Other activities are best done on your own – e.g. woodworking, using noisy power tools. Following on from this is the decision as to which parts of the house/flat are going to be used by which people for these activities. You may well find the answer in dual-purpose rooms (see above). Bedrooms in particular can be

and so on are more stimulating: good for rooms where movement is going on, e.g. playrooms (see pages 76–77 for colour-scheming notes).

HEATING AND LIGHTING

With adequate heating, many rooms can be used part-time for leisure activities. Extension leads are available for using electric fires or other equipment (e.g. power tools) far away from a power point. As always, ensure you have the right lighting for the tasks in hand.

pressed into service for use as day-time and early-evening leisure centres. It may also be possible to use a workbench in the garage; to kit out the attic; to equip the basement as a games room, or to add on a 'den' in the garden. There are certain basic points which you may find helpful to remember when planning for the leisure activities of your family.

COLOUR SCHEMES

Remember that colours create moods: blues, greys, neutrals and some greens tend to produce a restful effect, which makes a pleasing background for reading, or creative hobbies. Reds, oranges

'WORK' TOPS

When planning for activities at a table (sewing, typing, etc.) try and think about the chair and the work surface as one unit. Choose a chair which enables the user to sit upright, in an alert working position, with good support for the spine. The chair should allow the feet to rest naturally on the floor, whilst providing support for the underneath part of the thigh. When sitting naturally in a comfortable position, it should be possible to rest the forearms on the table top. If the user is going to type, the keyboard of the typewriter should be at hand height when elbows are bent. Similarly, if she is going to

sew by machine, the platform level should be at hand height. Work/table tops may have to be lower to accommodate this. And always make sure that there is comfortable knee room underneath. For notes on provision of work tops, see two-way rooms, above.

COMFORTABLE SEATING

For reading, listening to music, chatting, snoozing, watching television and so on, a wide variety of chairs and sofas are available, with prices ranging from a few pounds for a floor cushion, to hundreds of pounds for a leather-covered chesterfield. What you choose is mainly a matter of personal preference, influenced by your budget. Do you like to curl up? – make sure your chairs are big enough. Do you like to put your feet up? – consider footstools or reclining chairs. Do you like to rest your head? – you will need high-back chairs or sofas. Do you like to have a lot of snack meals, or endless cups of tea and coffee? – you will need shelves or low tables to cope with the crockery. Do you like sitting on the floor, in an ultra-casual fashion? – maybe floor cushions would suit you, and your family/friends. Have you got young children or pets? – choose chairs with removable covers.

PLANNING FOR PASTIMES
Watching television Many families spend a lot of time watching television but very little time thinking about the best way to plan their room accordingly. Which room is the best room for the television? Ideally, the set should go in a small separate sitting room, leaving your main living room free for undistracted family gatherings, entertaining friends and so on. Make sure that everybody has somewhere comfortable to sit where all can see. Most televisions are positioned far too low for comfortable viewing, including those sited on their manufacturer's stand. If possible, get your set up onto the wall on a special bracket sold for the purpose. Then you can swivel it to any angle, and you can arrange the wiring so that nobody trips over it. Ergonomic experts recommend a height of not less than 122 cm. (4 ft) from the floor to base of receiver. Never watch television in a room which is completely dark: this can strain your eyes. Have at least one low wattage fitting turned on and positioned so that it is not reflected in your screen.

Stereo equipment How best to accommodate your assortment of turntables, speakers, deck and so on? A good adjustable shelving system is the answer, having many advantages. You can get each piece of equipment at exactly the right level for your height and its function. The record-playing deck will not be affected by vibrations from springy floors. Some systems allow you to conceal the wiring in their wall channels and also to fix up useful lighting at strategic points, so that you can see what you are doing when you go to change a record.

What is the best position for the speakers? As always, the arrangement that *you* like best is the 'right' solution, but here are some guiding points. In general speakers should be on a level with the head of the listener. Imagine an equilateral triangle, with the speakers pointing inwards at either end of the base line. The listening head should then be at the apex (top) of the triangle. This is to say that the distance between each speaker, and the distance between each speaker and the listening head should be the same. As a further guide, within a room 4·5 m. by 3 m. (15 by 10 ft), the speakers should be positioned 2 m. to 2·5 m. (6 to 8 ft) apart. A simple test to see if you are sitting in the right position: you are sitting too close if the sound seems to move from speaker to speaker every time you turn your head, but you are too far away if you can detect no stereo effect at all.

Rooms for stereo listening should not have large areas of bare floor or wall, as it spoils the tone of the music. Walls can be broken up with shelf units, hangings, wall fabrics (e.g. paper backed hessians) and so on. Floors should be covered by carpeting plus underfelt.

It is a good idea to seal round the sides and tops of doors with self-adhesive foam-strip draught excluder to cut down on noise transmission to other parts of the house. Doors can be sound-proofed with a facing of 13 mm. (½ in.) blockboard on either side.

Home movies, slides, etc. If you like showing your slides and films, arrange your room so that you have easily accessible storage for the necessary equipment. Otherwise viewing sessions will not be as frequent as they could be, due to the inconvenience caused. Remember that lots of people may like to come and watch at the same time, and you may need extra seating. Stacking or folding chairs are useful, or small floor cushions for the kids.

5

1. A low storage unit separates the study from the sitting area in this room. The desk area is positioned to make maximum use of the natural light which may be supplemented by carefully positioned lamps. The continuous line of shelving and pictures create unity between the areas.
2. A high level platform bed leaves ample space beneath to be used as a living room. The spot lights may be adjusted according to which level of the room is being used.
3. Three purposes are combined

in this well-planned room. Low shelving provides a partial divider between the sitting and dining areas which may be further screened by a curtain. Beyond the dining area, a half wall, using open shelving, leads into the kitchen.
4. This kitchen has become a family leisure centre through the addition of a comfortable seating unit.
5. Cleverly shaped dividing walls and well-planned lighting make three self-contained units within this large room.

FLOORING

Floors take the hardest beating of any surface in the home. In the long run, economies on quality in floor coverings prove to be false economies. Always buy the best you can afford, unless you are aiming specifically for short-term or very light wear. You can save money by laying floor-coverings yourself but it is best to confine yourself to products designed specifically for 'do-it-yourself' laying. These include various kinds of tiles, such as vinyl, cork and ceramic; cushioned- and felt-backed vinyl sheet, carpet tiles and foam-backed carpeting. In most cases the manufacturer will provide clear and detailed instructions on or with the pack: read them, taking particular note of recommended adhesives. Particularly easy to lay are tiles with peel-off self-adhesive backings; you will find these in both vinyl and carpet ranges. Some types of quality floorings, e.g. woven (Wilton and Axminster) carpets, are not suitable for a woman to install on her own, as they require power stretching. Spending extra money on professional laying is recommended, to preserve the value of your initial and substantial investment.

TESTING BASIC FLOOR CONDITION

Before laying any kind of floor covering, make a thorough examination of your floor as it stands. To look attractive and to wear well, all floor coverings require a sub-floor which is sound, dry and level.

Damp test If you suspect that your floor could be damp, you should check up before going any further. New floor coverings will eventually be ruined by damp; and you will not be able to make good fixings with adhesives or sticky tapes. As a test, place a small piece of glass on the surface of the floor and seal around its edges with adhesive tape. A day or so later, peel away the tape and look under the surface of the glass. If you see traces of any moisture, this has been coming up through the floor. You should consult a firm which specializes in curing damp for a professional remedy. You should also call in the experts if you find any signs of

woodworm or dry rot in your floor. Remedies for more minor floor problems are within your own capabilities.

Squeaky floorboards You can usually cure the trouble by screwing through to the joist in two places for a tight fit. Be careful to avoid any pipes and wiring running underneath. Sometimes it helps to lubricate board edges with talcum powder.

Gaps between floorboards Gaps should be filled with a papier mâché mixture which you can make from torn squares of newspaper and glue size. Add wood stain if the filling will be on show. For really large gaps, you can cut fillets of wood and glue them into place with woodworking p.v.a. adhesive. Sand or plane flush to the surface of the floor.

Gaps at the skirting These could be causing nasty draughts, besides looking unsightly. You may be able to fill them with a proprietary filler, or you can nail quadrant moulding around the room, fixing it to the floor boards with panel pins at 150 mm. (6 in.) intervals (1). You should mitre the corners.

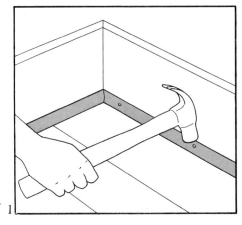

DEALING WITH UNEVEN FLOORS

Uneven floorboards These can be sanded smooth to provide the level sub-floor essential for satisfactory top coverings. Look in the Yellow Pages of your phone directory under Hire Contractors to find a firm which will hire you a floor drum-sanding machine. This will have a vacuum attachment to catch the dust. Before you start, nail down loose boards and punch down the heads of protruding nails. Scrape away old paint and varnish, and sweep the floor.

First sanding should be in diagonal strips, working at an angle of 45 degrees to the boards. Use a coarse abrasive (supplied with the machine) and overlap each strip by around

80 mm. (3 in.). Second sanding is in the direction of boards, and this time use a finer abrasive. For borders and corners use a small edge sander.

Sanded floors can be sealed with polyurethane varnish (shiny or matt) or painted with a floor paint or polyurethane paint for a low-cost floor finish. This type of floor tends to be rather noisy in use and can be chilly in winter. However, you can add rugs for softness and warmth. As an alternative to sanding level you can lay hardboard over uneven floorboards (see below).

It is also possible to paint old sheet floor coverings, e.g. lino, with special floor paints, sometimes called lino paints. Follow the directions on the can, and be sure to start painting in the corner furthest away from the door to avoid 'painting yourself in'. This is a tip to remember when you are varnishing wooden floors, too.

Uneven solid floors These may be made of concrete or quarry tiles. You can level them youself quite simply using a self-levelling screed which you can buy in powder form from a hardware shop or a builders' merchant. Mix with water in an old bucket according to directions on pack. Sweep floor thoroughly and wash with detergent solution. Prime non-absorbent surfaces, e.g. quarry tiles, with adhesive primer. Dampen absorbent surfaces, e.g. concrete, with water. Apply mix with steel trowel to thickness recommended by manufacturer. You only need to level out roughly; after a while, the screed finds its own level. On concrete, screed will dry in a couple of hours; on quarry tiles, screed takes up to 24 hours to dry.

Laying hardboard Hardboard makes a good underlay for vinyl sheet and tiles, cork tiles and so on, providing the smooth under-surface vital for their good appearance and hard wear. Hardboard for underlays should be fixed mesh side up. Hardboard laid smooth side up can be used without any further covering as an inexpensive flooring; it should be sealed with a clear varnish.

Hardboard is sold in standard sheets 2440 by 1220 mm. (8 by 4 ft), but small sheets 1220 mm. (4 ft) square and 1220 mm. by 610 mm. (4 by 2 ft) are also available and you will find these easier to handle. To prevent possible buckling through expansion after laying, you must 'condition' your hardboard before it is laid. Spread water with a large paint brush on the mesh side of the sheets, using about $\frac{1}{2}$ litre ($\frac{3}{4}$ pint) to a sheet 1220 mm. (4 ft) square. Leave the boards to dry, stacked flat, back to back for 48 hours in the room where they are to be laid. Once they are down the boards will tend to shrink rather than expand, but this movement will be restrained by the fixings. You should start laying your sheets from the centre of the room outwards: instructions for finding the centre are given under floor tiling, see page 31. Fix hardboard to wooden floors with annular nails, 19 mm. ($\frac{3}{4}$ in.) long. These have ridges around their shanks to stop them from working loose. Nail the first sheet through the centre first, and then put in other nails at 150–250 mm. (6–10 in.) intervals, working outwards all the time. Fix around the edges with nails spaced about 150 mm. (6 in.) apart. Lay the rest of your sheets in the order shown (2), staggering joins as indicated (do not stagger joins if hardboard is to be used as final flooring). Start nailing at the edge nearest to the previous board

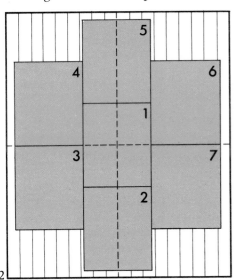

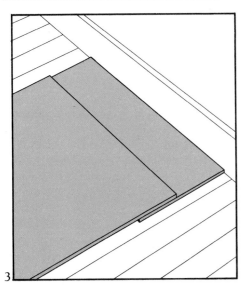

and work outwards across the sheet. Punch all nail heads slightly below the surface of the boards.

When you get to the outermost sheets, do not nail along the side nearest to the edge of the room; you can then slide a suitable sized off-cut underneath to trim to size for margins. Firstly, scribe the contours of your skirting onto the offcut, using a pencil and a small wooden block. Using a sharp knife, cut away the waste along your scribed line. Slide the scribed sheet under the edge of its adjoining sheet and run a sharp trimming knife along the edge where the two boards overlap to get an exact joint (3).

PLANNING

Before ordering any kind of flooring you will need to measure up your room to work out how much you need. If you find estimating difficult take your rough plan with you to your retailer. Vinyl and carpet tile leaflets often incorporate a special squared planning grid so that you can plan out special lay-outs.

WOOD FLOORS

Various types of wooden floor in strips or blocks are available for home laying. Fixing instructions vary with the different products: many of these floors are simple enough for the handywoman to tackle, particularly felt-backed self-adhesive wood blocks. In all cases use fixing methods and adhesives as recommended by the manufacturers in their usually very detailed and comprehensive instruction leaflets. If in any doubt, ask to see a specimen fixing leaflet before purchasing flooring to see whether you think you can tackle the job.

SHEET VINYL

Sheet vinyl has largely taken the place of the old-fashioned lino. It is available in a wide range of qualities at a range of prices to suit most budgets. Very few plain colours are available; marbled designs are about the nearest you will come to a 'plain' colour. The range of patterns however is good, including excellent ceramic tile imitations and photographic imitation mattings, brick and so on. More expensive, but kinder to the feet, are the felt- and cushion-backed sheet vinyls, which insulate against heat loss and noise.

Sheet vinyl comes in various widths; 1·8 metres is very common. Some

ranges are now available in extra wide width of 3·6 m, and these offer you a seam-free finish. But they are heavy and cumbersome to lay; two strong people are needed merely to lift the rolls.

Laying sheet vinyl This is at its best when laid over hardboard. An underlay of grey paper felt will also improve the finish and deaden noise transmission, particularly when the sheet covering is of poorer quality and thin. Remove any traces of old sheet coverings, including old nails, tacks, etc., before re-surfacing with new sheet vinyl. New sheet vinyl can be laid over old tiles provided they are firmly fixed; re-stick any loose tiles.

Measure up your room, and plan your floor. If you are laying straight onto floorboards (which preferably should be sanded smooth) you should try to lay your sheet vinyl at right angles to the boards. Obviously this point does not matter if you are putting down a hardboard underlay. You should allow for cutting into walls which are not square and allow about 150 mm. (6 in.) extra on each length of vinyl for trimming at the ends. In a large room, more than one length may be needed to cover the width: in this case, remember to allow for pattern matching, taking into account the size of the pattern repeat.

You will find sheet vinyls easier to lay if they are warm; so stand rolls on end in the room where they are to be laid the day before laying. Try and keep the room warm while you are working. Tools needed are minimal; many sheet vinyls can be cut with a large pair of household scissors, but you will also need a sharp knife for trimming into skirtings, and a long straight-edge, preferably metal, for seam trimming in larger rooms.

Measure and cut the first length from the roll, allowing for about 75 mm. (3 in.) overlap at the wall at each end. Lay this length along the wall, with a slight overlap up the skirting. Lay the second length to overlap the first length by about 15 mm. ($\frac{1}{2}$ in.). Cover the whole floor in this manner, overlapping each length as described. You will find that the manufacturer has made an allowance for this overlap when printing the pattern. Then leave the flooring to settle for as long as you can before trimming. Vinyl tends to shrink back after laying.

To trim the edges you will need first

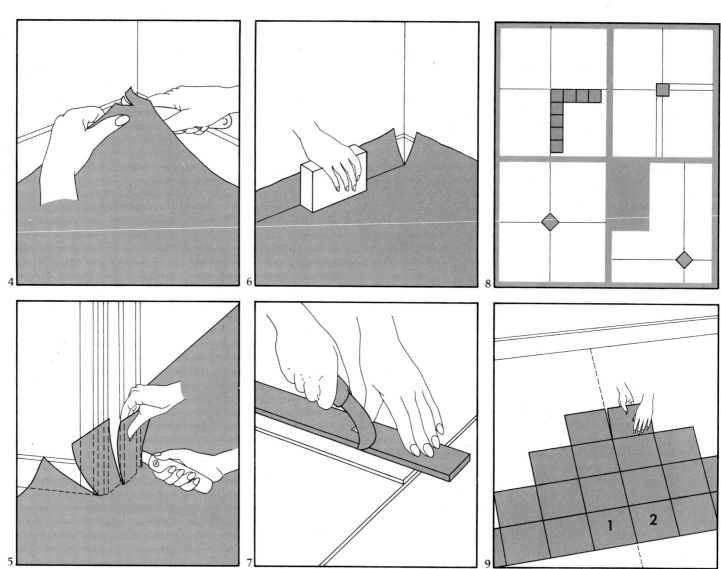

to make 'release cuts' to allow the vinyl to lie snugly up against the skirting board for trimming. At each corner snip away a triangular piece of material, taking away a little at a time, until flooring fits exactly (4). Also make cuts at all external corners, such as chimney breasts, fireplace surrounds and so on. And you will have to make release cuts before trimming around every angle of a door architrave (5). When all release cuts have been made, run a small wooden block around the room to provide a crease line ready for trimming (6). Cut along this line with a sharp knife, using hooked blade. Tear away cut strip when it becomes too cumbersome to manage.

In bathrooms, cloakrooms etc. you may need to trim around the base of a lavatory or wash basin pedestal. Do this before you trim in at the skirtings. Simply make one long release cut right to the front of the pedestal. Then, working outwards from this, make a series of release cuts all round the base of the pedestal until your floor covering lies flat enough for you to crease and

trim as described for trimming at skirtings.

To trim the seams, take the straight-edge and lay it along the overlapping thicknesses of vinyl sheet. Cut through both thicknesses in one operation with a sharp knife, and remove cut-away strips (7). In this way, you ensure edges fit perfectly together.

Vinyl sheet looks its best when stuck down. Use the adhesive which the makers specify for the job. Make sure your sub-floor is perfectly clean before laying. Turn back each trimmed length halfway. Spread floor with adhesive, turn down flooring and press into place. Repeat the process for the other half. It helps if you can then drag a smooth weighty object over the floor, for example, a bag of sand.

Or if you wish, you can merely stick the sheet down at seams and edges. You can use double-sided wide adhesive tape for this.

TILES

There are various types of tiles available for d-i-y laying, including vinyls

(plain and mottled colours, and tile patterns), cork (must be well sealed), ceramic (see notes below) and carpet. Tiles have various advantages over sheet coverings. The materials involved are in easy-to-handle units; you require no brute strength for lugging around heavy rolls. If you make a mistake trimming one tile, it is easy to arrange a replacement. When the floor is down, if a tile gets spoilt or stained in some way it is relatively easy to replace it. However tile floorings take longer to lay and you will not get the same effect of an 'unbroken' expanse of flooring as you do with sheet. On the other hand, you will find that the neat lines of the tile edges disguise dirt and staining to some extent.

Laying tiles Certain basic laying rules apply to all types of tiles. With the exception of some loose-lay carpet tiles, all tiles must be stuck down to a sound, dry, level sub-floor (see notes at beginning on getting your floor level, curing damp, etc.). Always use the adhesive recommended by the manufacturer. Indeed it is a good idea

8. Positioning first tile in centre cross. Variations show:
retaining right angle if central lines are adjusted
diagonal laying
laying in a passage

1. Vinyl sheet is colourful and practical
2. Choose carpet for its textural pattern as well as for colour

to open a pack of tiles in the flooring shop and read the laying instructions before you get home, so that you can get the right adhesive in the quantities recommended. Some vinyl and carpet tiles are self-adhesive; they have peel-off paper backings, which make them particularly quick and easy to lay.

All tile floors need careful planning. On squared paper, draw a plan of your room, each square representing one tile of the size you have chosen. This will help you to work out how many tiles you need. If you are planning any special effects (stripes, borders, one-colour inserts) a grid is essential. Many tile makers include a handy grid in their catalogues.

All tiles are laid from the centre of the room outward; to find the centre — measure and mark the centre points of the two opposite shorter walls (disregard fireplaces, alcoves, etc.). Drive in a nail at one centre point and fix a length of string firmly to it, long enough to stretch the width of the room. Rub chalk along the string until you reach the opposite centre point. Then stretch

your string tightly and fix at other centre point with second nail. Lift up the string and allow it to snap back onto the floor to give you a chalked line. Mark the mid-point of this line and place a tile on the floor with one side exactly on the chalk line and with a corner touching the centre point. Place another tile against the first tile on the other side of the chalk line and also touching the centre point. Draw a pencil line along the side of these two tiles to run through the centre point. This will give you a pencil line crossing the chalk at right angles. Re-position your chalked string and nails so that you can snap a second chalk line over the pencil line to form a cross with its centre in the middle of the room.

Place one tile so that one corner of it is exactly in the centre cross (8). Lay a row of tiles in all four directions, without any adhesive. Adjust your chalk guidelines if necessary, to give you a suitable size of cut tile at each border. When you have worked out your tile positions to your satisfaction, you can

start to apply your adhesive, carefully following the manufacturer's instructions. Start from where your lines cross at the centre. Lay the first two tiles side by side in right angles of the chalk lines. Work outwards on either side to form a pyramid pattern (9), spreading more adhesive as you need it. Cover about one square metre (10 sq. ft) of the floor at a time; use a separate spreader. Butt the edges of tiles together and position them precisely. Do not try and slide them. Always wipe off any adhesive on the face of the tiles immediately before it has a chance to set; use a damp cloth for this.

To cut borders (10): place a whole tile over the last complete tile laid (A). Place another tile (B) on top of tile (A), but pushed against the skirting. Draw a line across tile (A) using the tile (B) as a guide. Lift away tile (A) and cut it along marked line. The part of tile (A) that was uncovered will then fit neatly into the gap.

To finish your tiles, use the product (sealer or polish) recommended by the manufacturer. Cork for example, may be pre-finished, or you may have to apply two to three coats of polyurethane seal.

Ceramic tiles Some ranges of ceramic tiles are intended for d-i-y laying, having spacer lugs for easy fixing (11). Do not attempt to lay any other form of ceramic tile yourself. For d-i-y ceramic floor tiles, use adhesive recommended by the tile maker. Ensure that concrete floors are clean, dry and level. Timber floors will need an overlay of 9 mm. plywood fastened with countersunk screws at 300 mm. (12 in.) intervals. Old vinyl or lino tiles must be removed

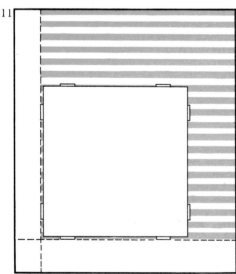

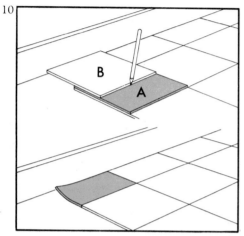

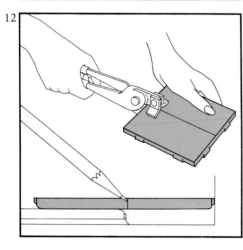

and the underfloor made clean and smooth. You should find the centre of your room, and plan out your tiles as described in the general notes on tile laying, above. Spread the adhesive and tile the floor in sections, working from the centre as already described. It is important to fix ceramic floor tiles with a solid backing of adhesive as any 'hollowness' will make them liable to damage by impact and pressure, e.g. chair legs. It is a good idea to coat the back of each tile with adhesive as well as the floor. To cut tiles for the border, use the overlapping techniques described above. Score the face of the tile with a tile cutter (12) which can then be used to break the tile cleanly. You will have to grout (i.e. fill the gaps) between your tiles when the adhesive has set and your tiles are rigid. Use a proprietary grouting mix as recommended by the manufacturer. Work into joints with sponge, and then sponge off any surplus on tile faces.

CARPETS

Carpets offer a soft, comfortable, appealing surface, but this of course makes them more vulnerable to wear and staining than other forms of 'hard' floor surfacing. You must buy carpeting of a suitable quality for the wear it is going to get; living rooms need better (and usually more expensive) qualities than bedrooms. You will find that British carpets are labelled with a quality grade which tells you whether a particular carpet is suitable for the location you have in mind.

Carpets can be made in various ways and here is an explanation of some of the confusing terms you will hear being bandied around the carpet shop.

Woven carpets The traditional method of making carpets is by weaving the pile at the same time as the backing. There are two types of woven carpets now on the market.

1. *Axminsters*, which are usually heavily patterned, as the special way they are made allows many colours to be used in any one design. The pile is usually cut.

2. *Wiltons*, usually in plain colours, in cut or looped piles.

The cut edges of all woven carpets will fray and therefore need binding. Woven carpets, which usually require an underlay, are best laid by professional carpet fitters, who will stretch them onto invisible tackless carpet grippers installed around the edges of

the room.

Tufted carpets The tufted way of making carpets is a newer development. The pile is needled into a hessian backing and then secured with adhesive. Better qualities then have a secondary foam backing added which cuts out the need for an underlay. The tufted method of manufacture is quicker and requires less labour than weaving. Quality tufteds therefore offer good value for money.

Cord carpets The carpets usually described in the shops as cord can in fact be made in a number of different ways. They can be woven rather like Wiltons, but with an uncut pile. Or they can be made from an unwoven 'mat' of fibres stuck to a hessian backing and then given a ridged surface. Alternatively, cords can be made from a tufted method of construction, with tightly packed uncut loops.

Carpet composition Perhaps more important for hard wear is not how your carpet is made, but what it is made of. So you need to consider the pile composition, plus its *density* (i.e. how much pile there is to every square inch of your carpet).

Wool the traditional and natural carpet fibre still remains unbeaten for warmth, resilience, hard wear and low flammability. However, the addition of 20 per cent of nylon increases wearing qualities up to five times.

Acrylic fibres (Acrilan, Courtelle) are the man-made group which most resembles wool in appearance and handle. They are resilient and hard-wearing, and may be found on their own, or in budget-priced triple blends with rayon and nylon.

Nylon (e.g. Enkalon, Bri-Nylon) man-made carpet fibres are hard-wearing and budget-priced. The disadvantage is that they tend to attract dirt; on the other hand, they can be easily cleaned by home shampooing.

Rayon (Evlan) man-made fibres are only suitable for areas of light wear, unless mixed in blends with other fibres. This is because of their tendency to flatten and soil.

You can also find attractive long-pile *polyester* (Terylene) carpets, and stain-resisting *polypropylenes*.

Choose a carpet with a dense firmly packed *pile*; it will wear better than a sparse pile which shows the backing when you bend the carpet back on itself.

Choosing a carpet You will be choosing a colour to suit your room scheme, but remember that light colours show dirt dreadfully: this part of your home is for walking on! Medium shades are probably the best bet, as very dark colours show up bits of white fluff, threads, crumbs, etc.

Fitted carpets make a room seem larger, but they are expensive, as you are paying for carpet at the edges and under furniture which is not actually being used. Carpet squares, available off broadloom rolls, or woven specially with patterned borders, can be turned from time to time to shift areas of wear. You could combine one of these with an inexpensive cord or with a hard flooring (e.g. sheet vinyl or tiles).

Remember that any carpet without a heavy-duty foam backing needs an underlay to cushion wear. An underlay also improves insulation against heat loss and noise transmission, and makes your carpet softer and more resilient. A good quality felt is fine, but you can also buy excellent foam rubber underlays.

Carpets are sold in standard widths. Woven carpets are still being made in imperial sizes on the old looms, which will exist for many years yet. 'Broadloom' carpets are made in widths of 15 ft (4·6 m.); 12 ft (3·7 m.); 10 ft 6 in. (3·2 m.); 9 ft (2·7 m.); 7 ft 6 in. (2·3 m.); and 6 ft (1·8 m.). Not all qualities will be made in all these widths however. Narrower 'body' widths of 36 in. (90 cm.) and 27 in. (70 cm.) ('three-quarter body' as it is called in the trade) are suitable for corridors and stairs. But some woven carpets (Wiltons in particular) are only made in three-quarter body and therefore have to be seamed up to cover any larger areas.

Before laying any carpet, inspect the floor for any unevenness, which will cause a patch of wear. Loose of uneven floorboards, protruding nails, electric flex etc. will, over the years, cause expensive damage.

As an alternative to expensive carpeting, you could consider *mattings*, including rush matting and coconut matting. These you can 'loose-lay' yourself without fixing; wearing properties will be improved if you can add an underlay. Any cut edges can be secured with latex adhesive or with carpet binding tape, stuck down with latex adhesive. Trim edges neatly first and on finishing, tap tape down lightly with a hammer to improve adhesion.

LAYING FOAM-BACKED CARPET

You may wish to tackle the laying of foam-backed carpets yourself. You should line the floor with paper felt to prevent foam backing sticking to the floor (this is particularly important if you think you may ever want to move the carpet to another room). Lay the carpet with the surface pile running away from the light: when you stroke the pile, this is the way that feels the smoothest. Then unroll your carpet, trying to keep the surface smooth and in line. If you run off true, with bad bulges resulting, you should roll up your carpet and start again.

If joins are necessary, use adhesive carpet tape (13). To fit carpet at skirtings, trim as necessary with a sharp knife. If large amounts need cutting away (this can happen at chimney breasts, for example) mark the estimated cutting line on the carpet with chalk. Cut this away, leaving a margin which allows you finally to trim for an exact fit. If you wish, you can secure your carpet at the edges with double-sided adhesive tape, or with a staple gun if you have one.

Doorways Doors must always be removed before laying carpet – this will also be necessary when laying thicker forms of hard flooring (e.g. hardboard plus vinyl sheet). You may well find it necessary to plane the bottom edge of the door to provide clearance for the new floor-covering: in which case use a plane or Surform, working from the sides to the middle. Fit a binder bar to the cut edges of carpets in doorways.

Stairs Stair carpets should be laid with care; any loose edges, ridges, etc., could cause a serious accident. If you doubt your abilities, it is wiser to enlist professional aid. Stair carpets are laid with their pile running downwards. (This is the way that feels the smoothest when you stroke the carpet). To estimate carpet quantities, measure depth of stair tread and height of riser. Add together these two measurements and then multiply by the number of stairs in the flight. Add 45 cm. (18 in.), to allow you to shift the carpet from time to time to even out the areas of wear. Choose a width of carpet suitable for your stairs: 27 in. (68·5 cm.) and 36 in. (91·5 cm.) are the most usual. You will need felt or rubber stair pads to cushion wear and deaden noise. The pads should fit against the riser on one side, and extend at least 50 mm. (2 in.) over the nosing of the tread. Tack pads in place, then screw sections of carpet

gripper into angles of each tread/riser on top of pads (14). Turn under edge of carpet and tack down at top of stairs. Unroll carpet down stairs, one tread at a time, pressing carpet into angle of gripper, using the tool provided with the gripper fixings, and keeping tension as tight as possible. On bends, keep the weave of the carpet in true with the line of the nosing (i.e. carpet's horizontal threads lying parallel to nosing) (15). This will mean folding up the surplus on the narrow side and making a neat pleat underneath. Tack this under the nosing. If stair has very little nosing, tack pleat in angle between tread and riser. At the bottom, tack surplus in large pleat against riser. Every six months or so you can shift your carpet upwards to even out the wear.

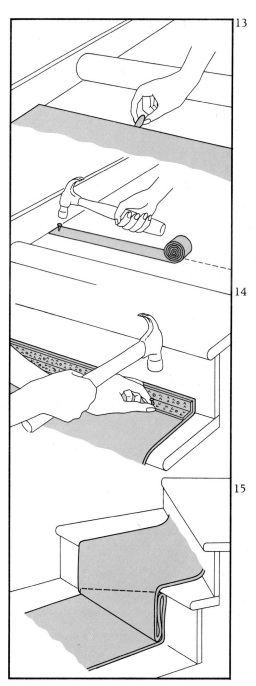

TILING WALLS

TILING YOUR WALLS

Tiled walls have distinct advantages especially where cleanliness and hygiene are of first importance. While vinyl floor tiles can be used as wall covering, the two most popular materials are cork and ceramics.

Cork has many advantages. It has the great attraction of being a natural material with much the same charm as attractively grained woods. Cork tiles can be bought with a bonded vinyl finish that requires no further treatment, or they can be treated with a wax polish or clear polyurethane varnish. Cork has great insulating properties, both thermal and acoustic and is pleasantly soft to touch.

Ceramic tiles are available in many delightful colours and designs and are relatively easy to fix. Because the procedure of cutting them to shape and fixing is slightly more complex than for cork tiles, it is dealt with below in some detail. Measuring for cork tiles is precisely the same as for ceramic but, of course, the adhesive is different and you should ask your supplier for the correct fixative. Rounded edge tiles (known as RE) are not required in cork as gentle sand papering will produce a rounded edge at window sills etc. Walls to which cork tiles are to be applied must be reasonably flat because you cannot compensate for hollows quite so easily as you can by using extra adhesive behind ceramic tiles.

PLANNING AND MATERIALS

If you have decided to tile a room the first job is to assess the quantity of tiles, fix and grout required. Measure up the total area to be covered with tiles and work this out in square metres or yards. The most common sizes of tiles available are 108 by 108 mm. ($4\frac{1}{4}$ by $4\frac{1}{4}$ in.) and 152 by 152 mm. (6 by 6 in.). Working in imperial measurements, the number of $4\frac{1}{4}$ in. tiles needed can be worked out assuming that 72 tiles will cover one square yard; in the case of 6 in. tiles 36 are needed for every square yard to be tiled.

A sufficient number of RE tiles (tiles having one edge round and glazed) will be required to go around any window recess being tiled or for the top edge of the tiling when this does not extend to the ceiling. For any panels of tiling which have two adjacent free edges at right angles (i.e. as occurs with a simple splash-back) a REX tile (having two adjacent sides rounded) will be needed for each panel corner (1, page 36).

Two types of adhesive are available, Polyfix which is a powder requiring to be mixed with water, and Polyfix Ready Mix for use straight from the container. The area of coverage or the number of tiles which can be fixed with the adhesive will be stated on the package. Similarly a quantity of grout will be required. This also can now be purchased in a ready mixed form (Ready Mixed Polygrout) although until recently it was mainly supplied as a powder to be mixed with water.

While for most internal tiling the standard types of adhesive will be found satisfactory, there are two circumstances to which special attention should be given. The first relates to any tiling on to wood (e.g. a window-sill). Unless this wood is very well sealed the moisture from the adhesive, or any subsequent ingress of moisture, can cause the wood to swell, followed by contraction when it dries. This movement can be sufficient to break the adhesive bond and to crack the tiles. It is advisable, therefore, to use Flexible Polyfix for any such areas.

Secondly, while most ready-mixed adhesives (those based on p.v.a.) are completely satisfactory in areas which are subject to intermittent wetting (i.e. most bathroom areas where splash-

2

1

supplied with Polygrout, a sponge or a rag. If no 'squeegee' is supplied an old car wiper blade is an effective means of removing excess grout;

clean cloths or paper for the final cleaning and polishing.

PREPARATION

In order to ensure good adhesion all walls to be tiled should be clean and free from any greasy deposits. Where necessary, care should be taken to remove any excessive unevenness in the surfaces, i.e. more than can be accommodated by the bed of adhesive which for most modern thin-bed adhesives should not exceed 3 mm. ($\frac{1}{8}$ in.). Any major cracks should be filled with Interior Polyfilla.

If a wall has been previously papered all paper should be thoroughly removed since it would constitute a weak layer between the wall and the adhesive and would result in an adhesion failure.

Any loose or flaking paint should also be removed by scraping so as to pro-

ing and condensation occur) they are not satisfactory for areas liable to remain permanently wet (e.g. in the base of a shower cubicle). For these areas it is advisable to use an adhesive which is claimed to withstand such conditions. This may be a cement-based powder adhesive, or a specially formulated ready-mixed product.

Other items required before commencing the work are:

a mixing bowl if adhesive or grout requires mixing with water;

a notched comb or trowel with which to apply the adhesive (a plastic comb is supplied with Polyfix, Polyfix Ready Mix and Flexible Polyfix);

a tile cutter;

a means of applying the grout, which may be a plastic 'squeegee' which is

1. A clean and practical effect
2. A collection of unusual tiles make an attractive feature
3. Tiles for colour and pattern
4. White tiling achieves a new and modern look in this bathroom

vide a sound surface for the fixing. If a wall has been previously distempered this should be removed by washing and if a layer still remains it should be bound by the application of a stabilising solution. New or very porous plaster walls can be sealed with a p.v.a.-based primer. When new plaster walls are being tiled adequate time should be allowed for drying before fixing the tiles. It is advisable to allow them to dry for at least one month, and to use a ready-mixed p.v.a.-type adhesive for the fixing.

If a powder adhesive is used it should be mixed with water according to the instructions on the pack, and left to develop for the recommended period before use. It is advisable to use any mixed adhesive within 3 hours of

mixing and certainly it should not be used after 4 hours unless it is specifically claimed on the pack that this is permissible.

HOW TO TILE

If the bath surround alone is being tiled, and provided the edge of the bath is horizontal (2), the bottom row of tiles may be placed directly against this edge and tiling continued above to the required height. The top edge should then be finished with RE tiles.

If a room is to be tiled on all walls it is necessary first to find the lowest point on the skirting board and to mark a point the height of one tile above this (3). A batten should be fixed to the wall with its top edge at the point marked, and should be checked as horizontal using a spirit level (4). If a batten is not available a horizontal line could be drawn in pencil at this level (5). It is desirable to set out the tiling so that approximately equal widths of tile have to be used at the two ends of the wall. One way to ensure this is to mark the centre line of the wall and to start tiling from this position. The centre line can be marked using a plumbline to ensure that it is vertical (6).

Adhesive should be applied to the wall above the batten and to one side of the vertical line. Do not apply more than 0·8 sq. m. (1 square yard) of adhesive at a time. Apply the adhesive to the wall with the comb or trowel and then holding the tool perpendicular to the wall and against it draw the serrated edge over the adhesive bed so as to comb it into ridges (7). This gives a correct and uniform bed thickness. Place the first tile above the batten and with one edge against the vertical pencil line. Continue placing the bottom row of tiles, following up with the next row above (8) and so on until the

area of adhesive has been covered with tiles.

British-made tiles have spacer lugs on their sides, so that by pushing each tile against the previous one they automatically space themselves to give a satisfactory grout line. When a number of tiles has been fixed it is advisable to examine the straightness of the grout lines since very minor adjustments may be necessary.

When tiles without spacer lugs are being fixed these must not be butted against each other or any minor wall-shrinkage or movement may then cause failure of the adhesion. In this

case it is necessary to space the tiles apart so that the grout lines are at least 1·5 mm. ($\frac{1}{16}$ in.) in thickness. This can be done by using matchsticks or pieces of card between tiles as spacers until the adhesive has set.

When the wall has been tiled as completely as possible pieces of tiles must be cut to fit the spaces remaining at the corners of the room (9). Finally the batten must be removed and the bottom row of tiles fixed in position cutting pieces off (10) as necessary to accommodate any unevenness of the skirting board.

Other walls should be dealt with in a

tile into two pieces along a line running through the centre of the pipe, and to score and nibble away two semi-circular sections, one from each piece so as to fit round the pipe (10).

Window ledges RE tiles (with one round edge) should be put around the window recess (11), i.e. on the horizontal ledge and the sides, so as to give a neat finish at the join up with the tiles on the walls.

GROUTING

When the tiling is completed it is advisable, but not essential, to leave it until the next day before grouting. The grout should be mixed to a paste as instructed on the pack if in powder form, or used straight from the container if ready-mixed. It should be applied over the face of the tiling using a plastic scraper, a sponge, or a cloth, rubbing it well into the joints (12). The excess is then removed with the scraper acting as a squeegee or with another cloth (13). For a professional finish go over the grout lines with a pointed stick and finally polish the surface with a dry cloth or a piece of paper.

FITTINGS

Some fittings, such as soap dishes, are available which are fixed in the same way as the tiles, replacing one of them. Where it is necessary to drill tiles a masonry drill must be used. Put a piece of sticky tape over the tile and mark the place to be drilled. The sticky tape prevents the drill slipping on the glazed surface until the hole has been started. Drill slowly and carefully so as not to generate too much heat.

ALUMINIUM TILES

Another interesting range of tiles is available in aluminium. Called Tyne-Plaqs they are available in two sizes and two forms. Those 108 by 108 mm. ($4\frac{1}{4}$ by $4\frac{1}{4}$ in.) are suitable for use in any situation in which conventional ceramic tiles of the same size could be used. The method of fixing is by means of adhesive pads and no grouting is required. These tiles are available in a whole range of three-dimensional patterns, in gold, polished aluminium and other colours and are capable of considerable pattern variations. The 152 by 152 mm. (6 by 6 in.) tiles in the same range are called cover tiles and are designed to be mounted by double-sided adhesive tabs over the top of standard 152 mm. (6 in.) tiles.

similar way ensuring that the horizontal grout lines are at the same level all round the room.

Cutting Where pieces need to be cut a tile cutter must be used. This may be a simple wheel or point in a handle or may be a more sophisticated type such as the Polycell tile cutter which has a scale indicating the width of the piece being cut. The essential action is to score the tile across on the glazed face with one continuous score line. Enough pressure must be put upon the cutter to score the glaze and it must be drawn across the piece; a good cutting action is denoted by the sound produced.

Having scored the tile the piece is broken along this line by exerting pressure so as to open up the scratch produced. One simple way to do this is to place the tile glazed face up on top of a matchstick located under the score line. By pressing down on both sides the tile should snap along the score.

When difficult shapes are required, e.g. when a piece has to be removed from one corner, score along the lines where the break is required and nip away the unwanted piece bit by bit using a pair of pliers or the notch which may be provided on the cutter. If a hole is needed for a pipe it is best to cut the

PLANNING YOUR KITCHEN

Kitchens – possibly the trickiest rooms to organise in the whole house. But the most worthwhile, as research has shown that the 'average' woman spends about $3\frac{1}{2}$ hours every day in the kitchen.

THE PROBLEMS

Firstly, every family wants different things out of their kitchen – the galley-type arrangement that suits the working couple will not be suitable for the family with young children who are aiming for a kitchen-cum-second living room. Secondly, you, the prime user of your kitchen, are also unique, with your own very personal likes and dislikes. Even your physical characteristics will make a difference to the kind of kitchen you want – if you are tall for example, you will want a higher sink (more about this later). Thirdly, everybody's kitchens are of differing sizes and shapes, with different arrangements of fixed features such as doors, windows, plumbing points, radiators and so on. And of course your plans will be limited by the amount of money you have available.

Getting your kitchen the way you want is no easy matter. But do not despair, because we have collected up the planning basics, and grouped them under easy-to-read headings. Here we deal mainly with starting from scratch, for those re-planning an existing kitchen, or organising the kitchen in a new or converted house. But at the end we give some easy-to-follow ways of improving any kitchen, when a basic re-plan is out of the question. (Maybe you cannot afford it, or you only plan to stay in your home for a couple more years and it is not worth it. Or maybe your accommodation is rented).

MAKING A PLAN

First job is to make a plan of the kitchen as it is at present. Kitchen unit and appliance manufacturers are now giving the dimensions of their products in metric measures, so we advise you to measure up in metric from the start, to avoid tedious conversions at a later stage. Make a rough plan first in pencil, so that alterations to it are simple. Mark everything that is going to affect your final plan: position of door(s) and the way they open; position of window(s) (with a separate 'elevation' to show sill heights); position of radiators or fireplaces; existing plumbing and gas points; position of existing power and lighting points.

Next step is to draw your plan out on squared paper (graph paper is easily obtained from any good stationer). Use a largish scale, for example a metric scale of 1:20.

DECIDING YOUR REQUIREMENTS

At this stage it is helpful to make some check lists.

1. Decide a) who will be using the kitchen (pretty obvious) and b) what they will be using the kitchen for (less obvious). For example under (b) you might have such activities as playing, eating, hobbies, chatting, homework and so on, depending on your type of family. And you may have a heading for 'laundry'. In which case you will need to allocate space for storage and use of washing machine and/or spin drier and tumble drier, and ironing board. You may also need racks for

drying clothes. (N.B. It is recommended that where possible another part of the house be allocated for laundry activities, as they do put rather a strain on the kitchen. Another point: the kitchen is not the best place for drying clothes, because of the fumes from cooking). Think about the type of cooking you prefer to do. Do you need lots of working surfaces for extended cookery sessions? Or do you need lots of storage for instant foods?

2. Make a list of all the equipment and furniture which already have to be accommodated in your new kitchen. The list should include all relevant

dimensions. You may find it helpful to draw the shapes of your equipment/furniture on squared paper to the same scale as your final plan; then cut them out. This way, you can move them around and see where they fit best. Remember to allow for equipment you hope to buy soon.

3. Make a rough list of everything your kitchen will have to store (see notes on storage below).

4. Decide what atmosphere you want your kitchen to have ... cool, uncluttered, efficient? Cosy country-style? This will make a big difference to the way you plan your final lay-out.

1. *A split-level cooker fits compactly into a corner*
2. *Sliding doors save space*
3. *Well-planned shelving provides storage space and an eating area in this long room*
4. *Bold use of colour in diagonal and vertical stripes*
5. *An effective combination of modern equipment and pine*
6. *Natural light, white paint and good planning can transform a small area into an efficient and pleasant kitchen*

4

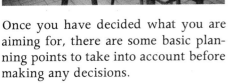

5

6

Once you have decided what you are aiming for, there are some basic planning points to take into account before making any decisions.

WORK-FLOW

When you are getting a meal, the pattern of your work is pretty much the same every time. You move from the *storage* area to the *preparation* area to the *sink* to the *cooker* to the *serving* area, not necessarily in a continuous sequence, as frequently you have to double back. You will find that it is most convenient if you can set your sink and cooker in one continuous run of worktop, so that there are no gaps and obstacles between them, and so that you have a place on both sides of the cooker to set things down. This will give you a sequence of work surface/cooker/work surface/sink/work surface (or the same in reverse order) which should be unbroken by full-height fitments, doors or passage ways. This working arrangement can take the form of a straight line, or it can be arranged as an 'L' shape, or in a 'U' shape. The most travelled route in your kitchen is from SINK to COOKER and this should not be disturbed by any through circulation.

You can accommodate storage under your work surfaces, and in wall cupboards. Your refrigerator will be a basic element of your storage – indeed professional kitchen planners talk about the 'work triangle' formed between the sink, cooker and 'fridge'. To avoid unnecessary trekking from one spot to another, it is recommended that the total length of the work triangle should be between 3600 mm. (12 ft) and 1800 mm. (6 ft) long. You can buy 'fridges' that will tuck underneath your working surface, but if you have or intend to buy a tall 'fridge', or 'fridge' freezer, then you should site it

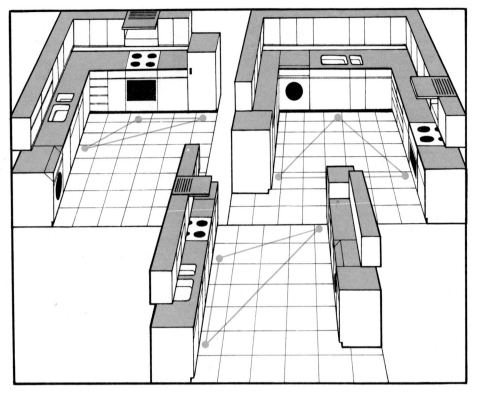

3 alternative working arrangements: L shape, U shape and straight lines

at the end of your run of working surface so that it does not interrupt your work flow. The same applies to tall units containing built-in ovens (see notes on split level, below). In larger kitchens, you will be able to arrange extra worktops and storage in addition to and separated from the main work sequence. You should aim to accommodate your serving area within your basic work sequence, to avoid the possibility of collisions with through traffic.

SINKS

A double sink with double drainers is ideal, but may take up too much space in smaller kitchens. Possible alternatives are: a) one large sink and one small sink suitable for rinsing, washing vegetables, etc; this small sink can also be fitted with a waste disposal if you wish. Or b) a single large sink (say 750 by 350 mm./2 ft 6 in. by 1 ft) with a mixer tap and two rectangular washing up bowls. Conventionally, draining boards are ridged, but if you opt for the unridged type, you can use the resulting flat counter for food preparation as well as for draining dishes. Sink-bowls are available for letting into work tops, with the advantage that you can arrange for one length of worktop to run continuously over a whole range of fitments, which makes it much easier to keep clean.

WORKTOPS

Unfortunately there is no single height level which is going to suit all of the people all of the time. This is fairly obvious, when you think how greatly people vary in height. A recommended height of 900 mm. (3 ft) for sink and worktop is specified in the metric British Standard for kitchen equipment. However research has shown that 75 per cent of women would be more comfortable with a sink rim and draining board height of 975 mm. (3 ft 3 in.), with 900 mm. for other worktops. If you are installing a new sink unit, you may therefore prefer to have it raised on a plinth. However, you will then have the problem of a change in levels between your draining board and other worktops; this should be avoided if it interrupts

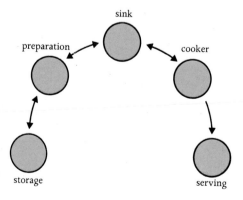

Pattern of work flow in the kitchen

a run of continuous worktops. You may therefore have to come to some kind of compromise.

Remember that your worktop alongside your cooker will be used for hot pans which will mark plastic laminates unless you provide a protective mat. Ceramic tiles, slate, or stainless steel are more suitable materials. You may like to incorporate a permanent 'chopping board' area into your work top, and the most suitable material for this is beech.

COOKERS

Electricity or gas? It is up to you, of course. The conventional *combined cooker* is space saving, and considerably cheaper than a split-level arrangement, where the hob and oven are installed separately. However, if you opt for a split level, it is possible to combine gas hobs with an electric oven/grill. It is also possible to have, say, 2 gas hobs and 2 electric. Your hobs can be built into a continuous run of worktop and you thus avoid dirt-collecting gaps and crannies. Your kitchen will look more streamlined.

Do not site your cooker or hob unit under a window if there is any danger of reaching over the hob to clean or open the window. Do not site your cooker or hob unit in a corner, as you will need room to stand comfortably in front, preferably with a working surface on either side of you, at the same height as the hob, so that you slide pans on and off as necessary.

STORAGE

The recommended front-to-back measurement for base cupboards is 600 mm. (2 ft); this will enable you to build in appliances such as washing-machines, washing-up machines and so on. You will find that you are actively using only the front part of the resulting working top; the back part can be used for the permanent storage of large bins or canisters or of often-used foodstuffs such as flour or bread and for appliances such as mixers or grinders. Wall cupboards or shelving units should be not more than 300 mm. (1 ft) deep, or you are going to start bumping into them. Wall cupboards should never be installed without a working space below them, if there is any danger of people bumping into them. You will need a height of between 400 and 450 mm. (15½ and 18 in.) between worktop and wall cupboard, but you could use the wallspace in between for extra narrow shelves not more than 100 mm. (4 in.) deep.

Remember that sliding doors can only be used effectively on cupboards longer than around 800 mm. (2 ft 6 in.). You will find sliding doors safer in use than hinged doors. So many people (particularly older people) have cracked their heads on the nasty sharp corner of hinged wall cupboards as they stand up. However: hinged doors allow you to see the whole contents of the cupboard at once and you can fit extra racks on the inside of the doors to improve storage facilities. Open shelving or box units are cheaper to provide than wall cupboards and perfectly satisfactory if you have no objection to everything being on view all the time. Adjustable shelves are the best solution for inside cupboards; this enables you easily to accommodate things like cereal packets or large bottles.

EATING

Most families like to be able to eat at least breakfasts and snacks in their kitchen. Families with young children will find a full-scale table with benches or chairs very useful, not only for easy-to-serve family meals but also for supervised painting and hobby sessions/homework. If you settle for a counter top and make it 900 mm. (3 ft) high, you can use it as extra working surface for jobs done standing up; but you must leave the knee space underneath open, unblocked by any storage or appliances. You will need to sit on tall stools and this arrangement is therefore not suitable for younger children, who could topple right over. Table tops are of course lower (around 700–760 mm./2ft 3 in.–2 ft 6 in.) and therefore can only be used as a worktop when you are sitting down. However, when you are not too pressed for time, it is very pleasant to sit down for some jobs, e.g. preparing vegetables for a stew, or fruits for a salad. If you are planning to have a table and chairs in your kitchen, do make sure you allow adequate space around the table for comfort. Round tables on a pedestal leg take up less room, and allow generous knee space.

You should allow easy-to-get-at storage near your eating area for foodstuffs needed regularly for the table (salt, pepper, sauces, cereals, marmalade, etc.) and for china, cutlery, table napkins and so on. This storage should

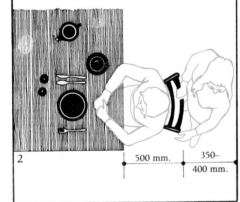

1. Measurements for storage space: a worktop height; b rarely used items; c lighter items; d frequently used items; e lighter items; f seldom used items
2. Space needed for eating area

be easily accessible from your sink/drainer, when the washing up is finished. If you have a washing-up machine, you can save space by allowing cutlery/chinaware to remain in the machine until needed for the next meal. Do you have any electrical appliances which you need near your eating area? A toaster or hot plate for example? If so, plan for a suitable surface for them, and also provide a power point.

FLOORING

Kitchen floors should be easy to clean, resilient, hard-wearing, quiet to walk on and slip-resistant. Suitable floorings include vinyl sheet or tiles, cork tiles (well sealed with polyurethane varnish), wood strip (will also need sealing). Ceramic and quarry tiles are not resilient or noise-deadening, but will provide a semi-permanent finish which is easy to look after.

LIGHTING

Good lighting is more important in the kitchen than in any room in the house.

Ceiling mounted fluorescents will provide a good overall level of illumination, but you may find the result rather flat and institutional. Cylinder downlighters would be a satisfactory alternative, or choose fittings which fit tight to the ceiling. Or you can conceal spotlights on the tops of cupboards and allow their light to bounce off the ceiling. Worktops can be lit with fluorescents mounted underneath an overhanging cupboard and concealed by a narrow wooden pelmet. In all cases, select fittings which are easy to clean.

WAYS TO IMPROVE ANY KITCHEN

If it is impossible for you to do a major re-plan on your kitchen, there are still various simple ways you may be able to make it work better for you.

1. The position of the sink is difficult to alter, but you may be able to have the position of your cooker changed (e.g. moving it out of the corner).

2. This might give you the chance to build an extra worktop, if possible to link sink and cooker.

3. Could you add any wall storage to your kitchen? Narrow wall-fixed shelves are simple and cheap, and provide handy storage for packets, bottles, jars. Fix cup-hooks to their undersides for mugs, etc.

4. Utensils hanging on the wall can be seen easily and will not clutter up worktops. Fix lengths of battens with hooks or simple dowel pegs. Fix small eyelet hooks into the wooden handles so that you can hang them up.

5. Is your sink too low, causing backache? You can raise a plastic washing-up bowl on a teak board, to bring it to a more comfortable level. Similarly, if the sink is too high for you, you can stand on a slatted wooden 'platform'. Always put your platform away when the washing up is finished, to avoid the possibility of tripping.

6. Could you improve your lighting? Jobs done in a good light seem much easier (see notes on lighting above).

7. Treat yourself to a few gadgets – for example, wall-mounted can opener, or wall-mounted kitchen scales.

8. Reorganise the insides of your cupboards. Fit racks to the insides of doors to take packets, saucepan lids, etc. Add extra shelves, hooks, etc.

9. Add on a cork pin-up area – for example, a few cork tiles. Use for messages, recipes, memos, receipts.

CHILDREN'S ROOMS

Conventional ideas about children die hard – none harder than the ones entertained by almost every expectant mother as she plans the room for her first baby.

A nursery can be very pretty indeed but if you have to organize your home on a tight budget and have a limited amount of time to spend on housework it is as well to realize that baby equipment will be unnecessary within nine months of birth and the decorations will look extremely shabby after a couple of years.

If you want to avoid the expense of constant re-furnishing and redecorating, rooms for children of *any* age must be planned cleverly to cater for future developments.

The first difficulty in creating such a room is that an inexperienced parent has very little idea of what a child's requirements are likely to be at any given stage. Here are a few guidelines and suggestions.

PLANNING ROUND A BABY

A new-born baby needs a room which is within earshot both day and night. Ideally it should be near his parents' bedroom, the bathroom and the area most occupied by his mother during the day (later she will discover that as a toddler he will not play happily for long if she is at a distance). This is simple enough in a small or one-storey home. In a large house a microphone can be placed near the baby to transmit sounds elsewhere.

Strictly speaking a young baby does not need a whole room to himself: a draught-free corner at the end of a passage or under the stairs is quite big enough. Expense and space can be saved by investing in a light pram consisting of a lift-out carrycot and fold-up frame. Nor does the baby need much storage space for clothes. He needs very few and these are speedily outgrown. The necessities are best kept on a mobile shelved unit which accompanies the baby wherever he is washed and fed.

If you intend to wash the baby in a portable bath, you need sufficient space in the bathroom to take the bath and its stand. When filled, these baths are quite heavy and easily spilled. For this reason, a baby bath for use in the nursery must be fitted with a removable plug, so that it can be emptied by means of a bucket. Quite frankly, it is probably quicker and easier to bath the baby in the kitchen sink.

It is equally important to feed the baby where you feel most comfortable. A restful, upholstered chair – the one you choose to knit or sew in – is better than a conventional armless nursing chair which is fit only for a spare bedroom when it is no longer needed. Instant heat during the night or at dawn is most quickly provided by a portable fan heater.

Once the baby begins to crawl, every potential danger below waist level must be removed. Trailing electric flexes and heavy objects which can easily be pulled over should no longer be within reach. Fix guards at the top and bottom of the staircase and in front of open fires. A play-pen with an integral floor – so that the baby cannot push it around – prevents him from getting into mischief and from spreading his toys all over the place when you cannot watch him.

A baby makes an indescribable mess when he is learning to feed himself. He needs a high chair placed on flooring that is easy to clean. Usually, but not always, it is most convenient to feed him in the kitchen.

By now quite a lot of baby equipment is being amassed. While choosing it remember that it cannot be sold profitably when outgrown and should, ideally, occupy the minimum amount

of storage space if you intend to save it for another child.

CATERING FOR THE TODDLER

By the time a baby is walking well – at around two years old – he becomes very energetic. He climbs out of his cot, prefers toys which develop his physical and mental abilities, builds with bricks and, given the chance, produces paintings with poster colour and drawings with indelible pens; books accumulate.

Buy a bed of standard length which will suit the child until he grows up rather than a so-called junior bed of lesser dimensions which will become just another item of outgrown equipment within a few years. If floor space is limited and you hope for another child, choose bunks which can be

4

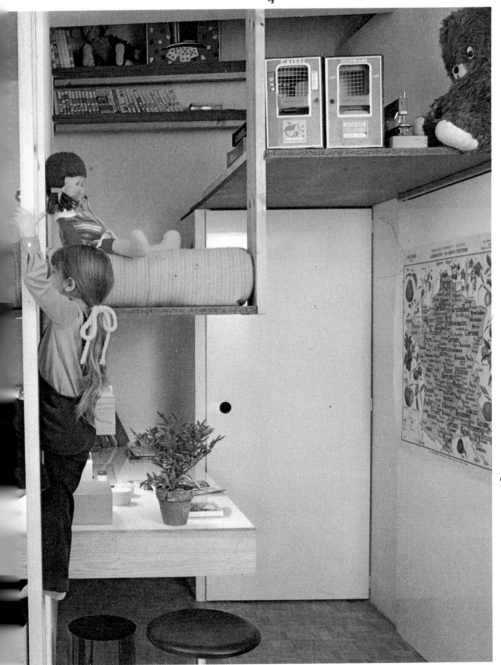

5

1. Bold colours are suitable for a wide age span
2. A 'grown-up' room for a small girl
3. Practically planned, this bedroom/playroom caters for all the children's needs
4. A single bunk bed makes maximum use of space
5. Wall patterns add decoration

separated later without looking too child-like. Invest in a flexible storage system with units for clothes, books and treasures plus a roomy locker in which toys can be dumped. If the system does not incorporate a suitable unit you will have to buy a table and some chairs.

This is the stage when walls and furnishings take a knocking. Choose tough finishes and fabrics which will not advertise dirt and are easily cleaned. Arrange the room so that it is easy to tidy. Picking up and putting away clothes and toys becomes a major occupation.

REQUIREMENTS OF THE OLDER CHILD

At around nine years old a child begins to value a certain amount of privacy. Soon – if not already – he will be burdened with homework and will need the facilities to get on with it. By the time he is a teenager, he will enjoy sitting in his room reading, listening to records, pursuing a hobby and entertaining his friends.

The adolescent appreciates a bed-sitting room. If there is not enough space in the room for more furniture, the bed can be converted into a settee by placing it beside a wall and adding wedge-shaped backrests or a quantity of cushions.

With a realistic idea of the equipment needed for a child's room from birth onwards, it is possible to plan further.

HEATING

Heating and lighting cannot be installed until you have selected – not necessarily bought – equipment and know where it will be arranged. If you have complete freedom of choice – in a newly built home, for example – choose a ceiling, underfloor or ducted warm air system. These leave the floors and walls free for furniture and present nothing on which a child can burn himself. Radiators and storage heaters are not so safe, can be unattractive and occupy valuable space. Radiant heaters, whether gas, oil or electricity should be avoided unless they are inaccessible to a child. It is better to have a fan heater, provided it has no trailing flex. Whatever the system, it should be able to produce a temperature of 22°C (72°F) which can be graded down to 16°C (60°F). All power points must be of the safety variety which are impregnable to probing fingers.

LIGHTING

Table lamps are unsuitable for children's rooms because they have dangling flexes and are easily overturned. A pendant lamp is safer but compares unfavourably with an adjustable spotlight – or several – which can slide along a track spanning the ceiling and may therefore be focused on any part of the room.

Lighting requirements differ at each stage: indirect light which will not hurt the baby's eyes is needed in the beginning. A very dim light will comfort a child who is frightened to sleep in the dark. Direct light that does not dazzle is required at the head of the bed, on parts of the storage system and on play or work areas. A dimmer switch, which is easily installed in place of the standard switch, allows for a fine adjustment to be made to the quality of the light.

FLOORING

Flooring should be easy to clean. It should also be hard-wearing, comfortable and not too cold for a baby to crawl on or for older children to sit on; smooth and firm enough to present a satisfactory track for wheeled toys. Carpet or matting does not fulfil these requirements. Vinyl tiles or sheeting or cork tiles do. Vinyl sheeting with insulated backing will deaden the noise made by running feet, bouncing balls and toys of all kinds when they are dropped. Alternatively, since most children enjoy the comfort of a carpet, it may be possible to cover part of the floor with a firm, smooth surface and another part with carpeting.

WALLS

As has been said before wall finishes should be hard-wearing and – as washing walls takes almost as long as decorating them – should disguise stains and dirt in general. Children lie on the floor or on their beds and put their feet on the wall. They lounge and bump against walls. They throw balls and other missiles at them, stick things on them, and, even if usually well-behaved, draw on them occasionally. Pale emulsion paint was not formulated to withstand treatment of this kind; the dark shades are also unsuitable as they develop shiny patches when rubbed. Gloss paint is certainly tougher and easier to clean but, from an aesthetic point of view, is not always satisfactory because it tends to make rather a hard impression on the walls.

There are many other wall finishes to choose from but if you do not want to invest in a robust permanent one such as wood panelling there is little doubt that a vinyl covering, patterned or textured, fills the bill perfectly.

DECORATING SCHEMES

It is reasonable to expect wall decorations to last five years and flooring to last twice as long. Before exposing yourself to tempting designs decide where you intend to add pattern. Few people can mix different patterns successfully. It is safer to stick to patterned walls and a plain floor and coverings or plain walls and a floor with patterned coverings. It you decide to cut down on bed-making by investing in a duvet with a pretty cover and matching pillow slips, choose a set which has matching fabric sold by the yard so that it can be used at the window as well. Such material will not be sturdy enough to upholster a chair but would be suitable for a cushion. With this you will need to find a plain vinyl paper and flooring that harmonizes with some colour in the pattern. Do not make your final decision until you have seen samples assembled together in both natural and artificial light. Following a five-year plan, you might decide to start with gently patterned walls then, for the next period, to switch to plain ones in a fairly strong colour which relates well to the original flooring. When the child is ten you will probably have to renew the floor and may be inclined to hang a more positive pattern than the first one on the walls. Avoid the large, harsh, would-be cheery designs that are produced in such profusion for children: they are unattractive when seen over a large area and the prospect of living with them for a long period is daunting. Nor should you try to duck the issue by choosing a washy, uncommitted design – these simply cease to register after a short time. Get your money's worth by investing in a really interesting design. By fifteen most teenagers have a pronounced sense of style (in fact children of less than ten usually have definite ideas about what they like). Any plain colour or pattern chosen is likely to be pretty sophisticated.

Before you unthinkingly hang curtains at the windows pause to consider a baby's requirements – you may have forgotten that in the beginning he is

unable to turn away from the light. Curtains, unless drawn completely, are not so effective as blinds in shading the sun from his eyes.

STORAGE

The storage system may well be the most expensive item on the agenda. If you choose a firmly established design, however, you can buy units as you need them. Look for a system that incorporates a mobile shelved unit to hold toilet necessities during the first stage – this will later prove invaluable as a bedside table or for holding such things as writing or painting materials, reference books or records and a record player. The system must also include capacious locker units for stowing away toys, a desk unit and, of course, cupboard and drawer units plus top storage. Do not be persuaded to invest in units less than 53 cm. (21 in.) deep; hanging space of adult proportions can be needed by a child

of twelve nowadays. You will find that only a system designed for living rooms and bedrooms is likely to contain all the units you need. Those intended for children's rooms look too juvenile to suit a child over ten and, being low, waste valuable top space which can be used to store such things as bedding and holiday clothes.

Near-indestructible finishes such as melamine have a definite advantage over more vulnerable ones but, unlike whitewood, they cannot be redecorated to blend with the rest of the room. Children stick painting, posters, photographs and postcards on walls with glue, Sellotape, drawing pins or anything else which offers a fixing. Provide a really big pinboard and set an example by organizing all pictures on it from the beginning.

ARRANGING THE ROOM

If you follow the suggestions we have made, arranging the room should not

With the right choice of decoration and furniture, one room can be made to meet the changing requirements of a growing child.

be a problem because you will not have innumerable pieces of free-standing furniture to include. Most small rooms arrange themselves: owing to the position of the door and window there is probably only one draught-free place for the bed and one free wall against which to install the storage system.

Complications arise when two or more children must share the room. All is simple while they are young. Trouble starts when they begin to want a little privacy, often leading to a request for their own rooms. If this is not possible, peace can only be preserved by dividing the room into well-defined areas. This can be achieved by either decorative or structural means.

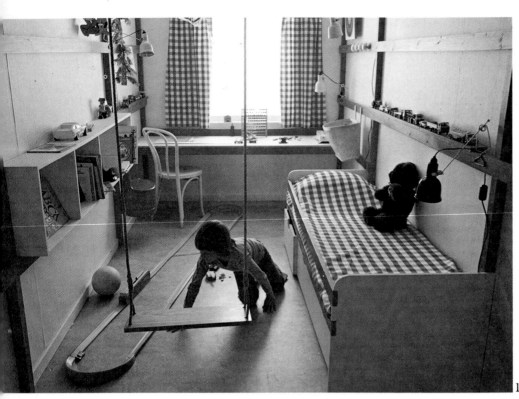

1

2

3

4

5

1. Using walls for storage space leaves a large floor area free for activities
2. Flooring should be hard-wearing
3. Improvised storage using unbreakable units is practical in a playroom
4. A large room simply divided by storage units to separate sleeping area from play area
5. A room adaptable for any age

THINGS TO MAKE

Just a working knowledge of some of the many materials available today, combined with practical common sense, will enable you to construct these items which may be used for functional or simply for fun purposes. It is not necessary to be a d-i-y expert: just follow instructions carefully.

SEWING TABLE

This sewing table can be made from Angleform components and other materials which are available from your local d-i-y shop. It can easily be made by anyone who is able to use a saw, screwdriver, drill and file. It is important, though, to work to accurate sizes and to keep your materials clean and protected while working. The unusual feature of Angleform is the aluminium tube, but as you will see, it is easy to work with and effective in use. It is advisable to protect the working area of the tube with adhesive tape to protect its excellent finish. N.B. When sawing chipboard it is a good idea to score the sawline with a sharp knife on both sides before sawing.

MATERIALS AND TOOLS REQUIRED

Wood or chipboard 17 mm. ($\frac{1}{2}$ in.) thick. 1 fixed top panel 37·46 cm. × 55·25 cm. ($14\frac{3}{4}$ in. × $21\frac{3}{4}$ in.); 1 slide top panel 30·48 cm. × 45·78 cm. (12 in. × 18 in.); 2 short side rails 10·16 cm. × 37·46 cm. (4 in. × $14\frac{3}{4}$ in.); 1 divider 10·16 cm. × 37·46 cm. (4 in. × $14\frac{3}{4}$ in.); 2 long side rails 10·16 cm. × 83·18 cm. (4 in. × $32\frac{3}{4}$ in.); 1 shelf 37·46 cm. × 86·36 cm. ($14\frac{3}{4}$ in. × 34 in.); 1 pattern rack back 37·46 cm. × 86·36 cm. ($14\frac{3}{4}$ in. × 34 in.); 2 pattern rack sides 15·24 cm. × 22·86 cm. (6 in. × 9 in.); 1 pattern rack front 37·46 cm. × 22·86 cm. ($14\frac{3}{4}$ in. × 9 in.); component base panel 45 cm. × 33 cm. ($17\frac{3}{4}$ in. × 13 in.); 2 pieces of plywood for slider 37·46 cm. × 4 cm. ($14\frac{3}{4}$ in. × $1\frac{1}{2}$ in.) and 36·8 cm. × 4 cm. ($14\frac{1}{2}$ in. × $1\frac{1}{2}$ in.); veneering edging strip for exposed edges if required.

Components 4 pieces of 71·12 cm. (28 in.) aluminium tube 15·9 mm. sq. ($\frac{5}{8}$ in. sq.); 3 × 30·48 cm. (12 in.) plastic channels; 4 box brackets; 4 large corner brackets; 24 shrinking brackets; 4 end plugs; 4 swivel glides; No. 6 and No. 8 screws. Screws required otherwise come with appropriate brackets.

Tools Round or V file; screwdriver; bradawl; ruler; tri-square; rubber mallet (hammer with block of wood would do); small hand drill with 0.238 cm. (3/32 in.) drill bit; sandpaper; work bench with vice is useful but not essential.

CONSTRUCTION

Stage 1 Take one *short side rail*, mark the centre of the top edge, and file a groove to a depth of at least 0·64 cm. ($\frac{1}{4}$ in.) with a round file.

Stage 2 *Shrinking brackets* are now fitted to the insides of the short side rail and long side rails. Fix screw through slotted hole first so that minor adjustments can be made before tightening all screws.

Stage 3 Now fix *plastic channels*. First drill fixing holes in channels for countersunk screws. Fix one piece centrally to the slide top panel and the other two to the rails to the depth of the slider. The *slider*, under the slide top panel, is made by mounting one piece of plywood upon another before screwing both to slide top. The longer piece, being on top, overlaps at either side, forming guide rails.

Stage 4 Assemble rails with *corner brackets* to form a frame. Make a V groove at each end of the side rails 4·76 cm. ($1\frac{7}{8}$ in.) down and 0·64 cm. ($\frac{1}{4}$ in.) deep across the inside corners. Position the brackets so that the centre hole lines up with the corner V groove in the side rails. Fix the brackets with screws provided.

Stage 5 *Shrinking brackets* should now be fixed to the divider as shown.

Stage 6 You are now ready to prepare the aluminium *legs*. Mark the position for two holes 0·238 cm. (3/32 in.) in diameter on the inside face of each leg, the top hole 15·2 cm. (6 in.) from the bottom and the other 1·27 cm. ($\frac{1}{2}$ in.) lower. Use a hand drill or low-speed power drill and protect the leg with tape while you are working. Fix a *box bracket* to each leg as shown. Position locking plate inside bracket and start the self-tapping screw. Make sure the bracket is square before the final tightening. The locking plate lug fits into the bottom hole.

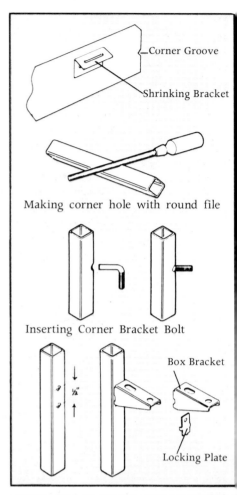

Corner Groove
Shrinking Bracket

Making corner hole with round file

Inserting Corner Bracket Bolt

Box Bracket
Locking Plate

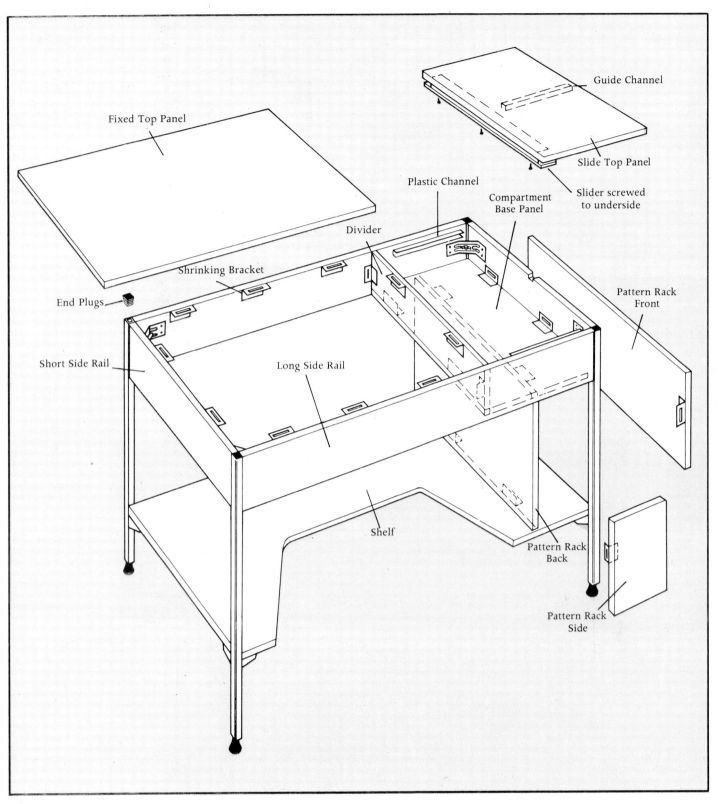

Fixed Top Panel

Guide Channel

Slide Top Panel

Slider screwed to underside

Plastic Channel

Compartment Base Panel

Divider

Shrinking Bracket

Pattern Rack Front

End Plugs

Short Side Rail

Long Side Rail

Shelf

Pattern Rack Back

Pattern Rack Side

Stage 7 To fix the *legs* to the rail frame, mark on each leg a point 5 cm. (2 in.) from the top and with a round file make a hole across the corner 0·64 cm. ($\frac{1}{4}$ in.) in diameter. These holes face inwards and it is a good idea to label the inside face of each leg to avoid confusion. Insert in each leg the *threaded L bolt*, short end in hole so that the long end protrudes horizontally. With rail frame upside down on your bench, attach each leg to the corner bracket by threading bolt through centre hole and tightening with butterfly nut (1).

Stage 8 The *slide top panel* with slider strips fitted should now be slid into position and the *fixed top panel* can now be fitted with the shrinking brackets (2).

Stage 9 Still keeping the assembly upside down, fit divider with shrinking brackets in the correct position and attach *compartment bottom panel*.

Stage 10 The bottom shelf can now be fixed to the box brackets with the screws provided (3). The cut-away section, giving foot room, has to be designed individually. Mark out the outline in pencil and either saw it yourself, or ask the timber merchant to do it for you.

Stage 11 You can now fit the *pattern rack compartment* by attaching the back panel first, then the side panels and finally the front panel.

Stage 12 Inset *end plugs* into the top of each leg and insert swivel glides into the bottom and tap firmly home.

49

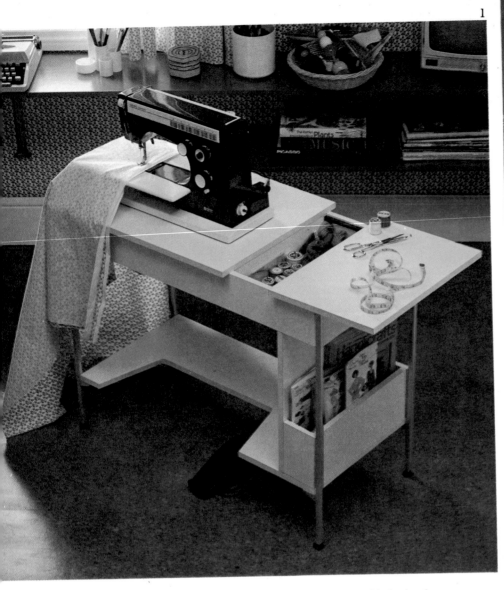

1. This sewing table is simple to assemble and will store all the accessories you need to have to hand
(Harrison Angleform)
2. A mirror house is fun to make for children
3. This panel can be made to fit any door or window recess; assemble your own arrangement from dried flowers, leaves and grasses

DRIED FLOWER DOOR PANEL

Materials

1 length of double-channelled whitewood, for frame, about 1–2 cm. ($\frac{1}{2}$–$\frac{3}{4}$ in.) deep

2 sheets of 4 mm. ($\frac{1}{8}$ in.) glass

2 wooden clothes pegs

dried grasses, flowers etc.

You will also need: a small roll of carpet tape or similar linen-backed sticky tape, and four small screws.

As this is intended to fit into a window recess, for instance in a back door, precise measurements are not given. The panel illustrated measures 58 × 48 cm. (23 × 19 in.), but larger or smaller sizes are made in the same way.

Method

It helps if you have a Jointmaster or some other means of cutting very accurately 90° angles in two planes at the same time. It is important that the frame sides butt together precisely, because no gluing is used: the idea is that you are able to change the arrangement of flowers etc.

Start the frame by marking the exact top and bottom measurements of the recess, cut them and mark which is top and bottom. Then measure the sides of the recess and subtract from each twice the depth of the whitewood channelling (1). Cut these pieces and assemble the frame in the recess to try for fit. The side members in particular must fit absolutely flush between the top and bottom members.

Glass With the frame in place measure up the size of the two sheets of glass required, allowing for the depth of the channels in the frame. Lay one sheet on a flat table, and slot the bottom frame member on the bottom edge, lower channel. Make your arrangement up, avoiding stems or flower heads which will not flatten out to about 4 mm. ($\frac{1}{8}$ in.) thickness. Also make sure that the glass surfaces are completely clean. When you are satisfied with the arrangement slot in the second sheet of glass and press it gently down. Now slot the top member in place, and add the sides. Secure the frame with strips of tape at the corners (2).

Fixing the picture Provided all your saw cuts are square and the tape is rubbed down firmly, the structure will be quite rigid and can be placed in the recess. Split each clothes peg and cut off the wedge ends: these are screwed onto the surrounding frame to hold the 'picture' in place, one at each corner (3). When you want to change the arrangement, simply remove these lock tabs, remove the picture, pull off the tape and remove the frame members. In reassembly, always use new pieces of tape. The frame may be left as natural wood, stained or painted.

1. For a recess 58 × 48 cm., using wood 1 cm. deep, A and B are 58 cm. long; C and D are 46 cm. For the size of the glass, take the inside measurements of the frame (56 × 46 cm.) and add on twice the depth of the channelling.

2. Use a strong tape, about 10 cm. long.

3. Use the two wedge ends of each peg.

3a. Peg hinges screwed to the frame.

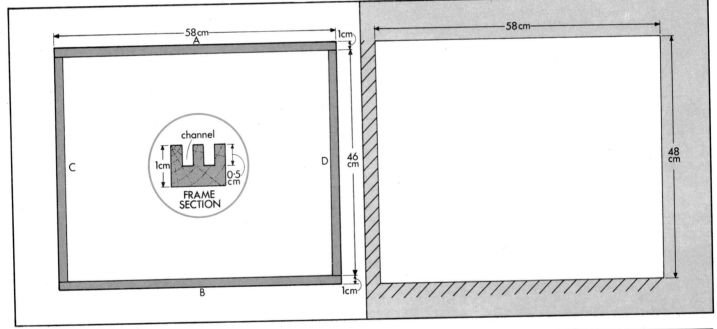

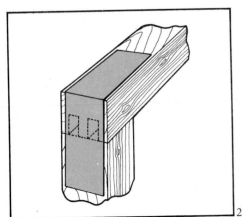

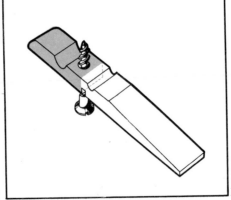

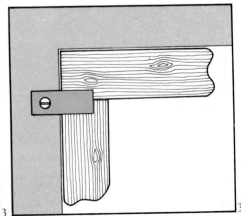

MIRROR HOUSE
Materials

1 sheet 3-ply (whitewood) 92 × 61 cm.
(36 × 24 in.)
4 pieces 675 g. (24 oz.) mirror glass
19 × 13 cm. (7½ × 5½ in.)
2 small hanging catches with 5 mm.
(¼ in.) screws
30 cm. (12 in.) picture wire
small roll double-sided sellotape
Evostik impact adhesive

You will also need: a clamp, a tenon saw and fretsaw, gloss paint (Caprice Yellow, Dulux), or see text, small can silver spray and small piece of Fablon or similar, for star stencils.

Method

Cut the ply sheet in half to give two pieces each 46 × 61 cm. (18 × 24 in.). Clamp the two halves together so that all edges are flush, and mark and cut the roof shape. Unclamp. Take the top piece and mark out the 'window' mirror positions as in the diagram. You can do this by positioning the mirrors and drawing round them, but remember to cut on the inside of the lines. Using the fretsaw, cut out the 'window' spaces and carefully sand all edges. Evostik the two halves together exactly flush, following the maker's instructions. Finish off by sanding.

Painting A quick system is to use an emulsion, giving the top face only two thinly-brushed coats with a light sanding in between. Paint the inside edges of the 'windows' but leave the house edges unpainted (brushing out towards an edge should ensure this). Now give the whole painted face a light sanding with four-grade paper, dust off, and spray on two coats of polyurethane

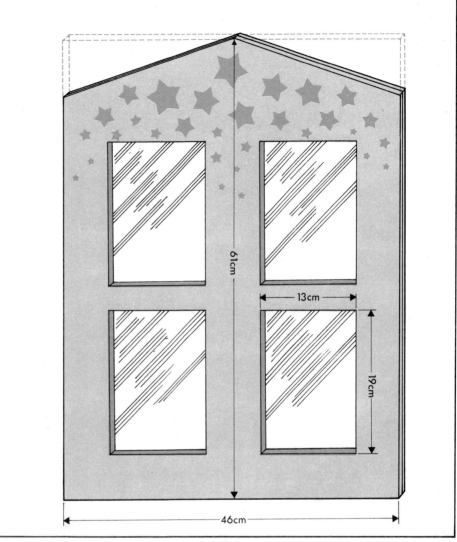

varnish. Leave to dry hard. Cut out star shapes from Fablon, stick in place, and spray silver paint over star area only, 'fading' gradually into the yellow. Allow to dry, peel off the star masks. Finish with spray varnish.

Place two or three strips of double-sided tape across each window space and stick in the mirrors. (Any small gaps can be filled in with coloured plasticine). Fix the two hanging catches on the back of the roof space (behind the mirrors), 30 cm. (12 in.) apart and attach cord or wire to hang.

KITCHEN TIDY
Materials

1 piece of hardboard or 4 mm. (⅛ in.)
ply, 60 × 80 cm. (24 × 31½ in.) for
backing
1 piece of hessian or sacking, approx.
70 × 90 cm. (27½ × 35½ in.) for
covering
1 length of 2 × 5 cm. (¾ × 2 in.) pine,
2·9 m (3 yds. 3 in.) long, for frame
1 offcut of 15 cm. (6 in.) width
Contiboard, approx. 50 cm. (20 in.)
long, for scribble area
Offcuts of 1 cm. (½ in.) chipboard to
make mirror 'envelope' backing
1 mirror tile 23 cm. (9 in.) square, with
self adhesive tabs
3 tins-225 g. (8 oz.) – e. g. coffee tins
1 ball of rough string

2 cork tiles 30·5 cm. (12 in.) square for
pinboard area, (tiles 23 cm. (9 in.)
square are preferable if available)
6 large tiling clouts for pegs.

You will also need: various glues (Evostik Resin W, Evostik impact adhesive and Araldite), a strong staple tack gun, filler, 2·5 cm. (1 in.) panel pins, 2 cm. (¾ in.) screws, and four small brass fixing plates for attaching the unit to your kitchen wall.

Method

Fix the hessian covering by lapping round the hardboard sheet and tacking with staples through the back. If these pierce through to the front, flatten over the ends. Staple about 2·5 cm. (1 in.) in from the edge of the board, starting in

the middle of one side, gradually working evenly out to the corners, and repeat the side opposite. Then do top and bottom. Keep the hessian evenly taut as you go.

The frame uses halved joints and is glued with Evostik Resin W. Take care when gluing the pieces together that any excess glue is immediately wiped off, otherwise the colour stain will not take evenly. Cut the pine length into two pieces of 60 cm. (24 in.) and two of 80 cm. (31½ in.), and make your halved joints (1). Do not use screws or nails at this stage. Sand the frame smooth and apply a thin coat of colour stain. Sand again when dried thoroughly, and repeat the staining. The shade of

53

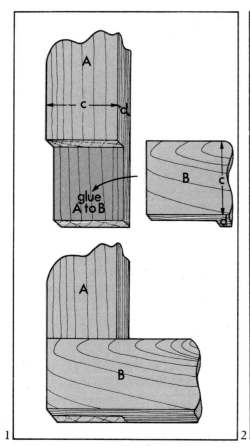

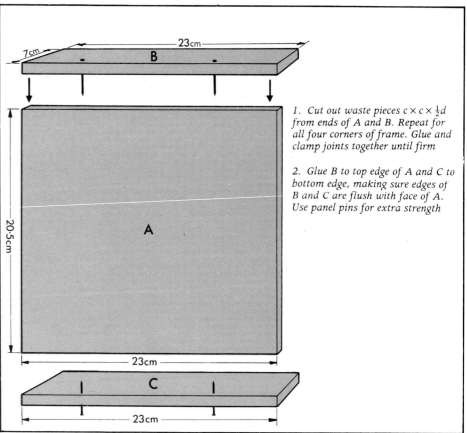

1. Cut out waste pieces c × c × ½d from ends of A and B. Repeat for all four corners of frame. Glue and clamp joints together until firm

2. Glue B to top edge of A and C to bottom edge, making sure edges of B and C are flush with face of A. Use panel pins for extra strength

colour achieved can be varied by applying more coats. Place the completed frame over the backing, and fix with screws from the back. Make sure that the screws will not break through to the front of the frame: they should be approximately 5 mm. (¼ in.) less than the total thickness of frame plus backing. Attach the four brass fixing plates (or brackets) on the back of the structure, one per corner.

To make the pinboard cut each cork tile down to 23 × 23 cm. (9 × 9 in.), seal with matt polyurethane and fix in place, butted together, with impact adhesive. It is a good idea to make sure that the glue layer spread on the hessian penetrates through to the hardboard. Allow ample time for this to get tacky before pressing on the cork.

To make the scribble board cut the Contiboard with a fine-toothed saw to between 45 cm. (18 in.) and 50 cm. (20 in.). Avoid chipping the laminate by sticking a strip of sellotape around the pencilled guide lines. Sand the edges smooth. Drill holes right through for the tile clouts which form the pegs, using a drill bit fractionally smaller than their diameter. Run a little Araldite into each hole before pressing the clouts in. The board is fixed in place in the same way as the pinboard, with the addition of two screws through from the back. Remember

once again not to allow the screws to break through to the front. Position left of centre to allow for the pencil holder.

Coffee tins Lightly score the back of each tin with an old Stanley blade, in criss-cross fashion, so as to get a good 'bite' surface for gluing. Make up three identical squares of hardboard from scrap, to fit against the scored surfaces, and glue in place with Araldite. Spray the insides with a few light coats of gloss colour, and bind round the outside of each tin with string. Use Araldite to glue all three flush together. When this has hardened out, glue the assembled tins in place with Evostik Resin W: brush it well into the hardboard squares, press the tins hard onto the backboard, then lift them off and apply more glue, and also brush in glue on the hessian surface to make good contact through to the hardboard backing. Finally, put the assembly back in position and leave to dry hard with a heavy weight placed across the tins.

The mirror 'envelope' From suitable offcuts of 1 cm. (½ in.) chipboard, cut the following sizes: two pieces 23 × 7 cm. (9 × 18 in.), one piece 23 × 20·5 cm. (9 × 8 in.). Using the Resin W and 2·5 cm. (1 in.) panel pins, glue and pin the large panel flush inside the two side panels to form the 'envelope' (2).

Note that the mirror tile should fit flush across the front, so that the front of the envelope must be 23 cm. (9 in.) square when assembled. Fill the edges with polyfilla, sand and paint. Emulsion followed with polyurethane is the simplest method, or a few coats of glossy emulsion. Place the envelope in position next to the tins, and very lightly trace the contact outline onto the hessian. Drill holes to take panel pins which are hammered in from the back. Make sure these holes are dead upright and central. Glue the envelope on with more Resin W, carefully turn the whole structure over and hammer through the panel pins. Peel the backing off the mirror tabs and press the glass firmly in place.

Pencil holder This can be made in all sorts of ways, from ready-made card tube containers which normally end up in the dustbin, or you can make up one specially with long paper strips, wallpaper paste and a thick broom handle as a mould. Remember to glue in a card disc for a base. The holder may be covered with coloured gummed paper, or painted with emulsion and polyurethaned. Make it 15 cm. (6 in.) deep to match up with the scribble board, and stick in place with impact adhesive at the right-hand end. If you are left-handed, you can alter the position of this or any other items.

6 eggs
milk
onions
Card 4.00

FUN WITH FURNITURE

'Having fun' is interpreted here as decorating the basic furniture. Decorating these days means more than just embellishing the surface with paint – it means solving problems too; with careful initial planning it is possible to make one article of furniture serve a multi-purpose function that in the long run will save on time, money and living space. To give some examples: a reading light and drawer clipped to a simple table transforms it into a desk – remove these clip-on accessories, throw over a luxurious cloth and you have an elegant dining table; open shelving units fitted with roller blinds can act as useful room-dividers in shared children's rooms or open-plan living rooms; conventional garden furniture can be brought inside the home and upholstered for all-the-year round use; office filing cabinets and purpose-built kitchen units can be fitted under a worktop or a counter anywhere in a home– the bedroom, bathroom or living room – often it is a question of changing the colour, handle or an inside fitting to suit a given situation. This is something that is best done with inexpensive furniture.

WHITEWOOD

What is really needed is flexible furniture that can 'grow' with your needs and the kind of furniture that lends itself to this is whitewood. You can adapt this to almost any decor situation and it lasts for years. Most large department stores have whitewood departments which stock basic designs, making it easy to match up and add items, as and when individual budgets allow.

Successful results in whitewood largely depend on a careful choice of accessories and colour schemes. You must decide exactly what period, style, colour and finish you are aiming for and, if necessary, do some homework on the subject. Wisely-chosen accessories can transform inexpensive whitewood into the luxury class: the difference is surprising when quite ordinary-looking furniture is fitted with good quality brass handles, smooth-running drawers, magnetic catches that close a cupboard door with minimum effort, and efficient castors. All these fittings are relatively inexpensive and not much trouble to fix.

Knobs and handles Plain, well-designed fittings always look good: white, coloured ceramic or brass knobs look better than plastic; so do military-chest, solid brass handles on a white-wood chest of drawers stained a rich mahogany. It is worth looking at alternative handles too: small chrome-plated towel rails and pieces of dowelling rod fixed to special screw-on plates make good pulls on heavy drawers or wardrobe doors. Some hardware shops stock unusual, inexpensive handles of the suitcase type.

Slide-on and build-up drawers The most flexible systems come in white polystyrene or clear perspex, or as plastic-coated wire 'baskets'. Drawers like these usually come complete with special runners and supports so that a complete bank of them can be built up to almost any height. You could also have drawers fitted under a living room or bathroom counter or in a kitchen instead of conventional built-in units.

Blinds can be used as an attractive and space-saving alternative to cupboard doors. You can buy made-to-measure roller and Venetian blinds and fix these to cupboard or shelving fronts. Or you can make your own roller blinds from a kit in your own choice of fabric, spray-treated to resist dirt and creasing. Pinoleum blinds look good on whitewood shelving units.

Mouldings D-i-y shops usually stock good ranges of these, particularly eighteenth-century designs that look extremely convincing painted over. Use a wood glue to stick these down.

Letters and numerals These are marvellous 'fun' decoration and brighten up bare expanses of panel. There are plenty about in different sizes and materials. Plastic, enamel and brass ones can be fixed up with self-adhesive tabs or screwed to a surface. Self-adhesive plastic letters and numbers come in a wide choice of colour and size and are available from most large art shops.

Miscellaneous hardware This includes clips, hooks and magnetic catches, castors and glides. Again, good-quality versions will make your whitewood work more efficiently. It is always a good idea to have a selection of clips and special racks (shoe and tie ones for the wardrobe; bottle racks for the kitchen); and remember, any castor or glide adds approximately 4 cm. (1½ in.) to the height of any piece of furniture.

Painting or staining If the wood is

Add a padded headrest to a deck chair

Stick a mirror in the lid of a whitewood box for a portable dressing table

Simple table h...

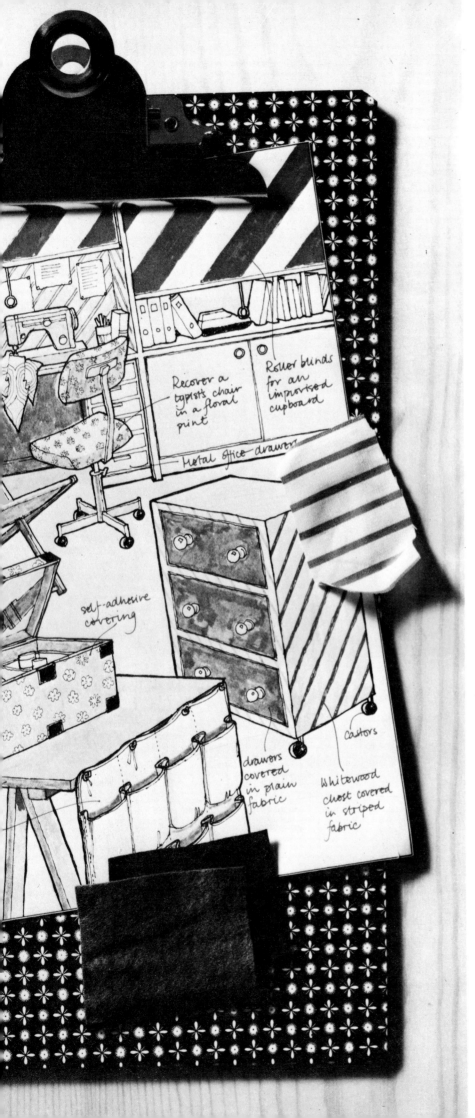

Recover a typist's chair in a floral print

Roller blinds for an improvised cupboard

Metal office drawers

self-adhesive covering

drawers covered in plain fabric

Castors

Whitewood chest covered in striped fabric

new and in good condition it might be an idea to show off the wood grain and for this, a wood stain or coloured polyurethane varnish can be used. There may be slight variations in colour on some pieces of furniture, but this can look rather attractive and in any case is unavoidable with whitewood, unless you are prepared to use French-polishing techniques. Painting is certainly one answer for less-than-perfect surfaces, but you will need to prime these with a wood or all-purpose primer before finishing with two coats of gloss paint. Always allow paint or varnish to dry out thoroughly between each coat and sand between each coat if necessary.

Self-adhesive coverings These rescue bad, pitted surfaces and are much easier and quicker to apply than paint; some come in plain, very shiny bright colours that look as good as the most expertly painted surface. There is a felt-covered one for lining cutlery drawers and a hessian one for door and cupboard linings as well as an enormous selection of patterned designs. Coverings are sold in various widths from approximately 30 cm. (12 in.) to 1 metre (39 in.) and it is advisable when buying coverings like these to buy slightly more than you think you will need, especially the patterned ones, as designs are liable to change.

Stick-on motifs These add instant decor impact – useful if you do not want to cover the whole surface or if you want a simple border pattern. Some motifs can be very sophisticated. Austrian Tyrol patterns, for example, can make a plain, stained-wood cupboard look almost as good as the genuine peasant article; Walt Disney characters, on the other hand, are always popular with children.

Fabric Professional window-dressers, display and exhibition designers have been covering furniture with this for some time. The job is made much easier these days with a staple gun. A staple remover is a handy accessory too as this enables you to take out tacks without damaging the fabric. Almost any lightweight fabric is suitable – cotton prints always look good and this covering is a pretty way of co-ordinating a piece of furniture with the rest of your room decor. If it appeals to you braid can be stuck over the staples afterwards. Special heavy-duty staple guns are available to order from larger stationery and d-i-y shops.

WINDOW TREATMENTS

There are numerous ways of treating every type of window. The problem is how to find out exactly what you want, basing your choice on a certain amount of knowledge.

Before we get down to the types of window dressing, here are a few general ideas; armed with these you will feel more confident of your own particular choice.

GENERAL POINTS TO CONSIDER

Always remember the outside of the house; the exterior should look as pleasant as possible. Consider uniformity, perhaps blinds all the way through the front of the house, so that the windows look neat and tidy from the outside. If you are using curtains, choose linings of the same colour, or even patterned lining throughout.

Plan your personal window treatments properly. You may live in a town, with a view onto a road, in which case you might need nets, or see-through blinds,

1. Café curtains for a pretty room
2. Vertical louvers used as a room divider and for windows
3. Classic French pleats
4. A plain window blind painted to decorate an exterior

to obscure the view in but allow you to see out quite clearly.

What do you and your family need, apart from good-looking treatments? Some people need a dark room to sleep in, in which case a black-out blind inside a curtain is the only answer, because curtains allow light to filter in from the top and sides, however careful you are.

ALTERNATIVES TO CURTAINS

Do not think only of curtains. There are so many alternatives – apart from nets, blinds and drapes. Consider painting a small window all over, or in a design, so that the light may still filter through, casting wonderful coloured shadows but leaving your privacy unimpaired. Think of using stained glass panes as a total treatment. If you have a kitchen window with an unattractive view, it might be better

to take out the bottom panes and replace them with mirrored glass, which reflects back into your room, giving extra light, but obscuring the view outside. A long tall window in a hall or landing, or in a place which really does not need a curtain or blind, could have glass or wooden shelves fitted across it at various intervals, on which to display a collection of glass or a mass of plants for a greenhouse effect.

Privacy may be preserved at the same time as letting in the light by using a hardboard panel with punctured patterns, painted white or a colour to suit your scheme, fastened to battens fitting neatly into the frame of the window. It is extremely effective. This can also be used on a low window looking out onto a street, in which only the lower portion of the window is treated in this way.

TYPES OF TREATMENT

Roller blinds These come in all sorts of shapes, sizes and fabric. D-i-y kits, giving full instructions for the particular system, are available from most large stores. It is important to buy the specially treated fabrics for roller blinds. These blinds do a splendid job and may be either highly decorative (you can draw your own designs on some) or plain, merely diffusing the light. When buying blinds you must first know how to measure your window (1). Secondly, consider the types of pull cords you may like (2). Lastly, consider braids and fringes, which add great panache to a simple style. Some manufacturers do shaped finishes with the base cut in certain styles for extra decoration.

Pinoleum blinds Formerly made of tiny strips of thin wood bound together by cotton, these are now made in plastic. They do the same job as roller blinds, are still cheap and are ideal for windows where you do not need total privacy. They let the light filter through into your room in a most agreeable fashion and allow you to see out. They were often used in the past in conservatories.

Venetian blinds These are very popular but should be seen as a long term buy because they are not cheap. They provide all the privacy you need, come in all shapes and sizes, and the slats are now available in slimline versions which are most attractive. They do need regular cleaning and there is a cleaner available in most stores. Venetian blinds look neat from both outside and in and last a life-time. You can also buy the old-fashioned blinds of wide slatted wood, which look very good, again last a life-time but cost a great deal. Cleaning these is not so easy.

Balastore blinds These are a cheap and charming type of window treatment. They are made of strong treated paper which is punched with holes to allow plenty of light to filter through, but retain privacy. They are ideal for short-term use because you can afford to install them while saving for a slightly more expensive scheme; ideal also if you are in a flat or rented house.

Pleatex Like balastore blinds these are made of strong paper, treated and permanently pleated. They are lightweight and can be fitted to odd-shaped windows such as those often found in attics. They are cheap and cheerful, but will not last for ever: as with most

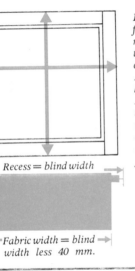

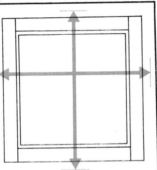

Recess = blind width

Fabric width = blind width less 40 mm.

1. Measuring your window for a roller blind. The blind may be fixed either inside the window recess (left) or outside the recess (right). Measure the width of the blind at the point of fitting. If fixing your blind inside the recess, give the full recess width and the drop dimension. Your blind will always be supplied with the fabric 40 mm. (1½ in.) narrower than the blind width. If fixing your blind outside the recess, decide by how much you wish the fabric to overlap at each side of the recess and measure the total width.

You should then add 40 mm. (1½ in.) to obtain the blind width. Your drop dimension should allow for your required overlap at the top and/or bottom of the window.

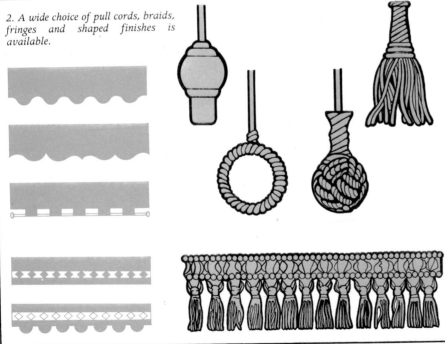

2. A wide choice of pull cords, braids, fringes and shaped finishes is available.

things, you get what you pay for.

Vertical louvers These are a lifetime investment, look cool, clinical and architectural, but are rarely cosy. They are beloved of architects and can look extremely effective. They are usually made of linen or treated canvas, hung vertically and opened to right or left. Alternatively they may be left in a closed position, when light is able to filter through easily. They can be used as a room divider, or in place of a door.

Roman blinds Extremely attractive, these are rather like pleatex but are made in the customer's own fabric. Usually a decorator will make them up to your own specifications, or you can try yourself, but they are not for beginners. When down, the fabric of the blind falls full-length to cover the window; when pulled up they concertina into pleats, and fold neatly against window or wall to form an attractive pelmet. They can, as in the case of most blinds, be wall or ceiling mounted.

Shutters These are entirely practical, but people in this country tend only to use them on the outside of their houses for decoration. They have far more practical uses, are excellent burglar deterrents, save on any other treatments, and fold back neatly during the day. At night they are extremely cosy.

Curtains and nets Finally we come to the most usual way of dressing windows, using curtains and nets. If you want to make your own you can save considerably on cost. The only real difficulty is if you have large areas to cover and not enough floor space to lay out your curtains while they are being made. If you want to do your own headings by hand, rather than using tapes, we give instructions below, but you should have some skill as a needlewoman. These headings, when hand sewn, do look marvellous, especially when they are interlined.

MAKING HEADINGS BY HAND

Pleated headings Behind the top edge of your curtain put stiffening that is the same width as the depth of your 'pockets'.

The pocket depth should relate to the length of the curtain; allow 4 cm. (1½ in.) per 30 cm. (12 in.) drop, e.g. 19 cm. (7½ in.) for a drop of 152 cm. (5 ft).

Draw vertical lines along the top edge of the curtain – these will be the guide lines for the pockets (3). Each pocket

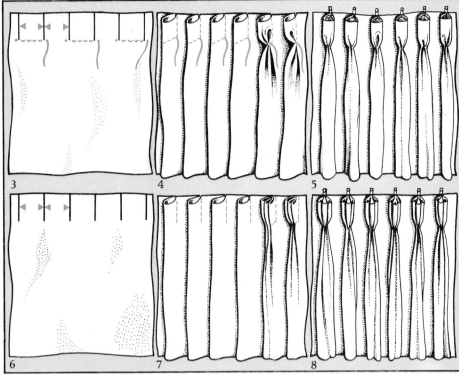

will take up to 10 cm. (4 in.) width of fabric; allow 10 cm. (4 in.) between each pocket. Put strong tacking stitches along the bottom of each pocket. Join pocket guide lines together and sew firmly (4). Draw up the tacking stitches and secure firmly. Fill the pockets with tissue paper or cotton wool (5). Sew hooks onto the back of each pocket and suspend from curtain rings.

French pleats The method for these is very similar and just as simple. Behind the top edge of the curtain put stiffening that is the same width as the depth of your pleat. The depth of the pleats should again be relative to the length of the curtain, allowing approximately 4 cm. (1½ in.) per foot drop, i.e. 19 cm. (7½ in.) for a drop of 152 cm. (5 ft). Draw vertical lines along the top edge of the curtain – these will be the guide lines for your pleats (6). Each pleat will take up to 10 cm. (4 in.) width of fabric; allow 10 cm. (4 in.) between each pleat. Join vertical pleat lines together and tack (7). 'Fan' the big pleat into three separate pleats and stitch the backs of all three pleats together (8). Stitch firmly at the base. Sew hooks onto the back of each pleat and suspend from curtain rings.

USING HEADING TAPES

These take the anguish out of curtain making. They are tapes threaded with string which are sewn along the top of the curtain. When the strings are pulled at one end, the tape draws up the fabric into the type of heading (9)

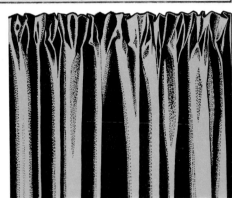

9

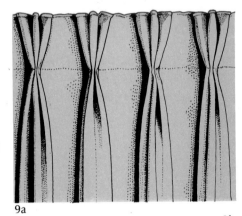

9a

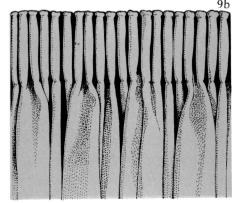

9b

1. Roman blinds used to
striking effect with matching
wall covering
2. Colour and pattern cleverly
co-ordinated for both curtain
and curtain sash
3. Stripes for a kitchen
window
4. Net curtains attractively
used to preserve privacy
without restricting the light
5. A simple and effective
solution for an unusual window
6. Blinds for a sunny bay
window
7. The window forms part of
your decor scheme
8. and 9. Day and night: a
blind recessed between alcove
wall and window lends itself
to differing effects

6

7

8

9

you have chosen. These tapes also hold the hooks, which in turn hang your curtains on a rail or pole.

Types of headings and tapes There are basically three main types of heading which you can make using standard heading tapes.

1. *Gathered heading*. These are the most simple and work best when hung from a pole. They literally make gathers along the top of the curtain. They take very little fabric, but can look skimped. If you do not wish to have a pole, then this is one time when we would suggest you use a track which covers the heading or even a pelmet. People are still inclined to use pelmets, for no better reason than the fact that they are already there (9). They are, however, often ugly and usually restrict the light.

2. *French or pinch pleats*. These are rather more sophisticated. You can buy them deep or shallow, depending on the length of your curtain. (For a short curtain, a shallow heading tape is suggested, similarly when used for nets which look well when heading tapes are used (9a)).

3. *Pencil pleats*. So called because they look like a row of pencils, these are ideal for lightweight nets, or fine fabrics. They are particularly effective for bedroom curtains (9b).

The choice, finally, is always yours. Take into consideration the room and the amount you have to spend on fabrics, remembering that some headings take far more material than others.

TRACKS AND POLES

Having decided on both tape and heading, you will need to decide on the type of track, rail or pole you like. This is a matter of personal taste – combined with suitability to your particular windows.

Hooks are attached to the heading tape, and onto the rail or pole, and actually hang the curtains. They are made in all shapes and sizes – in plastic, plastic-coated metal and rustproof metal – the latter a boon as the problem of rust was at one time very real. Normally you use a single hook, but when a more complicated heading tape is used, hooks can be two- and three-pronged. These fit into the pockets of the tape, to produce the desired heading; this is an alternative to pulling the tapes up tight on their strings and using a simple hook.

Poles The simplest and still the cheapest way to hang a curtain is on a

pole, using rings if your window will take it. This means that you should have space above the window and below the ceiling. In some cases, however, you can mount the pole in brackets fixed to the ceiling. You can buy lengths of wood, pole ends (wooden door handles are good alternatives) and brackets at hardware stores; when painted or varnished, they look spectacular and do a fine job. Alternatively you can buy brass poles which are very effective, but expensive. Finally some manufacturers make 'mock' poles, in plastic and metal, behind which you can hang your curtains, so that the headings are hidden, and a cording set may also be hidden away.

Tracks or rods There is a great variety of tracks on the market, to meet every different situation. Tracks, rods or rails can be wall or ceiling-mounted, according to your needs. Find out what suits your particular window and, armed with this information, visit your retailer.

A tension rod will work well in a difficult recessed window; it is sprung inside, the rod being pushed into the recess and held permanently there. It is best to use a light fabric, though, to avoid unnecessary strain. Then there are double tracks which make it possible to hang nets behind your heavy curtains. Bay windows no longer cause a problem, as there are tracks available which will bend to any curve. For difficult windows, like a dormer, a hinged track may be fitted. This swings back with the window when it is open.

It is also possible to buy tracks with a curtain overlap, so that when the curtains are drawn, they overlap; this looks attractive, and will not let any light in. Other tracks meet to make a perfect join, or are continuous, with the drapes breaking in the centre.

It is sometimes necessary to hang curtains away from the wall, to avoid a radiator, or shelf. You can get an extension bracket, which extends out as much as 15 cm. (6 in.) from the wall. There is a solution to every problem and any good retailer will find you your perfect track.

Finally, it is worth considering a cording set. This means that you do not have to handle curtains when opening and closing them, and you save on cleaning and wear. The set costs extra, but is worth it. Various styles are available.

HOW TO MEASURE AND MAKE CURTAINS

The following instructions are for making curtains using heading tapes. They may, however, be very simply adapted if you are sewing your headings by hand. The total width of finished curtains must be determined by the length of the curtain track, and not the window. Unless your window is wall to wall, you will require a curtain track which extends beyond each side of the window, to enable your curtains to be pulled well back. There are no set rules about the additional length of track required as this depends partly on the thickness of the curtain fabric and the additional thickness of the lining which will affect the bulk of the finished curtain. The following, however, provides a general guide line. For very small windows, allow at least 15 cm. (6 in.) extra track at each side of

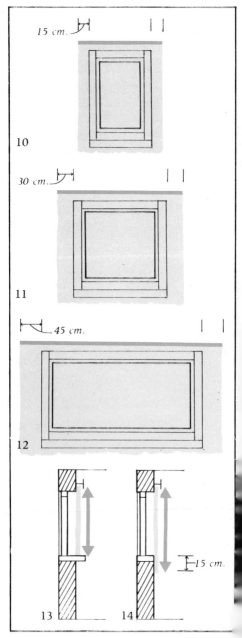

the window (10). For medium-sized windows (11), allow at least 30 cm. (12 in.); for wide windows (12), allow at least 45 cm. (18 in.). The type of heading dictates the total width of fabric needed. So choose your heading first, and work it out from there. It may sound difficult, but your retailer will always help you out on these occasions.

Remember to allow for a pattern repeat, which means that you have to make sure the patterns all join together at the seams. The patterns must also be matched so that they run on the same level on each curtain. If there is a large pattern repeat, i.e. a large gap between each pattern, you must remember to order extra fabric, or you will end up with not enough material. Floor-length curtains should finish 2·5 cm. (1 in.) from the carpet or floor. Sill-length curtains may either fall onto the window sill (13), in which case the curtains should finish 1·25 cm. (½ in.) above the sill. Alternatively, if your curtain hangs free from the sill, it is better finished at least 15 cm. (6 in.) below the sill (14).

To make unlined curtains Start by cutting your fabric to the right length, giving yourself an extra 10 cm. (4 in.) at the top, and 15 cm. (6 in.) at the bottom for hems. To prevent your fabric puckering, snip selvedges at intervals of 5–8 cm. (2–3 in.) before joining width. Join the widths together carefully, ensuring that the patterns all match. Use open seams (15) or French seams (16) to join width and press these seams. Always remember to press as you go.

Stitch down the top hem. If you are using a heading tape, rather than doing the headings by hand, ensure your tape is the right way up, and sew the top and bottom onto your curtain top, but only after you have hand-stitched the side seams loosely. Allow approximately 4 cm. (1½ in.) for each side hem; they should be double so that no raw edges show. We also suggest that you hand stitch the bottom hem, as it always looks better than machining. Another tip is to hang the curtains for a few days before finishing off the bottom hems, so that they have had a chance to drop.

To make lined curtains Most curtains look better with linings, and there are two ways of lining them. You can either loose line, or make it more professional and have a lining permanently sewn in.

For permanently attached linings you will need the same fullness of lining as of curtain fabric. The length should be 15 cm. (6 in.) less and 5 cm. (2 in.) narrower. Hem the lining with a 5-cm. (2-in.) hem. Lay your hemmed lining on the curtain with right sides together and tops lined up. Sew down each side of the lining, 2 cm. (½ in.) in from one edge (17). Turn inside out so that the right sides are now facing outwards. Turn over the top edge of the curtain and oversew to the lining (18). Attach the heading tape by machine. (19). Press carefully.

Loose linings are attached to the curtains by means of a special type of heading tape, which then hooks onto the curtain heading tape. It is best to allow 1½ times the fullness of the curtain. Loosely tack each side edge of the lining to the sides of the curtain.

A good finish If you want to make your curtains hang well, it is worth considering leadweight tape which pulls the curtain down, gives a professional finish, and is good with 'blow-away' nets. The tape comes in various sizes, encased in fabric, and is sold by the yard or box.

To finish off headings properly, when you also want to keep a couple of lengths of cord so that you can alter the tension if necessary, buy a cord tidy, wind round the extra cord, and hook it neatly onto the heading tape, out of sight (20).

Once you have your curtains in place, tie them with cord every 45 cm. (18 in.), so that all the pleats are well set, and leave for a minimum of 48 hours. When released you will be surprised how much better they will hang than if you had simply left them, and put them to use immediately.

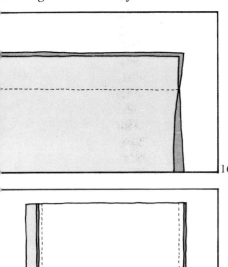

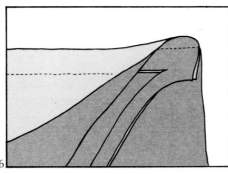

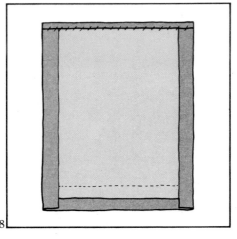

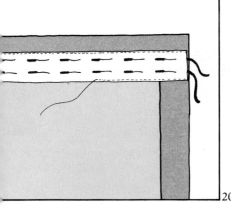

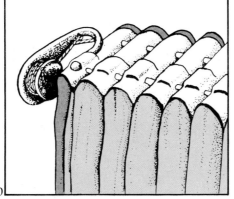

PLANNING COLOUR SCHEMES

The gentle art of colour scheming is not without its pitfalls and any of us can be forgiven for developing a mild phobia about the subject. Making the right colour decisions can be extremely difficult simply because there is such a wide range of choice and a multitude of possible permutations. But intelligently approached, the subject can be creative and rewarding. It certainly is not an exact science but that can be an advantage as the opportunities for personal expression are infinite.

While some people are lucky enough to be born with a natural colour sense, many of us have to work at acquiring the necessary skills. Anyone who has ever had the misfortune to be saddled with a scheme that has gone wrong will not begrudge time spent on gaining the requisite skills.

LOOK AND LEARN

To ask you to start looking around in search of colour knowledge seems almost insulting, but so many people seem to take only a passive interest in the colour of their surroundings that it is worth underlining the importance of active colour observation. Train yourself to observe your total environment, extending your vision above and below eye level. Looking at the colours in nature is not a bad starting point, for in the countryside or in a bed of mixed flowers, one is rarely aware of colour clashes. Emulating nature – or indeed just understanding nature's colour logic – takes a high degree of mastery. Still, with practice and acute observation it is possible to learn a great deal. And there is a lot of nature around to learn from; even relatively undistinguished birds like the common sparrow enjoy colour schemes that are full of inspiration for the decorator. More exotic birds show nature's consummate skill in the use of brilliant colours, often in the most unlikely combinations.

Then there is a great deal to be learned by looking at interiors other than your own. Visit stately homes and see how centuries of good taste have produced magnificence and perfect colour handling. Although your problems are likely to be on a smaller scale, the lessons are always there to be adapted for your own home. When you visit the homes of your friends try to decide what the factors are which contribute to relaxation and comfort – it will not be just the central heating! And if you go to houses where the atmosphere seems disturbed and restless, try to decide what factors introduce jarring notes.

Always listen to other people's views on colour. Anyone may come up with a fresh idea and a new point of view and new colour combinations. Ask for advice whenever you can, especially if it is free and always try to hear or read about the views of professional decorators. They are usually employed on grander schemes than those which confront you and their professional experience can be invaluable, as they have the experience that only constant application to the problem can provide. It is interesting to note in passing that even the professionals have their failures. It has been said that the work of the good interior decorator often elicits the comment from the client that they could have done the job themselves. This is usually an indication that he knows both his client and his job very well.

A great deal of design and colour expertise goes into the production of first-class magazines and printed brochures. Never ignore them, for while you can rarely take over a colour scheme exactly as it is reproduced, you can use this sort of material as a starting point. Cut out pictures which appeal and start a colour file. You will soon assemble enough material to enable you to decide your colour preferences. Add scraps of material, any bits of colour and start to assemble combinations which reflect your colour preferences. The act of consciously building up a file will heighten your awareness of colour.

COLOUR PSYCHOLOGY

However unaware of it, everyone is truly affected by colour and in recent years much research has been done into the creation of the correct colour environment for all sorts of activity. Hospitals, offices and public buildings, restaurants and shops are all carefully colour-schemed to promote the correct atmosphere for healing, work, eating and drinking, shopping or whatever is appropriate to the building concerned. For the identical reasons that apply to public buildings, your home environment needs the same close attention.

Let us take two basic examples: first a warm colour and then, from the opposite end of the colour scale, a cold colour. Red, say pillar-box red is a colour which is positive, excites the mental processes, causes the adrenalin to flow and tends generally to create an atmosphere in which, at first, more activity takes place in a shorter while. But after a time red can tend to upset your equilibrium, make you impatient and time will tend to drag. So do think twice before painting your kitchen a brilliant red, for by doing so you may create an accident prone environment. Red is aggressive, warm, vibrant and alive, full of action and liable to excite. In all its hues and tones, it has its decorative uses as well as its dangers.

Blue has the opposite effect. It tends to induce relaxation but many of the blues verge on coldness. These two extremes serve as a small illustration of some of the colour traps which abound. Happily there are innumerable compromises that can be enjoyably exploited.

There is, too, the question of an individual's personality. People react differently to colours according to the dictates of their own personalities.

Take the extrovert – the woman who dashes about all day, whose energy is breath-taking. She may need calming down and for her blue can be used to great effect. Put her in a blue room, or in tones of blue, and she will relax. Conversely, the slow, less active woman may need splashes of strong aggressive colours to pep her up and get her on the move. So we react, every one of us, to colour in an unconscious way. If we really want to get to grips with colour, we must try to become more aware of colour consciously. That is, by approaching the subject positively and thinking about it, observing and becoming aware and in time learning to master the creation of surroundings that enable us to live at one with ourselves. There are other factors that affect personal choice but, taken step by step, learning about colour is not difficult, merely a matter of careful observation.

Planning a colour scheme

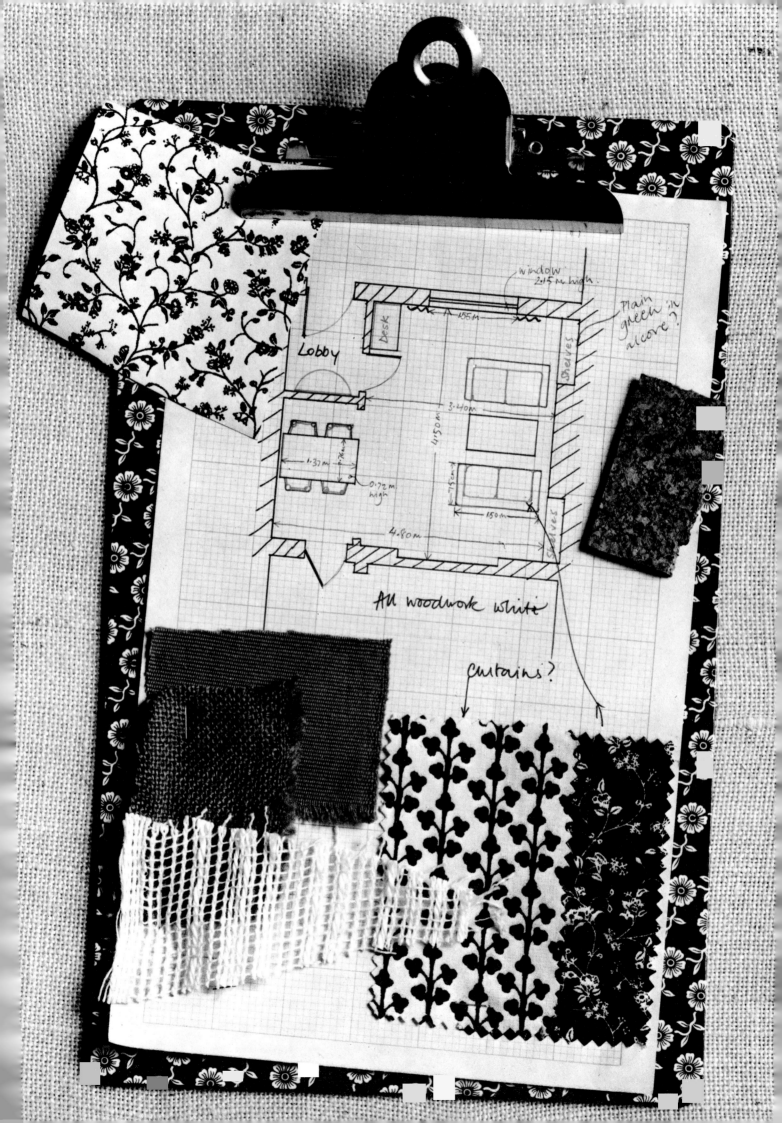

1. Just two colours, effectively combined in different ways, give depth to a scheme
2. Bold use of colour and contrast
3. Wall patterns contribute shape as well as colour
4. A subtle scheme accented by red
5. White, a colour in its own right as well as a vital component
6. Accessories to match the colours in a pattern give a co-ordinated effect

5

6

COLOUR PROPORTION

The proportion of one colour to another must be taken into account. If you do decide on say, gold as a main colour theme, secondary and accessory colours other than gold will be required in carefully considered proportions to enhance the main colour. Too much of any single colour rarely works. Combinations of two or more colours may be balanced as outlined below, see also our colour chart on page 77.

1. If you wish to choose two colours for your room scheme, colours which, in your opinion, complement each other – for example, orange – bright and strong, and green – softer and more muted, orange is obviously the dominant colour (remember that all shades of red are dominant). To keep the balance right you must use the orange as the *accent* colour, with green as the proportionately main colour. Use orange for your accessories – blinds, cushions and decorative objects. This is an example of a good general rule to follow.

2. If you prefer to use two colours of equal intensity (a perfectly reasonable choice), you should consider using them in exact proportions.

3. The use of multiple colours is much more difficult and requires a great deal of confidence. But though it is complex, the effect can be quite beautiful. Start with a fairly neutral base, on walls, carpet and furnishings. Faded colours, or traditional ones like eau de nil, magnolia or soft lemon form a good base to which many colours can be added in rugs, Persian carpets, an old shawl draped over a sofa, chairs with embroidered seats, multi-coloured cushions. The greater the variety, the better. To avoid too gaudy an effect, keep the colours soft and muted. The guiding rule here is that you need a lot of colour in detail. 'Busy' rooms are ideal for collectors and for people who regularly visit markets.

These three examples are obviously simplified, but they provide guidelines that work well in practice.

SHAPE AND TEXTURE

Once you have mastered colour proportion, you need to come to terms with shape and texture in relation to colour. The size and shape of objects can be accented or minimised – made to project into or recede from your scheme by means of colour and texture. Good decorating schemes mix matt with gloss, the texture of wood with gleaming glass, paper with paint. For a simple example of the effect of colour and texture on shape, take from the world of fashion the case of a fat lady who wants to make herself look slimmer. Wearing a long, well cut dress in a dark colour, with a matt texture, her bulk recedes; she looks slimmer and less obvious. On the other hand, a thin woman may take pains to show herself off to the best advantage in the opposite way; she can gain stature by wearing a flowery, shiny, two piece outfit.

To ensure that a decoration scheme works, all the surfaces should not look alike. Some must recede, others must be given prominence. Generally, soft, matt surfaces tend to be recessive. They blend into a scheme and become unobtrusive. Projective colours and surfaces in dominant colours have the opposite effect. They stand out and attract your attention. Glass tables, shiny PVC materials, gloss paints: all clearly define objects and draw the eye. Few schemes can work unless they

1. Use a stronger colour for accent

2. Two equally strong colours may be used in exact proportion

1

72

have a mixture of both dominant and recessive colours and matt and shiny and textured surfaces. Shape, texture and colour all contribute. An entirely matt scheme, which might, in theory, be stunning, could well be a dismal failure. If you have a high pile carpet upon which a wing chair stands (positive in shape), covered in a soft woolly fabric of the same colour and texture as the carpet, your chair will melt into the carpet. To emphasize the shape of the chair you should change either its texture or colour. You could cover it in hard, shiny leather, or PVC, or even silk, or a silk substitute. Even though the colour may still be the same, the different texture nevertheless makes your chair take shape and it will look clearly defined. You may, however, like the type of fabric on your chair and your carpet. It is easy enough to project your chair into the room simply by changing the colour. Use the same fabric, but in a different colour, say bright green or dark brown and the colour contrast will define the shape of the chair. We cannot stress enough the importance of texture in conjunction with colour as a means of making certain objects melt into the background, while others

project. Remember, cool colours tend to be recessive, hot ones project.

It is not advisable to break up a small room by painting one wall in a strong colour (popular in the unenlightened 50's). A wall so treated will come zooming out at you. Far better to give a small room an overall colour and add interest by clever lighting and by hanging pictures and objects in attractive groups on that wall.

There are, of course, exceptions to this rule. In a large room you may need to push a wall back, or bring another in by the simple use of colour. Box shaped rooms (the square) can look dreary and uninteresting, and by painting one wall, such a room will appear to be rectangular and more interesting.

Never make the mistake of painting two opposing walls in a small room the same strong colour, leaving the other two neutral. You will find yourself sandwiched between the strongly coloured walls in the most unpleasant way. The colour of ceilings is important. You may want to lower a high one. This is quite easily done simply by painting it in a strong warm colour, using gloss paint. But remember that this will only work if your room is large.

Small ceilings in a different colour from the walls can have the unpleasant effect of not only bringing the ceiling down, but also the walls in, making a small room seem smaller and uncomfortably cramped.

Pattern produces another dimension. An easy general rule to follow is that large patterns make a room look smaller, and small patterns make it look larger. If you are considering attacking the box room, loo or small bathroom, use pattern, large or small (but not too large, though this can work) over walls and ceilings. Small rooms cannot pretend to be anything else but small, and can gain unity and stature with an all-over pattern.

TAKE TIME TO PLAN
Before you start on a scheme, do make a plan of your room on graph paper, with measurements. You can even make several, drawing the room to scale and then colouring the drawings with felt tip pens, so that you have a rough idea of how it will look in several colour combinations. It is a good idea to use clip board, for easy jottings and drawings. Take snips of any fabrics and furnishings which you cannot change and glue or pin them to your

1. Texture, whether shiny or matt, forms part of a colour scheme
2. Cool colours combine with natural textures in simple yet sophisticated style
3. Colours of similar weight used in proportion
4. Brilliant use of an all-over colour, sharply offset by white
5. Accent colours achieve warmth and unity

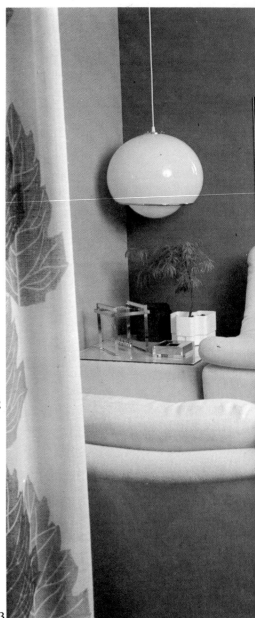

board. Armed with this, and all other relevant information, visit the shops. You will find that assistants are far more helpful if you can show them exactly what you are stuck with, and then what you have in mind. A planned approach helps you to gain confidence if you are unsure of your skill as

Consider the full range of tones within any one colour

a decorator. Do remember that once your scheme is on the clipboard and before it is on your walls, it is a good plan to live with large paint samples or paper patterns pinned up on the chosen walls for a week at least.

When you have papered and painted, remember that your room will not look right until you have got all your personal bits and pieces into place. Move back the furniture, the shelves and all accessories, take a deep breath and then assess the result.

POINTS TO REMEMBER

Do work out, when considering your scheme (especially if you live in a town and your only view is of the dustbins), whether you want an inward looking warm colour scheme, one which deliberately discards the unfriendly world outside. On the other hand, if there is a wonderful view out onto lawns, then incorporate this in your scheme; take your colours out into the garden.

Do remember to relate the colours you use through the house, especially if it is small, as too many patterns and colours can cause confusion. One idea is to have a fitted carpet throughout in the same texture and colour. Another is to keep halls and stairways, and landings, in one colour. This creates visual continuity.

Do always take into consideration the age of the person whose room you are decorating. Granny will not appreciate the same colours as young Tommy. Generally, the older the person, the more muted and softer the shades that should be used.

Do remember to make bedrooms restful, so that they do not aggravate. Soft, warm colours like terracotta and warm golden yellow are peaceful, glowing and relaxing. So, of course, are all neutral shades.

Do remember to think about the aspect your room faces: for example, if it is due north, do not paint it chilly blue, because it will just look chillier. Warm up cold rooms and tone down hot ones. If you must stick with safe and successful neutrals, then warm them up with small, bright splashes of colour, or darker tones of the same colour.

Do avoid dull greys, unless you are sure of your taste. They can so easily look dreary and lifeless, yet oddly these tones are still popular.

Do remember that the more neutral the colours used, the more you must be aware of shape and texture.

INSPIRED COLOUR COMBINATIONS

Colour scheming, as already pointed out, is a highly personal matter. Really your choice can never be wrong if it pleases you, for there are no hard and fast rules. But, as in cooking, time and tradition have contributed to a kind of folk-lore that indicates which ingredients are likely to produce harmonious results. Fashion plays a considerable part in this process and colours swing in and out of favour every few years. Today's popular mixes may be anathema in a few years' time, and today's 'old-fashioned' colours become popular again in time. That is why the principle of collecting colour samples to try with and against each other – for deliberate clashes can be spectacular – is so worthwhile.

Colours from the same family or segment of the spectrum usually live happily together. Thus a room in beige with creams and browns can be extremely successful, or, more stridently, a room with several reds can be spectacular. The earth colours, yellows, ochres, browns, oranges and reds combine as well in decoration as they do in nature. The essential first principle is to decide which colour or group of colours will make you happy, and then to assemble samples and try them in varying proportions together.

The importance of accent colours is paramount. Just as seasoning transforms bland food into a gastronomic delight, so the addition of sharp accent colour will transform an acceptable but bland colour combination into something really exciting. This chart is an assembly of colour schemes designed to start you thinking. It is divided into columns to indicate roughly in what proportion the colours should be used. The main colour will usually be the walls, but not necessarily. If you have vast areas of curtains in a room it may be that their area is greater than the wall space, in which case the curtains can be chosen from the main column. Similarly, the secondary colour will probably be suitable for the curtains, but if the windows are small and inconspicuous, the secondary colour can be applied to the furniture or the floor. No-one can arbitrate for you – you must collect the patterns and try your own combinations. Time used in the pursuit of perfection is time well spent.

	MAIN	SECONDARY	FLOOR	FURNITURE	ACCENT
RED	SCARLET	WHITE	STRING	WHITE OR RED	PINK OR SCARLET
	WHITE	SCARLET	WHITE	CITRON AND SCARLET	PLUM
	BEIGE	PINK	OATMEAL	RED & WHITE	PINK
	RED	WHITE	RED	RED	WHITE
WHITE	CAFE AU LAIT	WHITE	STRING	CREAM	BRIGHT GREEN SMOKY GREY
	WHITE	YELLOW	TURQUOISE	PATTERNED BROWN/YELLOW	BROWN
	BEIGE	WHITE	WHITE TEXTURED BEIGE	COFFEE	CHOCOLATE
	WHITE	CREAM		BEIGE & CREAM	BILBERRY
BLUE	AQUAMARINE	GOLD	DEEP YELLOW	AQUAMARINE	BRIGHT YELLOW
	OXFORD BLUE	CAMBRIDGE BLUE	BEIGE OR STRING	BITTER CHOCOLATE	WHITE
	NAVY	CEDAR GREEN	NAVY	GRASS GREEN	WHITE
	WHITE	OXFORD BLUE	LIGHT BLUE	BEIGE	OXFORD BLUE
BROWN	BITTER CHOCOLATE BEIGE	COFFEE	STRING	CHROME & COFFEE	HONEY
		TAN	BEECH	CHESTNUT	GOLD
	OATMEAL	CHOCOLATE	OATMEAL	CREAM	DUSKY PINK
	BROWN	ORANGE	BROWN	ORANGE	CREAM
YELLOW	DUSKY PINK	GOLDEN YELLOW	TAUPE	YELLOW	BITTER CHOCOLATE
	YELLOW OCHRE	ORANGE	DARK PINK	OCHRE	PINKS
	WHITE	YELLOW	BROWN & BEIGE PATTERN	GOLDEN BROWN	YELLOW
	BRIGHT YELLOW	CREAM	NEUTRAL	YELLOW & WHITE	ORANGE
GOLD	TAUPE	GOLD	BEECH BROWN	GOLD	SHARP BLUES
	GOLD	WHITE	STRING	BROWN	CITRON
	MUTED YELLOW	GOLD	BEIGE	WHITE & CREAM	GOLD
	GOLD	GOLD & OLIVE	GOLD	GOLD & OLIVE	OLIVE
GREEN	BOTTLE	LETTUCE	NEUTRAL	STRAW	AQUAMARINE
	LETTUCE	BOTTLE	GRASS	BOTTLE OR TURQUOISE	SHARP GREEN
	FOREST GREEN	WHITE	FOREST GREEN	BROWN & WHITE	GOLD
	EAU DE NIL	EAU DE NIL	BOTTLE GREEN	LAUREL	CORNFLOWER BLUE

PAINTING EQUIPMENT

Apart from brushes, rollers or paint pads for actually applying paint, you will need tools with which to prepare the surfaces. If you are hanging wallcoverings, you will need tools for this job also (see page 110).

walls and ceilings, a small trowel is often useful.

For applying filler to rough or uneven surfaces, use a wide filling knife; it looks like a stripping knife but has a much more flexible blade and should be kept for filling only; using it as a scraper will spoil the edge.

A dusting brush for removing dust before painting is not essential but it is more effective than a cloth duster.

To remove rust from ironwork, use a wirebrush – various sizes are available.

Other equipment that can be hired includes steam strippers for removing wallpaper and sanding machines of various sizes, as well as ladders, trestles, scaffold planks and staging.

BRUSHES
Brushing is still the most popular method of applying paint. The best brushes are made with 'pure bristle', i.e. hog bristle alone, and are the most expensive. But they will last longer and give a better finish than cheap brushes.

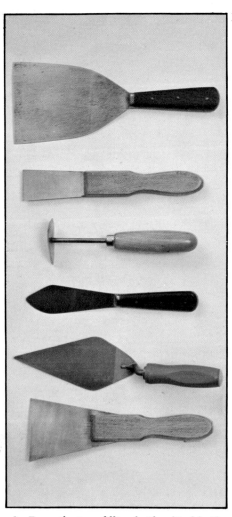

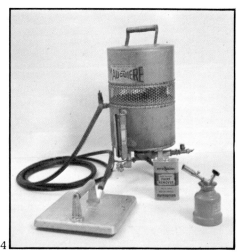
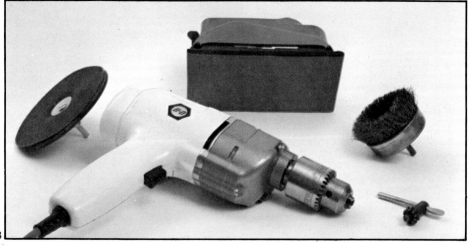

1. From the top: filling knife, chisel knife, shavehook, putty knife, trowel, scraper 2. Dusting brush and wire brush 3. Power drill with (from left) sanding disc, orbital sander, wirebrush 4. From the left: steam stripper, paint stripper, blow torch 5. Sanding machine

PREPARATION TOOLS
For removing wallpaper and paint, a 3-inch (76-mm.) stripping knife or scraper is used on wide surfaces; a 1½-inch (38-mm.) chisel knife does a similar job on narrow surfaces. Paint is removed from mouldings with a shavehook, either heart-shaped or triangular.

A putty knife is used for stopping up holes and small cracks as well as for repairing or replacing the putty around windows. For larger repair jobs on

Or, if you have a power drill, use a wirebrush attachment.

Other power drill attachments include sanding discs and orbital sanders, useful if you have flush doors and similar large areas to rub down.

Paint can be removed either with paint stripper or by burning off (see page 87) with a blow torch, usually fuelled by butane gas. Unless you have a lot of burning-off to do, it is probably not worth buying one but they can be hired.

Paint brushes, for use in oil-based paints, range in size from ½ inch (12·5 mm.) up to 4 inches (100 mm.) in ½-inch steps, these measurements referring to the width of the brush. A set of three, e.g. 1 inch (25 mm.), 2 inch (50 mm.) and 3 inch (75 mm.), is suitable for most jobs.

With emulsion paints, on walls and ceilings, distemper or wall brushes are used. These range in width from 4 inches (100 mm.) up to 7 or 8 inches (175–200 mm.). Professionals use the larger sizes but a 4-inch brush is a convenient size for the home decorator.

ROLLERS

These are excellent for ceilings and walls, especially with emulsion paint. Application is more rapid than by brush and many users find it requires less skill. However, a brush is still needed to paint into angles and corners. Rollers are usually 6 inches (150 mm.) or 7 inches (175 mm.) wide although narrower widths are available. Various

container which is pressurised with a built-in pump and forced through a tube to the inside of the roller.

PAINT PADS

Paint pads come in various shapes and sizes, the largest measuring about 6 by 4 inches (150 by 100 mm.). This method of application is rather slow but beginners often find them useful especially for painting window frames and similar narrow surfaces. Some types of pad are renewable.

LOOKING AFTER EQUIPMENT

It is worth buying good quality tools and equipment but you must look after them.

Keep knives and scrapers clean and bright and when you have finished using them, keep them in their own box or drawer. Jumbling them up with the general household tools means that edges will become blunted and damaged. Take particular care of filling knives.

Clean brushes, rollers and paint pads

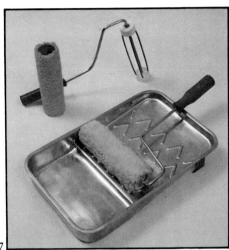

6. *Wall brush and paint brushes in sizes (from left) 3 in., 2 in., 1½ in., 1 in., ½ in. 7. Roller with short-pile fibre covering and long-pile covered roller in roller tray 8. Paint pads 9. A small electrically operated paint sprayer with a large model behind*

materials are used for roller coverings; a short-pile synthetic fibre covering is best for general-purpose use on flat surfaces. Use a long-pile type for rough or textured surfaces such as brickwork and pebbledash.

To hold the paint when using a roller you will need a tray or, for large jobs such as outside walls, a roller bucket. These are rather expensive but can often be hired.

Pressure-fed rollers save time in loading the roller; the paint is in a separate

PAINT SPRAYERS

Professional-size spray equipment can be hired but a fair amount of skill and experience is needed to use it competently. Small, electrically operated sprayers, suitable for amateur use, are available although, in speed of application, they may show no advantage over a roller; some of them require the paint to be thinned so much that it loses its hiding power. However, spray equipment of the type shown here gives excellent results with most paints.

immediately after use, before the paint has hardened, using white spirit, brush cleaner or water as appropriate. Some oil-based paints can be cleaned out with detergent or soap powder and water (see page 80). After cleaning, put the tools in a warm (not hot) place to dry and then wrap them in greaseproof paper. Pure bristle may be attacked by moths so it is a good idea to put moth-repellent in the box or other container in which the brushes should be stored. Never leave brushes to soak in water.

CHOOSING THE PAINT

With so many brands and apparently different types of paints available nowadays, it is not surprising if you are confused when it comes to making a choice. But do not despair; things are less complicated than they may seem.

Most of the paints you are likely to use around the house are of one of two main types:

(a) Oil-based
(b) Emulsion

OIL-BASED PAINTS

Oil-based paints have these features in common:

(a) They have a typical paint smell that may linger for some time.
(b) They normally take several hours to dry.
(c) They are generally thinnable with white spirit.
(d) They may be liquid or 'non-drip'.

Simple oil-based paints can be made by adding pigment to a drying oil, such as linseed oil. But they would dry very slowly, be low in gloss and not very wear-resistant. So, in house paints, resins are combined with drying oils for increased toughness and quicker hardening.

Natural resins were once widely used but they have mostly been replaced by man-made synthetic resins, more uniform in quality and having better wearing and lasting qualities. Alkyd resin is the most widely used, especially for gloss finishes. Some alkyd resin paints also contain polyurethane resin, usually in small quantities. This increases the resistance of the paint to knocks and scratches.

In non-drip oil-based paints, a special alkyd resin is used which is thixotropic; the paint looks thick in the can but becomes more liquid when it is stirred or brushed out. Left for a time, it thickens again. This allows heavier coats to be applied than with liquid paints and reduces the risk of 'runs' or 'drips'.

Some gloss finishes contain silicone, claimed to increase the 'slip' of the painted surface so that dust and dirt do not cling and cleaning is easier.

Usually, brushes that have been used in oil-based paint have to be cleaned in white spirit or brush cleaner. 'Easy brush clean' oil-based paints allow brushes to be cleaned out with household detergent or soap powder and water.

As you see, a paint might well be described as 'non-drip, easy brush-clean alkyd gloss with polyurethane and silicone'. But, basically, it is still oil-based.

EMULSION

Like oil-based paints, emulsions have some common features:

(a) They have little or no odour and this soon disappears.
(b) They dry quickly, usually in about an hour.
(c) They are thinned with water.
(d) They are usually non-drip.

Emulsion paints contain no drying oil; instead the pigment is mixed with a dispersion of synthetic resin particles in water. After the paint has been applied, the water evaporates and the resin particles flow together to form a continuous coating.

The synthetic resins most widely used in emulsion paint are vinyl and acrylic, either singly or together. Both resins are very tough and hard-wearing and have a wide variety of uses other than for paints. For example, similar vinyl resins are used for floor tiles, upholstery materials, wallcoverings and many other applications.

In North America, emulsion paints are often described as 'latex paints' and you may find this term used here sometimes.

OIL-BASED OR EMULSION?

As well as differences, there are some similarities between oil-based and emulsion paints. For instance, both are available as matt, eggshell or silk and glossy finishes. Some primers and undercoats may be either oil-based or emulsion.

Emulsion paints offer obvious advantages in speed of drying, absence of odour and ease of clean-up. But oil-based paints are generally more durable, give better protection and have more resistance to wear than their emulsion counterparts.

So choice will depend upon the job the paint has to do. For wood and metal, especially outside, oil-based paint is best. It is the first choice, also, for ceilings and walls in heavy-wear situations indoors, e.g. in kitchens and bathrooms where there is a lot of condensation or frequent cleaning down. Emulsion paints come into their own for ceilings and walls indoors in 'light' to 'medium-wear' conditions; or, as

Surfaces/locations	1st choice	2nd choice
Wood and metal, outside	Oil-based gloss	Perhaps emulsion gloss but check with dealer or manufacturer.
Brick, cement, stucco or pebbledash walls, outside	Emulsion 'masonry' paint	Cement-based paint
Wood and metal inside, 'heavy-wear' situations	Oil-based gloss	—
Wood and metal inside, 'medium' or 'light-wear' situations	Oil-based mid-sheen or matt	Emulsion gloss
Ceilings and walls inside, 'heavy-wear' situations	Oil-based gloss or mid-sheen	Emulsion mid-sheen
Ceilings and walls inside, 'medium' or 'light-wear' situations	Emulsion mid-sheen or matt	—

'masonry' paints, for outside walls.

As mentioned above, both types are made in matt, mid-sheen and glossy finishes, although the gloss emulsion paints do not, as yet, have quite the depth of gloss of the oil-based versions. Broadly speaking, durability and protective qualities increase with gloss level so the first choice for outside wood and metal, and for hard-wear situations indoors, is a full-gloss oil-based finish.

On the left we give a chart that indicates typical uses for the two types.

There is another factor that may have to be taken into account in making a choice and that is the type of paint on the surface already. Generally, it is all right to apply oil-based paint over existing emulsion paint, providing it is sound. Applying emulsion paint over oil-based is less satisfactory, especially if the old paint is glossy and there is likely to be steam and condensation, e.g. in a kitchen or bathroom. In these circumstances, the emulsion paint may peel or flake from the old gloss paint. If you do not want a glossy finish again, it is better to repaint with an oil-based mid-sheen or matt paint. Should you decide to take a chance with emulsion paint over oil-based gloss, make sure the latter is thoroughly cleaned and well rubbed down (see page 87).

HOW MANY COATS?

You will need to decide this because it will influence the quantity of paint to be purchased.

If you are painting new or bare wood, metal, plaster, etc., with oil-based paint, a minimum of three coats will be needed; i.e. a primer and two further coats – either an undercoat and a coat of finish or two coats of finish. For repaint work, you will probably get by with two coats or even one, if you are not making a great change in colour.

With emulsion paints, priming is not usually required on the normal new or bare wall and ceiling surfaces. If they are very porous or absorbent, a 'sealing' coat of thinned emulsion paint may be required, followed by one or two normal coats. Bare metal must always be primed with an oil-based metal primer (see page 88) before applying emulsion paint. On repaint work, one or two coats will usually suffice if the old paint is sound but a primer-sealer (see page 88) will be required if the surface is powdery or poorly-adhering. Exceptionally, more coats will be re-

	Average spreading rate for 1 litre	
	Square metres	Square yards
Wood primer	8	10
Metal primer	11	13
Primer sealer	9	11
Undercoat, oil-based	11	13
Gloss, oil-based, liquid	17	20
Gloss, oil based, non-drip	12	14
Mid-sheen, oil-based	16	19
Emulsion	15	17

quired than is indicated above with some colours. These are usually 'strong' or bright colours whose hiding properties or 'opacity' is relatively poor. Manufacturers usually indicate which colours on their colour cards are in this category and may recommend special 'first coat colours' to be used with these difficult colours.

The 'spreading rate' of paints, that is the amount required for a given area, varies according to type. It is usually shown on the can as so many square yards, feet or, nowadays, metres per litre. Typical figures are shown above. These are average figures for paints applied to smooth, non-porous surfaces. Spreading rates will be lower on rough or very absorbent surfaces. For example, on heavily-textured exterior walls, a masonry paint may have a spreading rate of only 3–7 square metres (3½–8½ square yards) per litre. Household paints are generally sold in 500 millilitre, 1 litre, 2½ litre and 5

litre sizes; smaller quantities, e.g. 250 ml., 100 ml. and 50 ml. are available in some brands. If you still find it difficult to 'think metric', it may help to remember that 500 ml. and 1 litre are about 12% *less* than 1 pint and 1 quart respectively; and that 2½ litres and 5 litres are about 10% *more* than the old ½ gallon and 1 gallon sizes.

Try to estimate your paint requirements reasonably accurately. Apart from the nuisance of having to go back for more if you run short, there is a chance that a later purchase will be from another batch and may be slightly different in colour. If you do find yourself running out, stop at a convenient corner, angle or other break whilst you still have some paint left. Never start with another can in the middle of a wall or ceiling. If you have bought several cans for a big job, it is a good idea to mix them together in a larger container to ensure uniformity of colour.

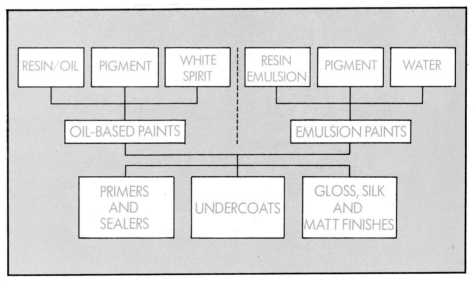

1. Clever use of contrasting colour and paint texture brightens up a narrow hallway.
2. Gloss paint provides a hardwearing surface for this chest of drawers.

3. Washable emulsion i.
most practical covering
the walls in a child's roc

4. Eggshell finish on
woodwork and walls ali
gives a sophisticated loo
this bathroom.

5. Paint with a very hig
gloss is an effective choi
a dividing door.

6. This vividly-painted
finish front door makes
great impact in a long h

7. Gloss paint on windo
frames and surrounds n
maximum use of light i.
bow window.

6

PREPARING TO PAINT

Preparation for painting or hanging wallcoverings is aimed at providing a clean, sound surface, free from major blemishes, so that the new decoration looks good and will last. It usually involves one or more of the following items:

    Cleaning
    Dealing with stains
    Removing old paint
    Removing old wallcoverings
    Rubbing down
    Filling cracks and holes
    Priming and sealing.

CLEANING

Washing down the old paint to remove light grime and surface dirt is about the simplest form of preparation and may be all that is required on paintwork in good condition. It helps to ensure that new paint will stick properly, as well as cover better, so that fewer coats are needed.

Sponging over with detergent and water or one of the general-purpose household cleaners will remove light grime effectively. More vigorous treatment will be needed on badly grimed areas over radiators, wall lights, etc., especially on matt-painted surfaces (1). A clean, well-worn 4-in. (100-mm.) paintbrush and a little powder cleaner can be used to scrub these areas. But be careful on emulsion paint and stop if it begins to soften or lift. After washing down, rinse with plain water, dry off and leave for a few hours before painting or papering.

Removing grease, oil, wax polish etc., is often necessary in kitchens or, if you have polished floors, along skirtings and the bottoms of doors. Another 'danger area' is around door handles (2) unless you have finger plates. Grease and wax spoil the adhesion of paint and may cause it to dry slowly or lose its gloss.

Heavy deposits should be scraped off; then scrub with white spirit and an old paint brush and wipe with a clean rag; repeat if necessary and finally wash with detergent.

Rust on iron and steel window frames, gutters, railings, etc., must be removed

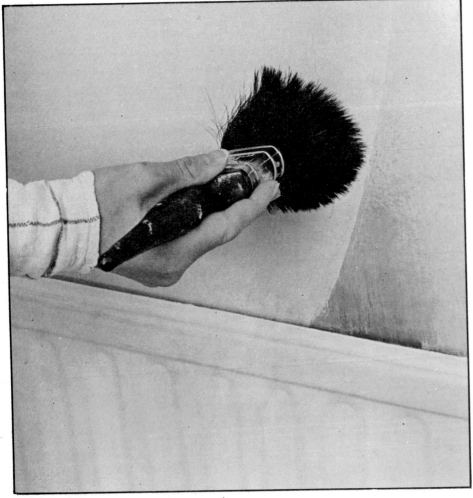

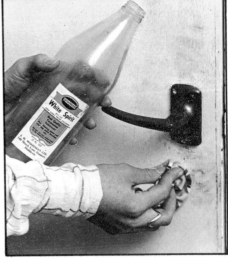

before painting otherwise it will spread beneath the new paint. Rust-removing solutions are available but thorough scraping and wirebrushing are usually equally effective. If you have a power drill, the rotary wire brush attachments are effective if there is a lot of derusting to do (3). Whatever method is used, prime with a good metal primer as soon as possible (see page 88).

DEALING WITH STAINS

Stains on decorated surfaces have a variety of causes, often difficult to

ing roof or defective gutter, for example), have this put right.

Tar staining often occurs if you paint over creosoted wood or tar varnished rainwater pipes. It shows as a brown discoloration and will 'bleed' into the new paint. One or two coats of aluminium primer-sealer (see page 89) usually effects a cure (5).

Knot or resin staining shows as a brown discoloration on woodwork painted in white or light colours. It may occur in streaks or, more often, in circular patches coinciding with knots in the wood (6) and is caused by resinous colouring matter in the wood. As with tar stains, knot stains may 'bleed' into the new paint if not treated. A coat of shellac knotting (see page 88) will prevent this.

REMOVING PAINT
The golden rule is:
Do not remove the old paint if it is in good condition; that is, adhering firmly and not badly cracked or blistered.

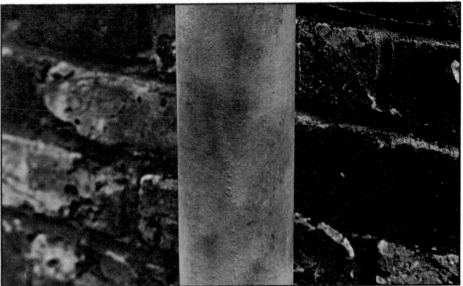
5

6

4

trace. Some stains may be removed by washing, others are persistent and may come through the new paint or paper.

Damp stains on ceilings and walls may be caused by bursts or overflows or from rain penetration or rising damp. Even when the ceiling or wall has dried out, the stain can come through again if the area is rewetted, for example with emulsion paint or wallpaper adhesive. To prevent this, apply a coat of oil-based primer sealer (see page 89) when the surface has dried out (4). If the stain is caused by a structural defect (a leak-

Paint removal is a messy job at the best of times and certainly is not necessary just because you are changing the colour.

When it is necessary to remove old paint, the main methods are:

    dry scraping
    with paint remover
    by burning off.

If you have to remove old non-washable ceiling distemper, this is washed off.

Dry scraping is the simplest way of removing blisters and areas of loose paint (7), using a scraper or shavehook (see page 78). On ceilings and walls,

application may be required. Try to avoid digging into the underlying surface, especially on woodwork.

When all the old paint has been removed, the surface must be thoroughly cleaned (8b) to remove residues of paint remover. With some removers, white spirit is used for final cleaning-up, whilst others are rinsed off with water; the latter are easier and cheaper to use. Observe any handling precautions recommended by the maker when using paint removers. In particular, ensure good ventilation, do not smoke and protect the eyes and skin against splashes.

it is about the only practicable method of removing loose or flaking washable distemper or emulsion paint – a snag is that, once having started on what appears to be a small patch of loose paint, you find that all of it is loose and can be scraped off in sheets. However, it is better to find this out before repainting or papering.

Paint removers work with most oil-based paints; some will remove emulsion paint. They can be used on wood, metal and plaster but are rather expensive to use on large areas. Fortunately, it is not often necessary to strip paint from ceilings and walls and, when it is, dry scraping is usually effective. Paint removers are based on strong paint solvents with a 'thickener' that enables a heavy coat to be put on and delays evaporation of the solvent. They are applied liberally (8), left until the paint softens and can be scraped off (8a). Tackle three or four square feet at a time; if the old paint film is very thick, more than one

10

0a

keep the flame away from the glass. After burning off, rub down the wood-work with medium glasspaper (see below) in the direction of the grain, paying particular attention to mould-ings.

Washing off is necessary on ceilings that have been coated with non-washable distemper. This can easily be identified because it is powdery and softens readily when wetted (10). It must be removed because paint and wallpaper will not stick over it. Tackle small areas at a time, use a large paint brush to wet the surface thoroughly, then scrape or sponge off the softened distemper (10a).

REMOVING WALLCOVERINGS

Unlike paint, wallcoverings should usually be removed, if possible, before re-papering. You can paint over wall-paper that is firmly attached or has previously been painted. However, once wallpaper has been painted, it is difficult to remove, especially if oil-based paints are used.

Ordinary wallpapers are removed by soaking with hot water until the paste softens and the paper can be scraped off easily. A little detergent or wallpaper stripper in the water helps it to soak in. Do not be in a hurry to start scraping; let the water do the work. When all the paper has been removed, wash the surface to remove residues of paste.

Painted or varnished paper is diffi-cult to remove because water will not penetrate. If it is sound and sticking properly, leave it. Rub down promi-nent joints and stick back any small loose areas. If it must be removed, try scoring or scratching the surface with wire wool or a wire brush so that water can penetrate (11). Or strip the paint with water-rinsable remover (see page opposite) and then soak the paper.

Vinyl wallcoverings cannot be soaked but the vinyl 'face' can be pulled off dry leaving the backing paper on the wall. If re-papering, and the backing is adhering firmly, hang the new paper over it. Otherwise, soak and scrape off in the usual way.

'Clean strip' papers are specially treated so that they can simply be pulled off. Wash the wall to remove paste residues.

RUBBING DOWN

Surfaces are rubbed down to make them smooth and level and to help adhesion. For most jobs, ordinary glasspaper or waterproof abrasive paper is used. Both come in various grades or degrees of roughness.

For rubbing down woodwork, new or stripped, use F.2 glasspaper if the wood is reasonably smooth; or M.2 grade, followed by F.2, on roughened wood. Rub down in the direction of the grain (12); rubbing across the grain makes

Burning off is the professional's way of removing paint from woodwork; it is not suitable for use on painted plaster or metal.

The term 'burning off' sounds rather alarming but the idea is to soften the paint with a hot flame so that it can be scraped off rather than actually setting fire to it. However, it does require care. To burn off a small area of defective paint you can use a handyman's torch with an attached container of butane gas. For larger jobs, professional-size equipment can be hired.

Wear an old pair of gloves to protect your hands against hot paint drop-pings. Remove anything inflammable, including curtains, from the vicinity. Have a bucket of water near at hand in case of fire.

Hold the torch in one hand and the scraper in the other (9); keep torch and scraper moving together. Use a shave-hook (9a) for scraping mouldings. Try not to scorch the wood or dig into it. If you are burning off window frames,

11

scratches which may show through.
Gloss paint can be rubbed down with F.2 glasspaper but waterproof abrasive paper, although a little more expensive, is more effective. It is also safer, because the old paint may contain lead and the 'dust' produced by dry rubbing could be harmful. And it lasts longer than ordinary glasspaper because it can be washed clean when it becomes clogged with paint.

Waterproof abrasive paper comes in various grades from 180 (coarse) to 320 (fine); 280 grade is satisfactory for most jobs.

'Wet' rubbing down is most conveniently done after washing the surface and whilst it is still wet. Dip the abrasive paper into water containing a little detergent or soap and rub in a circular motion (13). Sponge the paper from time to time to remove clogged paint. Finally, sponge the surface clean. Bare plaster and emulsion painted walls and ceilings do not need much rubbing down except to remove small lumps or 'nibs' of paint or paper. Use worn F.2 glasspaper for this.

When rubbing down flat surfaces, cut the sheets of abrasive paper into three equal strips and wrap each strip around a wood or cork block (14).

Large gaps, e.g. along the top of a skirting, can first be packed with damp newspaper to prevent the filler from dropping through (16); near power points, use strips of wood or hardboard in case there are exposed wires or terminals, as damp paper conducts electricity.

Exteriors For outside work, there are exterior-grade proprietary fillers but, for filling gaps and open joints in woodwork, linseed oil putty is better.

PRIMING AND SEALING

New or bare woodwork and metal usually need a primer. So do new or bare wall and ceiling surfaces if they are to be painted with oil-based paints; priming is *not* usually necessary if they are to be emulsion painted. Some previously-painted surfaces may need a primer or sealer. The treatment and types of primer required are as follows:
Wood A thin coat of shellac knotting is applied over each knot (see page 85);

12

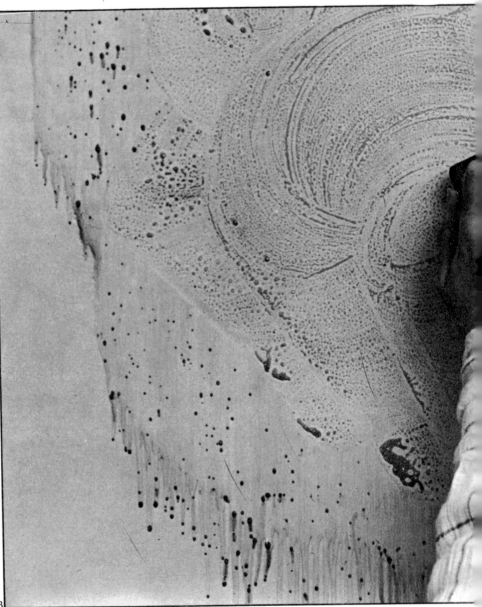

13

FILLING CRACKS AND HOLES

Interiors On interior woodwork, ceilings and walls, fill cracks and holes, as well as gaps along skirtings and around door and window frames, with one of the proprietary plaster-based fillers. Mix in accordance with the instructions on the packet and apply with a filling knife or putty knife (15). Leave the filling slightly 'proud' so that it can be rubbed down level when it has hardened.

Always use it for repairing or replacing the glazing putty around the glass. Bare woodwork must always be primed before you start the puttying or else the oil in the putty will be absorbed, leaving it crumbly and brittle.

For large cracks in exterior walls, or gaps around windows and door frames, use a cement/sand mix (1 part cement to 6 parts sharp sand) with water. Allow any repairs carried out with this mix to dry out properly before painting.

this dries in a few minutes. Then prime with proprietary white or pink wood primer (thinned slightly for hardwoods such as oak or beech) or, on very resinous woods, aluminium primer.
Metal, including iron, steel, aluminium and galvanised iron, is primed with a chromate metal primer. On iron and steel, prime as soon as possible after you have cleaned and derusted the metal (see page 84), especially on exterior surfaces; even overnight ex-

posure will cause rusting to start again.

Walls and ceilings of plaster, brick, cement rendering, etc., require priming if oil-based paints are to be used. On new work, allow ample time for complete drying out and then prime with an alkali-resisting primer. If the surfaces are mature and dry, prime with primer sealer.

Primer sealer is also used to seal water stains on walls and ceilings.

If unpainted walls and ceilings are to be prime these with the appropriate wood, metal or wall primer.

The exception is walls and ceilings from which old distemper or cement paint has been removed. However thoroughly you have prepared the surface, there is almost certain to be a residue of powdery material or the odd stubborn patch that defies removal. It would be unwise to paint or paper over this but priming with primer sealer will 'bind down' any residues.

Bituminous surfaces, e.g. creosoted wood or bitumen-coated metal, may give trouble if painted over directly (see page 85). If the creosote or bituminous coating was applied fairly recently, it is best left untreated for a year or so. Then apply one or two coats of aluminium sealer; when this has hardened, it can be over-painted.

If a bituminous coating is very thick and soft, it may never be practicable to paint it with normal paints.

14

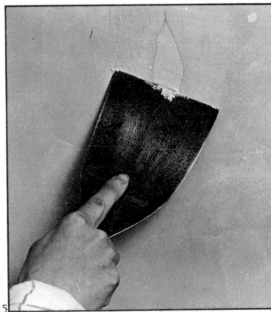

15

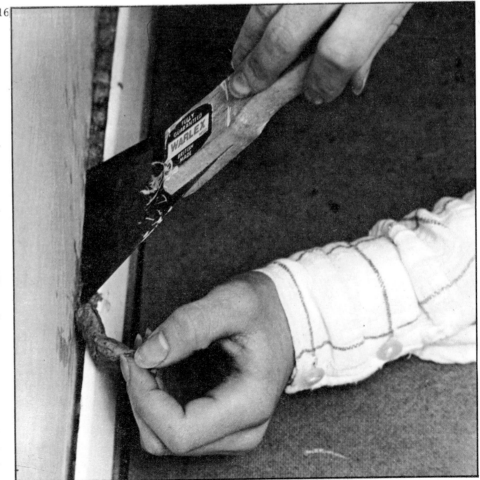

16

emulsion-painted, a primer is not usually necessary but the first coat of emulsion paint may require extra thinning, especially on very absorbent surfaces; the maker's instructions will guide you on this. Building boards, wallpaper and lining paper can be primed with emulsion paint.

Previously-painted surfaces do not usually need priming except where removal of small areas of defective paint has exposed the under-surface;

1

3

4

2

1. *A fresh start is given to a
room with a clean coat of
white paint for walls and
woodwork.*
2. *A room waiting to be
painted and papered.*
3. *A similar room
transformed with paint and
wallpaper.*

4. *Painted walls throw a magnificent fireplace into relief.*

5. *This room, with its elegant fireplace and panelling, can easily be restored to its former beauty.*

6. *Painted walls in a cleverly-chosen colour are a perfect foil for elegant furniture.*

5

6

LADDERS AND PLATFORMS

If you intend to paint or paper ceilings and walls, you will need some form of safe platform or scaffolding from which to work. It is possible to improvise with chairs, stools, boxes or the kitchen table but the right equipment makes for easier and, more important, safer working. Even amongst professional builders and decorators, a high proportion of accidents result from using makeshift or inadequate scaffolding. So do not take chances – they lead to accidents.

STEPLADDERS
The minimum you will need in the way of scaffolding is a stepladder tall enough to enable you to reach the ceiling comfortably and safely. In the average house built in the last 30 or 40 years, the ceiling height in rooms is likely to be around 244 cm. (8 ft.). In larger, older houses, it may be 305 cm. (10ft.) or even 366 cm. (12 ft.). For a 244 cm. (8 ft.) ceiling, a stepladder with 6 treads is adequate. You will need one with an extra tread for each 30 cm. (1 ft.) of ceiling height above 8 ft. Do not have a stepladder taller than you really need or you will find it awkward to use. And you will find a tubular metal stepladder with a folding platform on top lighter and more convenient than heavy wooden ones.

WORKING ON CEILINGS
It is possible to paint a ceiling from a stepladder but it means constant moving and makes it difficult to keep the painted edge 'alive' (see page 96). If you are papering a ceiling, working from a stepladder only is almost impossible. So, for either of these jobs, it's best to rig up a proper scaffolding with two stepladders and a stout plank. Or, for an 244 cm. (8 ft.) ceiling and if you have only one stepladder and do not want to buy, borrow or hire another, use a strong wooden box or a sturdy kitchen stool at one end. These have the advantage of taking up less room than a stepladder but do beware of stepping over the end of the plank whilst concentrating on the paint or paper you are applying. And do ensure that the stool or box is really firm and strong. The plank should be

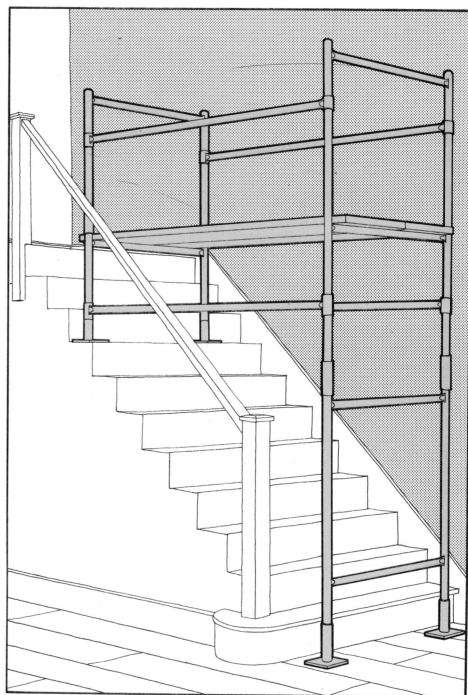

at least 228 mm. (9 in.) wide, 38 mm. (1½ in.) thick and about 750 mm. (2 ft. 6 in.) shorter than the span of the room.

STAIRCASES

Staircases, even in modern houses, can present problems especially in getting at the long wall in the staircase 'well' or the ceiling over it. For these areas, and depending on the configuration of the staircase, you will probably need an arrangement like that shown. Or you may find it helpful to use a tubular metal platform tower built up from demountable frames. There are special frames which allow the tower to be erected on the stairs. These towers, as well as ladders and planks, can be hired at quite reasonable charges.

Do take especial care in erecting scaffolding in a staircase. You may be working 305–366 cm. (10–12 ft.) or more from the floor and a fall could be very nasty. Ensure that all the equipment is sound and firm. If you use an arrangement similar to that shown in the diagram, place the foot of the ladder into the angle of the stair and secure it with a strip of wood nailed to the stair tread; similarly, nail a strip across the foot of the steps. Where one plank rests on another or on a support, avoid a 'trap end' i.e. one that projects over the support so that the plank tips up if you step on it. Get help in erecting and taking down the scaffolding. And do not tackle the job at all if you do not feel confident about working at heights.

1. For reaching a ceiling, arrange a platform by using two stepladders to support a plank.
2. Various types of platform tower may be hired: shown here, a staircase frame
3. A working platform in a staircase well should be securely arranged to give safe access to walls and ceiling.
Always ensure the foot of a ladder or any weight-bearing equipment is secure

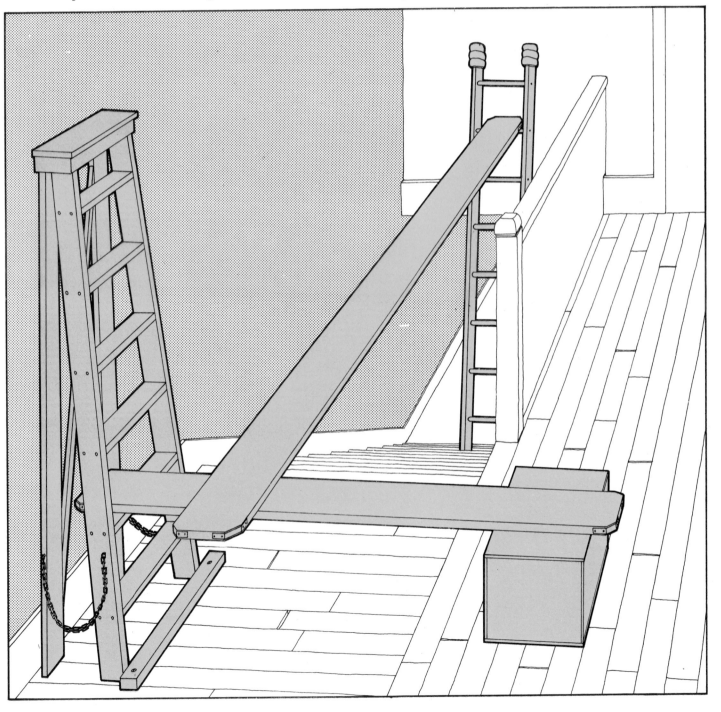

HOW TO APPLY PAINT

PREPARING THE PAINT

First, get the paint ready for use. Wipe the top of the can and around the rim so that dust does not fall into the paint when you take off the lid. Lever off the lid with a paint can opener or stiff knife blade taking care not to damage or distort it or you will not be able to replace it properly.

There should not be a 'skin' with a new can of paint but there may be in a part-used container, especially if the lid is not a good fit. If there is a skin, cut round it carefully and lift it out in one piece (1). Try not to 'lose' it or the paint may have to be strained.

The instructions on the can will tell you whether or not to stir the paint; non-drip paints are not normally stirred except for roller application. When stirring is required, the usual instruction is to 'stir thoroughly'; this means using a flat stick or chisel knife, long enough to reach the bottom of the can, and stirring with a lifting action (2) for a few minutes until all the 'solids' in the paint are mixed in. If the paint has 'settled' after long storage, pour half of it into a clean container, beat up the thick settlement and then add the remainder a little at a time.

If the paint has been used previously and is 'bitty', strain it through a double thickness of old nylon stocking tied over the top of a clean container (3). For a large job, you may have bought several cans of the same colour paint. To ensure uniformity of colour, mix the contents together in a larger container. Then pour the paint back into the original cans and replace the lids properly.

Follow the maker's instructions about thinning. Non-drip paints do not usually need thinning. Oil-based paints are generally thinned with white spirit; emulsion paints with water. Do not overthin, or the paint may not cover.

APPLYING PAINT BY BRUSH

See page 78 for general information on paint brushes. Use the sizes of brushes most suitable for the surface you are painting:

$\frac{1}{2}$ inch (12·5 mm.) and 1 inch (25 mm.) or 2 inch (50 mm.) for narrow sur-

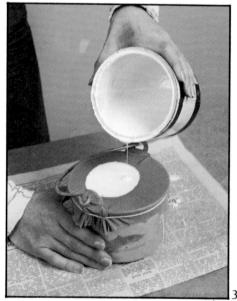

faces such as windows, picture rails and skirtings.

1 inch (25 mm.) and 2 inch (50 mm.) for broad surfaces like panelled doors or furniture.

1 inch (25 mm.) and 3 inch (75 mm.) for flush doors and similar surfaces.

4 inch (100 mm.) or 5 inch (125 mm.) for walls and ceilings.

The general principle is always to use the largest brush you can manage.

However, do not use one so big that it tires your wrist or is difficult to control. Ensure your brushes are clean. Newly-purchased brushes are *never* clean enough to use straightaway, particularly for gloss finishes. Wash them in soap and water the day before you start painting and lay them in a clean, warm place to dry.

Having prepared the paint and selected your brushes, you are ready to start

5

painting. Many people work straight from the can but it is better to pour a small quantity of paint into another container such as a clean empty paint can or painter's 'kettle' or, if you are using emulsion paint, a clean bucket. This means less paint to hold and, also, that if dirt is picked up with the paint brush, it does not spoil the rest of the paint. Non-drip paint does not pour but you can scoop it out and into the 'working' can with a broad scraper. With 'liquid' paints, charge the brush (4), dipping the bristles into the paint for about one-third of their length and then pressing them against the side of the container, just above the level of the paint. Do this each time you take a dip; it is cleaner and more 'professional' than wiping the brush against the rim of the can, after every dip, to remove surplus paint. With non-drip paints, dip the brush into the paint and straight out again.

Skill in applying paint by brush comes with practice. The general principle is to have a fairly well-charged brush of the right size and use long, 'wristy' strokes, spreading the paint evenly. Do not brush the paint out too far or it becomes difficult to spread and may not cover.

'Cutting in' Beginners often find it difficult to 'cut in' or paint to a straight line (5) e.g. when painting windows, door frames or the tops of skirtings. Use a small, well-charged, preferably part-worn brush for this job. Press the

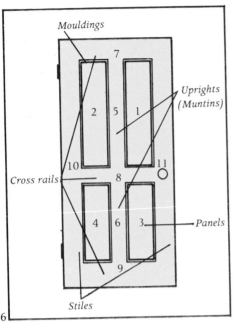

Mouldings

7

Uprights
(Muntins)

2 5 1

10 11

Cross rails

8

4 6 3 → Panels

9

Stiles

6

8

7

7a

8a

bristles firmly into the angle and draw the brush steadily along for 150–225 mm. (6–9 in.); repeat this stroke without re-charging the brush until the area is covered and the paint is evenly spread. If you cannot manage this at first, use a metal shield to prevent paint from straying.

Painting doors When painting panelled doors, paint the door edge first and then the remainder in the order shown (6); paint the frame last.

Flush doors require a different approach. Paint the top third of the door first, using vertical strokes; then, without re-charging the brush, draw it firmly across the painted area (7); finally, make light strokes with the tips of the bristles vertically up the painted area (7a). Paint the middle and bottom thirds in the same way, 'laying off' each section into the preceding one with light, vertical strokes.

Painting walls In painting walls, the main thing is to work quickly and methodically in order to 'keep the edge alive', as professional painters say; that is, to make joins before the paint has 'set'. This is especially important with oil-based gloss, egg-shell and matt paints if a patchy effect is to be avoided.

If you are painting by brush, use the largest one you can manage, preferably a 3 in. (75 mm.) brush for oil-based paints and a 4 in. (100 mm.) for emulsions. You will probably need a step-ladder in order to reach the top of the wall comfortably.

Apply the paint in sections, rather as described for flush doors. In painting only the upper part of the wall – for example, above the tiles in a kitchen or bathroom – apply the paint in vertical strips about 300 mm. (1 ft) wide if you are using oil-based paint or about double that width with emulsions. Each strip should extend the full height of the wall space. If you are right-handed, you will find it best to work from right to left across the wall; and, of course, the reverse way if you are left-handed.

Painting a large wall from ceiling to skirting is really a job for two people. A good method is for one to start by painting a strip extending from the ceiling halfway down the wall. Then the stepladder is moved on so that the next top strip can be painted whilst the helper moves in to paint the first lower strip (8). Work methodically across the wall in this way, keeping one strip ahead on the upper half of the wall until the whole area is completed. If you have to tackle the job on your own, follow the same principle of working in strips but let each occupy about one-third of the wall height. When painting walls with oil-based gloss finish, 'cross' and 'lay off' the paint as described for flush doors. But with emulsions and oil-based eggshell and matt finishes, apply and 'lay off' the paint with criss-cross strokes (8a).

Painting ceilings Paint in the way described for walls, working in strips 30–45 cm. (12–18 in.) along the shortest length of the ceiling. Work methodically from end to end of the strip, spreading the paint with criss-cross strokes, as for walls. Join up to the preceding strip as quickly as possible before the edge sets. If possible, arrange a proper scaffolding with a plank and stepladders so that you paint the full width of the ceiling. Again, a large ceiling is best tackled by two people.

After a time, especially when painting ceilings, the paint tends to creep up the bristles. Before it starts to run down the handle (and eventually down your arm), scrape excess paint out on the rim of the container, brush it down the inside and wipe rim clean.

Painting windows The tricky part of painting windows, until you are practised, is 'cutting in' neatly to the glass. Use a small, ½ or 1 in. (12.5 or 25 mm.) brush, preferably one that has had a fair amount of use so that the bristles have worn down to a chisel edge. If you have to use a new brush or one that has had little use, bind string around the bristles, or slip on small rubber bands, to shorten their effective length. Have the brush fairly well charged with paint, press it firmly into the 'rebate' or angle between the glass and the frame and draw it along in a long, steady stroke until the brush runs 'dry' (9). If there are 'misses', repeat the stroke, without re-charging your brush, until the paint is evenly spread. With practice, it does not take too long to become skilled at cutting-in but, if you are an absolute beginner, you can buy a metal shield to hold against the glass whilst you are painting. Wipe the edge of the shield after each stroke so that the paint does not creep under it and on to the glass.

As with doors, there is a sequence to be followed in painting windows. With casement windows (the ones with hinged sashes) open the window fully and paint the back of the casement edges and frame, then close the casement and cut-in the rebates as described above. Now open the casement and paint the broad parts (9a), first the cross-rails and then the uprights, using a larger brush, if necessary. Leave the casements open an inch or so, securing them with the casement stays, and paint the frame (9b) and, finally, the sill. If possible, leave the casements open a little until the paint is dry.

To paint double-hung sash windows, the kind that slide up and down, you start by 'crossing' the sashes; that is, pushing the bottom one up and pulling the top one down so that you can get at the meeting-rail. Paint this and as much as you can of the lower parts of the top sash (10). Also paint the bottom edge of the bottom sash. Now pull the bottom sash right down into its normal closed position and push the top sash to within about an inch of closing. Paint the rest of the top sash and also the top inside runners (10a). Raise the bottom sash slightly until its lower edge is clear of the frame and paint the whole sash including the top edge. Finally, paint the frame and sill (10c). As with casement windows, leave the sashes open a little until the paint is dry, if possible.

9

10

9a

10a

9b

10b

97

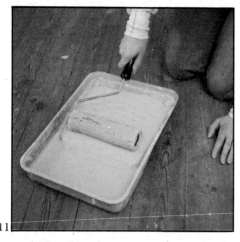

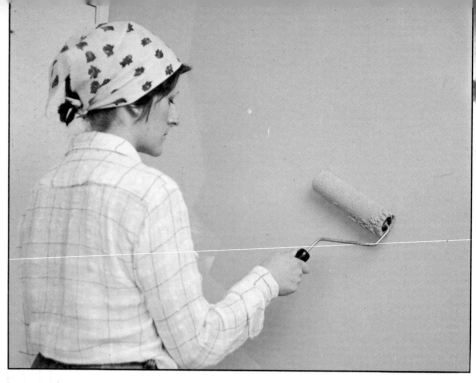

ROLLER APPLICATION

Rollers are excellent for broad areas such as ceilings, walls and flush doors; they enable you to cover the area much more quickly than by brush and you will probably find it easier to spread the paint evenly. Most types of paint, including gloss finishes, can be roller-applied and they are particularly effective for masonry paints on rough exterior walls. See page 78 for details of the different types of rollers.

To hold the paint, you will need a tray or, for big jobs, you may need a special bucket; these can often be hired. If you are using non-drip paint, make it liquid by stirring.

Pour the paint into the tray or bucket and charge the roller by dipping it about halfway into the paint (11). Then roll it backwards and forwards on the smaller end of the tray (or the grid, if you are using a bucket) so that the roller is coated all the way round.

Roll the paint on to the surface in even strokes, spreading it evenly (12). On ceilings and walls, use criss-cross strokes as described for brush application.

You will need a small paint brush to get into corners and angles. Paint these as you go along and get as close to the angle as you can with the roller so that any slight difference in the texture of the paint does not show.

PAINT PADS

Small paint pads (see page 78) are useful for narrow areas, like windows, if you are not too confident with a brush. Larger versions can be used for flush doors or even ceilings and walls although a roller would usually be quicker.

Paint pads are charged by dipping the fabric side into the paint and working the surplus out on a flat surface (13); a roller tray or shallow baking tin makes a convenient receptacle. Press the pad against the surface and draw it along in steady strokes (14).

CLEANING UP

When you have finished painting, there is still the job of cleaning up. Pour *clean* left-over paint back into the original container and replace the lid properly. But do not mix dirty or 'bitty' paint with clean, unused material; keep it in a separate container for less important work.

Wash brushes, rollers and pads that have been used for emulsion paint in warm water. Shake out and leave in a warm place to dry.

If oil-based paint has been used, wash brushes out first in white spirit or brush cleaner and then in soap and water. With some new types of oil-based paint, brushes, etc., can be washed in detergent or soap and water. If you are going to continue painting next day, brushes used in oil-paint can be stood overnight in sufficient water to cover the bristles to stop the paint from hardening. If they have been used for emulsion paint, wash them out immediately after use.

WALL PATTERNS

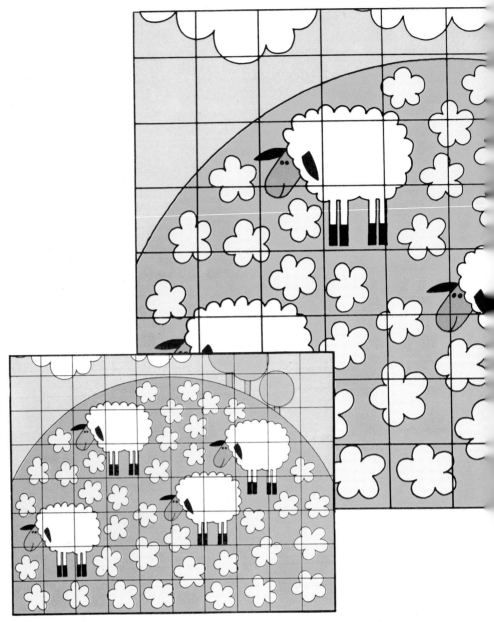

All over your home, there are large unbroken areas simply crying out for your own personal decorative treatment – they are, quite simply, your walls. Think of them as a series of huge 'canvasses' on which you are going to create your own 'pictures', however simple or abstract.

SUITING YOUR ROOM

If you are planning a wall spectacular, obviously the first thing to do is to consider carefully the rest of your decor – you want an effect that will be enhanced by its surroundings – not something violently in conflict with the rest of the room. Thus, you might steer clear of a pop art mural in a traditional setting. Simple abstracts, however, such as stripes and circles, can look right in many different styles of room, providing the colours blend in.

The most successful murals look as though they have been uniquely created for their setting, as indeed they have. You can achieve this effect by letting your mural flow off the wall at some point onto the rest of the room – taking part of the design (clouds, trees, etc.) up onto the ceiling, for example, or onto an adjacent wall. Let a broad stripe flow off the wall across the door, or onto a piece of furniture. Or you can use a stripe to outline the shape of a piece of furniture against the wall (secondhand junk finds often have interesting outlines that benefit from this treatment). A broad stripe running round a room can serve to link assorted alcoves, chimney breast and so on.

SIMPLE EFFECTS

Special paints can add interest without involving you in the intricacies of a mural. You can use aluminium paint for a silvery effect; or you can cover small areas with ordinary baking foil, which can be stuck down carefully with wallpaper paste. You can use blackboard paint on all or part of your wall – this is a matt black paint sold in most decorating, department and hardware stores. When it is dry, you can write and draw on it with white chalk,

and then wipe off the results. Use as a memo or message boards, or let your guests sign their names and add their drawings and jokes. Don't worry: the results are not permanent.

WORKING TO A LOW BUDGET

For special effects that cost next to nothing, you can paste magazines or newspapers on your wall, creating your own collage or mural as you go along. The best publications for this purpose are the very glossy monthly magazines. Creases can be ironed out before you start, but it is really best to use only newspapers or magazines in mint condition. First of all, you should size your wall with special sizing powder which can be bought from decorators' supply shops. Directions for use are on the packet. Then you can use ordinary wallpaper paste for sticking up your cuttings. If you can choose a theme (a colour, or a subject), and

stick to it, the results will be all the more effective. Try decorating just a portion of a wall (the part behind a sliding door for example) for a 'now you see it, now you don't' intriguing effect.

Newsprint tends to yellow rather quickly. To prevent this, coat your wall collage with a very weak solution of size. Allow to dry, and then brush on a clear spirit varnish (magazine collages also benefit from a coating of varnish).

You can also use old wallpaper sample books, often given away free when shops are clearing out, to make a giant patchwork for your wall. It looks stunning and costs next to nothing – just the price of a packet of paste! Regular shapes look best – diamonds, squares, or hexagons built up in repeating pattern. Choose your colours carefully to harmonise with each other and with the room.

Use a grid to enlarge your picture. Draw the large-scale grid onto the wall and transfer the picture one square at a time from the small-scale one.

PAINTS FOR MURALS

If you want to launch out into a mural, don't be timid. They are surprisingly easy to do. Murals can be painted onto any sound surface. Hardboard, plasterboard, plywood, insulating board, etc. should be sealed first as directed in the painting section. If you do your murals on panels, and then attach them to the wall, you can take them with you when you move. On previously painted walls, do not worry about small surface defects: they may well be disguised by your pattern, more so than if you were painting in a plain colour. If your wall is previously papered, you may be able to paint your mural over the top. Stick down all loose areas (especially examine for parting at the seams), and experiment with a small area of your background colour before proceeding with your main design.

You can use just about any paints you

like for murals. Emulsion from the various 'tint and mix systems', widely available from many stores, are ideal, because they offer a wide range of colours. Their shade cards are helpful: you can use them for planning a very sophisticated arrangement of graduated colours, which is nice for stripes. However, minimum quantities you can order are in general one litre of emulsions, and half a litre of gloss, so building up a big repertoire of colours could be costly.

First of all, therefore, turn out all the odds and ends of paint you already have in the house, and see what you can collect from friends: remember, you can strain old, lumpy paint through a pair of old stockings or tights. Bear in mind that you can mix your own colours as you get more confidence

on the job. You can also use artists' tubes of p.v.a. colours, which are cheaper to buy. You can use both oil- and water-based paints in your mural if you wish, but remember that for the former, you need spirit to cleanse your brushes.

Equipment You will need ordinary large wall brushes, rollers, or paint pads for large background areas. A selection of small brushes is useful for finer detailing; use small 1·25 cm. ($\frac{1}{2}$ in.) paint brushes and artists' brushes. A special brush called a fitch

has the head cut at an angle to facilitate 'cutting in' on straight lines, such as stripes.

You will need something to mix your colours in – a small dish, or foil pie containers are fine. For precise geometric designs, you will need a spirit level for true horizontals, and a plumb bob for true verticals. A set square is useful for right angles. Masking tape can be handy. If your walls have been papered, use a special low-tack drafting tape from a good stationer's, to avoid pulling off the paper when you remove the paint. Masking tape works best on a high-sheen base coat, such as an oil-based gloss, vinyl gloss, or vinyl silk.

TECHNIQUES

Where possible, paint paler colours

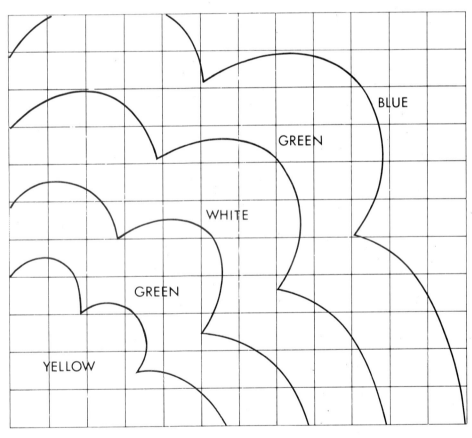

first, and then darker. Always allow adjoining areas to dry before proceeding to a fresh section. This won't take long (about one hour) if you are using water-based emulsions, but will take up to 8 hours for oil-based glosses (see notes on paints above). Use a very soft pencil for outlining your designs. Some people prefer charcoal; others use a brush and a thin wash of darkish paint. The important thing is not to have any preliminary outlining showing through the finished design, which would look most amateurish.

1. Simple curved shapes can be
traced quite easily using any
curved object as a guide.
Using a grid (see p. 101) makes
it easier to draw accurate
shapes.
2. Murals look stunning
carried right across doors and
onto the ceiling.
3. Your favourite picture or
cartoon can be scaled up and
copied onto a wall with
spectacular effect.

paper designs, or in advertisements – often there is the germ of an idea which is simple to copy. You can simply draw these designs onto the wall free-hand – no need to take the time planning out a grid.

Stars look good done in luminous paint (available in small cans from hardware stores). Children love them twinkling at night!

GEOMETRIC DESIGNS

Geometrics are simple. In old houses, where walls are out of true, it is often best to allow your stripe to follow the lines of the wall rather than emphasize architectural irregularities by making the stripe perfectly true with a spirit level.

For circles, you can use a soft pencil on the end of a piece of string as a large-scale compass. To make smaller circles, simply wind up your string around the pencil end. For a staggered bullseye effect, simply move the centre of your circles over a little each time.

You may find a pattern with curves easier than with stripes. You can draw large curved areas freehand, or cut out shapes in newspaper first as a guide. For a series of curves down a wall, or for the curved edges of stylised clouds or trees, use any suitable largish round or oval objects you may have around the house: large cans, oval trays, tennis racquets and so on all make good guides.

For a repeating design for a border, use a stencil. A selection of patterns is available from art and craft shops. Or make your own, cutting them out with a lino knife from thin card and varnishing the top, to prevent deterioration in use. Use a little paint on the end of a stub-headed stencil brush, and then pull the stencil away sharply. Inevitably, small amounts of paint find their way under the edge of the stencil, but this can add to the hand-crafted effect.

For large, plain, repeating patterns, e.g. clouds or stars, you can cut out a series of similar shapes from news-paper (cut through several layers at once). Lightly tape your shapes over your wall, spray around their edges, and allow paint to dry. Remove your paper guides, and fill in the interven-ing areas in a matching colour by hand. Very nice for cloudy ceilings.

The main thing to remember is: be bold! This is your wall, and you really can do what you like.

ENLARGING A DESIGN

If you wish to enlarge a sketch of your own design, or an idea from a book or magazine, onto the wall, use the grid technique. Work out a convenient grid system for your wall, e.g. 30 cm. (12 in.) squares. Count the number of squares you will need to fill the bottom of the wall on which you will be work-ing. Now measure the base of the picture area you wish to copy. Divide the second figure by the first. This will give you the square size for a small-scale grid which you draw over your picture for reference. Draw your large-scale grid onto your wall (very faintly: you don't want it to show at the end!) Now copy your picture one square at a time, from your small-scale picture reference to your large-scale wall grid. First mark all the points where the lines of the design cross the lines of the grid – then join up the lines, according to the original reference.

If you do not want an intricate picture, use stylised shapes instead – flowers, fruits, trees, clouds are all easy to do. Watch out for ideas on wrapping

103

ALTERNATIVE WALL COVERINGS

When it comes to wallcoverings, paper and paint are the most obvious answers. But what if you want something a bit different? There are lots of other things you can choose. You will probably have to spend both extra money and time on your special effects, but the result will be well worth it.

Listed below are the more unusual of the wallcoverings currently available. Many of them come with printed instructions in or on the pack; read these carefully before you start, noting carefully the brand of adhesive recommended by the maker. Some, e.g. paper-backed hessians, are readily available from many decorating shops and this is an indication that do-it-yourself hanging is relatively easy. Others, e.g. grass cloths and silks, may have to be ordered from a specialist and professional hanging is advisable.

VINYLS

Vinyls can be tackled with confidence by the amateur, proceeding in the same way as for wallpapers. Most vinyls are patterned to resemble wallpapers, although they are far more resistant to wear and easier to clean than ordinary papers. Colours tend to be brighter. Some vinyls, however, are plain coloured, but textured to imitate fabrics – rough-weave hessians for example, or smoother linens, or silks with an attractive slub weave. Using this type of textured vinyl, you can achieve the look of a fabric, at a cost considerably lower than the real thing. The hanging is far easier too (follow our guide to hanging wallpapers and vinyls on pages 110–117). Fabric-look vinyls wear well and can be cleaned easily. The new metallic vinyls are also worth mentioning as the designs look spectacular up on the wall, although they are not cheap to buy. N.B. For all unpasted vinyls, be sure to ask the shop for a heavy-duty paste containing fungicide. Ready-pasted vinyls should be supplied with a cardboard trough for easy soaking of each cut length. Be sure to allow excess water to drain away before applying lengths to the wall, otherwise you will rapidly flood your room with water.

TEXTURED PAPERS

Walls that are bumpy and uneven can be concealed with white textured papers, embossed to imitate a variety of natural and tiled surfaces. Although reasonable in price, these papers are usually given one or two coats of emulsion paint which you should allow for when budgeting. Relief papers – called 'the whites' by the trade – are best known by their individual brand names – Anaglypta, Supaglypta and Lincrusta. Anaglypta is the cheapest and is readily available; Supaglypta is more expensive, being stronger, thicker and heavier. Lincrusta is very expensive, being made from a thick mixture containing linseed oil, which is fused onto a backing paper. Once up, it will last virtually for ever, and the designs available include some very heavily textured effects such as imitation wood panelling. The hanging of Lincrusta requires considerable expertise and is best left to professionals. In general, Anaglyptas and Supaglyptas are hung in the same way as wallpaper (see pages 110–117), but there are various points to bear in mind.

Horizontal cross-lining is desirable under these types of paper. Use an ordinary lining paper, but hang the strips across the wall (starting from the top) rather than up-and-down. This is to prevent lining and top paper joins occurring in the same places (1). You will be working with long lengths of paper that may be a bit tricky to handle. Make a series of small, concertina-like folds (similar to the way you would for a ceiling paper). Then you can hold the bulk of the paper comfortably in the one hand, gradually easing it into place and brushing it out with the other.

Soaking time for relief papers is crucial; each length must be soaked for exactly the same amount of time, to ensure uniform stretching. Jot down on each length the exact time you finished pasting. Anaglyptas should soak from 5 to 10 minutes. Supaglyptas should soak from 15 to 20 minutes.

Brushing out After you hang each length, brush out immediately, before you trim top and bottom; until you have done this, the paper is absorbing paste, and still stretching. Use a paperhanger's brush, but do not press too hard or you will flatten the relief. Leave a very small 2 mm. ($\frac{1}{16}$ in.) gap between each length. Do not use a seam roller, as you will flatten the relief pattern.

Finishing Most people prefer to finish with paint; you will need one or two coats of any kind of emulsion. Silk finishes will effectively high-light the paper's texture. Allow the paper to dry out at least overnight before you start painting. Use a lambswool roller for applying the paint; it will take colour into the embossed pattern without flattening the relief.

FABRICS

Fabric wallcoverings are very appealing; they add a touch of softness to any room scheme, and thicker types will also make walls seem warmer. However, they are difficult to clean, tend to be expensive and, in most cases, the joins show prominently.

Before applying any type of fabric wallcovering it is necessary to prepare your wall, which should be sound and dry. New plaster should be allowed to dry out completely and this may take up to six months. Then coat with alkali-resisting primer, brushing in well. On papered walls, strip old paper, wash down to remove all traces of old paste and size and make good any crumbling areas. Apply a coat of diluted paste (according to directions on paste packet) to size the wall. Walls that have been painted must be washed down thoroughly, and then rubbed down with coarse glasspaper to provide a key for the adhesive. In all cases you will get a better finish if you cross-line (see above) your walls before applying your fabric.

Hessian This is perhaps the most popular fabric covering, providing a pleasant background for modern furniture. You can use it on one wall, or in alcoves, to great effect. It is available in a wide range of colours, but it is advisable to stick as nearly as possible to natural brown shades as they are the least prone to fading. Do not use blues, greens, purples and reds in very sunny rooms where the colours may dull from fading. Most decorating shops now stock ranges of paper-backed hessian. Rolls may be standard wallpaper width of 53–55 cm. (approx. 21 in.) or they may be wider. Check before ordering. You can also stick unbacked hessian straight on to your walls, following general instructions below for sticking unbacked fabrics to walls. Unbacked hessian will be cheaper, but you will not get such a good finish.

To hang paper-backed hessian: use adhesive as recommended by the manufacturer. Use very sharp paper-hangers' scissors for cutting to avoid fraying. Start in the middle of the most prominent wall, so that joins here are evenly distributed. N.B. Joins are always visible with hessian. Mark a vertical line, using a plumb bob. Measure wall, then measure and cut lengths, allowing 8 cm. (3 in.) at top and bottom for trimming. Apply paste evenly and liberally to first length, brushing out well. (Some manufacturers recommend pasting the wall; in all cases follow maker's directions.) Make sure edges are well pasted, brushing from middle outwards, but take care not to get any paste on the face of the fabric. Fold pasted surfaces together, as for wallpaper, and allow to soak for three to four minutes, but no longer. Unfold piece, position on wall and smooth down, starting from the centre and using a foam or felt-covered roller, *not a brush.* Run the roller well down the edges, but be careful to keep it clean, so that it does not transfer paste onto face of fabric. To trim, run back of scissors into ceiling angle, peel back hessian gently, and cut along score mark with sharp scissors. Press firmly back into place. Repeat at bottom skirting board edge. Alternatively, cut into edges with sharp knife.

Paste, hang and trim subsequent lengths in the same way. Make butt joints (i.e. do not overlap) and smooth joints over with roller. At inside corner angles, take hessian about 5 mm. ($\frac{3}{16}$ in.) round into angle. Strike a fresh plumb line and hang the next length well into corner, overlapping previous length (2). On outside corner angles, e.g. on a chimney breast, always wrap the hessian round the corner: never leave the edge of a length along the edge of a corner.

If you do get any paste onto the front of your fabric, wipe off immediately with a dry cloth, and then damp your cloth with methylated spirits and wipe again (caution: meths. is very inflammable).

Paper-backed silk, grass cloth and cork These are expensive luxury wallcoverings, costing a great deal for just one roll. Even professionals find them tricky to hang and it is not advisable for an amateur to tackle large areas. However you may want to create a special effect by lining an alcove, or a small wall area.

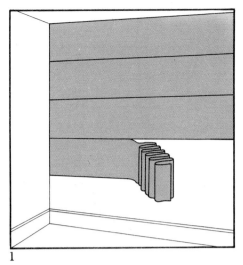

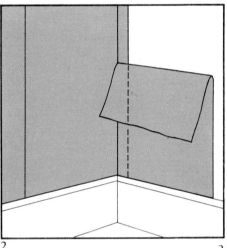

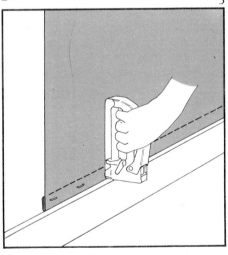

Silk has a subtle lustrous sheen, plus a pleasant natural effect created by variations in the weave; ideal to offset fine antiques or beautiful pictures. Japanese grasscloths come in soft shades of greens and browns in various weave patterns and give a room an oriental atmosphere. Cork wallcoverings come in various shades of browns, ranging from very pale to dark, and some have coloured or metallic ground. Here are some hints on hanging these wallcoverings. Always measure very carefully; you cannot afford to make mistakes with such expensive materials.

Use paste as recommended by manufacturer. If there is any metallic colouring in your wallcovering, add 55 g. (2 oz.) of washing soda to each bucket of paste. Prepare walls as outlined above; *cross-lining is essential.* Proceed in the same manner as for hanging wallpaper. You will probably find that these speciality wallcoverings have to be trimmed. Using a metal straight edge, and a sharp knife, remove about 16 mm. ($\frac{5}{8}$ in.) from along each edge. Press down on the straight edge hand, but use a light pressure on the knife. Leave pasted lengths to soak until supple, but do not oversoak. Very gently smooth into place with a paperhanger's felt-covered roller. On no account must any adhesive be allowed to reach the front of the coverings, as it will certainly stain. Be careful that no adhesive squeezes through the joins. Trim at top and bottom in usual way, using very sharp scissors and taking care to keep hands very clean.

Felt This adds a cosy, rich atmosphere to any room. It deadens sound and insulates against heat loss. Felt can be used with great effect to line a small room completely – e.g. a study, or a bedroom. Paper-backed felt can be hung in the same way as paper-backed hessian, above. You can conceal the joins by teasing the fabric a little after hanging and drying with a small wire brush. Unbacked felt can be applied direct to walls, see instructions below. Widths are available up to 190 cm. (6 ft. 3 in.) and hanging will be very much easier if there are two people working on the job.

Applying unbacked fabrics to walls (including unbacked hessians and unbacked felts)

1. Stapling. If your walls are covered in sound plaster, or you have partition walls, you may be able to staple fabric direct to them. Measure and cut fabric into lengths, taking care to match any pattern. Allow an extra 5 cm. (2 in.) on each length for turnings. Cut fabric with very sharp scissors to minimise fraying. Make narrow double hem along top of fabric, sticking it down with latex adhesive. Then staple fabric to wall along top, stretch down and staple along bottom (3). Repeat for each length and staple joins flat where necessary.

2. Stretching. Fabric can also be stretched tight over a wall over a framework of battens (see notes on panelling, below, for how to put up

1

3

4

2

on page 104. Cross-line using paper of a suitable colour, if the fabric has an open weave. Many fabrics, e.g. printed cottons, may shrink when they come in contact with the paste. Allow 20 cm. (8 in.) on each length for shrinkage and trimming, and 3 cm. (1 in.) on each width for shrinkage. Measure wall and cut fabric into lengths, taking care to match any pattern. Roll first length around a rod (e.g. a broom handle), with pattern inwards. Then mark your wall with chalk vertical guide lines, using a plumb bob. The first line should be the width of the fabric, minus 3 cm. from the corner of the wall. Continue to mark chalk vertical lines along the wall, each one the width of the fabric, minus 3 cm. (1 in.), away from the previous line. This allowance of 3 cm. allows you to over-lap your fabric when hanging, so that you can then cut through both thick-nesses for a neat butt joint (see below). Apply adhesive to the wall, but do not paste right up to your first chalk verti-cal guide line; leave a strip about 3 cm. wide free from paste (5). Take your first rolled-up length of fabric, and weight it along its bottom edge (you can use a thick strip of wood for this) (6). Unroll fabric gently up wall, posi-tioning edge against chalk line, so the

battens). You will not be able to hang any pictures on a wall treated in this way, unless your hanging points co-incide with the battens. The fabric can be attached to the battens with staples, or with small tacks, making narrow turnings top and bottom (see *Stapling*) and taking care to stretch fabric tight. You will need horizontal battens at the top and bottom of the wall, and at least one in the middle; and vertical battens at intervals the width of your fabric (4, page 108). You may be able to use your skirting board instead of the bottom horizontal batten.

3. Sticking. Fabric can also be stuck to walls, using a heavy duty paste. Walls should be prepared as described

1. Cork walls add warmth and complement wood
2. Felt provides a warm finish
3. Grass cloth gives a special, oriental effect which fits best in a simple decor
4. Co-ordinate the fabrics for your soft furnishings and wall-covering
5. Tongued and grooved boarding can be stained for a colourful effect

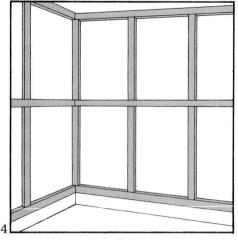

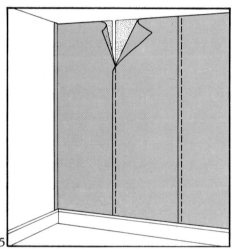

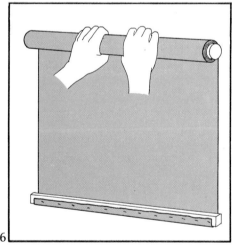

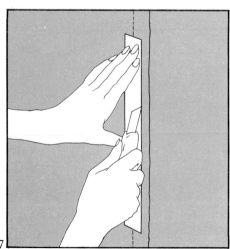

fabric overlaps around corner by 3 cm. (1 in.) – for this first length you will have to allow your fabric to extend beyond the edge of the rod so that it can overlap around corner. (It helps to have two people on the job). Use a foam roller to smooth *very lightly* into place. Paste next section of wall, taking care to leave 3 cm. strip free of paste, as before. Roll second length of fabric onto rod, and then unroll onto wall as before, positioning fabric edge along second chalk line; you will find that it overlaps the previous length. Continue in this fashion, allowing each length of fabric to overlap its neighbour. Before making any attempts to trim, leave fabric to dry thoroughly. It helps if your room is warm and well-ventilated as the longer the fabric takes to dry, the more it may shrink. For trimming you will need a long metal straight edge, and a very sharp knife. Trim away excess at corner. Then trim joints. Cut through the centre of both overlapping pieces, and peel away excess strips (7). This will give you neat butt joints. Using a small brush, paste wall on each side, underneath joint, and press fabric gently into place, taking care no glue seeps out of join. Trim at top and bottom with very sharp knife, cutting into angle of ceiling and along skirting, and adding extra touches of adhesive with fine brush if necessary. It is essential that your knife should be very sharp to minimise fraying.

Natural hessian, available cheaply from upholstery supply shops, in widths from 90–180 cm. (3–6 ft), may be painted with emulsion when thoroughly dry.

CORK TILES

Cork tiles made specifically for walls are now widely available; they are usually sold in packs in various sizes, including 30 cm. (12 in.) square, 60 by 30 cm. (24 by 12 in.) and 90 by 30 cm. (36 by 12 in.). Used for a small area, they make an attractive pin-up board. Used over a larger area, they will deaden noise, and improve insulation. Thinner types (3 mm. ($\frac{1}{8}$ in.) thick) are available plain or mottled. Thicker types (13 mm. $1\frac{1}{2}$ in.) are sold specifically for insulating purposes and have an attractive dark brown peaty colour and a rough granular texture.

Planning your tiling When tiling a whole wall, it looks better if the cut tiles at each end are of equal size. It is also important that the lines of the tiles should be truly horizontal and vertical, rather than following possibly uneven skirting and corner lines. So you must measure the centre of your wall, and mark a guiding vertical line with a plumb bob. Fix your first line of tiles against this, and tile outwards towards each corner. You will end up with an even section to trim at each end and you can cut the tiles with a sharp knife. Walls must be sound and dry; strip off old wallpaper and make good any crumbling areas.

Adhesives Cork wall tiles are stuck up with contact adhesive. Choose one of the 'thixotropic' (jelly) brands, as they are easier to work with. Your adhesive will cover around 5 square metres per litre and it will save you money to buy a five-litre can from a builders' merchant rather than separate litre tins from d-i-y shops. Very porous walls may require a preliminary 'sizing' with a coat of adhesive left to dry for at least four hours. This type of adhesive is very inflammable. Do not smoke or work with any kind of naked flame in the room; you should, for example, extinguish pilot lights. You will need to apply adhesive both to the wall and to the back of the tiles, waiting for a few minutes until both are touch dry before pressing into place. Be sure to coat tile edges to prevent shrinkage and ensure satisfactory butt joints; this is particularly important on chimney breasts and near radiators, where the heat may cause shrinkage.

FLOORING TILES

Vinyl and carpet tiles, sold as flooring, can be used effectively for small areas of wall. If you are furnishing with floor cushions, for example, you could use carpet tiles on the floor and then take them part of the way up your wall, removing the skirting board first for the best effect. In the kitchen, odd vinyl tiles left over from the floor could be used on the wall behind a working surface. You can stick these tiles in place with a contact adhesive, choosing a thixotropic (jelly) brand. It is essential that your wall is really sound, as these coverings are heavy and their weight is likely to drag away any loose plaster.

REAL WOOD

Wood finishes have a reassuring air of permanency. Pale woods tend to look less formal than darker finishes.

Tongued and grooved boarding is

justly popular, especially as a reasonably quick and long-lasting cover-up for walls in bad condition in older properties. It is very simple for a woman to put up, as at no time are you handling large heavy panels. Each board has a tongue running along its length on one side and a groove along its length on the other. The tongue from one board fits into the groove of the next, and so on. A common width for boards is 10 cm. (4 in.) but you should remember that each board will only cover 9 cm. (3½ in.) when interlocked with its neighbour.

Tongue and grooving is fixed one board at a time to softwood wall battens which should run at right angles to the boarding, i.e. your battens should be horizontal for vertical boarding, and vertical for horizontal boarding. The size of the battens should be 19 (or 25) by 50 mm. (¾ (or 1) by 2 in.) Battens should be spaced about 45–50 cm. (18–20 in.) apart (8). The quickest way to fix them is with masonry nails. Drive nails into batten, hold batten up to wall, then drive nails home. But if your plaster is very thick and crumbly, you may have to use screws and wallplugs to get a sufficiently firm fixing.

For vertical boarding, start in the corner and mark a true vertical line using a plumb bob. Measure wall height. Cut boards to fit. Remove groove of first board with plane or saw (this gives a neat edge) and position to follow vertical guide line. If the corner of your wall is out of true (it usually is) you can come back at the end and fill the gaps with small wood fillets or conceal the gap with a length of moulding; this can also be done at the ceiling to give a neat finish. If you are continuing your boarding around a corner, you will be able to butt the first board of the adjacent wall up tightly to conceal any gaps on first wall. Plane off grooved section neatly, for a perfect finish, and check as before that boards are truly vertical before proceeding to panel second wall.

Fix board to each batten with 19 mm. (¾ inch) rust-proof panel pins, driving pin in through tongue at an angle (9), and punching down below surface. Push groove of next boards as hard onto the tongue as you can (10), as the boards will probably shrink after they are up. Fix second board through tongue into each batten as before, and continue to cover wall in this fashion.

You can remove your skirting board before you start, if you wish, and take the boarding right down to the floor. A plain wood skirting can be fixed on top when you have finished. If you wish, you can remove door mouldings and take battens and boarding right up to the door edges. Or you can refix existing door frame onto battens, to bring it out to the same plane as the boarding. Treat your boarding with two coats of polyurethane varnish (matt or gloss) for a dirt-resistant finish. Alternatively paint it, or use a colour wood stain plus varnish.

Wood panels A wide variety of large wood panels are available in sizes up to 2400 by 1200 mm. (approx. 8 by 4 ft). These can be nailed to wooden battens, fixed horizontally at top and bottom of wall, and vertically to correspond with width of the board. Or they can be stuck direct to plaster, brick, concrete or wood using a new 'gap-filling' wallboard adhesive which has the ability to fill and abridge gaps of up to 6 mm. (¼ in.) caused by uneven walls. This adhesive is sold in cartridges by builders' merchants, who usually have free applicators on loan. Wall surfaces must be sound, clean and dry.

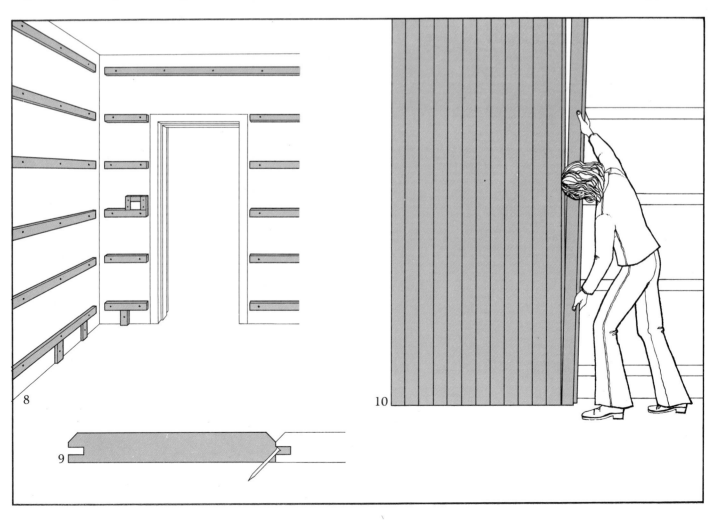

8

9

10

HOW TO HANG PAPER

Paperhanging is not too difficult if you have the right tools and equipment, work methodically and do not try to rush the job.

For your first attempt, choose a medium-price, ready-pasted vinyl or fairly stout wallpaper. Cheap wallpapers tear easily when wet and you will not want to risk spoiling expensive paper. It is best, also, to choose a semi-plain or 'free match' pattern, i.e. one that does not need matching. Avoid bold stripe patterns especially if the corners of the room are not 'true'.

TOOLS AND EQUIPMENT
You will need:

Scissors or shears Use as large a pair as you can manage; professional paperhangers' shears have 250–300 mm. (10–12 in.) blades. Ordinary household scissors are useful for fiddly cutting round light switches etc.

A folding 60 cm. or 1 m. (2 ft or 3 ft) rule

A soft lead pencil

A plumb-bob and line You can buy one or improvise with 3·6 m. (12 ft) of thin, soft string and a small weight.

A paperhanger's smoothing brush

A paperhanger's apron with a large pocket for shears, rule, smoothing brush, etc., is not essential but makes the job easier.

A hobbies knife with spare blades, useful for trimming round obstructions.

A synthetic sponge for removing paste from woodwork, etc.

With paper that is not ready-pasted, you will need a flat surface on which to paste the paper. Ordinary tables are usually too wide and not long enough so it is worth buying or hiring a proper folding pasteboard; these are usually 183 cm. (6 ft) long and about 61 cm. (2 ft) wide. Even if you are using ready-pasted wallcovering it is useful to have a pasteboard on which to cut it.

You will want a stepladder to reach to ceiling height. And if you have to paste the wallpaper, a bucket for the paste and a 4 in. (100 cm.) paint brush to put it on with; tie string across the handle of the bucket as a brush rest.

PREPARATION
A clean, sound, correctly prepared surface is essential if the new wallcovering is to look good and stay put. Refer to page 84 for information on how to prepare walls and ceilings.

Absorbent surfaces usually need a coat of 'size'; this makes hanging easier and helps adhesion. Use the size recommended by the manufacturer of the wallcovering or ordinary wallpaper adhesive suitably diluted. Apply the size freely with a large brush and allow it to dry before starting to hang the wallcovering.

MEASURING UP
The tables on page 112 will enable you to estimate how many rolls you need.

Left: Tools and equipment for paperhanging shown on a folding pasteboard. From the left: plumb-bob and line, hobbies knife, smoothing brush, scissors and shears, folding rule, pencil, synthetic sponge, chamois leather, paste bucket and brush
Above: Sophisticated use of colour and pattern makes a restful and elegant bedroom
Right: The bold flower design of this wall paper, with its white highlights emphasized by the white paintwork creates a light and cheerful effect

With large patterns, add one extra roll for every six shown in the tables to allow for waste in matching. 'Drop' patterns (see page 114) also tend to be wasteful. The main thing is not to run short before the job is completed. There can be slight colour variations between printing 'runs' and you may not get rolls from the same 'run' if you have to buy more at a later date.

A 'shade number' or 'roll number' is printed at the end of each roll or on a separate strip; all rolls with the same number should be identical in shade. Quote the number if you have to buy extra rolls later on.

Vinyls and most wallpapers are supplied trimmed nowadays, i.e. without a selvedge. If trimming is necessary, the dealer will probably do this for a small charge.

CHECKING THE ROLLS

The instructions may say 'Shade carefully before hanging'. This means checking for any differences in shade between rolls and also for shade variation from edge-to-edge across the width of the roll. Unroll three or four feet of each roll and drape them over the edge of the pasteboard (1). Do this in good daylight; differences in shade are difficult to see in artificial light.

With semi-plain or 'free match' patterns, the instructions may tell you to 'Reverse alternate lengths'. This takes care of any slight edge-to-edge variations in shade by bringing 'light' edges or 'dark' edges together on adjacent lengths. How to reverse alternate lengths is described on page 114.

Your dealer will usually replace unsatisfactory rolls if you return them promptly and in good condition. He will be less sympathetic if the material has been cut up or even hung before defects are spotted.

WHERE TO START

The general principle in paperhanging is to work 'from the light', i.e. from the largest window in the room so that slight overlaps at joints do not cast shadows making them more obvious. Taking a typical room, shown in the plan (2), a good place to start would be corner 'A'. From here, you would work from right to left until corner 'B' near the door was reached. Then you would start again at corner 'A' and work from left to right and back to corner 'B' again. It is not usually possible to keep a pattern matching all the

Chart for calculating number of rolls needed for walls

Height from skirting		Measurement round walls, including doors & windows									
Feet		28'0"	32'0"	36'0"	40'0"	44'0"	48'0"	52'0"	56'0"	60'0"	64'0"
	Metres	8·53	9·75	10·97	12·19	13·41	14·63	15·85	17·07	18·29	19·51
7'0"–7'6"	2·13–2·29	4	4	5	5	6	6	7	7	8	8
7'7"–8'0"	2·30–2·44	4	4	5	5	6	6	7	8	8	9
8'1"–8'6"	2·45–2·59	4	5	5	6	6	7	7	8	8	9
8'7"–9'0"	2·60–2·74	4	5	5	6	6	7	8	8	9	9
9'1"–9'6"	2·75–2·90	4	5	6	6	7	7	8	9	9	10
9'7"–10'0"	2·91–3·05	5	5	6	7	7	8	9	9	10	10
10'1"–10'6"	3·06–3·20	5	5	6	7	8	8	9	10	10	11
10'7"–11'0"	3·21–3·35	5	6	7	7	8	9	9	10	11	11
11'1"–11'6"	3·36–3·50	5	6	7	8	8	9	10	10	11	12
		Number of rolls required									

Chart for calculating number of rolls needed for ceiling

Measurement round room		Number of rolls	Measurement round room		Number of rolls
Feet	Metres		Feet	Metres	
28' 0"	8·53	1	48' 0"	14·63	3
30' 0"	9·14	2	50' 0"	15·24	4
32' 0"	9·75	2	52' 0"	15·85	4
34' 0"	10·36	2	54' 0"	16·46	4
36' 0"	10·97	2	56' 0"	17·07	4
38' 0"	11·58	2	58' 0"	17·68	4
40' 0"	12·19	2	60' 0"	18·29	5
42' 0"	12·80	3	62' 0"	18·90	5
44' 0"	13·41	3	64' 0"	19·51	5
46' 0"	14·02	3	66' 0"	20·12	5

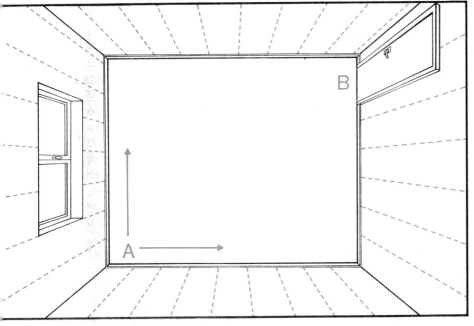

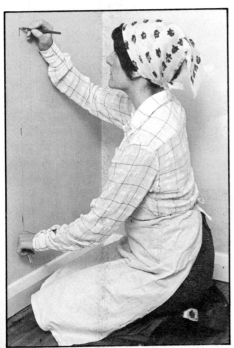

way round a room but, by working in two directions from corner 'A', the mismatch comes in an inconspicuous place. Also, of course, it follows the principle of 'working from the light'.

You may wish to hang a bold pattern on a feature wall or chimney breast. To achieve a balanced effect start from the centre and work out to right and left. Always start from a 'plumb' or truly vertical line. Do not rely on corners or your eye. If the first length is hung 'out of plumb', the remainder will follow it and you will find that the pattern runs off at top and bottom (3). Assuming you are starting at corner 'A' in the plan (2), mark a point at the top of the wall and to the left of the corner at a distance equal to the width of the wall-covering less 3 mm. ($\frac{1}{8}$ in.). Suspend your plumb-bob from this point, the full height of the wall. Have an assistant make a vertical mark behind the string a few inches above the skirting. Then, holding the string taut between the top and bottom marks, make a series of vertical marks behind the string (4). If you are on your own, tap in a small masonry nail at the top mark and tie the string of the plumb-bob to this (5). Now check that at no point is the distance between the marks and the corner greater than the width of the wallcovering less 3 mm. ($\frac{1}{8}$ in.) If it is, adjust the line of marks accordingly.

When starting in the centre of a wall or chimney breast, find the centre point and 'plumb' from there.

MEASURING AND CUTTING

With patterned papers, decide which is the 'top' and 'bottom'. Usually, the free end of the roll is the 'top' but if this is obviously not the case, rewind the roll in the reverse direction. With some patterns, 'top' and 'bottom' are a matter of choice.

Now measure and cut the first length of paper allowing 5–7·5 cm. (2–3 in.) for trimming off at top and bottom. Take care in measuring and cutting the first length because it will serve as a guide. Lay the first length on the pasteboard, pattern side up and with the 'top' at the left-hand end of the board and then cut the rest as follows:

(a) With semi-plain and 'free match' papers, align the free end of the roll with the top of the first length, unroll and cut off in line with the bottom. If the instructions say 'Reverse alternate lengths' (see opposite) then, for the second length, turn the roll round,

113

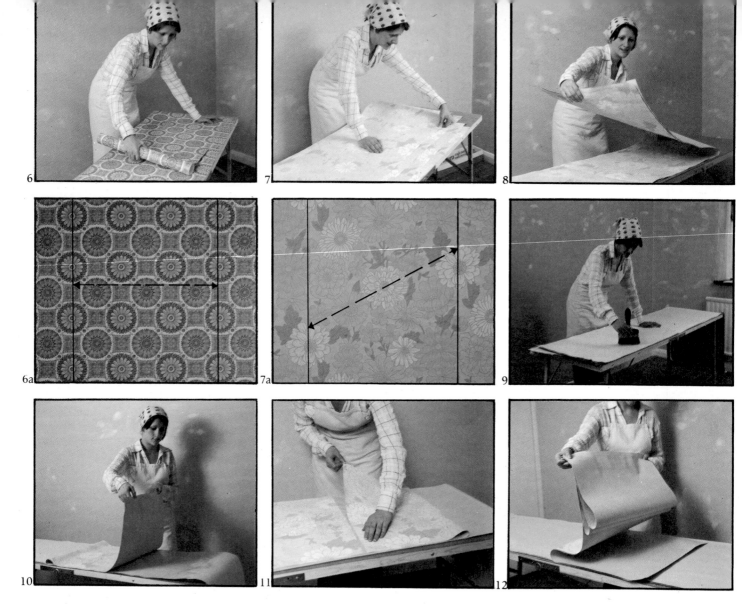

align the free end with the *bottom* of the first length and cut off in line with the top. For the third length, reverse the roll again and so on.

(b) With 'straight match' patterns, lay the second length over the first so that the pattern units coincide and the free end of the roll extends up to or beyond the top of the first length (6). Unroll and cut off level with the bottom of the first length. Cut all lengths in the same way so the pattern will match (6a).

(c) 'Drop' patterns match diagonally. Lay the second length over the first so that a pattern unit comes *exactly* midway between two identical units in the first length and the free end of the roll extends beyond the top of the first length (7). Unroll and cut off level with the bottom of the first length. The third length is a duplicate of the first, the fourth duplicates the second and so on, thus again ensuring pattern match (7a).

Professional paperhangers cut up two or more rolls in this way before starting to hang but it is better to start by cutting one at a time.

Turn the lengths over, plain side upper-most and with the 'tops' at the right-hand end of the pasteboard. To do this grasp the 'tops' (left-hand end of the pasteboard) with the right hand and fold them over to the right, at the same time inserting the left hand into the fold and drawing the 'bottoms' to the left (8).

PASTING

With ready-pasted wallcovering, you will have a 'trough' to hold water. Fill this about three-quarters full with cold water, roll up the cut length from the bottom, pattern side out, and immerse it in the trough for about a minute or as indicated on the instructions. It is then ready for hanging. If preferred, ready-pasted wallcoverings can be pasted in the normal way using well-diluted paste. This would be better for long lengths on staircases or ceilings.

For ordinary wallcoverings, use the recommended adhesive or, if there is no specific recommendation, any good brand. Make it up in a clean bucket. Arrange the lengths of paper in the

centre of the pasteboard with the 'tops' just overlapping the right-hand end. Push the first length away from you so that its edge is fractionally over the edge of the board. Apply the paste freely and evenly, working from the centre to the far edge (9) the length of the pasteboard. Next, draw the paper forward so that the edge slightly over-laps the edge of the board nearest to you and again paste from the centre outwards. Now fold the pasted portion over (10) and move the lengths to the right so that you can paste the re-mainder. Fold the bottom over to meet the top fold (11).

For lengths more than about 3 m. (10 ft) it is necessary to fold concertina-fashion (12). To do this, turn the first fold back and then continue making small concertina folds.

After pasting, vinyls can be hung straightaway. Ordinary wallpapers may need to stand for a few minutes to be-come supple, especially if they are fairly heavy. Do not oversoak, though, particularly with thin papers.

Dramatic use of wall paper

HANGING

If you need a stepladder to reach the top of the wall, place it about a foot away from the wall and forward of where the first length is to be hung.

Returning to the pasted length on the pasteboard, turn the top fold halfway back and then make a small reverse fold about 25 mm. (1 in.) from the top. Holding the length between fingers and thumbs (13), mount the steps and get into a comfortable position. Allow the top portion of the length to unfold and then locate the edge against the 'plumb' line (see page 113), holding the other edge away from the wall. When you are satisfied that the edge is running true to the line, smooth down with the smoothing brush using long, sweeping strokes. With vinyls, you can use a sponge instead for smoothing down. Make sure there are no bubbles or creases.

Press the paper well into the angle between the wall and ceiling, cornice or picture rail (14). Run the points of the shears along to make a sharp crease. The small reverse fold you made at the top will prevent paste from getting on to the ceiling. Pull the top away, open the small fold and cut accurately along the crease (15). Brush the top into position.

Step down, move the steps on for the next length, and open the bottom fold. Make a small reverse fold to keep paste off the skirting, then mark and cut as you did at the top. Sponge off any paste that has strayed on to the skirting then smooth down the paper.

If you are hanging ready-pasted paper, position the trough containing the rolled length against the skirting (16). Draw the free end out, and hang as already described, using a sponge for smoothing down.

Subsequent lengths are hung in the same way, carefully matching the pattern, if any, and making neat 'butt' joints.

TACKLING CORNERS

Eventually, you will come to a corner. It is not good practice to 'bend' any wallcovering more than about 12 mm. (½ in.) round an angle so you will need to cut a strip just fractionally wider than the greatest distance between the last full length and the corner.

Strips may be cut either 'wet', i.e. after pasting, or 'dry'; the latter would be best with ready-pasted wallcoverings. Always cut so that the correct 'matching edge' is left to join up to the edge of the preceding length. (17).

To cut a strip 'wet', align the matching edge of the folded length along the edge of the pasteboard. With the points of the shears, and using the edge of the pasteboard as a guide, make an indented line along the length, the correct distance in from the matching edge (18). If you find this method difficult at first, use a long straightedge and pencil *lightly*. Cut accurately to the line.

To cut 'dry', mark the line on the back of the paper using a pencil and straight-edge, taking care to work from the matching edge.

Hang the first strip in the usual way. Then 'plumb' a line (page 113) the appropriate distance from the corner and hang the second strip. If the corner is out of 'plumb' there may be some unavoidable overlap around the angle; cut this away if there is more than about 12 mm. (½ in.)

When you have completed half the room, e.g. from corner 'A' to corner 'B' in our imaginary room, go back to the starting point and work the other way round. How to deal with the window wall is shown (19). Finally, fill in small areas around windows, sides of the fireplace, etc.

WORKING ROUND OBSTRUCTIONS

Remove light fittings, switch plates, etc., if possible, but remember to switch off at the mains or remove fuses; wet paper conducts electricity. Put pieces of spent matchsticks in screwholes so that they protrude through the paper as a guide to refixing. When fittings and other obstructions cannot be removed, they will have to be cut round. How to cut round a switch plate is shown (20) and the general principle applies to other

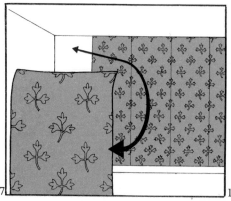

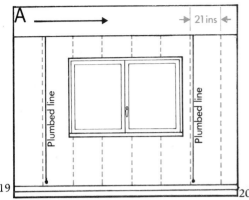

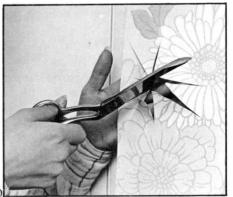

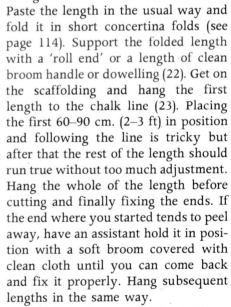

to 'work from the light', i.e. to hang the lengths parallel with the window wall. However, if working at right angles to the window wall means shorter lengths, work that way.

The first length is hung to a line struck across the ceiling. To strike a line, make pencil marks on the ceiling at each end at a distance from the angle or cornice 3 mm. ($\frac{1}{8}$ in.) less than the width of the paper. Then rub coloured chalk along a length of thin, soft string long enough to stretch between the pencil marks. With assistance, pull the string taut between the two marks, draw it away and let it snap smartly back (21). This will leave a chalk line on the ceiling. If you do not have an assistant, tap in a masonry nail at one mark and fix the string to this.

Paste the length in the usual way and fold it in short concertina folds (see page 114). Support the folded length with a 'roll end' or a length of clean broom handle or dowelling (22). Get on the scaffolding and hang the first length to the chalk line (23). Placing the first 60–90 cm. (2–3 ft) in position and following the line is tricky but after that the rest of the length should run true without too much adjustment. Hang the whole of the length before cutting and finally fixing the ends. If the end where you started tends to peel away, have an assistant hold it in position with a soft broom covered with clean cloth until you can come back and fix it properly. Hang subsequent lengths in the same way.

Remove light fittings completely if you can, first taking out the fuses or switching off at the mains. When you reach the position of the fitting, make a hole in the paper and pull the loose wires through. If the fitting cannot be removed, deal with it as above.

The last length will probably need cutting to width. This is best done 'dry' before pasting, as described on page 116.

obstructions. The paper is hung loosely over the switch and its centre located. From the centre, short radiating cuts are made, allowing the paper to be pressed flat. Then the outline of the switch is marked (20a) the paper eased away and the waste trimmed off with the shears. Paste is sponged off the switch and the paper pressed into position. With vinyls and stout wallpapers, the waste can be trimmed off with a sharp hobbies knife.

CEILINGS

To paper a ceiling, you will need to rig up a scaffolding with stout planks and suitable supports at each end (see page 92). You will be working overhead with nothing to hold on to so do not tackle the job unless you are confident 'off the ground'. And do not take chances with makeshift scaffolding which can be dangerous; see page 92 for ladders and scaffolding.

As with walls, the general principle is

117

SPECIAL EFFECTS

SPECTACULAR EFFECTS

There is such a wide variety of straight-forward finishes available to the home handywoman that special effects, achieved at the expense of considerable and painstaking labour, may seem superfluous. Paints are produced in vast colour ranges and many different finishes, while papers provide enough colour and diversity of pattern to satisfy most tastes.

However, if you are an adventurous decorator you can go further, devising your own special effects for walls, ceilings and furniture. You may, for example, wish to imitate wood grain on doors and skirting boards where the natural grain is either undistinguished or lost beneath layers of paint. You may even wish to simulate wood panelling on all the walls of a small room. This can be extremely effective, especially in small rooms – a tiny study, for example. Unless you have some ability as an artist, this may be rather difficult, because what you will be doing is literally drawing a free-hand representation of panelling and wood grains.

GRAINING COLOURS

These are known as scumbles and can be obtained from builders, merchants and shops supplying professional decorators. You will need a sample or colour picture of the wood grain you are going to imitate so that you have a clear idea of the nature of the wood you are aiming at. Preparation of the walls is exactly as for any other sort of painting. The next operation is to paint on the ground colour in the lightest tone of the grain you aim to achieve. This you allow to dry thoroughly before dabbing on the scumble which matches the darkest part of the grain with a brush, following the direction in which you intend the grain to run. While the scumble is still wet, draw a stiff dry brush across the surface to create an effect of grain, allowing the ground colour to show through. Then take a graining comb, which is either metal, rubber or leather and is available in a variety of grades for fine or coarse effects, and continue

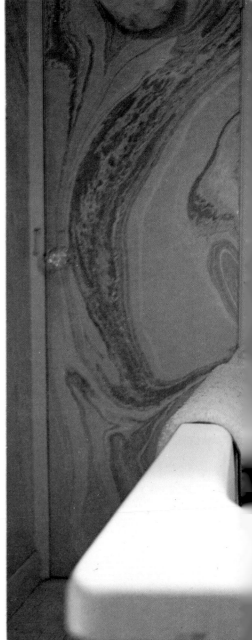

118

to elaborate the grain. Knots and burrs, if typical of the wood you are simulating, can be introduced by wrapping a piece of cloth round your thumb and twisting on the wet surface. Brushes and combs should be wiped between each stroke.

If you wish to imitate joins in the wood this is most effectively carried out by applying masking tape at the 'join', working to this and then leaving the scumble to dry before tackling the adjacent 'plank'.

A softening brush with a very gentle swatting action can be used to modify lines which are too harsh.

If you have a steady hand you can introduce moulding to give the effect of wood panelling on walls. The technique is similar to graining. After applying the ground coat, carefully draw in the panels and the moulding which surrounds them. Use masking tape to define the mouldings and then proceed as for graining, allowing the 'mouldings' to dry before graining the panels.

In a room which has panels of moulding, you can emphasize them by painting them first in the ground colour of the rest of the room, allowing this paint to dry and then painting the mouldings in a darker colour. While this paint is still wet, take a piece of clean cloth and wipe away the colour from the raised portions of the moulding so that the dry under-painting in the ground colour shows through. This technique of darkening the recessed parts of the moulding whilst lightening the raised portions is very effective, particularly in a large, formal room.

1. Stippling: according to your choice of colour, this gives a subtle, soft effect
2. Marbling can produce a highly coloured result
3. Sponging: another effective two-colour technique

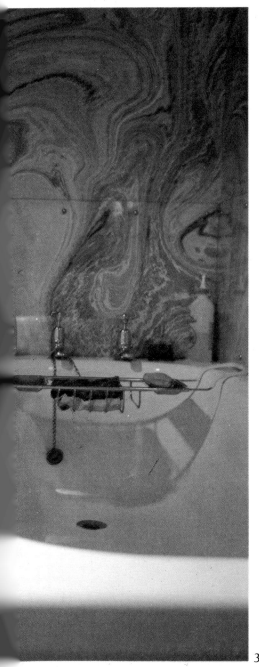

STIPPLING

This technique can be used to combine two colours on a painted wall in both subtle and strident combinations. The principle is similar to that of graining, in that you finish the basic painting of your walls in one colour and then apply a second colour which is broken up to allow the first colour to show through. The breaking up of the top coat is achieved with a stippling brush, using a dabbing action. It is best to work on one wall at a time. The amount of 'show through' can be controlled by

(artist's oil colours are excellent) and draw the veins on the painted surface holding the feather between thumb and forefinger. When a burr effect is required, roll the feather over to produce a broader stroke and back again to make a finer line. Harsh lines can be softened with a softening brush.

SPONGING

Another spectacular way to produce a two-colour effect is to use a sponge instead of a stippling brush. By gently dabbing the dry under-painting of your

*1. Top left to right:
flogger, softener, stippling
brush.
bottom left to right:
hog hair open grainer,
pencil over grainer, dotter,
hog hair mottler, graining
comb.*

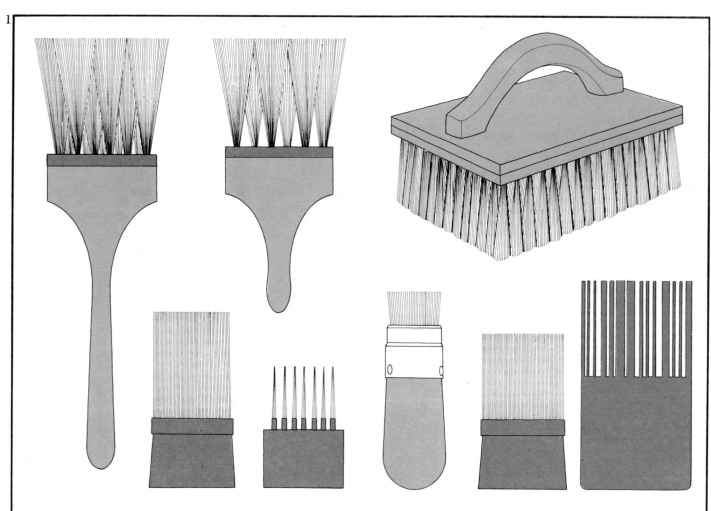

varying the vigour with which you use the stippling brush.

MARBLING

In decoration there are very often situations where the use of marble is appropriate. Marble can be quite successfully simulated, especially if you have a piece of marble handy to act as a source of inspiration and as a guide to the way the veins commonly occur. First paint the area to be marbled in a gloss or egg-shell finish in the main colour of the marble. Then apply the veins, using a pheasant's tail feather for the purpose. Dip this in the vein colour

walls with a sponge dipped in a second colour, charming mottled effects can be achieved. A slight twist to the sponge adds design motifs of great originality. Results may be modified with a softening brush. Towelling is a useful substitute for the sponge and gives interesting colour and pattern effects.

All these methods are a matter of trial and error and you would be wise to practise on a piece of board or unobtrusive piece of wall before tackling the main job. But results can be very rewarding and your decorative finishes will be unique.

*1. Disc ready to be screwed to
ceiling.
2. Batten is attached to the
walls.
3. Completed 'tube' of material.
4. Begin by attaching fabric
from disc to one corner.
5. Fabric pleated all round
onto disc.
6. Lower edge is pinned onto
batten.
7. Second disc is covered with
fabric and pinned onto first.
8. The tented room complete.*

TENTING

Modern paints and papers provide the home handywoman with an immense array of materials for exciting home decoration. There is practically no limit to the effects you can achieve. If you are already adept at colour-schemes, painting and paper-hanging and wish to go further into the realms of the decorator's art, here is a special technique that professionals sometimes use to stunning effect. It is called tenting.

It is an ideal technique to bring down a high ceiling and is best used in fairly small rooms, especially as the amount of material required is quite considerable. Tenting in sheer fabrics can be exquisite, creating an atmosphere which is at the same time feminine and slightly theatrical. Striped materials, too, are splendid for this effect, showing the stripes radiating like a sunburst from the centre to the corners of the room. Avoid patterns that require careful matching, as even a 3 × 3 m. (3 yd 10 in. square) room will require approximately twenty widths of 115 cm. (45 in.) fabric.

Measuring The technique which you will use for tenting is relatively simple, though the quantity of fabric used may call for more than one pair of hands while it is being fixed down. The first step is to measure the *width* of each wall and add these measurements together. You will need *double* this measurement as the total width of material required, to allow for the pleating (allow slightly less with a thick material). Thus a room measuring 3 m. × 3 m. (3 yd 10in. × 3 yd 10 in.)

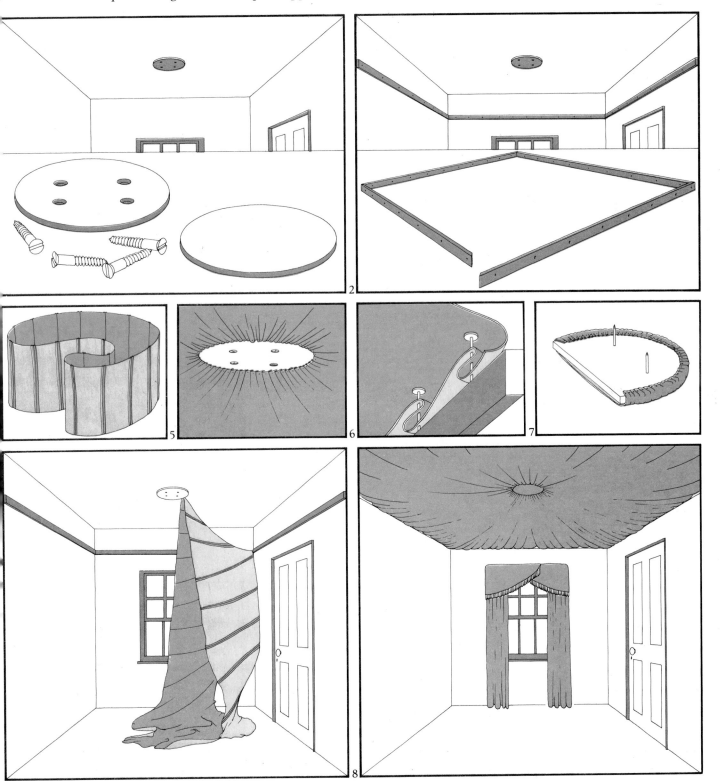

121

will take 24 m. (26 yd 1 ft). You must then work out how many widths of material are required to make up this total width. The length of the material is equivalent to the measurement of the furthest corner to the centre of the ceiling.

Ceiling Cut 2 circles of plywood about 20 cm. (8 in.) in diameter. Fix one to the centre of the ceiling by drilling 4 holes at 90° to each other in disc and ceiling, matching up the holes. Plug ceiling holes with Rawlplugs and screw on disc.

Wall To attach the material to the wall a batten like a picture rail will be required. This should be carefully mitred at the corners and pre-drilled to take screws that will fix it to the wall about 46 cm. (1 ft 6 in.) down from the ceiling. Carefully mark where the batten is to be fixed and prepare holes for Rawlplugs to coincide with the pre-drilled holes in the batten. Screw the batten to the walls and paint.

PLEATING

The selvedge edges of the material should be sewn together so that one enormous tube of material is created, pattern side in.

Start by attaching the material at one point on the ceiling disc. Then attach the trailing end to the batten at the corner of one wall, allowing room to work in the tube of material. A quarter of the total width of the material equals each wall's allotment if the room is square. Then start pleating at the ceiling disc one quarter of the circumference at a time, fastening the material either with tacks or a staple gun. Having finished the ceiling disc, now pleat each wall, either stapling or tacking the material to the wall batten, carefully cutting away surplus material as you go, to give a neat finish along the top of the rail.

The final step is to cover the second ceiling disc with surplus material and to nail this in position over the first disc in order to hide the ruching at the centre. First drive four nails at 90° to each other through the disc, and then cover with material so that the heads do not show. Tack or staple material down on wrong side to give a neat edge. Now tap this disc on top of the other.

The procedure is less difficult than it appears and the effect is delightful.

Tenting for an exotic effect

FRIEZES AND CUTOUTS

Highly decorative and very extravagant-looking effects can be achieved with patterned paper friezes at relatively little cost. We do not mean those narrow little borders with prissy designs that used to be pasted below picture rails but the ones of any width. They are pasted on any part of a wall to emulate a more expensive decorative material, to emphasize decorative features, to impose a decorative style where none exists or to relate one decoration to another.

EFFECTS WITH BORDERS

Take, for instance, a kitchen which you would like tiled to shoulder height for both decorative and practical reasons. The only thing that deters you is the price of patterned ceramic tiles and the fact that, once laid, they cannot be quickly removed when you want a change of decor. For a fraction of the cost you can hang, to the required height, a washable wallpaper printed with an equally attractive tile pattern (see below).

A room may have a plaster cornice round the ceiling which is not ornamental enough to be a stunning feature. A frieze of a suitable width pasted immediately below the cornice will supply the decorative element that is missing. A room without character can easily be decorated in the art nouveau or art déco style. A suitable border at the top and bottom of each wall and another extending down each corner will achieve your objective.

Then there is the room with walls of an intense colour highlighted by a brilliant white ceiling and woodwork. When finished the colour contrast is too harsh. Extensive re-decoration is triumphantly avoided and the whole effect softened by outlining the top of the walls and the edges of the woodwork with a border printed in both colours.

Choosing borders So, where do you discover such borders and friezes? If you cannot find them in the manufacturers' catalogues, select suitable wallpaper and cut it into strips either vertically or horizontally according to the pattern.

Finding the right design is the problem. It must be bold, because a relatively small amount of pattern must hold its own against large areas of wall and it is likely to be seen, not in close-up, but above or below eye-level at a distance. Bold, because in most cases the individual motifs will be cut out and they must make positive silhouettes against the wall. Because of this, the most suitable designs have a continuous repeat of simple but positively outlined shapes which can be cut round quickly with a pair of scissors. Motifs with spiky silhouettes tend to tear when pasted and curl when pressed on the wall.

Tiling borders Tile designs with diamond-shaped motifs which make good silhouettes when cut out, are the easiest to find (1). They are also produced on vinyl which is useful if you are decorating a kitchen or bathroom. Always pick a colour from the design for the rest of the walls and mix the paint to match exactly. Paint the walls beyond the level of the frieze. Cut round the motifs of the pattern and trim the other end to give a bit more depth than necessary. Mark a light pencil line along the wall to indicate the level of the top of the cut-out design. Paste the paper, coating the edges of the cut-out motifs carefully and, when in place on the wall, remove surplus paste immediately. Trim the plain end to fit the skirting and remove the pencil marks. You should try to use the same repeat at each corner of the wall; this is not always possible with large patterns.

EFFECTS WITH STRIPES

Some patterns can be cut out along the length of the paper. Striped papers fall into this category and, if you want to use the entire width, they do not have to be cut out

Perhaps the quickest way to achieve an ultra-modern décor is to paste a pattern of broad graduated stripes the

width of the roll all round a room or from the top to the bottom of the staircase at waist height (2).

Deck-chair stripes which match at each side of the paper make some of the best canopies if you mitre the pattern at the corners of the ceiling so that all stripes meet the tops of the walls vertically. After painting the walls to match the palest shade in the stripe pattern get some help in ruling a straight line diagonally from one corner of the ceiling to the other and then between the two remaining corners. Then find the middle of one side of the

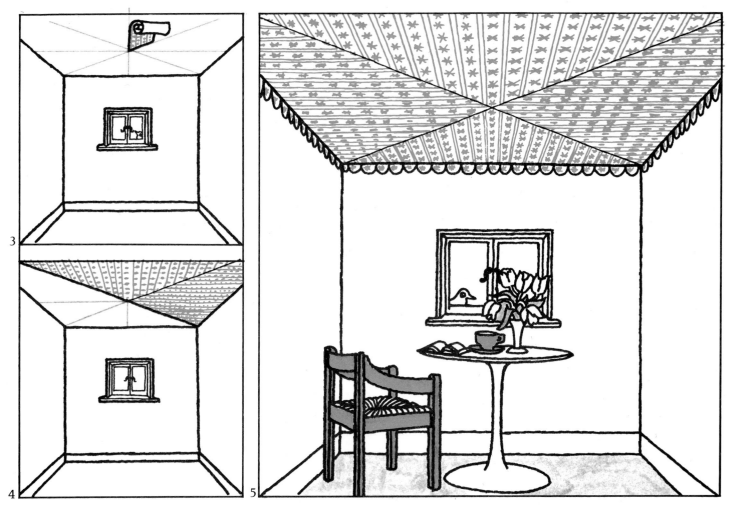

Personalized effects Cutting round patterns becomes a pastime with some people. After you have had a little practice you may want to personalize your rooms still further. If you find a suitable foliage design consider running it over the walls except in the vicinity of windows, doors and ceiling. Allow a few 'shoots' cut out to varying lengths to creep round them.

A large formalized flower pattern can make an amusing border along the bottom of a wall: paint the skirting to look like a long window box. Friezes along the tops of walls are usually more effective when the ceiling is papered all over in the same pattern giving a very opulent type of decor. Another idea makes good use of odd lengths of wallpaper which have different patterns: choose a selection of designs which all have light backgrounds or all have dark ones. If you choose light ones, paper a room entirely in a pattern with a dark background, and vice versa. Cut your collection of designs into 23 cm. (9 in.) squares and paste them over the previously papered walls in a checkerboard pattern. Paper patchwork walls are particularly effective in a small 'cosy' type of room.

ceiling and rule a line to the centre where the first lines cross. Repeat on the other three sides so that the ceiling is divided into eight triangles. Cut a piece of paper the length of one of the lines running from the middle of a side to the central meeting point. Paste and place with one side on one of these lines (3). Trim the end of the paper to fit against the diagonal ruled line. Fit the next length of paper parallel to the stripes on the first one trimming diagonally as before. Continue in this way to the corner then return to the starting point and work in the opposite direction (4). When the ceiling is complete scallop the bottom edge from short lengths of paper to make a frieze. Using a guide line marked on the wall, paste these pieces in place matching the stripes round the edge of the ceiling (5). Period patterns which can be cut to make satisfactory silhouettes can be more difficult to find. But a very satisfactory art déco border for the bottom of walls can be made from paper striped in appropriate colours. To add to the effect run the stripes up the corners of the walls at right angles trimming them to a point (6).

PROBLEM ROOMS

Many rooms in many homes are far from ideal in their proportions and inevitably pose decoration problems. Problem shapes and sizes may be accentuated – presumably unwittingly – by the users of the rooms. Small bedrooms are often cluttered up with heavy, dark wardrobes and busy patterned carpets which increase the claustrophobic atmosphere of the room. This example holds the key to the solution on many similar rooms – suitable furniture and fittings solve most space problems.

USING COLOUR

To make a small room seem larger you need as little interruption to a smooth visual effect as possible. Cool receding colours tend to push back the walls, and furniture that is similarly coloured blends into the background and becomes unobtrusive. A dark floor should be avoided as this, too, tends to make the room seem smaller than it is. A unified overall cool colour scheme does not lend to dullness when accent colours are used in small quantities to lend interest without adding heaviness. There are times when you *want* a room to look small and cosy, in which case the smallness should be emphasized by the use of warm advancing colours. Studies and dining alcoves lend themselves to this treatment. Cosiness can also be achieved by papering the walls and ceiling with an all-over mini-pattern which has a matching fabric for covers and curtains.

A tall room can be made to look lower by painting the ceiling in a heavy colour and clothing the walls in a horizontal pattern or by papering both walls and ceiling in an all-over pattern – this veils the distinction between them. Another trick is to install a picture-rail some distance below the ceiling and to run the ceiling decoration down to meet it. A contrasting colour finishes the walls below.

The adventurous decorator may decide to exaggerate the problems and provide a sophisticated solution by painting formalized trees with long trunks round the walls so that their leaves make a canopy over the ceiling.

1. *Different shapes in this long narrow passage utilize the space while preserving the overall effect*

2. *A frieze can be used effectively to lower a high ceiling*

3. *Mirrors extend the proportions of a room*

1

2

A room that is too low can represent more than a decoration problem, as the Building Regulations for newly built or converted properties do not permit anyone to live in a room with a ceiling height less than 206 cm. (6 ft. 9 in.). Low ceilings can make you feel that they are pressing on your head. Never decorate a low ceiling with a strong patterned or a dark advancing colour. Instead choose white or pale blue, pale green or grey. Low walls appear taller when papered with a strong vertical pattern which can run over the ceiling.

USING FURNITURE

A long room is a furnishing problem unless it is split into areas. This can be done by bisecting it with tall pieces of furniture such as open bookshelves, room-dividers or arrangements of cupboards (leaving the width of a door for access) or by erecting an arch between each area to mark a change of decor.

To make a long passage seem wider paint skirtings to match plain flooring or install along one wall a ceiling-to-floor mirror, mirror tiles, polished aluminium tiles or reflective paper. A passage, perhaps cave-like and depressing, can be amusingly exaggerated by installing a mirror on an end wall if there is one; this will create an impression of space.

If a small room must accommodate a lot of equipment, install built-in furniture, preferably light in colour. Select each item very carefully so that it earns its place by fulfilling its function, fits the space allotted and is attractive enough not to need extra bits added later. Visual harmony is very important. Use fittings that are all of the same height and design, so that you create long runs of regular, unbroken levels.

A big room always sounds like an advantage in an estate agent's advertisement but it can prove otherwise when you come to arrange it. Space is very desirable and may often be left to look after itself by concentrating on focal points in selected areas – the fireplace and conversation group closely arranged and full of interest balanced by the open space, perhaps punctuated with a piece of skilfully illuminated sculpture or a dramatically large plant. Not all spaces need to be filled.

A large dining room, however, is a problem because it has few necessities. There is something pathetic about a small number of people eating at a very big table. But a giant one you must

1. The smallness of a room may be emphasized and an intimate effect created by decorating walls and ceiling with the same, busily patterned wall paper

2. Lower the ceiling of a tall room by painting it in a dark colour and continuing the colour down to a picture rail

3. Use cool colours and built-in furniture to increase the proportions of a room

4. A large room should be split up into smaller areas

5. Strong vertical stripes make a low ceiling appear higher

have because a small one would make the room look like a restaurant. Fill up the rest of the room with bold objects. Try massing tall luxuriant indoor plants round the walls and ones of moderate growth in the space to spare on the table and sideboard. Line the walls with shelves bearing anything decorative. Paint the ceiling in a strong warm colour such as terra-cotta and curb any inclinations you may have to delineate the skirting boards and picture rail with a contrasting colour. If you are not a collector, paper the walls and ceiling in a bold, close pattern containing hot and heavy colours. Pack one wall with closely arranged pictures.

USING CAMOUFLAGE

Camouflage is your best ally in the battle with awkward rooms. Many people have something to hide. Too many doors in one room is a common problem. Paint them, including the surrounds, in the same colour as the walls and their effect is minimised. Do not emphasize radiators by picking out in white; they – and unsightly pipes – will tend to vanish if painted to match the walls.

Odd combinations of windows often occur, especially in older houses. The dotty effect of these can often be overcome by organising long curtains that cover several irregularly placed windows.

It is worth repeating basic colour rules. Receding colours, pale and cool, tend to push out the walls. Use them to increase the apparent space in any room. Heavy advancing colours tend to reduce apparent space and are invaluable in reducing height and space when required. Stripes hung vertically appear to increase height and when used horizontally they appear to condense space.

If you have an old bathroom with many exposed pipes which cannot be re-routed, you have two alternatives. Either paint them to match the walls – camouflage them to make them disappear – or paint them in bright contrasting colours to make a feature of their eccentricity! This can work wonderfully well.

Most rooms with awkward alcoves, chimney breasts and similar intrusive features are susceptible to simple logical treatment. Alcoves and buttresses form an excellent base for fitted cupboards and walls with interrupted surfaces can usually be 'flushed' – with cupboard fronts and shelves to form surfaces that are pleasing to the eye and useful as well. One interior decorator is famous for saying 'there are no problem rooms – only difficult solutions!'

ASSESSING FURNITURE

Even if you are not fond of old furniture, you cannot help noticing that much of it is more strongly constructed and better finished than its present-day equivalent.

TYPES OF FURNITURE

The kind of old furniture that we are mainly considering includes all the solidly-built, stylish pieces made be-between 1875 and the Second World War, when nearly all craftsmen took pleasure in their work and provided more than was strictly necessary for the wages they received.

Solid Victorian furniture from the beginning of this period is plentiful.

Art nouveau furniture, with its distinctive, curvilinear decorations and rhythmic shapes, made around the end of the nineteenth century, is eagerly sought by connoisseurs and is still to be found; look out for oak chairs and cabinets which can still be picked up quite cheaply.

Edwardian Most of the furniture from the turn of this century, simply known as Edwardian, is quite different. It is not so heavy or florid as Victorian nor has it the flowing forms of art nouveau designs, and it is not so expensive. Look for wardrobes, dressing-tables, chaise-longues and upholstered chairs, dining-chairs, tables and sideboards.

Twenties and Thirties The better made furniture from the twenties and thirties is well worth having, and many stylish sideboards, dining-tables, three-piece suites and bedroom suites, of the kind being snapped up by collectors, can still be picked up for a song.

Used furniture of more recent manufacture is simply termed 'second-hand'. It lacks period charm for most of us, but many pieces are worth buying if they can be brought up to date.

Utility The war resulted in a shortage of materials and only so-called 'utility' furniture was produced. This serviceable, austere stuff, entirely lacking in embellishment, is now enjoying a certain vogue among sophisticates who like its uncompromising style.

Post-war After the war, furniture continued to be based on the new con-

structional principles, but its simple shapes were often glamourized by the use of new materials and finishes.

MAKING A GOOD BUY

Whether you choose to buy old furniture for economic or decorative reasons, you can end up with a homeful of debris if you neglect to subject every piece you fancy to a close examination. This is sometimes difficult. A typical second-hand furniture shop is often stuffed to the ceiling with everything under the sun. It is impossible to browse round and the contents seldom bear a price tag. This leads you to suppose that the cost may fluctuate according to the customer. For this reason it is wise to ask the price of anything that interests you before it is disinterred.

BUYING AT AUCTIONS

The biggest bargains are found at auction sales. These are, in general, haunted by people who have got a fair idea of the value of most things and by dealers who know the buying and selling market inside out. Do not buy anything yourself until you have been to one or two sales for experience. Before bidding, decide the maximum amount that you are prepared to pay. Furniture can usually be viewed the day before the sale. Buy a catalogue in the office and read the descriptions of each lot – one item or a group of items offered together – with great attention. To protect the buyer, it is illegal for the vendor or auctioneer to describe, say, a chair as Chippendale when it was not made in his workroom but only in the

style that he created.

The laws governing description change from time to time, so make a point of reading the *Conditions of Sale* which hang in every saleroom.

LOOKING FOR WOODWORM

Wooden furniture should first be examined all over for woodworm. This pest lays its eggs under the surface; when hatched, the young eat away their surroundings until these can become completely weakened. Furniture inhabited by woodworm will introduce it to other wood – although oak and mahogany are usually immune – in the vicinity. Sometimes woodworm deserts timber altogether. In this case, the holes look old and when the wood is knocked no sawdust is dislodged. Sawdust beneath holes is a sure sign of unwelcome activity above. Being rotten, badly-infected furniture is obviously to be avoided. A slight infestation is nothing to worry about but should be treated the moment you get home.

TESTING FOR WEAKNESS AND BROKEN JOINTS

Next, test furniture by rocking it about. If any part is unsteady see whether the frame is broken and if so, whether the wood looks brittle throughout. Do not buy anything in the latter category because it will soon disintegrate. Some breaks and splits can be riveted with a straight or a T-shaped steel plate, but this kind of repair is unsightly and should be reserved for parts that are generally invisible.

Furniture is a bad investment when

1. *A typically stylish Thirties wardrobe.*

2. *An Edwardian dressing-table well worth restoring.*

3. *A Victorian sofa would look splendid recovered.*

4. *A pair of typical Art Nouveau chairs.*

5. *The distinctive shape of Utility furniture of the Forties.*

instability is due to a broken joint. Learn to distinguish between joints that have worked loose and ones that have snapped – unless you are willing to undertake carpentry. A kitchen-chair leg that has come out of its hole in the seat frame can obviously be re-glued in place; a damaged dovetail joint in a series of sound ones which are closely spaced is not worth worrying about, unless it leaves a hole that can be seen; but a joint that has been broken off usually means that the whole part must be made again.

Make further investigations if you en-counter an item which has been held together with a screw, in a place where you would not expect to find one. This kind of thing suggests that a bodger has been on the job, and he has probably been indulging in other makeshift repairs to get the item speedily off his hands with the mini-mum of effort. These profiteers are responsible for a lot of damage. One of their principal occupations is immers-ing pine furniture in tanks of caustic soda to strip off paint. They often leave the furniture in too long and consequently the wood shrinks when dry, so that all the joints pull apart.

CHECKING FITTINGS AND DECORATION

Always check moveable elements. You are not likely to buy a bureau without ensuring that the drawers slide smoothly, or a drop-leaf table without finding out if the leaf when raised is steady and level with the rest of the top. But a draw-leaf dining-table can be more difficult to check because it is often quite a performance to assemble it to its full extent.

Always make sure that an item which is assembled in sections is complete. A wardrobe, for instance, is often found to lack a decorative rail round the top. This is a difficult detail to replace if the wood cannot be identified. You will often find that a piece of furniture is lacking part of its decora-tion. Strips of simple moulding may be easy to obtain but carved motifs are not. If it is a small, very simple section that is missing you may be able to mould a replacement in plaster or carve one if you can match the wood.

Missing fittings can be a problem. If hinges must be replaced, make sure that the wood is sound enough to hold screws. Some fittings, once common, are not reproduced nowadays even by specialist firms (this, believe it or not, includes most wooden knobs!). A miss-ing metal drop handle on a chest of drawers may entail buying a new set which could cost more than the chest.

Blemishes It is unreasonable to expect old furniture to be unblemished. Chipped feet, etc., can be filled and will be undetectable under a coat of paint. Gashes, scratches, dents, holes and stains that do not affect the wood under the finish are no deterrent, even if the item is to have a transparent finish, because they can be removed. Deep burns or other blemishes are another matter, however. The finish on the top of a table or bureau will have to be removed completely, and the wood will have to be sanded down until the burn has disappeared, before you can apply a new finish such as water-proof and heatproof seal, wax polish or French polish. Blisters or cracks in veneer can be remedied without diffi-culty but replacing missing patches of veneer is a fiddly job.

Upholstered furniture can involve you in more expense and work than you expect. When you invest in a tattered settee you are usually only buying the wooden frame. To have it re-sprung and covered professionally will cost the same as buying a new one. You can buy cane to re-seat a chair but rush is no longer obtainable; sea-grass has to be substituted.

KNOWING ABOUT WOODS

As you will see from our photographs, many woods that you think you recognized turn out to be something else. One of the difficulties in identifying wood is that there are many varieties of each kind. Another difficulty is that any variety may be sawn either along the grain, straight across it or diagonally across it, and the results will look entirely different. To top it all, the appearance of any given wood can be transformed by a multitude of stains and finishes.

It is interesting to know what kind of wood your personal treasures are made of. It is not essential, however, to be able to identify uncommon timbers in order to recognize the everyday varieties that were used for the kind of furniture that was inexpensive when it was produced and is still cheap today. It is a good idea to collect odd bits of oak, mahogany, walnut, beech and pine to use when patching or replacing parts of furniture, but you do need a dry place to store such material. You will probably find that you can generally make do with either wood filler for a minor repair or, if the damage is more extensive, with new wood which may be finished to match the rest of the piece.

When you get an old piece of furniture home, place it in a good light and, if the surface has been neglected or damaged, try to discover what the finish consists of.

FINISHES

French Polish is a finish applied to fine furniture. It is composed of shellac dissolved in methylated spirit. The distinctive deep gloss is achieved by rubbing on one layer of polish after another.

Wax is the oldest finish and was traditionally a mixture of beeswax, carnauba wax and turpentine. Modern wax is softer and loses its shine more quickly.

Oil darkens and enriches the colour of wood, emphasises the texture and provides a modicum of protection against penetration by moisture. Oak, pine and beech were generally rubbed with linseed oil as a preliminary to waxing or finished with a varnish not used nowadays based on oil and turpentine gum.

Varnish comes in a variety of types and none is easy for an amateur to identify. Old furniture was often finished in spirit varnish. Mass-produced furniture made in the last 40 years is finished with cellulose lacquer or, for extra toughness, polyurethane lacquer.

Paint is easy enough to see but it is more difficult to recognize the different types. Before it was prohibited, oil paint was made which contained a large proportion of lead. This kind of paint is poisonous if chewed and can be recognized on old furniture because its gloss fades with age.

IDENTIFYING A FINISH

You probably know that a piano is French-polished. But what you may not know is that not all French-polished furniture has such a mirror-like gloss. The grain of items which have only been given a few coats of polish can still be felt in some cases. This kind of French-polished finish is often difficult to distinguish from an oiled- and-waxed finish.

To tell the difference, take a rag and rub a little methylated spirit onto a small area that does not normally show. If the wood has been French-polished this will dissolve, leaving a sticky patch. If nothing happens, dry off the methylated spirit and repeat the process using turpentine (the real thing, not the substitute called 'white spirit'). A patch of naked wood should result if the wood has been waxed unless a cheap, old-fashioned varnish or a modern seal has been applied.

There is an instant test – often used surreptitiously by unscrupulous people before they invest in an item – which may give you an indication without the use of methylated spirit or turpentine. Take a razor blade and scratch off a portion of the finish right back to the wood. French polish leaves the surface in the form of very fine curled shavings; wax deposit feels 'waxy' between your fingers; oil varnish forms coarse curls; cellulose varnish just turns to powder.

RESTORING FRENCH-POLISHED FURNITURE

Cleaning If your piece is merely dirty it will simply need refreshing. French polish is cleaned by wiping it with a cloth *barely* moistened in a solution of

1. Rosewood was often used for small pieces like this beautifully-carved box.
2. Well-polished old oak furniture has a distinctive lustre.

detergent and luke-warm water. If there is a build-up of grubby polish, clean it off with a rag moistened in pure turpentine before polishing with the hard wax formulated for antiques. In future, wipe it over regularly using detergent and water before shining it with a soft duster. Wax it once a year and remove the build-up every five years.

Renovating After removing old wax, a French-polished finish which is shabby can be revived by working in a mixture made up from 5 parts alcohol, 2 parts linseed oil and 1 part pure turpentine. Use a circular motion and take care not to overdo the treatment as the mixture will soften the polish. Leave several hours, then apply wax polish.

Marks left by hot plates, dishes or mugs are not easily eradicated. Several treatments, each consisting of a hard rub with an equal mixture of linseed oil and turpentine, may remove them. Clean up the oily residue with vinegar.

Alcohol Marks made by alcoholic drinks are serious: spirits dissolve the polish. Wipe up spills instantly. If harm has already been done and cannot be disguised by wax polish, just rub the whole surface of the piece to an even finish with the finest sandpaper and then re-wax; this course will produce a finish with a soft sheen rather

3. *Pine furniture is often stripped of its paint and varnish to achieve a simpler effect.*
4. *Elaborate Victorian sideboards like this are often made of mahogany.*
5. *Walnut was a favourite for more elegant furniture.*

2

3

than a high gloss.

Scratches in the polish can be filled in with proprietary fillers but a better result is obtained by abrading scratches with the finest sandpaper and then, after removing every speck of dust, giving the area very thin successive coats of French polish with an artist's sable brush. Allow each coat to dry before applying the next. Substitute French polish can also be used as described on page 154.

Burns that have not affected the wood can be erased like scratches. If, however, the wood is charred, a patch treatment is likely to show because, after the burnt wood has been removed, the crater will have to be filled with a compound, coloured to match the surrounding wood. This is a very difficult task because the slightest discrepancy in tone is magnified by the polish which follows.

Fading Furniture may fade when exposed to sunlight. This may be because the wood was treated with a stain which has turned paler or the wood itself has bleached. An even colour cannot be achieved without stripping off the finish.

RESTORING WAXED FURNITURE

A piece of waxed furniture which has been well-cared-for has a rich patina unmatched by any other transparent

4

5

finish. A wax finish is by no means impregnable however; liquid and stains can be absorbed by the wood underneath in spite of the fact that before polishing it was probably rubbed with linseed oil to enrich the colour and to emphasise the grain.

Dirt If the wax is grubby, clean it off with pure turpentine and then wax again, using antique wax.

Stains If the wood is marred by stains, however, you will get the best result in the end if you sand it down until clean. If there are only a few isolated marks you may be able to bleach them out. Black and grey stains made by water can be removed by painting them with the strongest possible solution of oxalic acid crystals in water.

Ink stains may be eradicated by alternately treating them with vinegar and sodium hypochlorite.

OTHER FINISHES

Spot treatments for wood covered with other transparent finishes are not feasible unless you know what the finish is so that it can be re-applied. A painted finish which is damaged needs stripping entirely because, even if it comes from the same tin, a patch of new paint will not match paint applied in the past, as the colour will have changed through exposure to sunlight. The only exception would be brand-new paintwork.

MINOR REPAIRS

Your policy should be to avoid buying a piece of furniture in need of repair unless it is a bargain. However, sometimes you will be tempted to buy a damaged item because you like it so much, or you may be unfortunate enough to have a fresh acquisition damaged in transit. If you collect old furniture the ability to undertake minor repairs is invaluable.

TOOLS
A practical, careful person with a small stock of tools should be able to mend simple breaks, replace fittings and sort out small functional problems without specialized training. Your tools should include: a power drill with a selection of bits; screwdrivers; a mitre box; a tenon saw; a hacksaw; a plane; a milled file; a Stanley knife; chisels; mallet; a hammer; pliers; a vice; a steel rule; a steel measuring tape; a spirit level. Tools should never be neglected.

MENDING LEGS AND FEET
A break in a curved leg or foot can rarely be repaired without re-making the whole part. However, a break in a straight leg can generally be mended by making a dowelled joint (1). To find the right position to drill the holes, tap a

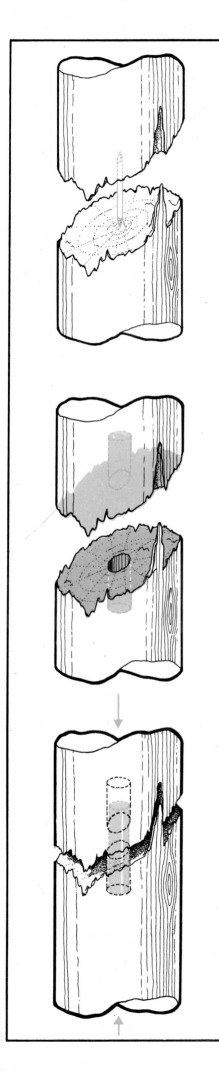

fine panel pin into one section of the break and press the other section to it so that a mark is left. Remove the pin and drill a hole of the same diameter as the hardwood dowel in each section. Bevel each end of the dowel and make a score down one side to accommodate excess adhesive. Paste the holes thinly with carpentry adhesive according to the directions, tap the dowel almost home in each section but apply adhesive to the raw edges of any ragged pieces on the outside of the leg before completing the job.

Legs and feet that break can sometimes be mended with a very useful screw which is threaded at both ends with a plain part between (2). Choose a big double-ended screw for a big leg and *vice versa*. Mark the centre of each section with a panel pin as before. Drill a hole in each to fit the screw snugly. Grasping the plain part of the screw with a pair of pliers, twist the screw into the section that has not broken off. Finally twist the remaining section onto the projecting end of the screw.

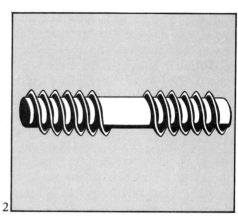

CASTORS

Old-fashioned castors should be oiled once a year. Many break because they have been neglected. Moreover, when a castor breaks and is not replaced instantly, a great strain is thrown on the whole piece.

There are two types of castor. The first is screwed up into the leg (3) and commonly breaks just below, leaving the threaded portion inside. If you cannot get this portion out by twisting the projecting part with a pair of pliers, or if no part projects, make a slot in the snapped-off end with a hacksaw and turn it anti-clockwise with a screwdriver.

Take the old castor with you when buying a new one, as the only replacement of the same pattern that you can find may turn out to have a smaller screw. This will make it necessary to plug the hole in the leg with a dowel into which a new screw hole of suitable dimensions will have to be bored. The second type of castor has a cup into which the bottom of the leg fits and is held by screws (4). If the bottom of the leg cracks the screws lose their hold and you have got to saw the leg off at the top of the cup and add a new piece. Cut a leg bottom of the same size as the discarded one and join with a dowel as described before.

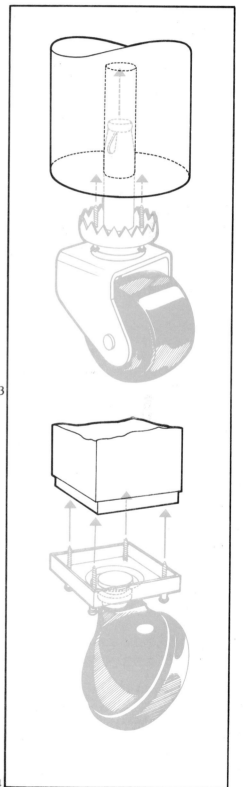

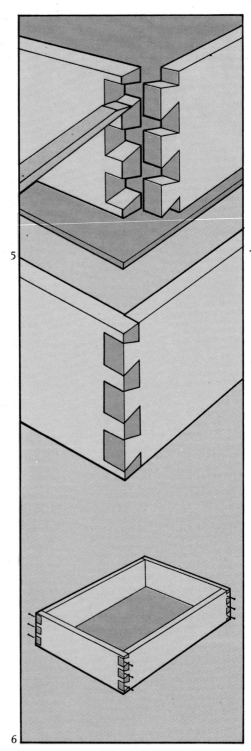

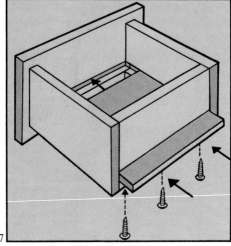

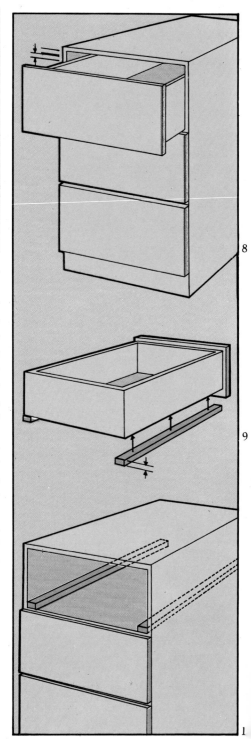

REPAIRING DRAWERS

Dovetailing A jammed drawer may be due to the fact that the dovetail in one of the corners has come unstuck. If so, remove the bottom of the drawer and pull the damaged corner apart gently (5). Clean the old glue from the dovetailing gently, using a chisel. If it proves obstinate, try damping with a little hot water. Then apply carpentry adhesive to the interlocking parts and reassemble. Hold securely with panel pins (6). The joints in the other corners will have to be re-glued in the same way if they have loosened in the process of fixing the first.

Refitting the bottom Many a drawer sticks after liquid has been spilled in it. The bottom of a drawer is held by screws at the back but fits into a groove at the front (7). When it dries, the bottom shrinks and falls out of the groove. Try taking the bottom out, re-fitting it in the groove and re-fixing the screws in a fresh position. If the bottom will not fit satisfactorily you will have to cut a new one.

Runners Some old drawers are somewhat naïve in construction; they amount to no more than an open shallow box which is pushed into another box which is not quite so shallow and is open at the front. When new, such a drawer has a strip of wood at either side of the underside which slides along corresponding strips underneath; through the years these may have disappeared. A repair of this kind is very satisfying. It is quick and easy to glue and pin on new runners and the result can make an appreciable difference to your everyday life.

Take off any remnants of wood from the bottom of the drawer and the bottom of the drawer cavity that may have been put there in a half-hearted effort to cure the problem. Put the drawer back and measure the height of the gap above it (8). Half this measurement minus 1·6 mm. ($\frac{1}{16}$ in.) is the thickness of the wood runners that are needed; their width is not particularly important. Cut four pieces of wood which are the length of the drawer. With carpentry adhesive, attach one runner to each side of the underside of the drawer to exclude the face (9). When the glue is dry push the drawer into the drawer space and mark the position of the runners on the front. Fix the bottom runners on the floor of the drawer space accordingly (10). Coat them all with candle wax.

Grooves Some drawers are grooved along the sides; these grooves accommodate a slide-rail at either side of the drawer space. If a coating of candlewax does not help the drawer to run smoothly and if the rails are intact, it is possible that the sides of the drawer or drawer space have warped; this is a sticky problem best left to a professional.

A mahogany chest of drawers that has been beautifully restored. The brass handles were removed for cleaning and then lacquered.

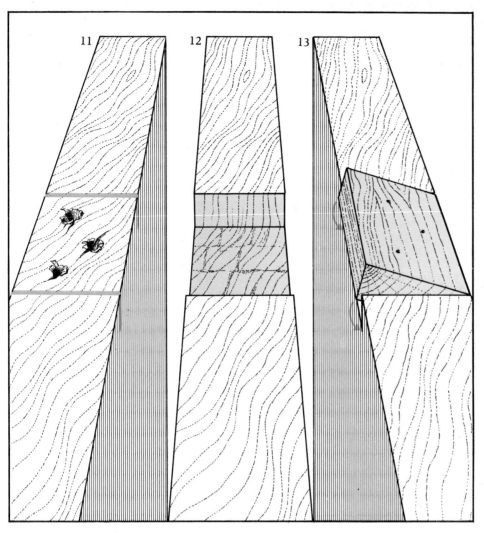

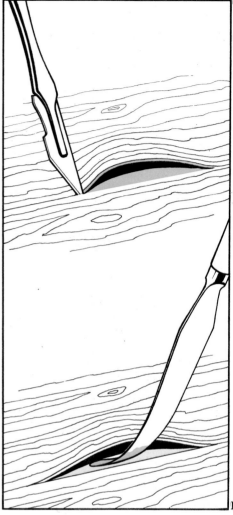

CRACKS

Heaters near wooden furniture cause the wood to dry out and shrink. A fine crack in the middle of a panel can be stopped with matching plastic wood, but if the crack is wide the panel will have to be replaced if you are not prepared to paint it. Stop furniture from shrinking by placing a humidifier or bowl of water near radiators and heaters.

HINGES

A lot of damage is caused to doors and door-frames by hinges with loose screws. When you come to tighten them you often find that you cannot get a fixing because the wood has been chewed up by numerous screws in the past. In this case, do not try to solve the problem by using longer and longer screws; you will only compound the problem. The damaged wood must be cut out and replaced by a 'patch'.

Patching You will need a sharp tenon saw, a chisel and a mallet. Mark the section to be cut out and saw the top and bottom at an exact right angle to the edge (11). Chisel out the wood from the back very carefully indeed until

each edge of the cavity is perfectly square and clean (12). Take a piece of wood of the same thickness as the damaged wood that has been removed, cut it to match the height of the cavity and tap it into place. If it projects a little, mark off the projecting part and cut off the surplus. Apply carpentry adhesive inside the cavity, tap the patch home (13) and for extra security hold it with a couple of fine panel pins. When the adhesive has set, fix the hinges.

BEADING AND MOULDING

These are very easily damaged and nowadays it is almost impossible to match anything but the commonest classical patterns. If the piece is a particular treasure you can have a length of moulding cut to match, otherwise the simplest solution is to replace the whole lot with a suitable substitute.

MENDING AND REPLACING VENEER

Veneer is vulnerable; it blisters if damp, lifts if subjected to heat and, as it is wafer-thin, splinters if knocked.

Blisters can be eliminated by cutting

through them with a sharp razor blade (14). Slip impact adhesive into the cavity on the tip of a pointed knife or a match stick (15). A palette knife is particularly good, being flexible. Press the veneer back in place. Cover the place with greaseproof paper and place a heavy weight on top until the adhesive has set. Tap with your finger: if it sounds hollow, the veneer is still raised.

Missing veneer must be replaced. You will probably have to strip away some more in order to buy some to match. Veneer is bought by the sheet. New veneer is usually slightly buckled and it should be flattened by soaking in warm water, then placed between two sheets of blockboard held down evenly by weights. Allow it to dry out naturally; if used damp, adhesive will not hold.

Holes To replace a chipped piece of veneer is a fiddly job. Cut back any complicated irregular edges of the veneer surrounding the bare area but avoid creating a geometric shape which, when patched, will show because the graining will not match exactly (16). Take a piece of tracing paper, place it over the bare patch and make a tracing

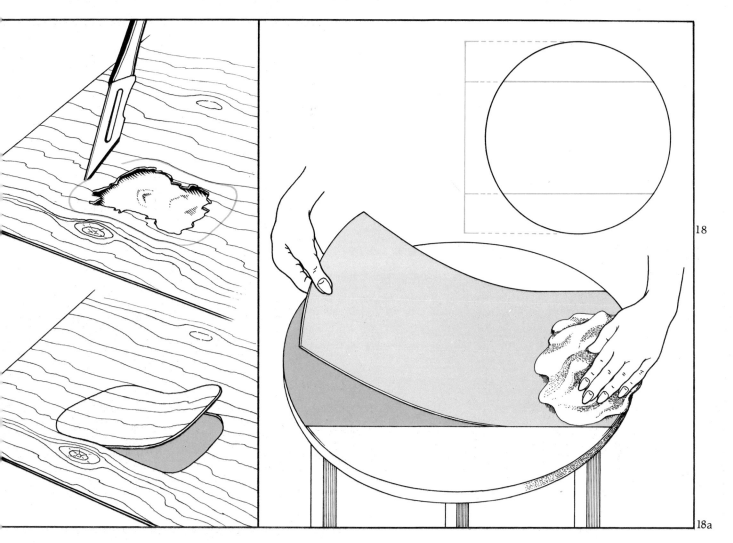

18

18a

of the edges of the veneer. Trace this very exactly onto part of the new veneer with similar graining (17). Cut out the shape very patiently with a fret-saw. Making sure to press out air bubbles, stick down the patch using a synthetic rubber and resin adhesive which dries quickly and is unaffected by heat or damp. Place a piece of greaseproof paper over the patch and weight it so that the whole of the patch is under pressure. When it has set hard smooth away any unevenness with finest glasspaper. Sanded areas will have to be repolished and may, before-hand, need to be touched up with stain.
Varying thicknesses The procedure is not always as simple as this because new veneer is thinner than some old veneers. If you are not aware of this to begin with, your patch will end up below the level of adjoining areas, with the result that it cannot be weighted whilst the adhesive is setting. If the piece of furniture is covered by thick veneer and you have not got any to match, try using two thicknesses of new veneer. If this does not solve the problem you will have to strip off the existing veneer and cover the whole

surface with the new veneer.
To lift old veneer, do not try to dig under it with a scraper. You will only damage the wood underneath which must provide a perfectly smooth, level base for the new finish. Clean off the varnish, polish or wax from the old veneer. Place a damp cloth over it and press with a warm iron to promote steam. The moisture should soak through the veneer and melt the old glue underneath. Persist until the veneer can be lifted without difficulty.
Replacing shaped sections While removing the veneer you will have noticed how it was arranged. Circular tabletops, for instance, often have a band of veneer which is applied first, running over the centre, with a narrower band at each side, much of which is cut away due to the curved edge. The Victorians and Edwardians liked veneer and large tables were some-times covered in shaped sections to form a pattern.
Having cleaned all the glue off the area to be covered, take a ruler and a very sharp pencil and mark off the sections on the surface (18). With the utmost accuracy, mark out one section on the

underside of a sheet of veneer making sure that the grain runs in the right direction. Cut it out. Cover the under-side thinly with adhesive and also the corresponding section on the surface. After about 10–15 minutes, or when the adhesive is ready, place one edge of the veneer on the corresponding line on the surface and roll down the rest of the veneer very slowly, pressing out the air bubbles (18a). Cover with hardboard and press down evenly. Remove any surplus adhesive before proceeding to the next section. If your calculations have been correct you should have no problems when you come to the last section to be laid.
Inlaid bands of veneer often come adrift and may be troublesome to re-place if they are the thick variety. As suggested before, try to resolve the problem by using a double thickness of new veneer. Paste two sheets of thin veneer together, cut to the appropriate shape, stick in place and press under a weight. When the adhesive is hard, sand down the patch, and finish as necessary with the appropriate stain. Polish to match up with the rest of the piece.

STRIPPING AND PREPARING

Traditionally, hardwoods were always polished. Softwoods – considered inferior – were stained to emulate them, or painted. Nowadays most younger people have cast aside these prejudices and can see, for instance, that the colour and grain of pine have a beautiful simplicity when the wood is stripped and well-finished. Indeed, the so-called luxury hardwoods, such as mahogany and rosewood, with their dark colourings and pronounced graining, are considered by some to be too grandiose to fit into today's more informal interiors.

Do not hesitate to fly in the face of convention unless a piece is valuable. The older generation are still horrified if you paint 'good wood' or strip the original finish off it and bleach the colour away. But what is the point of preserving a piece of stuffy furniture you detest when you could enjoy the sight of it with a different finish? Of course, you may prefer your furniture with a traditional finish; your only concern then is to restore it to its former glory. Old finish must still always be removed if any type of new one is to be completely successful.

Stripping any finish from wood is a messy business whatever method you adopt. If you can, reserve this activity for warm, dry weather and take your furniture outside. Before getting down to work remove all metal fittings and knobs.

METHODS OF STRIPPING FURNITURE

There are three ways to get rid of an unwanted finish: by using a blow lamp, by using chemical strippers including a caustic soda bath or by sanding.

Blow lamp A painted finish on a large plain surface can be burned off roughly with a blow lamp (1). Choose one powered by propane gas and keep it moving backwards and forwards over a small area at a time until the warmed paint lifts. Scrape it away keeping the lamp turned away from anything that may burn. It is impossible to avoid scorching the wood slightly, so this method is best used on furniture that is to be re-painted.

Chemical strippers These, called solvents, break down paint and other finishes really efficiently *but are mostly dangerous*. Do not entertain the foolish idea that a manufacturer would not produce a proprietary solvent that could harm you. Powerful strippers

1. A simple Victorian bedroom chair in a poor state of repair is a rewarding piece to strip and reseat.
2. Similar chairs, stripped of their varnish, become a charming, light feature in an attractive living room.

which will poison, burn and overcome you with their fumes are on sale all over the place. So, however impatient you are to begin, take time to read the instructions on cans and bottles and place the recommended antidote at hand in case of accidents. Keep children and animals well out of the way and clean up debris and tools when you are finished. Chemical strippers result in a lot of goo which sticks to everything if you do not clear up the mess as you go.

Caustic soda bath The quickest way to strip off oil paint or varnish is to dump the item in a galvanized tank filled with caustic soda solution. When the paint or varnish has dissolved to a cream, hoist the piece out, scrub it and hose it down with cold water. The disadvantage of this method is that the whole piece will be saturated and, unless it is removed from the tank in time, the wood will be roughened, the adhesives in the joints will give way, the wood will swell and then crack and,

when dry, will warp. Caustic soda and solvents like it are, therefore, reserved for furniture of robust construction, such as kitchen chairs, kitchen tables and kitchen cupboards.

In solution, caustic soda is a jelly-like mixture that damages foliage, flooring and clothes and will burn if it gets on your skin. Avoid breathing the fumes and never use it in an enclosed space. When handling it, gird yourself in wellington boots, a rubber apron and rubber gloves – these will perish if used regularly for the purpose – and have water near at hand to neutralize spills and splashes.

Caustic soda as stripper (2). Few people own a tank large enough to hold furniture and it is certainly not worth buying one unless you will use it regularly. Caustic soda is produced in crystal form and dissolved in water. It can be made up in a bucket and will cost you less than a proprietary stripper which is probably based on the same ingredient. The crystals spit if

water is poured onto them. To avoid this, fill the bucket with water first, and then add the caustic soda at the rate instructed on the tin. Take a mop or a paint brush, depending on the size of the piece of furniture, and coat your item with solution. Almost immediately the top coat of finish will start to blister (2a). Have two paint scrapers at hand: one with a wide flat blade and one with a curved blade. When the finish is thoroughly soft scrape it off, dumping the mess into a cardboard carton (2b).

In general, one coat of stripper removes one coat of finish and the process has to be repeated several times. Finish from corners, crevices and carvings can be difficult to remove. Be careful not to score the wood with your scraper; a stiff brush on a handle can help. When all the finish has been removed you must prevent the caustic soda from making grey stains on the wood by quickly scrubbing the piece with cold water until every trace of solvent is removed (2c). Dry off surplus moisture so that the water will not seep into the joints. Leave the article to dry overnight away from artificial heat. It will then need to be sanded as described below.

STRIPPING OFF FRENCH POLISH AND OTHER FINISHES

A French-polished finish should be cleaned off with a cloth dipped in methylated spirits. Paint it on with a brush and rub the finish off equally over the whole of the table top, chair leg, covered door, etc., before applying the methylated spirit again and repeating the operation. If you remove the polish from one part entirely before tackling the next, you risk scratching and staining the exposed wood whilst erasing the surrounding finish. When the polish has gone, rub the wood gently to a smooth, even surface using fine sandpaper.

Using the same method, wax polish is removed with turpentine, and cellulose lacquer is lifted with ammonia. If an unknown finish fails to respond to any

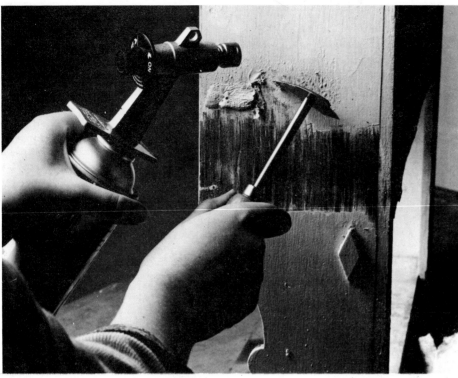

of the solvents mentioned, seek the advice of an experienced assistant in a decorator's shop that sells to the trade.

Sanding It is a common experience to find that, having got rid of paint and varnish, a dark brown stain remains which was applied when the item was made. You may want to leave this if you are painting or polishing the article. However, if you intend to exploit the beauty of the wood's natural colour, the stain must go. Stain sinks into the wood and cannot be removed by chemical means. It has to be sanded away.

Whether it is stained or not, you will find that the moisture involved in the stripping procedure already described will have raised the grain and roughened the wood. Rub the whole piece down with medium and then finest grade sandpaper, paying particular attention to all the places that are difficult to get at (remember that all transparent finishes magnify the quality of the surface underneath). If your hand is so light that you can be sure you will not make ridges, you may use a power drill fitted with a fine sanding disc in order to smooth the plain areas more quickly. Avoid using it on curved surfaces.

Any finish can, in fact, be sanded off. It is a good, if slow, method to adopt on furniture of fine construction with delicate joints or fine-grained wood which would be damaged by moisture of any kind. The biggest drawback is that sandpaper becomes clogged by varnish, seal or paint very quickly and must be replaced with a fresh piece.

Also, dry stripping with sandpaper produces a fine dust which gets in your hair, mouth, nose, eyes, throat and clothes. You should work in a mask that can be bought at a chemist's shop and, if you do not want to wash your hair when you have finished, cover it with a scarf. A vacuum cleaner close by saves a lot of clearing up when you have to work inside.

Sanding blocks (3) Abrasive paper wrapped round a block with a flat base will only grind down bumps or splinters projecting from a flat surface. The blocks that are produced with a convex base allow you more latitude when sanding curved surfaces. You will find that in awkward places, abrasive paper is most effective when wrapped round your fingers.

Sanding machines As has been mentioned, a mechanical sander can grind

ridges in wood. Because the head rotates at such a pace, an inexperienced person can cause a great deal of damage before it is realized. The circular rubber attachment for a power drill, produced to support sanding discs, is particularly dangerous in this respect because it is so flexible. Machines fitted with a firmly-fixed orbital pad, made for sanding alone, are the easiest to use effectively (4).

Whatever machine you use, always switch it on before touching the surface to be sanded and always remove it before switching off. Be careful when rubbing down an edge because the machine can 'take off'; and beware if you hear a flapping noise: this indicates that the abrasive paper has split and is likely to spin off. It could hurt you if it struck your face. If the body of your sander heats up, the ventilation holes may be blocked with sawdust. Taking care not to interfere with the mechanism, clear them with a fine knitting needle, having first unplugged your machine. It is a good idea to buy an extension lead for your sander so that it can be used out of doors.

3

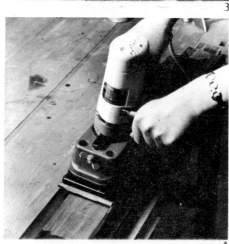

4

PREPARING A STRIPPED WOOD SURFACE

Now we hope your hard, careful work has been rewarded. Your piece of furniture should look exactly as it did in the craftsman's workshop before he applied the original finish. When you run your hand over the surface it should feel satisfyingly clean and smooth. Or does it? Are there now open pores on the surface or are there still a few dents, scratches or stains? Did the solvent darken the wood, or did the wood turn out to be a disappointing colour?

Filling dents and scores Odd marks can be bleached out as described on page 146. Open pores, dents, scores and holes that still remain must be levelled. Cut a pad of wet blotting paper to cover a small dent exactly. Leave it there for several hours until the spot is thoroughly damp. Remove the blotting paper and cover the dent with a metal screw-on bottle cap, hollow side up. Rest an iron on it lightly with the thermostat set low. Every now and then steal a look at the dent and continue the treatment until the wood has swollen level with the rest of the surface. A large dent should be pricked with a fine needle before wet blotting paper is applied and the bottle cap exchanged for a cap that fits the blemish.

Filling a score, hole or knot-hole is easy if you intend to apply a painted finish. Roughen the inside of the blemish to provide a key and then, using a flexible knife, stop the indentation with white cellulose woodwork filler applied in thin layers until it stands proud over the surface. When dry, rub down the mound with finest sandpaper until the patch is indistinguishable from its surroundings when you run your fingers over the surface. Filling a blemish in wood that is to receive a transparent finish is another story: the stopping may match the surrounding wood when bare, but when the wood has absorbed the finish, the patch that has been filled looks much paler.

Plastic wood is the easiest filler to use. It is produced in several colours but do not assume that the one called mahogany, for instance, matches mahogany. Try walnut for dark woods and natural for pale ones. If these are not satisfactory buy a selection of wood stains and mix your own shade. After dusting the surface of the furniture, select a small area and rub in a little finish until the wood will absorb no more. Put some plastic wood on a saucer, and tint with stain if necessary until it matches the finished wood. Fill the blemish as described before. If the plastic wood dries to a lighter colour, tint the top of the patch with a little more stain. Use a fine artist's sable brush taking care to keep the stain off the wood. Clean off the patch of finish before proceeding to the next stage.

Bleaching wood In recent years stripped pine furniture, either left bare or protected by an unobtrusive finish, has become so fashionable that it is bound to become more difficult to find and more expensive. Other woods can be bleached to give a similar effect or, if reduced to an even paler shade, make perfect subjects for staining or lacquering with the brightly-coloured translucent finishes now available.

Domestic bleach is not strong enough to make an appreciable change in the colour of wood. Very effective two-pack bleaching kits can be bought in specialist shops. The chemicals involved are powerful and should be

1. It is worth browsing round shops like this for old, neglected pieces of furniture to restore.
2. Junk shop finds, like this chest of drawers, can look most impressive once they have been stripped and polished.

used with great care, following the instructions because, unless neutralized at the correct time, they attack the wood until the fibres and glue in the joints are weakened. Reduce the colour stage by stage, allowing the wood to dry in between – when wet it gives no indication of the colour it will be

when dry.

If you cannot locate a proprietary furniture bleach you can make your own. Mix 56 g. (2 oz.) of oxalic acid crystals into $\frac{1}{2}$ l. (1 pint) of hot water (this mixture is poisonous and the acid contained will burn your skin). Apply the mixture with the aid of a paint brush, repeating the operation between drying-off periods until the required colour is reached. Pine that has become greyish should attain its normal colour with one or two applications; oak is more resistant and, providing it has not been artificially darkened, will take about twice as many. Mahogany will need perhaps half a dozen applications to become pale enough to look perfectly suitable in a country kitchen.

When the wood has dried to the required colour, neutralize the impregnation of acid with a weak solution of vinegar. When dry again, smooth the surface with fine sandpaper.

Liming This is a method of emphasizing the beauty of the pores and grain of oak which also imparts a paler appearance. To raise the graining, the wood is scratched with a wire brush. Lime, mixed to a cream, is then rubbed into the pores with a rag. When dry, the surplus on the surface of the wood is removed with a fine sandpaper. It is much easier to follow the same process using ordinary cellulose filler; the unwanted residue when dry can be wiped off with a damp cloth.

Fuming oak If you are determined to be different you may decide to darken your oak instead. If you are really enthusiastic you may even insist on fuming it which gives a very ancient-looking finish. Fuming is done in ammonia vapour – a gas which will make your eyes stream and is very unpleasant if inhaled. The operation should only be undertaken in the open air. Find an airtight wooden or metal container which will easily accommodate the piece. After placing some wooden chocks in the bottom to prop the piece clear of the fluid, put the item inside, pour in the ammonia (ask for 0·880) and close the lid.

Various types of oak react to a different degree but you cannot open up your fuming chamber to peep at your work because the fumes will escape. Abandon the chamber for half a day if you hope to achieve a rich brown shade. No neutralizing is necessary, but it is as well to leave the object in the open air for a while to get rid of the smell.

ADHESIVES

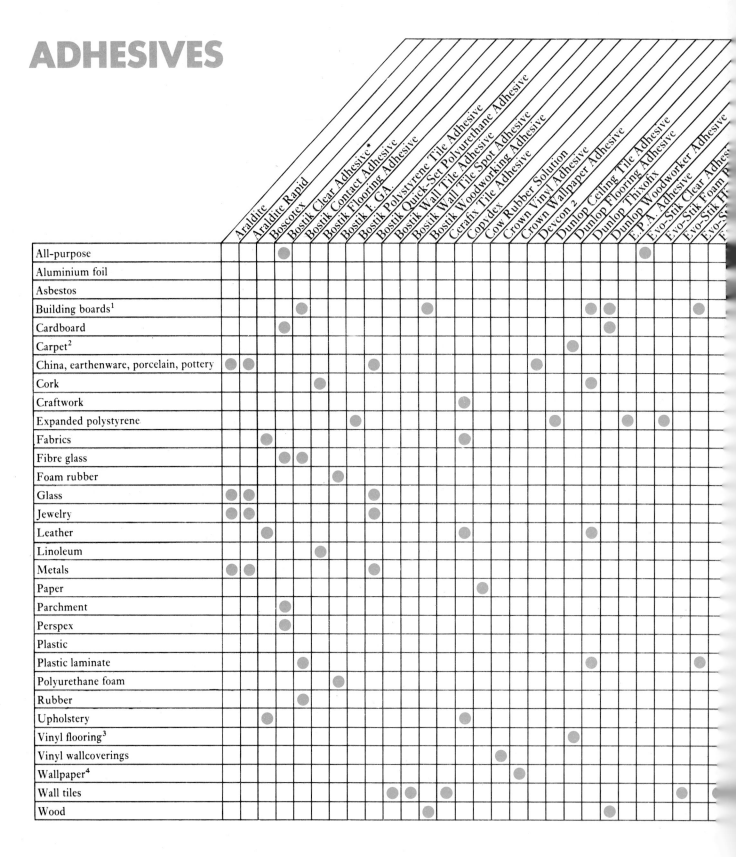

Column headers (left to right):
Araldite · Araldite Rapid · Boscotex · Bostik Clear Adhesive* · Bostik Contact Adhesive · Bostik Flooring Adhesive · Bostik F.GA. · Bostik Polystyrene Tile Adhesive · Bostik Quick-Set Polyurethane Adhesive · Bostik Wall Tile Adhesive · Bostik Wall Tile Spot Adhesive · Bostik Woodworking Adhesive · Cerafix Tile Adhesive · Copydex · Cow Rubber Solution · Crown Vinyl Adhesive · Crown Wallpaper Adhesive · Devcon 2 · Dunlop Ceiling Tile Adhesive · Dunlop Flooring Adhesive · Dunlop Thixofix · Dunlop Woodworker Adhesive · E.P.A. Adhesive · Evo-Stik Clear Adhesive · Evo-Stik Foam... · Evo-Stik H...

	Araldite	Araldite Rapid	Boscotex	Bostik Clear Adh.*	Bostik Contact Adh.	Bostik Flooring Adh.	Bostik F.GA.	Bostik Polystyrene Tile	Bostik Quick-Set Polyur.	Bostik Wall Tile Adh.	Bostik Wall Tile Spot	Bostik Woodworking	Cerafix Tile Adh.	Copydex	Cow Rubber Solution	Crown Vinyl Adh.	Crown Wallpaper Adh.	Devcon 2	Dunlop Ceiling Tile	Dunlop Flooring Adh.	Dunlop Thixofix	Dunlop Woodworker	E.P.A. Adhesive	Evo-Stik Clear	Evo-Stik Foam	Evo-Stik H.
All-purpose			●																				●			
Aluminium foil																										
Asbestos																										
Building boards[1]				●				●											●	●						●
Cardboard				●																●						
Carpet[2]																				●						
China, earthenware, porcelain, pottery	●	●							●									●								
Cork						●															●					
Craftwork														●												
Expanded polystyrene								●											●					●	●	
Fabrics			●											●												
Fibre glass				●	●																					
Foam rubber						●																				
Glass	●	●							●																	
Jewelry	●	●							●																	
Leather			●											●							●					
Linoleum						●																				
Metals	●	●							●																	
Paper															●											
Parchment				●																						
Perspex				●																						
Plastic																										
Plastic laminate					●																●					●
Polyurethane foam							●																			
Rubber					●																					
Upholstery			●											●												
Vinyl flooring[3]																				●						
Vinyl wallcoverings																●										
Wallpaper[4]																	●									
Wall tiles										●	●		●											●		
Wood												●									●					

* Bostik Clear Adhesive can be used with all plastics except polyester, polyamide, laminates, polystyrene

1. as, blockboard, chipboard, hardboard, plywood

2. hessian- or felt-backed to wood or cement sub-floor *or* foam-backed to wood or cement sub-floor

3. unbacked vinyl or vinyl asbestos tiles or sheet to hardboard, plywood, chipboard or cement sub-floor *or* felt- or foam-backed vinyl and vinyl asbestos

4. lightweight and medium weight; washable and heavyweight

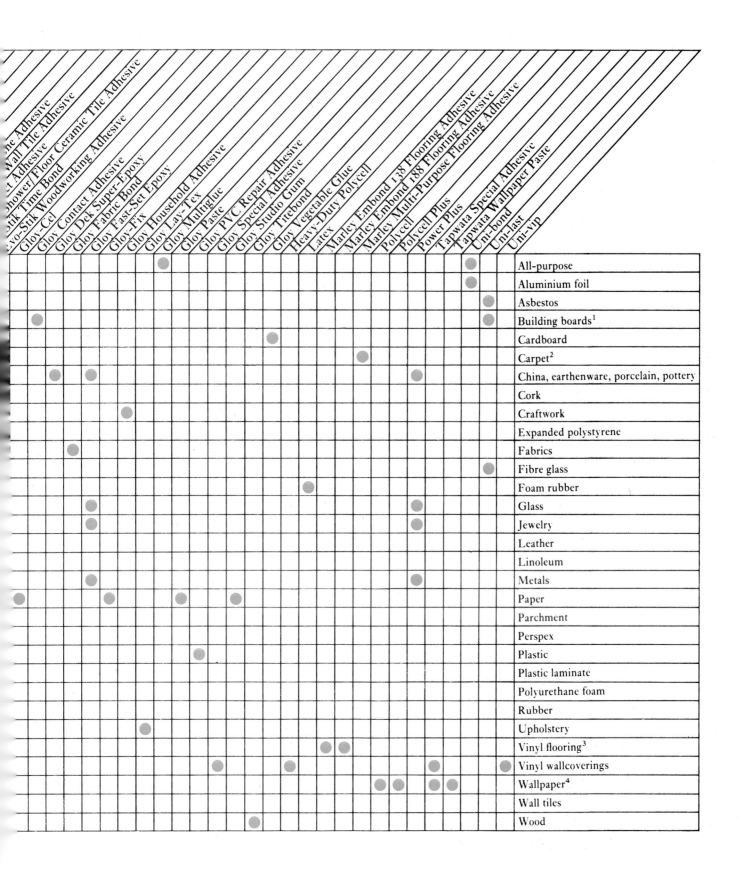

	ne Adhesive	Wall Tile Adhesive	t Adhesive	hower/Floor Ceramic Tile Adhesive	tik Time Bond	vo-Stik Woodworking Adhesive	Gloy-Cel	Gloy Contact Adhesive	Gloy Dek Super-Epoxy	Gloy Fabric Bond	Gloy Fast-Set Epoxy	Gloy-Fix	Gloy Household Adhesive	Gloy Lay-Tex	Gloy Multiglue	Gloy Paste	Gloy PVC Repair Adhesive	Gloy Special Adhesive	Gloy Studio Gum	Gloy Titebond	Gloy Vegetable Glue	Heavy-Duty Polycell	Latex	Marley Embond 138 Flooring Adhesive	Marley Embond 188 Flooring Adhesive	Marley Multi-Purpose Flooring Adhesive	Polycell	Polycell Plus	Power Plus	Tapwata Special Adhesive	Tapwata Wallpaper Paste	Uni-bond	Uni-last	Uni-vip
All-purpose															●																	●		
Aluminium foil																																●		
Asbestos																																	●	
Building boards[1]								●																									●	
Cardboard																					●													
Carpet[2]																										●								
China, earthenware, porcelain, pottery									●		●																		●					
Cork																																		
Craftwork													●																					
Expanded polystyrene																																		
Fabrics										●																								
Fibre glass																																	●	
Foam rubber																							●											
Glass											●																		●					
Jewelry											●																		●					
Leather																																		
Linoleum																																		
Metals											●																		●					
Paper							●					●				●			●															
Parchment																																		
Perspex																																		
Plastic																	●																	
Plastic laminate																																		
Polyurethane foam																																		
Rubber																																		
Upholstery														●																				
Vinyl flooring[3]																								●	●									
Vinyl wallcoverings																		●				●								●				●
Wallpaper[4]																											●	●		●	●			
Wall tiles																																		
Wood																				●														

PAINTS AND FINISHES

Some days you wake up with the urge to transform a room by nightfall. And what easier way to do it than to paint the furniture in bright colours? Manufacturers know all about this kind of reaction and, in consequence, they try to make their paints virtually foolproof. They know that in a mood like this you will not wait to read instructions and, although you might pause to wipe away obtrusive lumps of dirt, or even stop a few holes if you have got the filler handy, you will not hesitate to sling a coat of gloss paint straight onto a surface covered with greasy marks. So they make sure that their product will stick to anything.

And we are not going to damp your enthusiasm when you are in that mood either. The preparation that proceeds finish is so finicky, time-consuming and deadly dull that, unless we sometimes ignored it and slapped on the finish when we felt like it, there are some jobs that would never be done. Anyway, if this is the mood you are in do not read the previous chapter because it is all about preparation. And do not read this one either. Just get out your paint and brushes – hope you cleaned them after your last bout – and get on with it. Incidentally, the finish will last longer if you sand off old, peeling paint first!

In another mood you can be sickened by the results of this kind of painting. Perfectly good pieces of furniture which could have looked so glamorous with slick, mirror-smooth finishes, reveal all too clearly the blistered paint, dust, grit and hairs trapped beneath their streaky, slapdash coats of colour. You decide that you would rather surround yourself with a roomful of perfectly-finished furniture that you can be proud of, even if it takes you three times as long to finish. The fact is that with a perfectly-prepared surface you are already well on the way to success.

TOOLS AND MATERIALS

One of the most maddening proverbs in the English language proclaims that 'a bad workman blames his tools'. It should go 'a good workman never has bad tools!' Anyway you will never get

1. A magnificent example of eighteenth century French-polished furniture
2. Detail of veneering and inlay
3. Detail of veneering
4. Portable writing-desk of Chinese camphor-wood with an oil and wax finish
5. Detail to show how waxing brings out the grain of the wood
6. French-polished mahogany sideboard
7. Detail of French-polished surface showing how stain brings out the beauty of the wood

satisfactory results if you are hampered by brushes with coarse bristles, ones that moult, ones that are the wrong size, etc. Everything has to be just so. To achieve a perfect painted finish on, say, a chest of drawers, you will need fine sandpaper, a tack rag (obtainable from decorators' shops), a selection of brushes ranging from 7·5 cm. (3 in.) down to 2 cm. ($\frac{3}{4}$ in.) wide plus an artist's water-colour brush size 4.

The brushes should be thickly packed with fine quality bristles and, when pressed lightly on a flat surface, the edge of the bristles should be level with no separations. To keep brushes in new condition you should have a plentiful supply of white spirit – also needed for thinning oil paint and other materials – and a vessel to hold it, allowing space to clean the bristles immediately after use. You will need primer (and possibly knotting), undercoat, finishing paint, something clean to stir them all with and a clean tin to pour them into with a mouth at least 12·5 cm. (5 in.) wide. There is no quicker way to ruin a brush than to force it into a small tin.

New brushes always moult slightly. Soak them in lukewarm water when you get them, then swish them about

4

5

6

7

and strip the water out between finger and thumb. Always shape them after use and store wrapped in paper to keep them free from dust and grit.

PRIMING
When the finish of a piece of furniture has been stripped away leaving bare wood, this must be sealed with primer before painting. If you neglect to do so, the wood will soak up the bonding in the paint – the adhesive ingredient – leaving only a powdery sediment of pigment on the surface. This wastes expensive paint at the best and provides an unreliable base coat at the worst. To save time spent on applying both a primer and then an undercoat, manufacturers produce what is called a primer/undercoat or sealer/undercoat.
Knotting If you are dealing with new wood you should take one precaution before brushing it with wood primer. Knots, which show where a branch or twig grew out of the trunk of the tree, are likely to ooze resin as the wood dries out over the years. To prevent resin softening or discolouring the paint, you should cover the knots in hardwood with two coats of knotting. *Pine woods* which are, of course, softwood, are particularly resinous. Do not treat the knots separately but brush all the wood with aluminium primer. Do not make the mistake of using aluminium paint; it is not the same.
New whitewood furniture, which is mostly made of plywood, should be coated with acrylic emulsion primer/sealer undercoat after being rubbed down with fine sandpaper.
Teak If you have a piece of teak furniture, you are probably aware that when unfinished, the wood is naturally oily and you may have assumed that it would never hold a coat of paint. This is not true. Oily wood can be primed with teak sealer to accept any paint. When the primer is bone dry rub down your work with finest sandpaper.

PROTECTING YOUR SURFACE FROM DUST
'Dust is the enemy' said a much-respected master painter now, sadly, dead. 'The best gloss finish that I ever encountered was painted by a friend of mine in ideal, if extreme conditions. He took the work and his gear, which included his tacky duster, into an empty room, hung a wet blanket over the door and retired until the dust settled. Then he stripped to the buff,

re-entered the room stealthily and got down to work. He repeated the performance for five days until the job was finished, by which time he had caught pneumonia, enabling me to take over his lucrative business whilst he recovered in hospital.'
The fact is that currents of air in a room eddy with dust stirred up from fabric of most kinds and also with minute particles of grit carried in by draughts. Do not work in a room which needs cleaning. Do not work in one with ill-fitting windows and doors. Do not work surrounded by other people or move around yourself more than you can help. We are not suggesting that you work naked but we do advise you to avoid wearing knitted or hairy clothes. Clean your work down when it is dry after each process using a vacuum cleaner fitting with a soft brush, and then wipe the surface over meticulously with your tack rag. This is impregnated with a sticky substance which traps dust.
It is very difficult to achieve a perfect finish in artificial light, and impossible to do so when using a dark colour.

PAINTING UNDERCOAT AND TOPCOAT
Having prepared your wood, it is ready for an undercoat. The undercoat covers the colour of the surface underneath and, having a matt finish, provides an excellent key for the paint that follows. Use the colour recommended as a base by the manufacturer of the topcoat and apply it so that a super-smooth finish results. It is only possible to achieve this with paint of the correct consistency. Brush marks are inevitable if paint is too thick. Practically all paint must be thinned. On each facet of the work, brush across the grain of the wood and then brush out the paint to follow the grain. This must be done fast to avoid 'slithering' over dried edges. Take care to prevent paint dribbling over rims and round corners – drips of this kind often go unnoticed until it is too late to remove them without creating further damage. Leave the work to dry thoroughly, then sand it down with super-fine paper to provide a key for the next coat and clean up as before. If the original colour is not completely obliterated, a second application of undercoat will be necessary.
The topcoat is applied in exactly the same way. It is useful to have a dress-

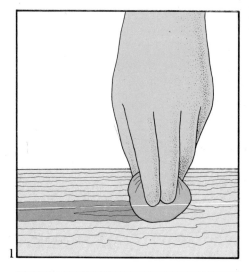

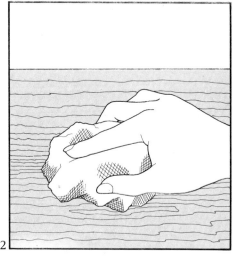

maker's pin at hand to remove foreign bodies from your work the moment they appear. Topcoats vary. Some give a completely opaque finish with one application. Others need two. Yellows and reds are notoriously transparent. If an additional coat must be applied you will have to wait a week or more until the previous one is bone dry before sanding it to provide a key for the final finish. Avoid placing anything on your completed work for at least a week.

TYPES OF PAINT
There are so many different types of paint nowadays that confusion is inevitable. Most paints which have to be thinned with white spirit are based on alkyd resin.
Alkyd paint for topcoats is produced with a high gloss and an egg-shell finish. Egg-shell finish has a slight sheen.
Some alkyd paints are described as non-drip or thixotropic. These have a jelly-like consistency, drop instead of drip and should be brushed out as little as possible because they liquify if overworked.

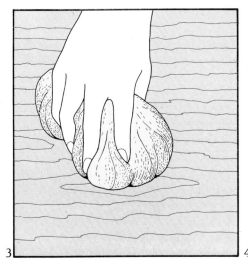
3

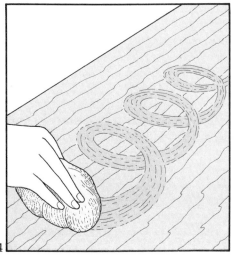
4

5

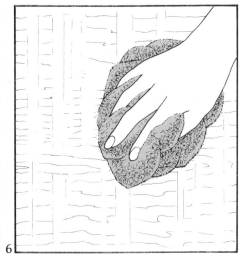
6

One-coat paints have their place. If you have some furniture with, say, a white finish which you want to remain immaculate, one-coat white paint applied without an undercoat, etc., at regular intervals will do the trick. It will not, however, cover a different colour very satisfactorily. If you do decide to follow a one-coat system for this you must use the same paint right from the beginning, and the first coat will probably need to follow an undercoat and primer as described in the traditional three-coat system.

Polyurethane paints are based differently. They dry more quickly, are more resistant to knocks and scratches and are, therefore, eminently suitable for furniture. They are, however, only as good as the base beneath so that adequate preparation is essential. Both gloss and egg-shell finishes are obtainable.

Cellulose paint has a high gloss and, because it dries so quickly, is better applied with a spray. Many aerosol paints fall into this category and are handy for using on small objects. Hold the can as instructed; if you spray too close the paint will 'puddle'.

In the main, you choose a painted finish to make a colourful effect, to bring old-fashioned furniture up to date or to cover a wood surface with nothing to recommend it.

WOOD STAINS

A translucent finish adds glow rather than brilliance to an interior, emphasises fine craftmanship and accentuates the rhythmic beauty of wood grain in perfect condition or accentuates its imperfections.

In the old days craftsmen stained wood if they considered the natural colour pallid, or they wanted to produce an imitation of a more expensive wood. Today, you sometimes realise that a piece of furniture would look much more attractive if the wood were darker or brighter. When deciding to stain an item, it is important to envisage the precise shade that you wish to achieve.

There are two types of stain recommended for amateurs, water-based and spirit-based. Stains made up with water are the oldest kind and are reckoned by craftsmen to be the best, despite the fact that they raise the grain of the wood. As they are not always stocked by local stores you might like to have a few formulas for making your own.

Making up your own wood stains

Bichromate of potash will darken mahogany or oak by chemical reaction. Using an earthenware basin add enough of these poisonous crystals to hot water to make a strong solution.

Sulphate of iron To induce a greyish cast to mahogany, oak or maple, dissolve sulphate of iron in boiling water to make a weak solution.

Vandyke crystals To give hard or softwoods a rich brown coloration use Vandyke crystals. Mix them with ammonia for mahogany; with bichromate of potash for oak; with Bismark brown for beech, birch or whitewood. All the stains, of course, are applied cold. They should be strained through muslin if they contain sediment and tested for their effect on a portion of the wood that is not normally seen.

Applying the stain The danger when staining is of overdoing it or of overlapping, which causes streakiness. Personally, we have had unfailing success by making up the stain in a fairly weak solution and, unlike professionals who apply it with a brush, rubbing it on with a lint-free cloth folded up to make a creaseless pad (1). The pad is moistened evenly in the stain – hands are protected by rubber gloves – and wiped on the wood following the direction of the grain. The colouring is light at first and no hard edges are left providing you cover the whole area swiftly and the pad is moist rather than saturated. The wood is left to dry before repeating the procedure until the right colour is attained. You will find that the parts of an item where the wood has been sawn across the grain absorb the stain quicker and need less of it to reach the right shade.

The same technique is equally successful with the spirit stains that are sold ready-made and also with the colourful wood stains that have recently appeared.

Sealing pores with grain filler The disadvantage of staining is that it opens up the pores of woods such as oak, walnut and mahogany. These pores must be sealed with special filler otherwise a great many coats of finish will have to be added, involving extra time and expense.

The materials used for grain filling are many and varied. Some fillings only

153

accept certain finishes and others must be stained to match the wood. Most require the surplus to be sanded off which, if the wood has been stained, can affect the colour. Paste grain fillers are the easiest to use. They can be used under any finish and are available in many shades. You just mix them to a creamy consistency with turpentine and apply them by brush. After about ten minutes you rub the mixture into the wood with a coarse rag and then wipe the surplus away (2). Leave for 24 hours to harden.

FINISHING WITH A FRENCH POLISH

Stained furniture was generally French-polished. French-polishing entails the use of varnish on a pad which readily sticks to the surface in inexperienced hands. Efforts to lubricate the pad with linseed oil – as a professional does – usually results in churning up the previous finish.

But professionals admit that the easy-to-handle substitute polishes now produced can, if conscientiously applied, equal a traditional French-polished finish. There are two kinds of home French polish that can be bought from well-stocked decorating shops.

The first type provides a finish which, like its forbear, is not particularly resistant to heat, water or spirit. The pack contains a bottle of glaze and a bottle of burnish. After preparing the wood it is polished all over, using a spiral movement, with a pad of lint-free cotton moistened with methylated spirits and packed with cotton wool moistened in the glaze (3 and 4). The work is then lightly sanded (5) following the grain and the whole process repeated three or four times. The finish will have spiralling smears. These are eradicated by rubbing firmly in the direction of the grain of the wood with a new pad of the same construction moistened in the burnish. When dry and polished with an ordinary yellow duster (6) the result is extremely brilliant. As an additional bonus, this polish can be used to fill scratches or to eradicate heat, water and spirit marks in traditional French-polished finishes.

In view of the fact that vulnerable finishes are such a worry, we tend to prefer the second type of polish. This is applied using much the same technique but, because it contains polyurethane, it is resistant to spills and other carelessness. The method itself has its advantages and disadvantages. The need for grain filling is obviated by the special polyurethane mixture which is painted on as a preliminary. The need for methylated spirit is also obviated but more coats of glaze must be applied. Sanding is minimal but 8 hours must elapse before applying the burnish, which obliterates the smears.

OIL AND WAX FINISHES

It may surprise you to learn that French polish is a relatively modern finish. Before the nineteenth century oil or wax, or a mixture of the two, were the only transparent finishes for furniture. Being free from the somewhat artificial glaze imparted by varnishes of any kind, an oil-and-wax finish gives the deepest and richest patina of all – especially treasured by the person who lovingly polishes it day after day to maintain the sheen which provides some protection against normal wear and tear.

Oiling First you feed the wood with oil to provide a degree of resistance against heat and water, but mainly to enrich the colour of the wood without raising the grain. Add 1 teaspoonful terebene to 290 ml. ($\frac{1}{2}$ pt.) raw linseed oil. Moisten, but do not saturate, a cloth in this mixture, and scrub it into the wood evenly. When it has absorbed a certain amount, to save energy, wrap the cloth around a heavy block and polish in the direction of the grain. The wood will continue to absorb oil indefinitely but stop feeding and polishing it once a day after several weeks. This process can be speeded up if you replace the glasspaper on an

1

orbital sanding machine with several thicknesses of oily rag.

Waxing When your wood looks sleek and well-fed, but is free of oil residue, spread a liberal coat of antique wax polish over the surface with a clean, stiff boot brush so that it penetrates into the grain and into all the corners and crevices without clogging them. Leave to harden for several hours. Polish with a clean brush – a floor-polishing machine makes an excellent job of a table top – and finish with a soft duster. Repeat the performance several times and at regular intervals thereafter.

A fair imitation of an oil-and-wax finish can be achieved by applying a thin covering of polyurethane home French polish and then rubbing it down with the finest glasspaper before polishing with wax. The patina will be shallower but the finish will be resistant to accidents.

The brightly-coloured stains mentioned earlier cannot, of course, be finished with French polish, oil and wax or even ordinary polyurethane lacquer. All these finishes leave a tinge of brown or yellow which would spoil the clarity of the colours. You have got to insist on a special colourless polyurethane lacquer which is not easy to find.

LACQUERS

More convenient altogether are the translucent, coloured, polyurethane lacquers which are produced in a number of natural and pop-art shades. These have all the resistant properties you would expect, dry quickly and, of course, save a lot of fiddling about with stain and grain filler.

1. Modern wood stains are much more colourful than their Victorian counterparts
2. Polyurethane lacquer stains are very quick and easy to apply, and produce a hard-wearing, resistant surface

UPHOLSTERY

As has been said before, you can innocently pick up a shabby upholstered chair or settee quite cheaply, only to find that the cost of re-covering it is twenty times more than you expected to pay. The prospect of doing it yourself is daunting. It is a slow job but, providing you understand the basic principles, carry out the work conscientiously and equip yourself with the correct materials, you should be able to congratulate yourself on the result and save a great deal of money into the bargain.

UPHOLSTERING A DINING-CHAIR
Start with a small and relatively simple job. Victorian and Edwardian dining-chairs are often inexpensive. The following instructions are for re-upholstering what is called an upholstered-over chair. These are very common. They have upholstered seats which are carried down the sides of the frame to a polished ridge round the lower edge. When the chair illustrated was found, the upholstery was in such bad condition that some of the springs were missing and the horsehair stuffing was so dirty that it was disposed of straight away. It was decided to replace the traditional springing materials with their modern equivalents. These are easier to manage and fewer processes are needed, which saves time.

Modern materials Traditional webbing, with its distinctive black and white herringbone weave, rots after a time and has largely been replaced by Pirelli webbing which is stronger and elasticized. Pirelli webbing has an additional advantage: it provides 'bounce' and consequently makes the use of traditional metal springs unnecessary. Springs take time to secure and the twine used to lash them is short-lived. Foam sheeting in various densities and thicknesses tends now to take the place of the various traditional waddings which are difficult to spread evenly. With a certain amount of experience foam is fairly easily managed and the layers of fabric to keep wadding in place are no longer necessary.

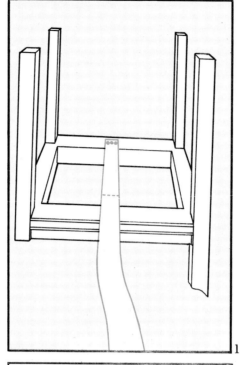

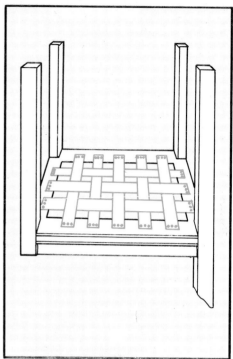

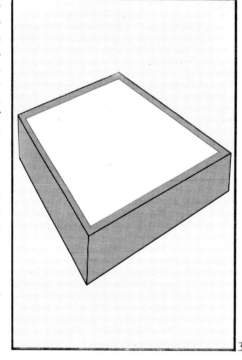

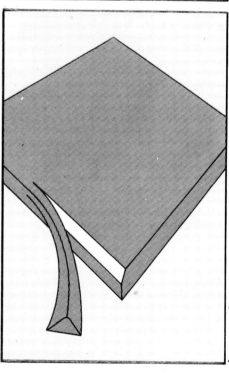

Tools and Materials: 4–5 cm. ($1\frac{1}{2}$–2 in.) Pirelli webbing; 5 cm. (2 in.) polyether foam sheet; 2·5 cm. (1 in.) solid foam sheet; 90 cm. (1 yd.) bleached calico; 90 cm. (1 yd.) cotton wadding; one pack each of 0·95 cm. ($\frac{3}{8}$ in.) and 1·5 cm. ($\frac{5}{8}$ in.) upholstery tacks; foam rubber adhesive for upholstery; 90 cm. (1 yd.) covering fabric; gimp to match; brass upholstery studs.

Buy enough Pirelli webbing to total five times the length of the seat plus three times its width. Buy enough foam sheet of each thickness to cover the top and sides of the seat and enough wadding to pad the sides of the seat all

round. A pack of tacks in each size will probably be enough. It is often impossible to find gimp of a suitable colour to trim the edge of your cover. We have had great success in dyeing strong, 1·25 cm. ($\frac{1}{2}$ in.) wide braid to match. It tends to shrink, so buy a couple of metres to be on the safe side.
Tools: a cabriole hammer which has a small head, enabling you to knock in tacks in a restricted space without damaging the finish of the chair frame (avoid a hammer which is too light to drive in anything heavier than a dressmaker's pin); a stripping chisel, which has a sharp, narrow blade to fit under the heads of tacks that are

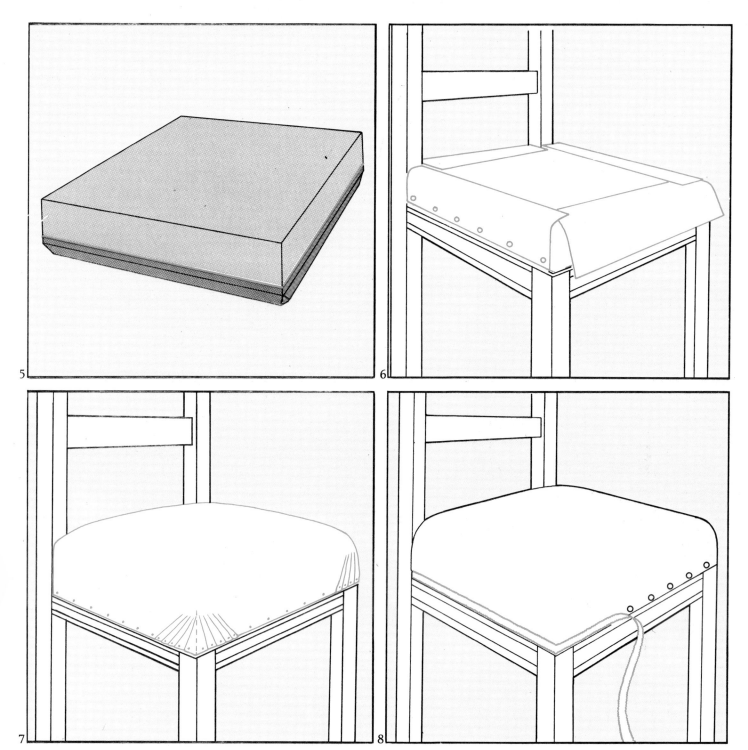

difficult to remove; a tack lifter which will lever up easy ones; pincers; a pair of dressmaker's scissors; a sharp carving knife with a plain blade; a felt pen to mark the foam without cutting into it; a ruler.

Stripping the frame If possible, remove the old upholstery out of doors clothed in an overall, with a scarf over your hair as a protection against dust. Then remove the tacks securing the upholstery to the frame by levering them up with the tack lifter. Place the chisel under the heads of tacks that refuse to be shifted so that, when tapped with a hammer, it is driven underneath, following the direction of

the wood grain. If you work across the grain it is very easy to knock out a section of the frame or to split it. The pincers will be particularly useful with tacks that have been bent.

Once the seat has been stripped you will probably find that numerous tackholes proclaim the fact that it has been upholstered many times before. Examine the frame and renovate or refinish it as necessary. Do not proceed to the next stage until the new finish is completely dry.

Webbing Take the Pirelli webbing and place across the centre of the seat widthways with the end 0.5 cm. ($\frac{1}{4}$ in.) from the outside edge of the

frame. Secure it by driving three 1.5 cm. ($\frac{5}{8}$ in.) tacks vertically into the wood (1). Mark the webbing where it reaches the opposite edge unstretched. Mark back 0.1 ($\frac{1}{10}$ in.) of its length. Stretch it so that the second mark occurs at the edge of the frame, tack it down, stretching as before, and cut off the surplus 0.5 cm. ($\frac{1}{4}$ in.) beyond the tacks. Tack down a strip of webbing from centre back to centre front in exactly the same way. The rest of the strips are woven in and out of the previous ones and stretched and tacked down as before (2). Allow no more than a 5 cm. (2 in.) gap between each strip.

157

Foam Using a light cardboard, cut a scale plan of the top of the seat ignoring the cut-out skirting the base of each back upright. Lay this template on the thick foam and, with the help of a ruler, mark a 0·5 cm. (¼ in.) wide border outside it and cut along the lines with a sharp knife (3). Do the same with the thin foam, but cut it 5 cm. (2 in.) smaller than the template on each side. With scissors, bevel the edge of the thin foam all round so that it resembles a shallow dome (4). Stick the flat side centrally onto the pad of thick foam and then, dome face down, stick the whole thing onto the webbing with spots of adhesive (5).

Calico border The foam pad must be secured to the chair. But, as it cannot be tacked without splitting or distorting, a border of calico is stuck round it. Tear four 9 cm. (3½ in.) wide strips of calico to fit the sides of the frame. Spread a 3 cm. (1¼ in.) wide strip of adhesive along one edge of each strip

and then another, 2.5 cm. (1 in.) wide, round the top edge of the foam seat. When the adhesive is tacky stick the calico strips to the foam (sticky sides together) as evenly as possible, snipping away a small amount to accommodate the back supports. Tack the calico to the sides of the frame with the smaller tacks so that the seat is held firm without pulling the foam out of shape (6). Trim away any surplus calico. Smear the sides of the frame lightly with adhesive and press four strips of wadding round them, leaving the back supports exposed.

Undercover and cover Cut an undercover in calico, 15 cm. (6 in.) bigger than the template on all sides. Place it centrally over the seat and, using small tacks, secure it to the sides of the frame at back and front and at each side so that it holds the foam firmly without distorting it. Make a fairly shallow diagonal slash at each corner at the back, pull the calico tightly into

Where the upholstery fabric has a distinct stripe, the front corners can be trimmed and folded as shown on this chair.

the corner between the foam and each back support and tack down. Pleat the undercover neatly round each front corner and tack (7). Cut the cover and fit in the same way, pulling it tight.

Gimp makes a tidy finish which covers the tacked edge of the cover where it meets the polished ridge round the sides. Tack one end to the back hard up to one of the back supports. Take it round the front of the support, tucking it down so that it is trapped behind the upholstery and invisible. Tack it down to the side of the seat below, stretch right round the frame to the other side and tack (8). Take up in front of the back support again, down to the back and tack. Stretch to the other corner, turn in, cut and tack in place over the raw end. Decorate with brass studs.

UPHOLSTERING A DROP-IN SEAT

Many dining chairs have drop-in seats. These are easy to upholster, which is encouraging if you have six to do. Usually this type of seat has developed an uncomfortable hollow in the middle with a hard ridge of stuffing round the outside. Generally, such seats are not domed but are given a firm flat finish. They are best cut from 2·5 cm. (1 in.) thick solid foam. It is most important that the outside dimensions of the frame are not made any bigger than they were with the original upholstery. If foam creeps over the edge or a heavier fabric is used for the cover, the seat may very well refuse to fit into the chair frame.

Fabric needed Most seat frames measure approximately 46 cm. (18 in.) from back to front. Generally 1·4 m. (1½ yds.) of 122 cm. (48 in.) wide fabric is quite sufficient to cover four seats, but more may be needed if the pattern is large so that the same motif needs to appear on each seat.

Webbing Strip away the old cover and upholstery. If necessary smooth the frame with sandpaper. Using 1·5 cm. (⅝ in.) tacks, fix three strips of 4 cm. (1½ in.) wide Pirelli webbing from the back to the front of the frame, stretching them as described before. Weave two crosswise. Turn the frame over and place it on a sheet of 2·5 cm (1 in.) solid foam. Trace round it. Draw another line 1 cm. (½ in.) outside the first and cut round this. Bevel the foam to half its depth. Mark a 4 cm. (1½ in.) border all round the unbevelled edge and spread thinly with adhesive. Tear four 7·5 cm. (3 in.) wide strips of calico to fit the sides of the frame. Mark a border 3 cm. (1¼ in.) from one torn edge on each strip and spread with adhesive. When tacky, stick the strips round the foam so that the edges that are free from adhesive can be wrapped round the frame to the back when the foam is in place.

Fitting the seat Mark the centre of each side of the frame on the underside and mark the centre of each side of the foam pad on the calico. Place the foam on a table, calico side down, set the seat frame on top of it, matching the marks. Wrap one strip of calico onto the underside of the frame and tack. Tack the opposite side evenly without compressing the foam unduly. Tack the other two sides in the same way (1). The surplus calico at the corners must be neatly mitred without creating extra bulk. Slash the two thicknesses at each corner. Wrap them onto the other side of the frame, trim away surplus and tack neatly in place.

Cover Cut the cover 7·5 cm. (3 in.) larger than the template all round. Tack it to the underside of the frame to hold the foam firmly. Pleat the corners neatly, trim as necessary and tack down.

A drop-in seat is the easiest form of upholstery for a beginner.

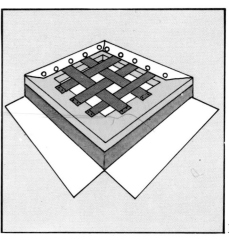

1

UPHOLSTERING THE SEAT OF A BENTWOOD CHAIR

It is common to find a bentwood chair with a broken plywood seat. These circular seats, which were punched with an attractive pattern, were simply tacked onto a rebate running round the inside of the frame. They were relatively short-lived but it did not matter because replacements in many sizes were then stocked by any iron-monger. Today they are no longer obtainable, but an upholstered seat can be made instead which, in suitable fabric, looks just as pretty, if not prettier, and is a lot more comfortable.

Making a template Remove the old seat but do not try to use it as a template because it will probably be mis-shapen. Instead, make a template of the area it occupied. Place this on a small sheet of 0·95 cm. ($\frac{3}{8}$ in.) plywood, pencil round it and saw round the inside of the mark. Pierce a few holes for ventilation. Sand down rough edges and fix to the rebate with panel pins (1).

Foam Cut out a circle of 4 cm. ($1\frac{1}{2}$ in.) thick solid foam which is 0·5 cm. ($\frac{1}{4}$ in.) smaller than the template all round. Bevel one edge and stick the domed side onto the wooden seat so that there is a small channel running round the peri-meter onto which the covers can be tacked (2).

Undercover and cover Cut the under-cover from unbleached calico making it 4 cm. ($1\frac{1}{2}$ in.) bigger than the tem-plate all round. Fit it over the foam and, pleating the edge neatly and evenly, tack it round the edge of the seat; trim away any surplus (3). Cut and fit the cover in the same way. Tack suitable gimp round the edge and, placing them closely, finish with brass studs.

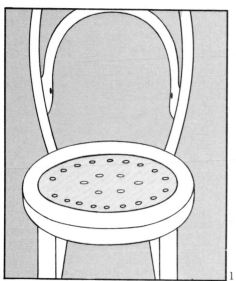

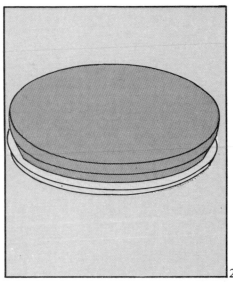

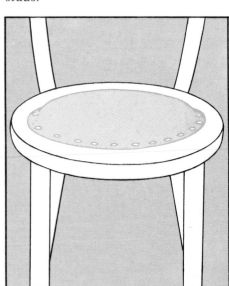

UPHOLSTERING A BUTTON-BACKED CHESTERFIELD

Many people like a buttoned chester-field. If you are fortunate enough to find a cheap one it will almost certainly need re-upholstering. Usually the springs have come unleashed, the old-fashioned webbing has broken, the padding is escaping and the canvas that separates each layer of upholstery has rotted. If you aim to re-cover it your-self, do not buy a chesterfield with upholstery which is in worse condition than this or a frame from which all the upholstery has been stripped right away. Your chesterfield will have to be completely re-upholstered, but as this is quite an ambitious undertaking, and not all chesterfields are precisely alike, it will help you to have an inti-mate knowledge of the previous up-holstery and the techniques employed throughout. For this reason our instruc-tions cover the classic upholstery methods, using traditional materials as far as possible.

Stripping the frame Remove the old upholstery very carefully, layer by layer, noting the construction minu-tely as you go. Label the coverings and preserve them as patterns, and as a guide to the amount of new fabric that you will need. Note which part of the frame each covering is fixed to. Note how the stuffing is arranged, how much and where; keep the horse-hair and wash it. It can be washed in a machine if tied up securely in an old pillow-slip. Note how the springs are secured, where they are placed and keep them. Mark the frame where the strips of webbing were tacked. Note anything else you are likely to forget; make diagrams if you can.

Tools and materials In addition to the tools required previously you will need a webbing stretcher; a regulator (to adjust the stuffing during stitching); a large curved needle to sew down the springs; a smaller 7·5 cm. (3 in.) needle for finishing joins in the fabric; a strong 25 cm. (10 in.) mattress needle for the main stitching; a finer 25 cm. (10 in.) needle to secure the buttons. You will also need enough webbing (not Pirelli) to cover the underside of the frame (measure the original webbing to calculate this); springs if any are missing; 360 g. (12 oz.) canvas; 225 g. (7½ oz.) canvas; extra horsehair if necessary; upholstery wadding; tacks; 3-ply sisal cord for lashing the springs; flax twine for stitching and buttoning;

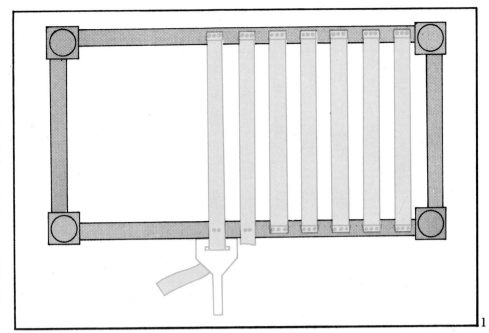

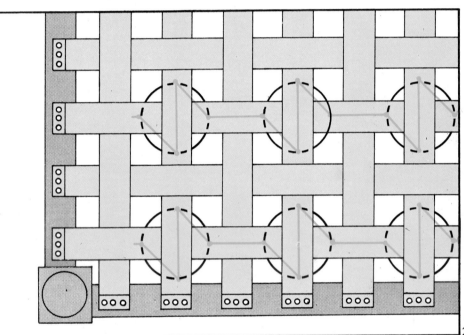

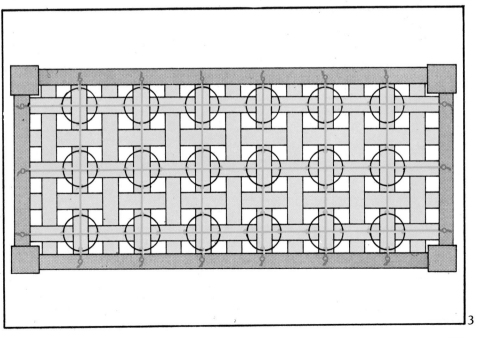

fabric for the cover; calico; button moulds securely covered to match; piping cord.

Webbing Remove any tacks remaining in the frame and the arm rail and turn the chesterfield upside down. The webbing running from the back to the front of the seat is attached first. Leaving a couple of inches free, tack down the end of the webbing with two 1·5 cm. ($\frac{5}{8}$ in.) tacks, 1 cm. ($\frac{1}{2}$ in.) from the outside edge of the frame. Turn back the loose end and using three tacks, tack it down 1 cm. ($\frac{1}{2}$ in.) from the inside edge (1). Use the stretcher to pull the webbing as taut as possible before tacking down the other end. Complete the parallel webbing. In the same way, fix webbing from side to side of the frame but interlace it in a basket-weave pattern for added security.

Tying the springs Set the chesterfield back on its feet. Arrange the springs – broad base down – in rows on the webbing. Situate each on a spot where the webbing intersects, spacing them evenly. Using the long curved needle threaded with sisal cord, stitch each spring down to the webbing by the bottom wire, knotting it securely in four places (2).

The springs must be secured upright so that the upholstery above is not pushed out of shape. Cut a length of sisal cord twice the width of the seat. Secure it temporarily to the frame with a large tack opposite a row of springs. Tie it over the row of springs, knotting each in two places. Drive in another tack at the other end, pull the cord until the springs are upright, twist the cord round the tacks and drive down so that the head secures the cord. Fasten off the ends of the cord to the springs. Continue to tie the springs in rows and then do the same in the opposite direction until each spring is secured north, south, east and west (3).

Canvas cover Cut out the heavier canvas leaving 2·5 cm. (1 in.) margin all round and lay it over the springs. Tack it all round the frame folding over the margin, without compressing the springs. Stitch the canvas to the top of the springs with the curved needle stitching each spring in three places (4). Tip the frame on its front. Web the back behind the uprights and then the sides. Turn the frame on its back and fix the springs vertically to the webbing and then lash them as before. Tack a covering of canvas over the back and

sides, tacking it to the frame in such a way that the stuffing that follows will not escape through any gaps.

Bridles Using the curved needle threaded with twine, knot securely to the edge of the canvas, then take large stitches 7·5–10 cm. (3–4 in.) in rows all over the seat, back and sides, including the arm rail. These stitches should be loose: they will help to anchor the horsehair stuffing (5).

Horsehair Pick over the horsehair to get ride of any lumps and spread it evenly over the seat, pushing it under the bridles as much as possible. You need a good, deep layer of horsehair – 5–7 cm. (2–3 in.). Tease it between your fingers to spread it evenly. Make sure there is enough round the edges of the seat.

Wadding Now cover with a layer of cotton wadding, smoothing it over the horsehair.

Undercover Cut out the undercover for the seat in the lighter canvas, allowing 2·5 cm. (1 in.) margin all round. Turn up the raw edges and drive in a few tacks temporarily to centre it on the seat. Now tack it down firmly to the seat, pulling it as taut as you can. Pull it down particularly firmly at the corners. Turn the corner by pulling and tacking the canvas as far round the corner as you can, then bring the top of the corner down and secure with a tack. Check that the stuffing is as even as you can make it before finally tacking down.

Back and sides Mould horsehair over the arm rail running round the top of the frame, tucking it under the bridles, then cover with wadding. Turn the frame on its back and spread horsehair round the back and sides tucking under the bridles as before. Cover with wadding. Cut out the canvas pieces for the back and sides allowing plenty to cover the arm rail. Pin in place, adjusting the shaped seams at the corners if necessary. Remove the pieces and sew the seams by machine. Pin the undercover in place to secure the wadding. Set the chesterfield on its legs and tack the undercover to the bottom of the back of the arm rail, pleating as necessary. Pull the undercover down behind the seat all round and tack. Pleat the front evenly round the faces of the arm rail and tack (6). Cut canvas pieces to cover the webbing on the outside back and sides. Tack them in place after sewing the seams by machine as before.

A chesterfield needs slow, patient work. Your reward, if you follow the instructions carefully, will be a lovely piece like this. This one has been finished off with brass studs rather than piping.

4. Stitching the canvas cover to the tops of the springs in three places.
5. Bridle stitches to hold the horsehair in place.
6. Pleating the undercover round the arm face.

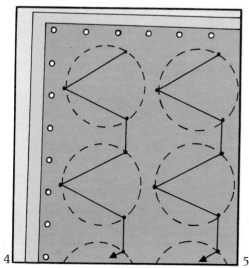

4

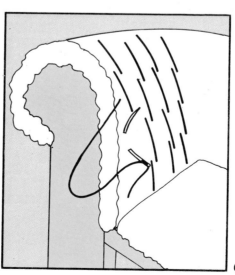

5

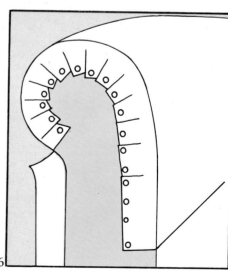

6

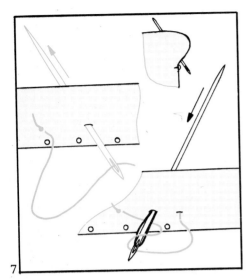

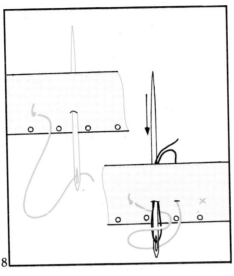

Blind stitching The seat should now be stitched through to make a stuffed 'roll' along the front edge. This stitching is a slow and laborious job, but it must be done. Your seat will need at least three rows of stitching to give it a really firm edge. Wear an old leather glove to help you pull the twine firmly enough after each stitch.

First row Thread the mattress needle with the twine, put a slip-knot at the end, and take a stitch about 2·5 cm. (1 in.) from the left-hand corner. Now push the needle into the canvas at an angle of 45 degrees, inserting the needle as near the tacks as possible. Pull the needle through till you can see the eye, then push it back through the canvas so that the point appears 2·5 cm. (1 in.) to the left of the point of entry. When the eye of the needle appears, wrap the loop of twine round it once, pull the needle through and tighten the twine (7). Insert the needle again 5 cm. (2 in.) to the right and continue along the seat.

Second row Before beginning the second row, use the regulator to pull the stuffing up towards the edge: push the sharp edge into the canvas and rake the hair towards the edge to make it firm. Start the second row 1 cm. ($\frac{1}{2}$ in.) above the first. Slope the needle as before, but this time bring the needle right through. Push back eye-end first about 2 cm. ($\frac{3}{4}$ in.) from where it came out. Twist the twine round the needle and pull through, pulling hard on the twine (8). Insert the needle again 5 cm. (2 in.) to the right and repeat.

Third row Repeat the second row, first raking up the stuffing with the regulator to give a firm edge. Keep the stitching as even as possible, to give the seat a straight edge.

Second stuffing Put on another thin layer of horsehair, filling up the 'ditch' formed by the stitching, and cover with another layer of wadding.

Calico cover Cut out the calico cover as for the undercover. Tack it down in the same way, centering it on the seat and pulling it as taut as possible. Pull down firmly at the corners and pleat. The surface should now be smooth, taut and springy, with no bumps, wrinkles or hollows. Correct any faults before the top cover is put on.

Buttoning Cut out the seat cover and mark the points where the buttons came – if there were any – with a cross in white chalk. Fit it over the seat and pin to the undercover distributing the fullness evenly. Place the chesterfield gently on its back. Using the fine 25 cm. (10 in.) needle plus flax twine, stitch through the seat from underneath, pick up a button and stitch back. The slip knot allows the button to be pulled really taut before both ends of thread are tied in a reef knot. A disc with two slits, made of either fabric or leather, prevents the thread from pulling through the stuffing (9). Knot the ends of the twine underneath so that the button is tightly indented in the padding. Tie off all your buttons, then pleat and pin the surplus fabric from each buttoning into the front, back and sides. Pull the pleated cover through the back and sides of the seat. Tack to back and sides of the seat frame.

Front frame Instead of tacking the pleated cover to the front of the frame, cut a 30 cm. (12 in.) deep panel of fabric slightly wider than the width of the front of the frame. This is attached to the seat cover by means of a piped seam. Cut bias strips of fabric, about 5 cm (2 in.) wide and seam together to make a long strip. Baste the edges together to enclose piping

cord and machine to one long side of the panel. Stitch this side of the panel to the front of the cover just below the seat 'roll' through the piping – stitch by hand, using the small curved needle. Trim away surplus fabric. Tack the bottom of the panel to the underside of the frame and to the side of the face of each armrail. Tie in a single row of buttons along the panel without pleating.

Cut the cover for the back and sides, mark as before and seam together. Tie in your buttons and tack to the armrail pleating as before. Pull the bottom of the cover tightly behind the seat at back and sides, pleat and tack to the frame. Pleat round the faces of each armrail and tack.

Facings Cut out a pair of armrail facings. Cut 5 cm. (2 in.) wide bias strips out of cover fabric, baste the edges together to enclose piping cord. Sew the piping all the way round the facings except at the bottom. Hold a piece in place against each face of the armrail with a few dabs of suitable adhesive. Pin them over the tacking of the fabric round the faces of the armrail. Join the facings to the cover by sewing through the piped seam with the small curved needle. Tack the bottom of the facings to the underside of the frame.

There is, of course, nothing nicer than a leather chesterfield, but to cover in leather is beyond the ability of an amateur. Do not hesitate however, to carry out the work in vinyl of a suitable type and weight. In some ways it is easier to handle than fabric. You would be unwise to try to sew up the seams with the average domestic sewing machine; they are better done by hand. Whatever fabric you choose it should obviously be hard-wearing.

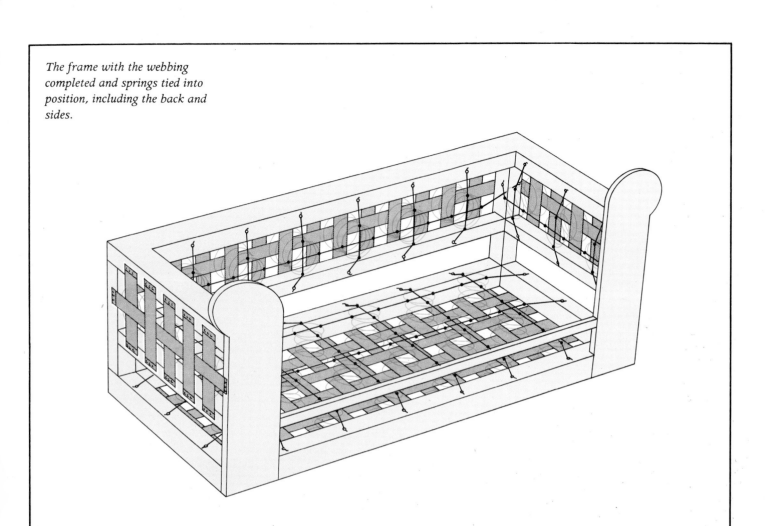

The frame with the webbing completed and springs tied into position, including the back and sides.

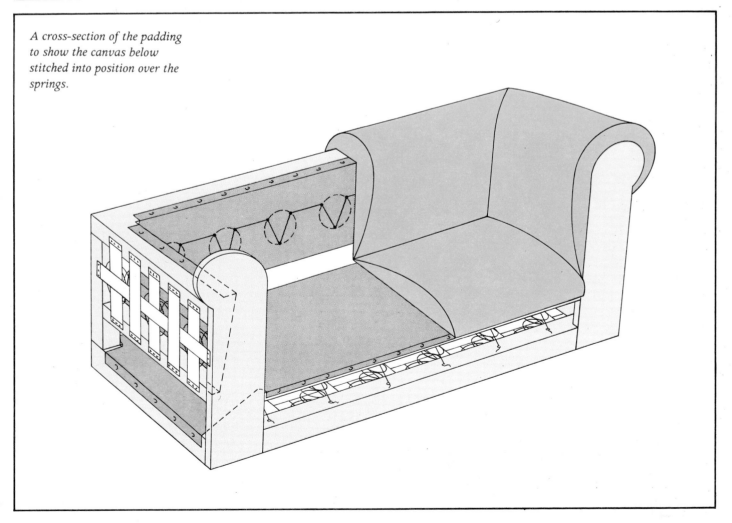

A cross-section of the padding to show the canvas below stitched into position over the springs.

MAKING LOOSE COVERS

Frequently you can pick up a comfortable armchair cheaply. The upholstery is perfectly sound but the fitted cover is worn and often hidden under an unattractive stretch cover. If you want to cover the chair with fabric in a pale colour you would be wiser to make a loose cover which can be washed by machine. Fitted covers can, of course, be cleaned with upholstery cleaner but the result, where light colours are concerned, is not always entirely satisfactory.

A loose cover is easy to make if you are an adequate home dressmaker and have a sewing machine with a piping foot attachment which can cope with several layers of heavy material simultaneously.

CHOOSING A SUITABLE FABRIC

Do not waste time making a loose cover which will not take rough treatment in its stride. Fabric with an open weave stretches, hangs limply and after a time the threads pull away from the seams. In addition, the fibres will rub against each other wearing out in the process. Similarly, fabrics with a marked slub roughen in wear and attract dirt. Select a heavy, colour-fast, machine-washable fabric with a pattern: plain material shows dirt and stains too easily. Heavy linen is one of the best choices as far as wear is concerned. It hangs crisply, retains its shape, wears indefinitely and its smooth surface repels dirt. However, it does tend to move about on a slippery chair and it will crush and shrink unless it is guaranteed to resist both.

Shrinkage is an important consideration. A tailored cover that fits perfectly when new can prove much too small when washed. Indeed, many linens and cottons that are said to be shrink-resistant turn out to shrink by 5% or so, if you read the manufacturer's guarantee. It is a nuisance to have to send fabric to the laundry, and it is very awkward to wash and dry yards of heavy material in the piece at home, but to avoid disappointment later you are strongly advised to do one or the other before making your cover up.

CALCULATING AMOUNT OF MATERIAL NEEDED

A loose cover takes more material than you might expect. The standard width of upholstery fabric is 122 cm. (48 in.). As a rough estimate you will need a length measuring five times the height of your chair. But before buying fabric you should calculate the amount needed accurately. The following instructions are for a loose cover to fit a common type of armchair. They provide the basic know-how so that, if your chair is different, you should be able to make the necessary adjustments in the shape or number of pieces without difficulty.

Measuring depth Referring to diagram 1 take the following measurements. (1) Outside back from A to floor + 5 cm. (2 in.) for seams. (2) Inside back from A to B + 20 cm. (8 in.) for tuck-in and seams. (3) Inside arm from G to J + 20 cm. (8 in.) for tuck-in and seams. (4) Outside arm from G to H + 5 cm. (2 in.) for seams. (5) Seat from B to C + 20 cm. (8 in.) for tuck-in and seams. (6) Front from C to D + 5 cm. (2 in.) for seams. (7) Front facing from U to V + 5 cm. (2 in.) for seams. Add up these measurements and convert into metres. Remember to count inside arm, outside arm and front facing twice.

Measuring width Now take your width measurements. (1) Outside back K to L + 5 cm. (2 in.) for seams. (2) Inside back K to L + 5 cm. (2 in.) for seams. (2) Inside back K to L + 5 cm. (2 in.) for seams. (3) Inside arm O to P + 13 cm. (5 in.) for tuck-in and seams. (4) Outside arm Q to R + 5 cm. (2 in.) for seams. (5) Seat E to F + 25 cm. (10 in.) for tuck-in and seams. (6) Front M to N + 5 cm. (2 in.) for seams. (7) Front facing W to X + 5 cm. (2 in.) for seams.

As a rule, after the pieces have been

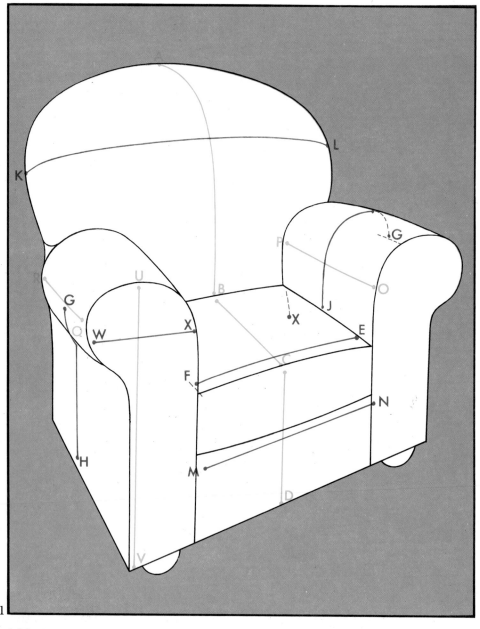

1

cut to fit large chairs, there are only narrow strips left down the selvedges. These are sometimes sufficient for the piping. Occasionally, there is enough to make a pleated frill in which seams can be hidden under the pleats. Pieces for small chairs can occasionally be cut from half the width of the fabric, which is a great economy.

To avoid confusion, make two diagrams, marking your width measurements on one and the length measurement on the other.

A frill to finish You must now decide whether you want a frill. Frankly, a loose cover without one looks somewhat unfinished. If you feel that a pleated frill all round will look too fancy, consider a plain one with a deep pleat at each corner. This gives a slick, strictly tailored finish. The average depth of a frill is 20 cm. (8 in.) with an allowance of 8 cm. (3 in.) for the hem and seam. For an all-round frill, you will need 1·5 times the circumference of the base of the chair. For a box-pleated frill you will need 2·5 times the circumference of the chair. The selvedge must run towards the floor. Add this length to the previous amount, plus at least one metre for piping, plus at least one more if there is a pattern.

CUTTING OUT

Making a pattern Before cutting your fabric you must make a life-size pattern of each piece and for this you will need six sheets of brown paper. Chairs are not always symmetrical, owing to uneven stuffing in the upholstery, therefore do not duplicate parts automatically. Check your previous measurements and take more to include the shaping. 2·5 cm. (1 in.) is allowed for all seams.

Cutting Pin your pattern on the fabric.

All the lengthwise measurements correspond to the lengthwise grain of your fabric. Make sure to centralize the design of the material and arrange it to the best advantage. A giant posy of flowers, for instance, will spoil the appearance of your finished cover if it is placed to one side of the inside back, seat or front. The main design motif should appear on the centre back and centre seat. Make sure that the pattern matches on the two inside arms, outside arms and arm facings. Be generous when cutting. It is easy to trim cloth away but generally impossible to join it on without making an unsightly seam where there should not be one.

As you cut each piece, mark the centre of it with a tack line down the lengthwise grain of the material. This will prevent fitting the pieces askew on the chair at the next stage. Label each piece for identification purposes.

FITTING THE PIECES

The pieces must now be fitted on the chair. Find the centre lines down the inside back of the chair, the outside back, the seat, the front and the inside and outside arms. Mark with chalk.

Inside back With the right side outwards, place the inside back piece on the back of the chair, matching the centre lines so that there is a 2·5 cm. (1 in.) seam allowance at the top of the highest point of the back. Smooth the piece downwards and widthways. From the centre line at B to a point T, as seen on diagram 2, chalk a curved line. Point T can be fixed on your chair by pushing your hand down the tuck-in at the junction of the arm, seat and back. Feel, from the construction of the chair, what tuck-in allowance must be made at that spot. Cut off this piece.

Arm junction In the same way the

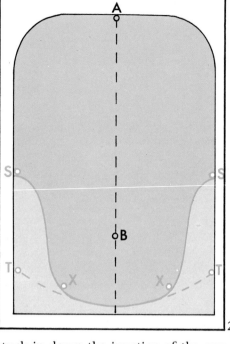

tuck-in down the junction of the arm and back must be shaped from the point marked X, tapering to the seam allowance only at the top of the arm at S. Mark and cut. Repeat the procedure on the other side.

Seat Place the seat piece on the chair. Match the centre lines, pin in place and shape the tuck-in at the back and at the side where it will join the arm. Point X on diagrams 1 and 2 must be the meeting point of all the tuck-in seams (3).

Outside back Pin along the tuck-in seams and trim surplus fabric away neatly. Place the outside back piece on the chair and match the centre lines. Match and pin the top centre of the outside back to the top centre of the inside back. Following the line of the chair top, pin the two sections together so that the edges match. Pleat the fullness at the corners of the inside back symmetrically and continue pinning down each side to the top of each

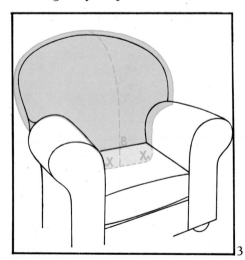

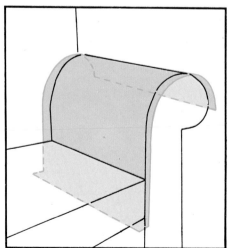

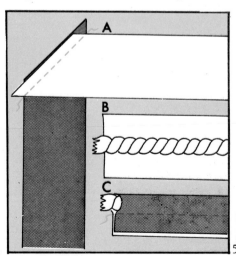

arm.

Inside arm Place the inside arm pieces in position matching the centre lines and shape the tuck-ins to fit the back and seat tuck-ins. Where the arm sections meet the back, the tuck-ins should taper to the seam allowance at the top again. This seam allowance must be clipped round the curve. Pin and fit the tuck-ins of the back and arms and push deep into the crevice round the seat.

Outside arm Pin the outside arms to the inside arms from Q to R. Fit the seams on either side of the outside back section to those of the outside arms (4).

Front facings Pin front facings to the inside and outside arm pieces, pleating evenly, where necessary, so that each arm matches. Trim away any surplus material to make neat seam allowances and clip them round the curves. Pin on the front piece.

The cover should fit your chair snugly. The fabric should not pucker or pull anywhere. All seams should follow the contours of your chair so that, when sewn, seams will be straight. Adjust your pins accordingly.

Slip off the cover by unpinning one of the back seams from the bottom to within about 10 cm. (4 in.) of the top where it begins to curve.

Measure this opening from top to bottom and buy a strong zip to fit. With basting stitches, identify matching points on all the seams. Take special care to mark the pleated seams closely. Clip through basting so that threads are left on each seam allowance. Unpin the cover.

PIPING SEAMS

You must now make your piping. To give a crisp finish all seams on loose covers are piped except those involving tuck-ins. As a rough guide, half a metre of 122 cm. (48 in.) fabric will make 10 metres of piping. Measure the lengths of your seams which have to be piped and buy a corresponding length of medium thick piping cord, plus a little extra to allow for shrinkage. This too must be washed before use.

Cutting strips To find the bias of your fabric fold the material diagonally so that the straight-cut edge across the top lies down one of the selvedges. Crease this fold. Lie the fabric flat and mark the crease using a piece of sharpened chalk and a ruler. Now rule parallel lines. The distance between them should measure 5 cm. (2 in.) plus the girth of the cord. Cut along the chalk marks. The ends of the strips will be at an angle to the edges. Do not try to cut them off square. To join the strips, lay them out so that the ends overlap, take up a small seam allowance then seam together (5). Press the seams flat. Fold the strip round the piping cord so that the edges meet. With the piping foot on your sewing machine, stitch as close to the cord as possible. Trim off to leave a 1 cm. (½ in.) seam allowance. Smooth out the piping. The stitched line of the piping is placed on the seam line, raw edges to raw edges of the fabric, with the piping facing inwards on the right side of the fabric.

Tacking the cover Turn the cover inside out and, inserting the piping, pin all seams matching identification points. Tack. Clip the piping seam allowance to correspond with the curves particularly round a shaped section like the front arm facing (6). Do not pull the piping too tight. Try the cover on the chair. Make any adjustments necessary.

With the piping attachment still on the machine, stitch all the seams, taking care to keep close to the piping where it is inserted. Sew piping to one side of the back opening and starting from this opening, pin piping all round the bottom in readiness for the frill, making sure that the lower edge of the cover is level. Slip the cover on to check again the depth of frill.

The frill Join the pieces for the frill together. Make a 5 cm. (2 in.) hem and press. If the frill is to be box-pleated, pin and press the pleats. Pin the frill round the bottom so that the piping is visible. Juggle the pleats a little so that an inverted pleat occurs at each corner (7). Turn in the ends at the opening so that there is plenty of fullness at these points to prevent gaping. Machine the frill to the bottom of the cover. Sew in the zip. Sew a strong hook and eye to hold the ends of the piped seams together above the frill.

CUSHION COVERS

To make a loose cushion cover, prepare the pieces in the same way as described for the chair. Stitch the plain seam joining either end of the border first, placing this at the back of the cushion. Pipe in the usual way leaving one back seam open for the zip. In the case of a very firm cushion it may be necessary to extend the opening round the second side.

SETTEE COVERS

Settee covers are treated like very wide chairs. You will probably need a double width of fabric on the seat, front and backs plus a zip at each back corner. Avoid a seam down the centres, however: better to have a full width panel in this position, flanked by a half-width one at either side (8). These should be joined together by machine before the fitting stage.

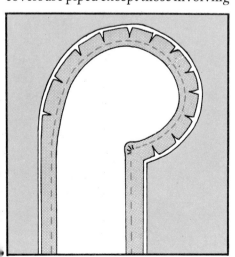

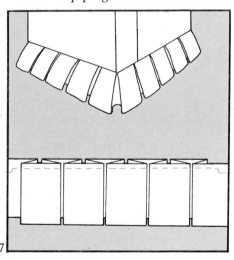

7

8

169

CANING AND RUSHING

Many antique occasional chairs have cane seats and many stools and dining chairs with a rustic character have seats which are woven from rushes. Unfortunately, neither material is very long-lived, and it is common to see chairs of either type with their seats caved-in standing outside antique dealers' shops.

Cane-workers are becoming scarcer and scarcer, and often the work of those who can be found is unsatisfactory. Quite soon everyone who owns cane-seated chairs will have to re-seat them themselves.

The encouraging thing about caning is that if you follow the instructions, and only aim to do an ordinary chair, your first effort will look marvellous. Do not try to cane one of the eighteenth-century chairs with a spider-web-caned back until you are pretty experienced.

TOOLS AND MATERIALS

For the classic caning pattern you need a clearer (1), which is a rod fitted to a wooden handle, used to push old cane out of the holes punched round the frame of the seat. You also need a doubler (1a), which holds the new cane tight in a hole whilst you are threading it through the next hole, and a shell bodkin (1b) which helps you to carry the cane under strands which are already tightly-woven. In addition, you will need a caning bodkin (1c): this

opens up a space for threading further canes through the holes in the seat frame when these become packed with several strands of cane towards the end of the job.

Seating cane is a hard, glossy cane which is split lengthways and supplied in various sizes. You will need about 56 g. (2 oz.) for an average seat. Before use, it should be soaked for two or three minutes to make it pliable.

HOW TO CANE

Take a one-sided razor blade, and cut away the old cane. The holes will still be filled with short fragments: knock them out by poking the blade of the clearer into the holes and hitting the top of it with a mallet.

The classic caning pattern is worked in seven stages. The first four stages are carried out in No. 2 cane. No. 3 cane is used for the next two stages and the work is completed with No. 6 beading cane.

If the seat is wider at the front than the back there will be more holes in the frame at the front. Because of this, it is usual to start working outwards from the central holes. Count the number of holes along the back and

front of the seat. Mark the centre hole in each case. If there are an even number of holes, mark the corresponding ones nearest to the centre.

Stage one Take a long strand of cane and thread it to about half its length down through the central hole at the back and then up through the neighbouring hole on the left. Bring the two ends to the front of the seat and thread each down through its corresponding hole (2). Place the doubler in the right-hand hole to keep that length of the cane firmly in position whilst you proceed to work with the left-hand one. Take it up through the next hole on the left, down through the corresponding hole at the back, up through the next one and so on (3).

Always place the doubler in the hole you have just threaded to hold the cane firmly. The tension should be taut, but not as tight as you can possibly pull it. In later stages it can be very difficult to weave the cane if the tension of the preliminary work is excessive. The canes must remain parallel, so – assuming that the seat is wider in front – when you have reached the corner hole at the back give it a miss and thread the cane through the hole

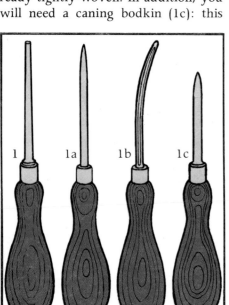

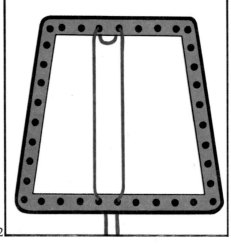

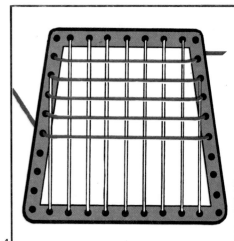

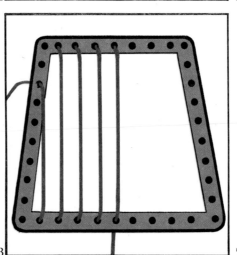

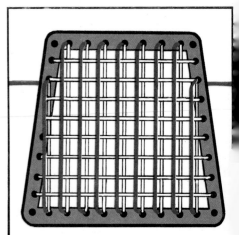

in the side frame which will preserve the pattern. Continue to do this until all the front holes except the corner ones have been used.

Repeat the procedure working to the right. The smooth side of the cane must always remain uppermost and care must be taken that it is not twisted underneath the frame.

Joining canes Whenever you need a new strand of cane, the end of the old and the beginning of the new are spiralled twice round one of the short sections between the holes under the frame and then pulled tight.

Stage two In the second stage, using the same method as before, the cane is threaded from side to side of the seat over the previous work (4).

Stage three When this is finished, the cane is again threaded from the back to the front of the seat over the previous canes, duplicating the first stage (5).

Stage four You take the cane from side to side of the seat again, but this time it is woven under and over the previous strands, one by one (6). You can do this with your fingers but it is easier to use the shell bodkin. Make a point of keeping the strands close together in their pairs so that there are clearly-defined square spaces in between.

Stage five Weave the cane diagonally, treating the twin strands as if they were one. Push the bodkin up through the left-hand corner hole in the front and then weave under the caning until you reach the opposite diagonal hole. Thread down it and up through the next on the right (7). Continue to weave diagonally. To retain the pattern when commencing the left-hand sector of the seat, cane must again be threaded through the left-hand corner hole in the front and woven to the right-hand corner hole at the back.

Stage six The cane is woven diagonally in the opposite direction using the same method, but weaving over the horizontal canes if you wove under them in the previous stage, or vice versa. Start from the right-hand corner hole in the front of the seat (8). The weaving, this time, will take in the three previous strands.

Stage seven Many commercial caners conveniently 'forget' to fix the beading cane round the seat. This hides the holes, and puts the finishing touch to your work (9).

Take a length of No. 6 beading cane

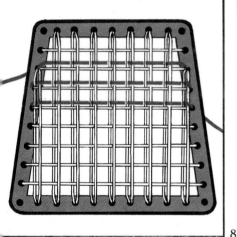

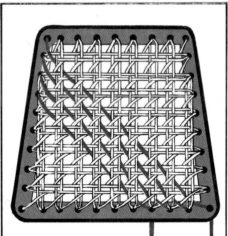

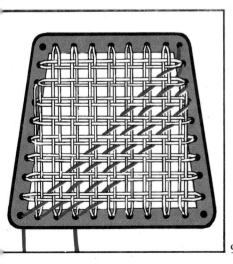

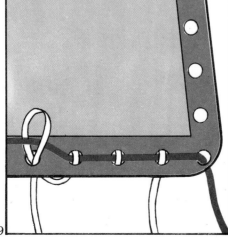

and trim one end to a point. Insert it into one of the corner holes and bring the spare end beside the next hole on the left. Insert a strand of No. 2 cane down through this hole and secure the end under the frame. Now carry the other end over the beading cane and back through the same hole so that it has formed a loop entrapping the beading cane. Take the beading cane to the neighbouring hole on the left, bring the No. 2 cane up through it, loop over the beading cane and back again through the same hole. The beading cane just lies over the holes all round the seat and is secured by the No. 2 cane at all except the corner holes. As the beading cane might split if it were made to turn sharply at the corners, it is always renewed at each corner hole. Try to keep your work neat underneath if only for your own satisfaction.

TWILL CANING

If you have a square drop-in-seated stool or dining-chair, there is a particularly beautiful and rare type of caning that you might like to try. The cane is closely-woven in a twill pattern and gives an effect which will set your chair well apart from any other.

You need about 170 g. (6 oz.) of glossy wrapping cane, a long, steel seating needle and two slats of 1·25 cm. (½ in.) thick wood which are longer than the sides of the seat.

Stage one Tie a slat along the outside of each side bar (1). These are removed during the second stage to loosen the tension when the cane worked in the first stage becomes too tight to be interlaced.

Moisten your cane as before and, preparatory to working from side to side of the frame, secure the end of a length to the inside of one of the side bars in a corner, using a tack. Now wrap the cane neatly round and round the frame so that each cane lies close to the previous one and the top and underside of the frame are indistinguishable (2). Canes are joined invisibly on the edge of the frame: wrong side up, thread the new cane under three of the previous strands, using a bodkin to raise them. Allowing 2·5 cm (1 in.) to project, lay the old end across the new length and twist them together so that the new piece is on top of the other which lies flat

against the frame.

When the frame has been covered, secure the end of the cane with a tack. **Stage two** In the second stage, working from the back to the front of the frame, the cane is woven over and under four strands of cane at a time, in staggered rounds, to achieve the pattern. With a side bar of the seat facing you, secure a fresh length of cane with a tack under the frame so that you can start weaving at the far right-hand corner. Work the seating needle under four strands, over four strands and so on to the far left-hand corner (3). Turn the frame over and continue weaving in the same way on the underside.

At the beginning of the next round, start by weaving under three strands before proceeding with four at a time again (4). The following rounds, start with two and one (5 and 6) and then start again with four (7). Take care to press each strand close to the last one. When the cane worked in the first stage becomes inconveniently tight, carefully remove the slat on the edge where you started weaving. Remove the other when the tension again becomes too tight. Towards the end the cane cannot be threaded from side

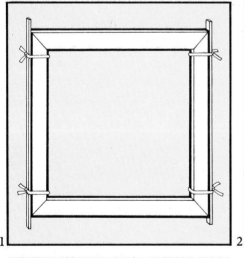

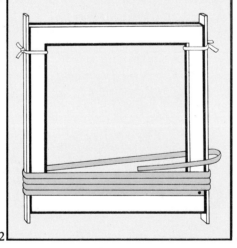

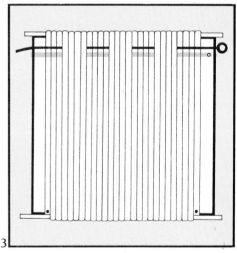

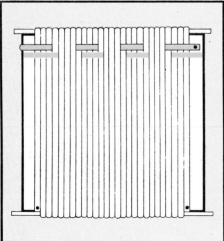

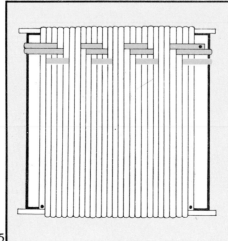

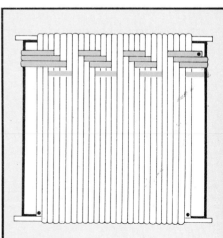

1 2 3

4 5 6

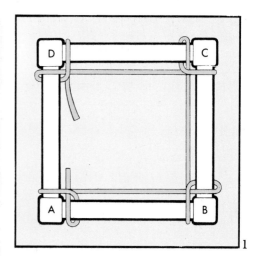

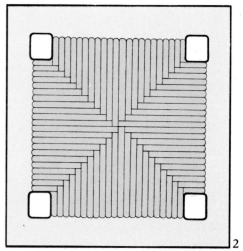

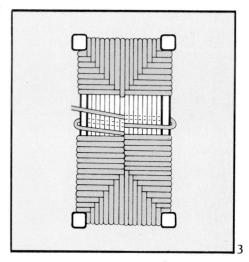

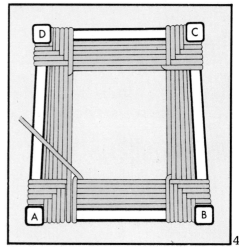

A rush stool in need of re-covering.

to side in one movement: you can only weave it under four canes at a time with the help of a bodkin.

RUSHING

Rush seating is worked quite differently, being wound over and under the frame. In the last twenty years rushes have become virtually unobtainable, so it is now usual to use sea-grass instead. This does not give quite the same traditional impression but it is easier to use.

Unlike rushes, which have to be twisted tightly together to make a 'cord' of uniform thickness, sea-grass is of equal thickness throughout and is continuous. It should be wound onto a special shuttle which is obtainable from craft shops.

Method Label each corner support of your stool or chair A, B, C and D, work-

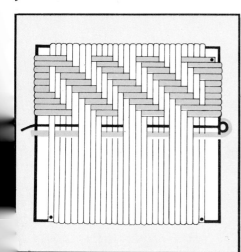

ing anti-clockwise from the left front leg with the seat facing you. With the left hand, hold the end of the sea-grass at A pointing to D. Bring the shuttle *over* the front bar close to A, *under* the bar and *over* the end of the sea-grass and the side bar close to A. Take it *under* the bar, *over* and round the side bar close to B and *over* the sea-grass and front bar close to B (1). Pass it *under* the bar, *over* and *under* the back bar close to C, then *over* the sea-grass and side bar close to C. Take it *under* the bar and then *over* and *under* the side bar close to D. Take it *over* the sea-grass and back bar and then repeat again from A working the next round neatly beside the first. When the seat is completed (2) secure the end of the sea-grass round an adjacent strand on the underside and thread the end out of sight.

If your seat is oblong the sides of the seat will be finished before the frame at the back and front are filled. Using the space between the two central strands running between the side bars, weave the sea-grass in a figure of eight between the back and front bars (3). Thus: up through the centre of the seat over the front bar, up through the centre, over the back bar and up through the centre etc.

A seat that is wider in front than at the back is no problem. Follow the directions for the square seat, but on the second round, and alternate rounds thereafter until it is no longer necessary, take up the extra space by wrapping the sea-grass round the front bar twice at A and B (4).

CUSHIONS

Gentlemen in the trade assess the worth of a pillow by supporting it under the middle with an outspread hand. Inferior pillows, i.e. inexpensive ones, sag sadly on each side. They are either filled with fibre that does not cling together and consequently slips away from a pressure centre, or they are filled with material which would be perfectly satisfactory if there were more of it.

As with pillows, so with cushions. Looking around one comes to the conclusion that most people do not realize that a cushion should present an extremely buoyant appearance. It should be plump, and it should be well-filled in the corners.

But there is more to it as far as your own cushions are concerned. You may need a softly-yielding cushion, a soft, bouncy cushion or a relatively hard, resilient cushion, depending on the circumstances. If you buy a second-hand cushion because you like the cover, you are likely to be repelled by the dust that emerges when you give the whole thing a good shaking. For hygienic reasons you will probably remove the cover immediately and send it to be cleaned if it cannot be washed at home.

CLEANING OLD CUSHION FILLING

The cushion itself is more of a problem. Old filling is not worth keeping unless it happens to be feathers or horsehair.

Feathers can be sterilized: wrap them in aluminium foil, prick it with a needle and put your parcel in a low oven (Regulo 1 or 290°F.) for an hour.

Horsehair is an unusual filling but is sometimes found in very firm Victorian cushions. It can be washed in warm suds, rinsed and then dried on a tray in an airing cupboard or some similar place which is not draughty.

Ticking Feathers or down make the best filling for super-soft cushions provided that the quills are prevented from piercing the fabric. To eliminate this problem, the cushion undercover must be made of pillow ticking. In times gone by, this was rubbed inside with beeswax as an extra precaution, an additional dressing being applied to

the seams: it is still worth trying.

RE-STUFFING A CUSHION

A finished undercover should measure 5 mm. ($\frac{1}{4}$ in.) less than the cover on every side. Join the seams by machine, leaving a gap in the centre of one of the shorter sides (if there are any) which is wide enough to put your filling through.

The down in feather filling wafts up your nose, floats all over the room and clings to your clothes. Wear an overall and take any precautions that you can think of to reduce the mess. Holding the undercover between your knees with the open seam at the top, push the first few handfuls of feathers into the bottom corners and force them to stay there permanently by prodding them with a knife handle or anything else with a blunt point which is convenient to use. Fill up the undercover to bursting point and then manipulate the feathers into the upper corners by the same method you used for the bottom ones. Close the opening in the seam by hand.

'CURING' FEATHERS

It is more than likely that you will not have enough of the old feathers to follow these directions. New feathers are astronomically expensive, so try curing your own with the method described in Cassell's 'Book of the Household' published in 1888:

'Mix a quantity of lime-water to the proportion of one pound of quicklime to a gallon of water [250 g. to 4·5 litres]. Stir it thoroughly and put it aside to settle. Pour the clear water off into a shallow vessel in which the feathers have been laid. The water should be three or four inches [7·5–10 cm.] deep so that the feathers are thoroughly covered. Stir them about so that they become well soaked and sink to the bottom of the pan. They should be frequently moved about in the water, but must be left in it not less than three days. The water is then poured off and the feathers rinsed in clear, cold water and then laid out to dry in bags of coarse net which will keep them safely while allowing the air to circulate round and amongst them. The net bags

must be frequently shaken, in order that any superfluous dust or dirt may be rubbed off the feathers.'

When the feathers are thoroughly dry they are ready for use. Quicklime must be handled with care as it 'boils' when placed in water. It can be obtained from some builders' merchants.

ALTERNATIVE FILLINGS

Kapok The usual substitute for feathers is kapok. This flocculent vegetable fibre does not work its way through the undercover, so that unbleached calico may be used instead of pillow ticking. Kapok is stuffed into the cushion in the same way as feathers but a larger quantity must be used. Friction causes loosely-packed kapok to form pellets. Unfortunately, even the plumpest kapok cushion becomes floppy and lumpy in the end. When this happens you have either to intro-

duce more filling, or to re-stuff the cushion from scratch.

Shredded polyether foam is widely sold. It makes a very resilient filling which is particularly suitable for a cushion that has a cover made of tapestry, for instance, which you want to remain relatively unwrinkled in use. It must be handled correctly, however. The granules must be packed into an undercover made of pillow-ticking otherwise their shapes will show through the cover. It is messy to use. Unlike feathers or kapok, which 'fly' everywhere, shredded foam sticks tenaciously to all but the smoothest fabrics. When working with it, wear an overall made of slippery fabric and remove any fragments clinging to the undercover before introducing the cushion into the cover. To compensate for these inconveniences, foam-filled cushions can be washed.

A solid foam cushion shape gives a firmer and smoother finish. It is also more expensive but does not need a ticking undercover. Do not dispense with an undercover altogether, how-

ever, or the foam will cling to the inside of the cover and will rot if the light filters through it.

A polyether or foam rubber squab must be used inside a tailored cushion cover. These can be bought ready-made but you will probably have to cut one out of solid foam yourself if it is to fit an existing cover. Foam is produced in numerous thicknesses and is sold by the square metre. Measure your cover and choose the thickness of the foam according to the depth of the panel separating the top and bottom of the cover minus 0·5 cm. ($\frac{1}{4}$ in.). The amount you need is governed by the width and length of the cover minus 0·5 cm. ($\frac{1}{4}$ in.) on each dimension. The size of a squab for a circular cover is calculated in the same way.

There are different types of foam to give a variety of resistances from firm to soft. When cutting foam, mark your cutting line with a felt tip pen and ruler. Cut through it with a very sharp carving knife (with an unserrated edge) guided by a metal ruler. Do not compress the foam whilst cutting it.

REPAIRING CHINA

However careful you are, sooner or later a favourite piece of china or glass slips out of your hand and . . . It has happened. There it lies in pieces. Professionals can undetectably rebuild an item from hundreds of fragments. Of course, this is an expensive business but if the break is simple you can mend it successfully yourself with the easily-managed materials that are at your disposal today.

Sticking china used to be much more difficult than it is now. The old adhesives were unsatisfactory: they were not resistant to heat or water; they were vulnerable to fungus and they were incapable of mending anything invisibly. The invention of cellulose glues and epoxy resin adhesive revolutionized china and glass repairing with the result that items which would once have had to be riveted, dowelled or pinned, can now be stuck together strongly and permanently.

Restoring china is delicate work which requires infinite patience. An item that is to spend the rest of its life on a shelf need not be so strongly mended as one that is used regularly, but any difference will be in the adhesive used, not in the finish. However, when you are inexperienced, do not ask too much of yourself. You cannot expect to be able to mend an article so that, when finished, no trace of an accident remains. Nor can you expect old china to look as good as new.

PREPARING THE BROKEN PIECES
Begin by re-assembling the pieces of the broken item. Let us hope that they are all present and that the bits fit cleanly together so that you will only have to stick them together carefully. You cannot, however, just smear new adhesive onto the pieces and wait for it to set. They must first be cleaned so that the broken edges offer a perfect base for the glue.

Cleaning If the porcelain or pottery was about to be washed up before the accident, each piece must be washed in warm soapy water. Even if the pieces appear to be clean they must be wiped over with methylated spirit. For this task, use a scrap of delicate silk because

it does not catch on jagged edges, leaving little bits of fluff which have to be picked off by hand.

Stains Quite often an item breaks because it has been badly cracked for a long time. The breakage is not so much an accident as a final separation. In this case the broken edges will be badly stained and, unless bleached to their original colour, will emphasize the repair and thereby mark it as the work of an amateur. If the item is made of continental porcelain clean the faces of the cracks with a pad of cotton wool moistened in hydrogen peroxide and then lay pads of it over the stained parts for several days, moistening them as necessary. When the stains have completely disappeared, scrub the parts very gently with a soft toothbrush and rinse. Peroxide will not have any effect on earthenware or English porcelain which are more porous, so that stains are more deeply absorbed. Such pieces must be immersed in a solution of domestic bleach for a week or more. This should eradicate stubborn stains without damaging the glaze.

SEPARATING PIECES PREVIOUSLY CRACKED
The pieces may include ones which were previously cracked and mended (1) and not mended very well. If this is the case, you may as well take them apart and make a good job of the whole item whilst you are about it. First of all soak the pieces in boiling water and detergent, holding back any pieces which you doubt your capacity to reassemble. This should soften the types of adhesive that people used to use for china restoration, such as Seccotine,

shellac and Durofix. After a few minutes the pieces that were joined with these should pull apart (2).

Solvents If this method is of no avail, the cracks must be swabbed liberally with solvent. In turn, try methylated spirit, which dissolves types of shellac that are invulnerable to boiling water; amyl acetate (highly inflammable with toxic fumes) which dissolves cellulose adhesives such as Durofix; acetone (highly inflammable) which dissolves cement mixtures; Dissolvex which is versatile and dissolves all sorts of adhesives including hardened Araldite and other epoxy resin adhesives; benzine (highly inflammable) which dissolves Evostik. The latter should not have been used in the first place as it is unsuitable for repairing china. If you are still out of luck put the pieces in a pan of water and slowly bring it to the boil.

The solvents should remove every trace of adhesive from the cracked edges. If, after all your efforts, some still remains it must be very carefully scraped off and picked away with a needle. The tiniest remnant is sufficient to prevent the broken surfaces from meeting perfectly.

TYPES OF ADHESIVES
There are literally hundreds of different china adhesives on the market. Each will be enthusiastically recommended by someone, when you enquire for the best.

Epoxy glue Professionals use rapid-setting epoxy resin adhesive. You can buy a rapid- or a slow-setting epoxy resin adhesive. Beginners should use the slow-setting type which allows for

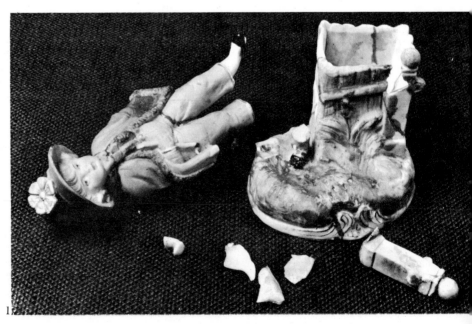

some adjustment.

Epoxy resin adhesive is sold in a pack containing two tubes: one holds the adhesive and the other the hardener. An equal length of each is squeezed separately onto a small sheet of glass. When mixed with a palette knife the setting process begins. The adhesive will be sufficiently hard within twelve hours to join china firmly but will not reach its ultimate strength for a week, unless subject to a high temperature. Before epoxy adhesive is set it can be dissolved with ethyl alcohol (highly inflammable) and the residue cleaned off with acetone. Dissolvex will break down the adhesive at all stages if the article is immersed in it.

Epoxy brands English epoxy adhesives (Araldite, Bostik 7, Power Pack) are more viscous and difficult to spread – unless kept in a warm room – than some foreign brands. Worse, they dry to a dirty grey-green. Professionals use them, however, if they cannot get hold of the German equivalent Uhu Plus or the Canadian one called Devcon 2. The latter, which is on sale in Britain, is opaque white when dry and can be used for filling tiny holes which makes it invaluable.

Whilst working with these adhesives you will get them on any tools you may use and on your fingers. To deal with the mess before it gets out of control keep a rag and a bottle of methylated or surgical spirit at hand.

JOINING THE PIECES

An amateur will take a cracked plate, paste the broken edges with glue and then hold the larger section in one hand whilst he juggles the other piece

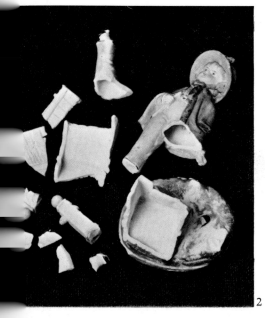

into position as best he may. You really need two hands just to align the broken edges (in addition, one of those adjustable magnifying glasses fixed to a stand will help). You must devise a method of holding your work steady, so that both hands are left free and parts that are being joined are not pulled asunder by the force of gravity.

Supports A plentiful supply of plasticine, plus a board to stick it to, are essential for propping up cups etc. at the required angle. A plate or saucer may be wedged upright in a drawer which has been gently closed. Some people find that a box of sand 7·5–10 cm. (3–4 in.) deep holds some things effectively. Tilt the article at the required angle and push down into the sand, being careful not to get sand on the glue.

Repairing techniques When repairing broken china never try to stick more than two edges together at the same time unless you have no alternative as, for instance, when joining a handle to a cup or a triangular chip to the top of a basin.

Bed the main part of the item down securely in sand or plasticine so that the broken surface faces upwards. Squeeze 0·25 cm. ($\frac{1}{8}$ in.) epoxy resin adhesive plus 0·25 cm. ($\frac{1}{8}$ in.) hardener onto your mixing surface, replace the caps on the respective tubes and mix the adhesive until it becomes uniformly cloudy. Take the tiniest portion of glue on your finger and just 'grease' each edge with it so that every part is covered but there is no surplus. There is one position in which the top edges will interlock perfectly. And one position only. Press the two pieces together firmly and examine them. In spite of the care you took in applying the adhesive a little may have squeezed out in one or two places. Do not try to wipe it off with solvent because this will seep into the join and, at this stage, weaken the adhesive. Scrape it off with the end of a matchstick and four hours later take the rest off with a wisp of cotton wool moistened in ethyl alcohol. If you dare not do this in case the join is disturbed, wait for fifteen hours and pare off the excess with a razor blade before finishing with finest sandpaper.

TAPING THE JOINS

It is very inconvenient to have dribbles of glue round the break. When you have stuck the two surfaces together

they must be held firmly whilst the adhesive sets. This is not done with cellulose tape, which stretches, but with gummed brown paper tape. Cut it into short lengths, damp them and stick them smoothly over the join at right angles and fairly close together. When dry, the tape shrinks so that the broken edges are tightly clasped together.

Some joins must be taped differently. A cup with a broken handle is anchored on its side with plasticine so that the handle is uppermost. After the parts are stuck together, the tape is pasted over the middle of the handle and onto the bowl of the cup at either side. A triangular piece broken out of the rim of a bowl has to have seven lengths of tape radiating at right angles round the join.

BUILDING UP FRAGMENTED PIECES

An item such as a plate which is broken in fragments must be built up piece by piece. It is most important to assemble it before sticking it together. If you go ahead regardless, you will probably find that you are left with a hole in the centre of the jigsaw plus the missing piece which cannot be fitted. The hole is either too small – because the dimensions of the item have been infinitesimally altered by the addition of the adhesive – or the missing piece cannot be slipped in because the contours of the edges will not allow it.

Barbola In this kind of repair it is common to find that there are a few splinters of china missing or, if present, that they are too small to work with. These tiny holes are best filled with barbola paste, which is easy to handle in its fresh, putty-like state. Put a piece, no larger than a pea, on a piece of glass, roll it flat and cut it into strips. Moisten the edges of the hole, take a morsel of barbola on the end of the fine blade of a modelling tool and paste it into place. If the barbola stands proud of the surface it can be wiped smooth with a wet finger. Leave the item for a day for the filling to dry. The patches of barbola, which will be white when dry, can be painted to match the rest of the piece.

Make a small pool of Chintex glaze on a tile and add oil paint generously. After each application of colour harden off in the oven at 100°C (230°F). Avoid using hot water or detergent on pieces mended and painted in this way.

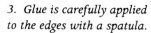

3   4

3. Glue is carefully applied to the edges with a spatula.
4. The mended figurine is supported by plasticine and brown paper strips while the glue sets.
5. The completed piece with no mend showing.
6. The piece to be repaired is bedded down in a sand box.
7. Barbola paste is moulded round the edge with a spatula to fill the gap.
8. Painting over the filled cracks and remodelled tip of the plate. Use oil paints and Chintex glaze, applying one coat at a time and hardening off in the oven at 100°C (230°F).
9. A gorgeous assembly of carefully-mended china.

5

6

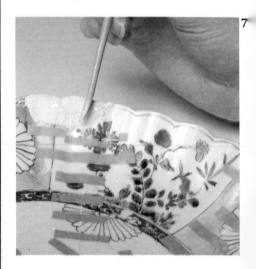

7

9

8

SILVER AND OTHER METALS

Any dealer knows that silverware is either over- or undervalued by its owner. A fact that you will confirm if you eavesdrop in a shop where people are trying to sell their treasures.

VALUING SILVER

Silver is valued according to its weight, workmanship and rarity of design or, if it has no aesthetic or historical worth, by its weight alone. If you happen to have some which has not been appraised you should have this done for insurance purposes, if not for your own interest.

Composition Silver is a soft metal. Sterling standard 925 contains 925 parts of silver plus 75 parts of a harder alloy which is mainly copper. Without the assistance of this alloy the silver would be too soft to use.

When is silver not silver? The law in this country is explicit. A silver hallmark is only stamped on an item by an assay office if the content is no less than 925 parts in 1000. Anything less – and this will include pieces that would be accepted as silver on the continent – is designated as silver plate. Checking the precise content is difficult.

Testing Most jewellers keep a small pot of nitric acid and, if asked to make an assessment, will scratch a tiny indentation on the underside of an item. This will change colour when the acid is applied: green means that it is not silver at all; dark grey means that it contains some silver; black means that it will pass the sterling standard.

Hallmarks If a hallmark wears off – items are sometimes ostentatiously stamped on a particularly exposed area – it is a complicated business to get it re-stamped if the maker's mark is not registered at the selected assay office.

REPAIRING SILVER

Obviously, repairing silver is not a job for an amateur.

Dents It is usually more difficult to straighten out a dent than it is to solder on a new part. It is not just a matter of knocking out the dent from the inside. The dent has caused the silver to stretch or thicken and it must be re-formed to assume a uniform thickness with the aid of a special hammer – a process which is called 'plenishing'. As you can imagine, plenishing something such as a jug with a narrow neck can be very awkward.

Splits and holes must be repaired with hard solder. *Soft* solder is a mixture of lead and tin which can be melted at a low temperature by an ordinary soldering-iron. Before soft solder is polished it resembles silver, but afterwards it darkens, making the repair very obvious. Worse is to come. The lead content amalgamates with the silver, and the resulting alloy is corroded by the sulphides and oxygen in the air so that the silver is rotted. Before an attempt is made to mend silver that has been previously repaired with soft solder, every scrap of solder must be removed or it will unite permanently with the silver when the hard solder is applied.

When silver is hard-soldered the heat that must be applied oxidizes some of the copper, which rises to the surface in the form of copper oxide. Underneath, a film of pure silver is left. Both these deposits must be polished away to achieve an even-coloured surface. If this is not done properly, a coppery sheen will remain which can be seen in a clear light.

Repairing a candlestick is a problem. It consists of a very thin silver mould filled with pitch or plaster. The filling has to be removed without creating further damage. As the silver is so fragile it is very difficult to file and polish the solder to an undetectible finish.

CLEANING SILVER

Tarnish is caused by hydrogen sulphide in the air activated by humidity. If allowed to develop, tarnish will build up until an item is composed of more silver sulphide than silver. But people who take pride in cleaning their silver every week may be doing more harm than good. Proprietary cleaners contain abrasives which, when removing tarnish, also erase a minute quantity of silver with it. Over the years this can amount to quite a bit.

Probably no better are the two traditional cleaning methods followed by butlers of the old school who cleaned silver by rubbing tarnish off with their thumbs, or with a paste made out of French chalk, methylated spirit and a few drops of ammonia.

The cleaners which demand that silver is dipped into them are the best. To make your own put a little washing soda plus an aluminium milk bottle top into hot water. Immerse the silver in it, leave until the tarnish has disappeared, rinse in clear water and dry with a soft cloth free from anything that could scratch the surface.

Silver should be stored wrapped in anti-tarnish paper, sealed in a plastic bag containing a sachet of silica gel or sheathed in a dry cloth previously soaked in a pint of water in which 283·5 g. (10 oz.) of zinc acetate was dissolved.

SILVER PLATE

Sheffield-plated items were individually designed and made between 1720 and 1830, and many are almost as valuable as their silver equivalents. Plated silver of this period was made by welding a thin sheet of silver onto a thin sheet of copper. The two layers can be seen where an edge is turned under or overlapped.

Sheffield plate had such a reputation that many mass-produced electroplated articles of later date were unscrupulously stamped 'Sheffield' and sold abroad. Indeed many can still be found in this country which are merely made of copper with silver electroplating.

If you happen to own a Sheffield-plated article with copper patches appearing where the silver is beginning to wear off, you would be wise to postpone the moment when it must be electrically re-plated until the whole article is definitely unsightly.

Electroplated articles are usually made of nickel (EPNS or NS) or Brittania metal – usually unmarked – which is a mixture of tin and antimony. When a plated article is worn, the base metal begins to show through the silver in patches. It may not be worth re-plating articles that are in poor condition. Fragile metal may split when fittings such as wooden knobs and handles are removed before plating. Tarnish on items which have been neglected may have corroded the plating or base metal, which will cause green spots or scars to break through the new plating.

Base metal that is split cannot be re-plated without increasing the damage unless it is soldered and copper-plated first. Nickel, being a strong metal, is

less likely to give trouble than Britannia metal which is particularly vulnerable to oxidization and knocks. Indeed, many plating firms will not accept it.

For these reasons, when buying shabby plate examine the condition of areas subject to strain: above and below handles, round bases and on either side of hinges.

COPPER

Copper that is not cleaned turns bright green. Decorative items usually have a polished finish. Remove tarnish with a soft cloth dipped in a weak solution of oxalic acid. Thereafter, keep the surface bright by rubbing it with half a lemon dipped in salt, rinsing it in hot water, drying it thoroughly and polishing it with brass cleaner.

Copper cooking utensils are generally given a satin finish and all, except basins for beating eggs and preserving pans for making jam, are lined inside with tin to prevent the copper, which is a soft metal, from being worn away. Professional culinary-ware shops undertake the repair of saucepans. An effective way of cleaning copper is to take a big enamelled pan, fill it with as much cheap vinegar as you can afford, add a ladleful of cooking salt

and heat until the salt dissolves. When cold, dump your filthy copper pan inside and watch the colour change. Wash it in detergent, rinse in hot water and dry thoroughly. Keep a salt and vinegar solution beside the kitchen sink and wipe copper utensils with it before washing them up as usual.

BRASS

Brass, which is an alloy of copper and zinc, corrodes unattractively. If the surface is very bad, try rubbing it down with fine steel wool before dipping and brushing it in a fairly strong solution of washing soda or giving it the salt-and-vinegar treatment. The polished finish can be restored if you rub the surface energetically with whiting or jeweller's rouge.

You will find that some brass polishes are more abrasive than others and often leave an unsightly white deposit in the crevices of door knockers, name-plates etc. This is a particular problem when cleaning Benares ware, which is beautifully chased, engraved and embossed. Scrub the deposit with a soft toothbrush dipped in a solution of ammonia – avoid splashing skin and eyes or inhaling the fumes. Follow by brushing with detergent solution. Heavily-tarnished brass decorations on

Silver, pewter, brass and copper all respond to proper care and cleaning

furniture are best removed for cleaning. They can, like other decorative brass and copper articles, be lacquered so that cleaning is no longer necessary. First take the precaution of washing off all deposits of polish; if you do not the brass will turn green.

BRONZE

Bronze is not always the colour that you expect. Sometimes the copper it contains, in company with tin, lends a reddish tinge which makes it look like brass. Never clean it with metal polish, however, as you will remove the all-important patina which should be deep, rich brown. Instead, buff it with dark brown shoe polish to build up a protective sheen against corrosion. Prior to this a green rash on the surface can be washed away in a solution of sodium sesquicarbonate.

PEWTER

When cleaning pewter never dip it in acid: it will develop a pink sheen that is very difficult to get rid of. Rub it down with finest steel wool and boil it in a large pan with some hay.

MIRRORS AND GLASS

Glass is basically made from a mixture of sand, lime and soda. Glass which contains lead is called crystal. It is much clearer, more brilliant, heavier and of course more expensive.

People tend to think that glass is an immutable material which only changes its character when it is broken. In fact, to a certain degree it is absorbent and soluble in water. It also reacts to chemicals in the air and to changes of temperature.

Chemical reaction can sometimes increase the value of glass. You may have noticed iridescent patches on old windows. These develop over a long period in a humid atmosphere when a substance in the glass reacts to the carbon dioxide in the air to produce sodium carbonate and calcium silicate. This is considered a highly desirable patinization by connoisseurs and is one of the reasons why ancient glass is so highly prized.

REMOVING STAINS FROM GLASS

The fact that glass is soluble and absorbent is demonstrated by the greenish tide-marks seen inside glass vases and by the wine stains left on the inside of decanters. These marks are not simply residues imparted by flower stalks or deposits left by dehydrated wine. The stains are not only on the surface. Liquid has dissolved some of the glass inside the vessels and, at the same time, the glass has reacted to lime and other salts from plant stalks or to the tartrates in wine.

The usual remedy is to use scouring powder on the vase and lead shot plus water inside the decanter. These abrasives are well enough suited to glass of the more everyday kind. But diamonds are not the only things that scratch glass; coarse abrasives will also scratch the surface. Fine glass or crystal should be rubbed with a fine abrasive such as pumice powder. If you cannot get your hand inside the object, use a stick with a cloth wrapped round the end. Dip it in the pumice and rub it on the stain energetically. Rinse the article, allow it to dry and then finish off by polishing the damaged areas with jeweller's rouge. Brass polish is also a gentle

abrasive and can be used in the same way. When you have finished, you may find that the surface is slightly greasy. Wash it with hot water containing detergent.

These procedures work quite well when the damage is superficial. If stains are stubborn, however, try rubbing them with ammonia or vinegar. Then polish the surface with a soft cloth moistened in methylated spirit and dipped in crocus powder; the latter is obtainable from chemists. If the result is still unsatisfactory, avoid compounding the problem by using powerful acids. Valuable glass which is badly stained can be renovated by an expert glass restorer who will probably employ corrosive liquids, but he knows how far he can go without ruining an item.

CLEANING AND CARING FOR GLASS AND MIRRORS

Glass can sometimes suffer from a defect in the manufacturing process. Inexplicable cracks will appear; the glass is said to have 'flown'. In fact, stresses implicit at one stage of the production process were not released at a later stage and the glass has fragmented when subjected to warmth from the sun, from smoke or some other source. In the past, housewives always boiled new glassware because they believed it imparted a certain protection against breakages. They put the glass into a pan full of cold water, brought it slowly to the boil, then allowed it to cool until the contents could be lifted out by hand. When glass stoppers are stuck in a bottle or decanter it is tempting to

force them out. Do not try. Stand the bottle on a radiator or somewhere that is warm. The air inside the bottle will expand and force the stopper loose. If this is not effective, paint a mixture of two parts of methylated spirit, one part of glycerine and one part cooking salt round the stopper and leave for a day. A few gentle taps should then shift it.

Methods of cleaning glass are many and varied. Proprietary glass cleaners are certainly expensive and the fact that a good window cleaner can get sparkling results with only plain water and lint-free cloths shows that other aids are unnecessary. However, if you are a little short on elbow-grease, it may be worth cleaning your glassware and mirrors with cold tea and polishing your best glasses with fuller's earth.

Any method of cleaning windows applies equally to glassware or mirrors. The anonymous Victorian author of a household manual entitled 'Cookery For Every Household' has the last word: 'Take some tepid water and add enough liquid ammonia to make it smell slightly, or a small quantity of paraffin. Wring a chamois leather out of this and wash over the window with it, paying particular attention to the sides and corners. Then finish off with a soft cloth or dry leather. No material of a fluffy nature must be used. Clean soft paper makes a very good polishing pad. Paint or other stains can be removed from the glass with vinegar or oxalic acid.'

REPAIRING BROKEN GLASS
Not so long ago it was impossible to

1. An old decanter can be cleaned to spectacular effect
2. Mirrors can be restored to look as good as new

repair glass effectively at home. The arrival of epoxy resin adhesives has made it quite feasible to mend simple breaks yourself. The tools required and procedure are the same as for china (see page 176) except that if adhesive oozes out of the crack when the broken surfaces are pressed together it must be rubbed off when hardened with steel wool and not with glasspaper which scratches glass.

Wine glasses commonly break across the stem. Such breaks can be mended with epoxy adhesive but owing to the structure of the glass they may break again elsewhere. Stainless steel bands are often wrapped round instead, but look unattractive. It is better to dowel the stem: a corresponding hole is bored in each section and a pin introduced to hold them together. The pin will show – not so much in cut-glass – but is not unsightly as it is swathed in a frosting of adhesive.

If you take glass to be repaired by a professional he will warn you that he cannot guarantee the piece against breakage. If your glass is not valuable you may as well take the risk of mending it yourself, on the principle that a shattered glass is no worse than one without a foot.

Bed the bowl of the glass firmly in plasticine. The danger in drilling glass is that it breaks if overheated, so that a method of keeping it cool must be used. Build a 0·5 cm. ($\frac{1}{4}$ in.) high wall of plasticine round the perimeter of the broken stem (1). Fill the well that has been formed with cold water. Fit your power drill with a 2·5 mm. ($\frac{1}{8}$ in.) spear-point bit. Hold the bit within 2·5 cm. (1 in.) of the centre of the broken surface, switch on and bring it very, very gently down onto the hole. Hold it very steadily and when it bites, lift it to make sure that you are drilling straight up the centre of the stem (1a). Taking frequent rests to keep the bit cool, drill until the hole is 5 mm. ($\frac{1}{4}$ in.) deep. Remove the plasticine. The part of the stem that has broken off must now be marked so that the holes will be aligned. Poke the tip of an indelible pencil into the hole already made and then press the undrilled part against it in exactly the right position. The former should now bear a mark into which you can drill using the same method as before.

Take 1·25 cm. ($\frac{1}{2}$ in.) of half-hard brass wire 132 and flatten one side slightly so that a small channel is formed

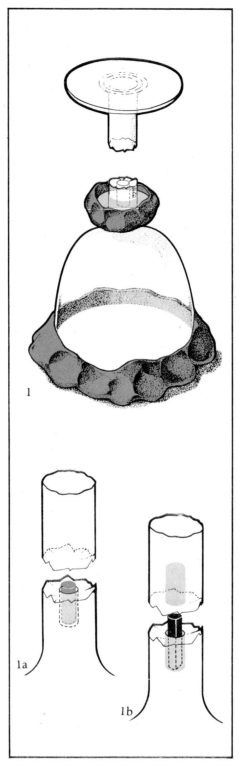

1

1a

1b

through which surplus adhesive can escape when the wire is inserted. Push it home into one of the holes and fit the other over it (1b). If you have done your work well the holes will face each other precisely and the wire will slip in without a hitch. Take out the wire and score the sides of it with a file to provide a key for the adhesive.

Make up some cement composed of epoxy resin adhesive mixed with titanium dioxide – the latter is obtainable from craft shops specializing in pottery. Fill the first hole with cement and insert the pin. Clear all the surplus

cement away immediately. The following day, fill the other hole with freshly made cement and fit the other part of the stem over it. If the broken edges fit together perfectly you will not need to glue between them. Wipe away the excess cement quickly. Now bind the pieces together with gummed paper tape in the same way as you would if the item were made of china (see page 176).

To hasten the setting process your glass, if it is not coloured, can be put in the oven. Lay it on a bed of raw rice so that it is supported throughout by something of uniform temperature when heated. Switch on the oven to 150°F. or Mark $\frac{1}{4}$. When the oven has achieved this temperature switch it off without opening the door which could cause a sharp drop in temperature, cracking your glass. Within two hours the cement should be dry.

CUTTING GLASS

It is useful to be able to cut glass yourself. After practising on some spare pieces you should find it easy. You need a table and a sheet of thick hardboard to rest over it covered by a blanket. You also need a T-square, a long ruler and a glass cutter. You should keep the latter in a pot of turpentine to prevent it from rusting.

Lay the glass on the hardboard and the T-square on the glass. Slide the T-square along until the space between the edge of the long arm and the edge of the glass is 0·25 cm. ($\frac{1}{8}$ in.) less than the width that you want cut. The long arm of the T-square forms a right angle with the edge of the glass touching the short arm. You cannot be sure that the edge of the glass is parallel to the long arm unless you check the distance between each at several points.

Hold the T-square firmly and with the cutter held like a pencil, but more upright, draw it from the further edge clearly towards you until it slides off the near edge. Use a steady, firm stroke in order to score the glass and keep your hand at the same angle. Do not cut down onto the edges or the glass will chip. Only a clean score will result in a clean break. If, at first, you run into difficulties, try dipping the cutter in light oil and smearing a film of paraffin on the projected cutting line. Holding the largest section, lift the glass carefully. Tap each end of the score with the handle of the cutter and then the underside of the smaller sec-

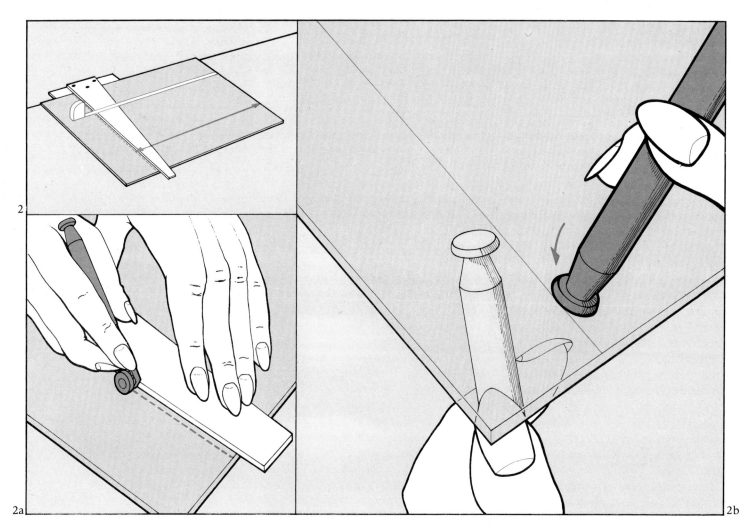

2

2a

2b

1. *The bowl of the glass must be secured and the area to be drilled must be kept cool.*
1a. *Check to ensure your drilling line is straight.*
1b. *Use wire as a key for the adhesive.*
2. *Cutting glass. First position the T-square with the long arm parallel to the edge of the glass.*
2a. *Hold the cutter like a pencil to make the score.*
2b. *Tap each end of the score with the cutter handle, and the underside of the smaller section.*

tion beside the score. The glass should split. To grind the sharp edges smooth, rub them at an angle of 45 degrees with an oilstone dampened in water. Use a circular motion.

RE-SILVERING MIRROR GLASS

Mirror glass is expensive and so is resilvering. If you have a small, un-important mirror which you are fond of but which is not worth sending to be professionally re-silvered, you might like to do it yourself.

Remove the mirror from its frame and place it on a stand of some kind so that it overlaps the edges. Spread newspapers thickly underneath. Rub off the old silver and paint with caustic soda solution (this is corrosive and gives off strong fumes: wear gloves and work in a well-ventilated room). Now all traces of grease must be removed – even a fingerprint will reappear as an unpleasant spot on the silvering. Wipe the surface over with a solution made up of one part nitric acid to four parts of water (corrosive and fuming again). Rinse in distilled water.

Silvering solutions are of several types. The simpler ones have to be brushed on and the result is usually uneven. The following solution (a mix-ture of three separate solutions) is quite complicated to mix and must be used immediately, but it achieves an impres-sive finish. Make plenty, because it is flooded over the glass.

Take a sufficient quantity of a solution made up of one part silver nitrate to ten parts of distilled water and add ammonia to it drop by drop, stirring constantly, until the precipitate which is first formed only just re-dissolves. Now add an equal amount of a solution made separately from one part of caustic potash to ten parts of distilled water and, stirring constantly, dissolve the precipitate which has formed again with a few more drops of ammonia. Lastly, make another solution to equal the original amount of the previous ones using 0·5 ($\frac{1}{2}$) parts of glycerine to ten parts of distilled water. Drop just sufficient of this into the main brew to turn it slightly thicker – the rest will be added later.

Now make a 10% solution of stannous chloride and flow it over the glass swiftly. Pour the rest of the glycerine solution into the silvering solution, stir rapidly and pour evenly over the sur-face. Wipe away any that seeps onto the other side of the glass.

The silvering process should be com-plete in three or four minutes. Rinse the mirror in distilled water and dry slowly. Silvering is very easily scratched. Melt a tin of wax polish and spread this over the back of the mirror with a soft brush. Cover with a sheet of greaseproof paper before replacing the mirror in the frame and pinning on the backing. Silvering is blemished by damp which is often introduced acci-dently through the back of the frame when cleaning or by hanging over a damp patch.

185

RESTORING PICTURES

Good pictures in good condition are expensive. But dilapidated pictures of the same calibre are often sold cheaply. Some are very well worth buying if you know how to restore them yourself. Do *not* use any of these techniques on a family heirloom, or on any picture that might be valuable, without consulting an expert first.

OILS
Damage to oil paintings comes into several categories. The canvas may be torn or punctured by holes; or, if the painting is on wood, this may have split. Alternatively the varnish may have discoloured, mildewed or crazed, or the paint blistered or cracked.

Composition An oil painting is composed of a number of layers. First there is the canvas made of linen which is stretched and tacked round a wooden frame. Traditionally, the canvas is primed with a seal, made up of gesso or glue and water. Sometimes a coat of white lead paint is then applied. The picture itself is painted with pigments ground into a thick cream with linseed or poppy oil. This may be thinned further with more oil. Finally, the picture is coated with varnish which intensifies and protects the colours. A painting on a wood panel is generally built up in a similar way but, whereas blemished canvas can be renovated, wood which is split or damaged can only be repaired if you are skilled at retouching.

Unfortunately for the restorer, some artists do not work in a traditional fashion. All painters hope that they are working for posterity, but few are convinced that this is a definite possibility. Consequently, most tend to concentrate on the immediate demands of their subject and some use unconventional techniques in the process. In other words you cannot always know what has gone on between the canvas and the final coat of varnish.

Earlier renovations Nor can you rely on the fact that any previous renovation has been carried out according to the rules. In this century, picture restoration has been brought to a fine

art with the introduction of scientific cleaning methods. Previously, many restorers indulged in all kinds of practices which can complicate work today. When you look at a blemished oil painting, the cause and extent of the damage is not always obvious. Unless you have experience in the use of oil paint you should leave a picture alone if it is obvious that the paint must be re-touched.

CLEANING AN OIL PAINTING
If the painting is intact, clean the grime

1. *Large frames can be cut down and used to show off a favourite print or to make a surround for a mirror.*

2. *Junk shops, specializing in old pictures, can be sources of unexpected treasures needing just a little care and attention.*

off the surface of the varnish. There are many lubricants and solvents recommended for this but avoid linseed oil because it darkens, hardens when dry, proves completely insoluble when you want to clean it off and, in consequence, can only be picked away bit by bit. Use turpentine or white spirit only with the greatest caution because, although these will lift dirt and grease, they dissolve some varnishes and, if this happens, the original paintwork may be disturbed. Preferably, use a proprietary cleaner such

as CRP or wipe the picture with a swab of cotton wool dipped in a cup of cold water containing $\frac{1}{2}$ teaspoonful of ammonia. Your painting may be satisfactorily freshened by this treatment although the surface and colours still look dull. Either wipe a little wax polish over the finish and rub gently to a shine later, or brush on a coat of synthetic resin varnish which will not yellow with age.

Dealing with mildew Due to being hung or stored in a damp atmosphere some pictures are mildewed. The

187

fungus should be wiped off and a sheet of thick cartridge paper soaked in a 5% solution of Sanobrite should be inserted between the canvas and the back of the frame to discourage further attacks. Pictures should be hung in a room which is neither damp nor too dry. Keep them away from central heating and the heat from open fires or stoves, etc. A bloom on old varnish indicates that it was applied in unsuitable conditions. Polish it off the surface with Renaissance Wax Polish.

REMOVING BLEMISHED VARNISH
If, after cleaning, the picture remains brown and dull or the varnish is blemished, the latter will have to be removed. There are several types of varnish and you will have to experiment with different solvents on a part of the painting which will not show until you find one that dissolves the finish satisfactorily. In turn, try turpentine, white spirit, methylated spirit and refined pyridine on a pad of cotton wool. When you have discovered one which works (if there is more than one, choose the solvent which dissolves the varnish *slowest*) place a swab of cotton wool and a bottle of castor oil at hand. The castor oil must be dabbed on the work immediately to stop the action of the solvent if a suspicion of colour is seen on the pad – a chemical capable of dissolving varnish can also soften the paint – or if something odd starts to materialise. In the past, some restorers covered up damage under the varnish by painting and re-touching on top of it. They then varnished over that.
Start removing the varnish at one corner and work across the picture, finishing one patch at a time. Do not take off all the varnish; try to leave a thin layer to protect the paint. When you have finished, wipe the whole picture over with turpentine and leave the paint for a couple of days to harden. To revive the colours, apply a thin coat of pure copaiva balsam mixed with turpentine. When dry, varnish it with dammer varnish, picture mastic varnish or a modern synthetic varnish.

REPAIRING DAMAGED CANVAS
To repair an isolated hole or tear in the canvas cut a patch of new canvas slightly bigger than the blemish. Coat it on one side with a mixture made up of one part turpentine to five parts beeswax and five parts resin which has previously been heated and stirred gently in a saucepan. Stick this on to the back of the picture and press the torn canvas into its original position on the front. Now protect the front with several layers of greaseproof paper, put several more on the back and press the patch lightly with a very cool iron; if this is too hot the paint will blister.

RELINING A PAINTING
So often you find a really exciting painting with the canvas in poor condition generally. In an effort to prevent further degeneration the picture can be re-lined.
Remove the canvas very, very carefully from the stretcher, cutting it out with a razor blade if there is no other way to avoid bending or pulling the canvas and thus causing the paint to crack. Take a new piece of canvas of the required size, stretch it on a wooden frame and size it with a solution of gelatine previously melted in hot water. Paint it with a coat of the beeswax-resin-turpentine mixture described above. When dry, apply another coat and brush a coat on the back of the old canvas as well. Coated surfaces together, place the old canvas carefully on top of the new one, smooth over the surface to remove any air bubbles and press any ripped canvas into its original position. Protecting both sides with several layers of greaseproof paper and with the painting face down, press the whole canvas with the coolest of irons. When the sandwich of adhesive is set, the canvas may be returned to its original stretcher. If it had to be cut out you may have to get a smaller one. If this would mean that a portion of the painting was lost, you could trim the edges of the canvas and stick it onto a sheet of blockboard using the adhesive already mentioned.

CLEANING WATER-COLOURS AND PRINTS
Water-colours and Japanese prints are very difficult to clean because the colours run and leave tide-marks if they come into contact with water. Moreover, dry pigment can rub off if subjected to pressure.
Dirt Do not try to remove dirty marks with a rubber. Try erasing them by rolling fairly fresh breadcrumbs gently over the paper.
Grease To remove grease marks place a sheet of clean white blotting paper underneath the picture if it is un-mounted, and paint the spots with a fine sable brush dipped in petrol, benzene or pyridine.
Foxing causes those small, rusty-brown stains seen on old paper. They can be touched out with a fine brush dipped in equal parts of hydrogen peroxide and industrial methylated spirit. Alternatively, brush the stains and blot the liquid up with white blotting paper.
Miscellaneous stains may be shifted with chlorine solution which is then brushed away with distilled water, but you must be prepared to retouch and match the colours, which is a skilled job.
Mildew Most of the discolourations on old water-colours, prints, pastels and drawings come from the thoughtless way in which they were mounted. Very often the back of the paper was pasted with flour paste or glue which immediately attracted mould and fungus and often introduced colouring from the mounting board onto the water-colour paper. If the trouble is extensive there is no point in renovating further. But if you want to prevent a slight growth from developing further, the best way to remove the picture is to cut the mounting board very carefully away. If you can manage to insert a razor blade between the two you may make enough leeway to get to the point when you can soften the adhesive with steam. Hold the back of the picture near a boiling kettle and, when free, sterilize the back of the picture with Sanobrite.
Pastels are even more difficult to restore because the chalk is only a loose residue on the paper. If it is already shedding to the point where there is a deposit behind the glass at the bottom of the frame, take out the picture and spray it with a PVA fixitive.
Prints are easier to deal with altogether. Providing the colours are insoluble, the mounting can be soaked off if the print is immersed in water and dirt can be washed off in detergent solution, followed by a thorough rinse. Remember to handle the print very gently indeed. Never rub at marks while the paper is wet and easily torn. Prints should be dried naturally between sheets of clean white blotting paper and creases can be removed from dry prints if these are placed on a dry sheet of blotting paper, covered with a damp one and pressed with a cool iron.

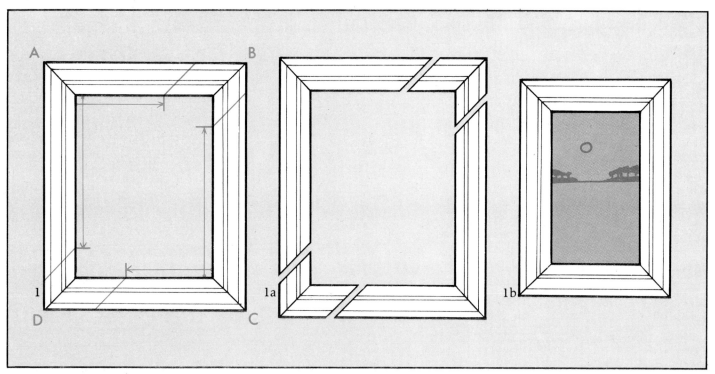

REPAIRING FRAMES

Having restored or at least improved your picture, it is time to turn your attention to the frame. If you bought the frame separately you may be disappointed to discover that it does not fit. Let us hope it is too big as, if it is made of wood, cutting it down should cause no problem. When measuring frames, always remember that the edge of the frame overlaps the picture, and that you must allow for this. Measure your picture and then measure the frame at the inside edge of the rebate which accommodates the glass. For simplicity's sake we will label the corners of your frame A, B, C and D. Only two of these corners, B and D, which are diagonally opposite each other, need be cut. Measure from corner of rebate A to corner of rebate B marking off the width of picture. Measure from C to D marking off the width. Measure from A to D marking off the length (1). Using a mitre box, cut the corners as marked (1a). Paste the cut edges with epoxy resin adhesive, bring together according to the directions and hold the two corners fast with corner cramps (1b).

A frame which fits, but has weak corners, can be strengthened with triangular or L-shaped steel plates. Secure them to the frame with short screws (2). A frame in this condition is probably dilapidated throughout. It can be made to look as good as new if you follow the directions for stripping and finishing given elsewhere. When stripping it, rather than using chemicals

which might weaken the joints further you would be wise to sand off the finish.

REGILDING A FRAME

Gilding with gold leaf is a professional job. This does not mean that you cannot achieve a very passable imitation yourself. Do not try to do it with gold paint, however, because even if the colour is right, the finish is wrong. Instead, use one of the gold waxes that are on the market, to imitate gold leaf when it is worn a little so that the gold size underneath is exposed (gold size

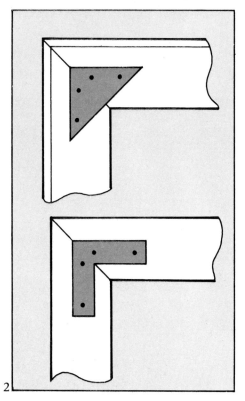

is commonly a dull, Chinese red). Look at some old gilding and then you will be able to buy the appropriate colour. If you can find the right shade in a polymer paint, so much the better. These are obtainable from art shops, are soluble in water but are insoluble when dry. Having painted your frame, buy some Restoration Wax or Treasure Wax Gilt in a convincing shade of gold and rub it into the frame with your finger; more in some parts than others.

REMOUNTING A PICTURE

Your print may have to be mounted and you may want a contrasting border or 'slip' round it before enclosing it in a frame.

A plain board slip is bevelled on the inside edge. To cut this edge you need a mount cutter's knife and a bevelled ruler to cut the 45 degree angle. Smooth any roughness that remains with finest sandpaper. To cover the slip with material, it is not necessary to bevel the edge of the mounting board. Stick a rectangle of fabric right over the front, cut mitred corners, stick the fabric onto the back of the board and trim away any surplus.

If you glue a print or picture to a mount permanently you automatically decrease its value. If the paper is not too fragile, smear an appropriate rubber solution over the back of the print and place it on the mounting board. Smooth the picture flat. Any solution that has squeezed out can be rubbed off when hard with an eraser formed from hardened rubber solution.

OLD PIECES TO NEW USES

People who like to browse in junk shops often buy objects which were once indispensible but have since fallen into disuse because their purpose has passed. Thus, a gophering iron, because it is attractive in itself, may be found ornamenting an occasional table instead of pressing fine pleats into a cotton or linen blouse or cap.

Enthusiasts sometimes find new uses for such relics: a Victorian chamber pot sprouts spring bulbs; a hefty copper tub, unearthed from an outhouse laundry, bears geraniums, nasturtiums, fuchsia, a mist of blue lobelia and sweet alyssum; old brass weights become doorstops.

Some of these byegones are very expensive. Much more expensive, say,

1

2

than a modern bulb bowl, urn or doorstop. But that is not the point. The older objects are valued because they are more interesting. Improvisation highlights their charm.

If you keep your eyes open and use your imagination, it is possible to find old pieces for conversion which will cost you nothing – or at least very little. The countryside is a fertile hunting-ground for such things. The inhabitants tend to hang on to items that have become obsolete or even, in some cases, put them to another use for practical reasons until fashion turns full circle and they come into favour in their original role. Country people are often amazed to find that someone has a use for the junk lying about at home.

1. *This spectacular drinks cabinet was once a rusty old iron stove. It was sandblasted to get rid of the old paint and rust, then sealed.*

2. *A very continental-looking sideboard adapted from a marble washstand.*

3. *An iron bedhead which has been renovated and screwed to the wall.*

4. *An old oak chest makes an interesting hall table.*

5. *The base of an old wardrobe, the top filled in with a cushion, makes a good chest for the end of the bed.*

DOING UP OLD BEDSTEADS

Old iron bedsteads are attractive and worth reviving. If you find an old one it will probably be covered in rust and much else. Wipe off the loose debris, then clean off as much rust as you can with a power drill plus a wire brush attachment. Finish with fine sandpaper. The iron will rust again unless you apply a rust preventive before painting. Do not necessarily paint it black – crimson, purple, brown, royal blue or emerald gloss would all give an equally glamorous effect.

It is possible that some brass knobs will be revealed in the preliminary stages of de-rusting. If so, keep the wire brush away from them, and unscrew them if possible. Attack the tarnish with a pad of fine steel wool dipped in scouring powder. Next, rub them with a similar pad moistened in harsh vinegar, then dipped in scouring powder and cooking salt. When the last of the tarnish has disappeared wash off the cleaning compound with soapy water and dry the knobs thoroughly. Buff them with metal polish and, if you want to avoid cleaning them in the future, wash off the invisible film left by the polish, dry the knobs once again and give them a coat of clear polyurethane lacquer.

The main structure of your bedhead is likely to be made of mild steel tube with cast-iron bars and embellishments. If this is so, the main supports at the side will be hollow and can be drilled so that the bedhead may be screwed to a divan with a wooden frame or to a wall behind. If you try to drill the steel tubing with an ordinary high-speed tungsten bit this will skid on the surface and you may simply make a dent in it. First provide a starting point by giving the spot a sharp bang with a spear-point bit.

Cast iron is very heavy, brittle and is easily cracked or snapped if dropped. None of the bars on a bed made entirely of cast iron are likely to be hollow. If your bedhead is entirely made of iron you could risk weakening the main supports if you drilled them. If you want to take the chance use a high-speed twist drill. Otherwise lash the bedhead to the frame of your divan or secure it to the wall behind with bayonet clips. It will probably be easier to manage if any castors are first removed. You can always replace them afterwards if it is convenient to have your bed on castors.

OLD PIECES TO CONVERT

Treasures may be found among disused farm implements. Look out, in particular, for old iron driver's seats of the ribbed kind so often fixed to horse-drawn agricultural machinery. When unscrewed and de-rusted such seats make very handsome, sculptural dishes for displaying fruit.

Junk yards Discoveries are also to be made in junk yards. Old earthenware sinks make ideal containers for a collection of alpine plants because, if the plug is left out, the drainage is suitable. For the same reason an old lavatory, even if it is not prettily patterned, can make a satisfactory container for a plant arrangement against an outside wall. It will look amusing instead of astonishing if you blur the silhouette slightly with trailing evergreens.

Galvanized metal tubs and baths with a handle at each end abound in junk yards. If sound and undented, these can be cleaned and given a coat of paint to great effect. Try decorating them with graduated stripes in a combination of Victorian colours such as bottle green and plum, and fill them with indoor plants.

Washstands Look out for washstands in such places. Some make marvellous sideboards. Large white enamelled metal jugs with blue rims are a common discovery. These used to be produced in a variety of graceful shapes and, if unchipped, make very attractive containers for flower arrangements of the simple, informal kind.

Mantels Second-hand furniture shops often have useful things put aside. Victorian and Edwardian mantels made of mahogany – or cunningly faked to look as if they were – are occasionally found. They often have elegant proportions and interesting shapes. Sometimes they include bevelled mirrors, little drawers and even lamps. Cleaned up or painted they make impressive bedheads when screwed to a wall. If, as may happen, you encounter one with a big space where the mirror was, fill it in with buttoned upholstery. In the absence of lamps, bore a hole at either side of the board through which to pass the electric flex. Connect the flex to brass brackets screwed to the board and fit them with perky little fringed shades.

Wardrobes Look for the base of an old-fashioned wardrobe. It will contain a roomy drawer and will make a good substitute for a chest at the end of a bed or for a long seat in a living room. The solid top will have a polished rim but the area where the top of the wardrobe was lodged will be unfinished. Hide it under a squab cushion with an attractive cover.

MAKING LAMP BASES

People get a lot of satisfaction out of converting unlikely objects into lamp bases. These usually fail to charm because the base does not make a well-proportioned support for the shade, or flex dangles untidily from the bulb holder which is a makeshift arrangement. A flex connected to the side of a holder fixed into a cork screwed into the bottleneck is unsightly and will make the lamp top-heavy.

Try to temper imagination with discrimination, therefore, by choosing a base which is hollow, heavy or capable of being weighted with sand. Near the bottom a hole will have to be drilled through which the flex can be threaded to connect to the bulb holder before this is firmly fixed in to the top. Cork-type bulb holders of this pattern are on sale.

When a hole is drilled in china or glass there is a risk that it will overheat and break. To keep the area cool whilst it is being bored, stick a little wall of plasticine or putty round the proposed hole which should be 5 mm. ($\frac{1}{4}$ in.) in diameter. Fill the resulting crater with cold water. Fit your power drill with a 5 mm. ($\frac{1}{4}$ in.) spear-point bit and start to drill gently, turning the whole drill round full circle at the beginning. To get the required delicacy of touch think about sitting in the dentist's chair. Rest frequently to keep the bit cool and be even more careful than before when you are almost finished. This is when most breakages occur.

Metal objects and figurines often make graceful lamp bases. The only difficulty in drilling any non-ferrous metal is to prevent the bit from skidding about and damaging the surface before it gets a hold. Even if the metal is solid, follow the instructions previously given for drilling a hole in a tubular steel bedhead.

BOTTLE CUTTING

Other things besides lamp bases can be made out of glass bottles by slicing them into sections. An effective ashtray, for instance, can be made out of a bottle with an indented base. The

1. Edwardian mantels like this, covered in dark varnish, can often be found in junk shops.

2. Stripped and painted a more cheerful colour it looks most attractive mounted on the wall.

bottle is held by a patent tool fitted with a blade which scratches a line round the bottle when it is rotated. The scratch is heated by turning the bottle above a candle. It is then rubbed with ice. If the bottle does not separate when pulled lightly apart the hot and cold process is repeated. Sharp edges are smoothed with fine emery paper.

TREADLE SEWING-MACHINES

Confirmed converters are usually keen to transform the metal stands of old treadle sewing-machines into tables. These stands are made of cast iron and when richly ornamented make very pretty tables if fitted to a suitable top. Remove the unsightly leather band which activates the wheel and immobilize the latter by binding it with wire to an immovable part elsewhere.

Sometimes the wooden top which incorporates a useful drawer is still fitted to the stand. The gap in which the machine was lodged may be filled with a sheet of plate glass.

If you want to fit a larger table you will find that the stand has four screw holes for fixing it. There is no doubt that a marble one will look best. If you happen to have a marble slab you will find that it is relatively easy to cut a square or rectangular top out of it. Mark the cutting line along the top, bottom and sides very accurately and then score all round with a carbide-tipped tile-cutting tool. Saw a deep notch at either end with a hacksaw. Leave the slab unsupported where you want the break to occur and stand on this part. Finish the edges with a sanding disc fitted to your power drill.

2

YOUR TOOL KIT

Look after your tools: keep them together in one bag or box, so you can find them when necessary. Protect them from damp and grease lightly to protect against rust.

TOOLS YOU MAY NEED

Bradawl (1) Use the spiked end to make a small hole in wood before driving in a screw with a screwdriver. Alternatively use a gimlet.

Clamps (2) Two or three 'G' clamps in various sizes are used for holding sections of wood together while glue sets, handy for repairing furniture as well as for new constructions. Clamping is essential when repairing wood which has broken across the grain.

Drill (3) Hand or electric drill fitted with the appropriate 'bit' can be used for making holes in timber, masonry, etc., when building furniture or putting up shelves. The drill bit (3a) is the part that actually bores the hole and you change your bit according to the type of work you are doing. *Twist* drill bits are used for making holes in wood and *masonry* drill bits are for making holes in brick or stone. Drill bits come in various sizes to make holes of differing diameters: you have to match your bit to the size of your screw.

To operate a hand drill (3b): first insert the appropriate bit by twisting the outer cover to open the chuck jaws. Use your left hand to hold the drill steady and your right hand to turn the handle at the side. Before drilling wood make a small indentation with hammer and nail to prevent drill from wandering. On walls, drill into plaster through sticky tape to prevent plaster flaking away or cracking.

Electric drill Particularly useful for women, as it takes the strain out of many heavier jobs. A two-speed, or variable-speed drill, is a better buy as you will find that you can use it for a wider range of surfaces (you will need to use the slower speed for making holes in hard masonry).

The manufacturer's instructions will show you how to fit different bits into the drill chuck (3c) – the part that holds the bits. There are several different types of bits, including carbon steel twist drills for wood, and high-speed steel twist drills for metal. Your supplier or manufacturer will advise on the correct bit for the job. Always make sure you are drilling at right angles to the work surface; you can line up your work with a try-square standing on its end, or you can buy a special drill stand. Various attachments are available for your basic drill unit: these include sanding and polishing discs, and circular saw attachments.

Rawldrill Inexpensive alternative to a drill for making holes in masonry. Tap gently with a hammer, turn and tap again. Tap a bit harder when you are through the plaster.

Hammer (4) Every home should have one! Most useful type is a claw hammer with a 454 g. (16 oz.) head firmly fastened to the handle. You can use the 'claw' end to lever out old or crooked nails. For light work, use a Warrington hammer (4a) which has a narrow tapered end (the pein) for starting small panel pins, etc.

Nailing hints: place the head of the hammer squarely on the nail, which is held in the left hand, and start off with a few light taps, holding the hammer near the head. Then remove your left hand, change your grip to the end of the hammer and strike firm blows from the elbow. Nails with glue will give a strong joint. Always join the thinner pieces of wood to the thicker. Reduce the possibility of splitting by starting each nail in a hole made with a bradawl. Do not fix nails in a line along the grain of a piece of timber, but stagger them. This reduces the risk of splitting the wood.

Hacksaw (5) Multi-purpose saw with removable blade; useful for many small cutting jobs, in particular for sawing through metal pipes and rods. Replace blades frequently and try and keep saw horizontal as you work. Do not attempt to cut too quickly.

Small general purpose hand-saw (6) This has a stiff blade and small cutting teeth, for cutting timber. Always mark your timber with a cutting guide line, and saw on the waste side of this line. Place your work at knee level, and make a few backward upward strokes to start off. Then do the real work with downward long slow easy strokes, keeping the saw at an angle of about 45 degrees to the board. As you finish your work support the waste or it may break away and splinter.

Tenon saw (7) With stiffened back this is used for cutting joints; use in conjunction with a mitre block for cutting mitres (45 degree cuts), for framing, etc.

Pliers (8) A useful cutting, pulling and levering tool. The head tip will grip small objects such as protruding nails; the cut-away circular section will grip small pipes, etc; the cutter blades will sever wire.

Screwdriver (9) It is essential to have at least two – a medium size carpenter's screwdriver with tapered tip will do for most general work. The ratchet

kind (9a), though more expensive, is easier for women to use, as less strength is needed in the wrist. A screw always needs to be started with a hole in the wood. Sizes up to number 6 can be started with a bradawl or gimlet. For larger sizes, you must drill a pilot hole first, slightly smaller than the size of your screw. Ideally the tip of your screwdriver blade should be slightly less than the length of your screw slot. You can mark your work if it is wider; if it is not wide enough, you will not be able to apply sufficient pressure. Watch

out for screws with cross-cut heads, e.g. Pozidrive; these need a special screwdriver to undo them, or to drive them in. You will need a small electrical screwdriver for fiddly work such as changing plugs.

Small portable vice (10) Holds work steady while you drill, cut, etc. It makes your job much easier, and leaves you two hands free. Can be fixed to any convenient surface.

Staplegun (11) Useful tool for re-covering chair seats, covering walls with fabric, stapling carpet edge, etc.

Steel rule (12) Essential for all types of measuring. Cloth tapes can sag.

Surform (13) An easy-to-use range of tools for shaping wood. Use a Surform plane at a 45 degree angle to the grain of the wood, with most of the pressure on the forward stroke.

Trimming knife (14) Useful multi-purpose tool for trimming all kinds of sheet materials, including hardboard, plastic laminates, etc. Blades can be changed to suit work: e.g. use a hooked blade for cutting sheet vinyl. Most have retractible blades for safety.

HEATING THE HOME

OPEN FIRES

The open fire, which many people regard as Britain's greatest contribution to home comfort, has made a comeback. For a time it went out of favour, displaced by heating methods which were said to be more flexible, more convenient and more efficient, but many families cherish an open fire's comforting red glow and flickering flames.

In any case, solid fuel has to some extent caught up with the competition, for its heaters are now much more efficient, much better to look at, not as troublesome to stoke and clean out as they were and have acquired some form of automatic control, for they can now be fitted with thermostats.

TYPES OF FIRE

A solid fuel fire has to burn in a grate so that air can come up through its bars, and 'feed' the combustion. The old-fashioned kind – the 'stool bottom' grates – merely stand in position on the back hearth, surrounded by the fireback. They also have a movable ashpit cover, of which the main function is to hide the untidiness of the pile of ash that has gathered on the back hearth, or in the ash pan. The ashpit covers usually have a grille that can be opened or closed to effect a rudimentary form of air control. These grates are an inefficient way of burning solid fuel, and are better replaced by something more modern.

There are two possibilities. First, there is the modern inset open fire, which is the updated version of the stool-bottom grate. This used to be known as the 'all-night fire' when it was first introduced just after the war, because the fact that it could burn continuously seemed then to be its outstanding attribute. Alternatively, you can have a room heater, an enclosed stove-like appliance with a glass front, which may or may not be an opening door. Both are very efficient appliances. In addition to heating the room, they can have a back boiler that will provide not only hot water, but also, especially in the case of the room heater, power several radiators as well.

Both types of appliance are fixed, and if you are getting a new one then make sure it is properly installed by an approved dealer.

The important point about these modern appliances is that the flow of air can be adjusted more effectively. You increase the supply of air when you want to speed up the rate of burning, and shut it down when you want the fire merely to 'idle'. To effect this control, usually you turn a knob on the front, and that opens a section of the ashpit cover. Some of the appliances are much more sophisticated than that, however, for they have electrically operated fans which give you even greater air control. Some room heaters, too, have hoppers that stoke the fire automatically, and thermostatic controls (when you reach the desired temperature, they shut down the flow of air) can also be fitted. Heaters where you end up with just one lump of clinker instead of a pan full of ash, thus making cleaning out a lot easier, can also be bought. If you want to see what is currently available on the market, go and visit your local builder's merchant.

EFFICIENT OPERATION

For these appliances to work properly, they must be well sealed where they meet the fireplace and hearth. Check the seal on yours this way. Have the fire well alight, close the air control, then run a lighted taper all round the joint. The seal needs attention at any point where the flame is drawn inwards. If you find any defects, point them with fire cement.

A throat restrictor is well worth fitting to an open fire without a boiler. The throat of a fireplace is that part just over the fire opening through which smoke passes on its way to the flue. Get your builder to fit the restrictor, which is a metal plate with an adjustable opening. You can then cut down on the flow of air taken up the flue by the draught of the fire. Thus, less cold air will be drawn into the room, which will be warmer as a result.

FIRE LIGHTING

The best way to light a fire is with gas. Many authorities insist that you use gas in a smokeless zone, although some do not, especially if there is no gas supply to the house. A possible alternative is the electric fire lighter.

Some modern appliances come with gas ignition fitted, but a gas poker will do instead. When using gas, always apply the light before you turn on the gas.

Of course, there is always the old method of using newspaper and firewood, which are cheaper than commercial firelighters, though perhaps a little more trouble.

When using sticks and paper, first clear the grate and ashpan entirely of cinders. If the fuel is coal, enough must be put on top of the paper and sticks to light the fire, but not so much that you smother it. With coke and other smokeless fuels, pile on as much as the grate will hold. These fuels also need more paper and sticks than coal.

Whichever method you adopt, open up the air fully, then apply the light. When the fire is going well add more fuel. Turn down the air control when it starts to burn brightly.

THE FUELS

There are two basic types – the natural fuels, which come straight from the mines after being washed and sized, and the processed ones. House coal is an instance of the former. It is cheaper than most other solid fuels, and burns with the long, bright flames that make an open fire so attractive. However, it cannot normally be used in a smokeless zone. But some modern room heaters – known as the Smoke Eater type – can burn coal and still comply with the smoke control regulations. Anthracite is a natural smokeless fuel, more suited to room heaters and boilers than open fires.

The processed fuels (e.g. Sunbrite and Phumacite) are manufactured from the natural ones, to produce special characteristics, among which smokeless burning will figure prominently. Ask your dealer what he has available, and consult with him on what will be the most suitable for your appliance.

Coke is becoming harder to get as the gas works that used to produce it close down with the advent of natural gas.

At one time, you controlled the heat of the fire by the size of the coal you placed on it. Nowadays we have the more accurate method of using the air supply to get a fast or slow burning fire.

STOKING

It is false economy to try to control

Modern storage heaters fit
very well into an elegant
setting.

198

your fire by the amount of fuel you place on it. Better to keep the grate always well full, and adjust the amount of heat with the air control. Modern smokeless fuels need a high temperature for burning, and if you let the fire go down too low before you refuel it, it might take a long time to get going again, and could burn out.

Be sparing with the poker. A long thin poker is best, as it helps you to push the ash through the grate bars without disturbing the firebed too much.

If you have a back boiler, try to avoid attempting to boost the hot water supply by short periods of intense burning. This can damage the grate. It is more economical in fuel to keep the fire burning at a steady rate, ensuring a constant supply of hot water. Brush down the boiler surfaces and flueway at least once a fortnight to keep them clear of soot and ash, for these deposits can reduce the amount of heat getting to the boiler.

ROOM HEATERS

The firedoor and ashpit cover should fit snugly – have them attended to if they do not. Any broken glass should be replaced immediately.

Keep the firebox well filled, and the ashpit cover on. As with an open fire, regulate the burning with the air control – not the amount of fuel on the fire.

Some heaters are fitted with firebrick linings. If these get damaged, repair them with fire cement.

OVERNIGHT BURNING

It is more economic to keep your fire burning slowly all night than to heat the room up from cold next morning. It helps to avoid condensation, too.

CHIMNEY SWEEPING

One of the advantages of smokeless fuels is that the chimney does not need sweeping so often – perhaps no more than once every two or three years. But with a coal fire, you should call in the sweep at the end of every heating season – preferably in the summer when you can do without a fire.

REMOVING A FIREPLACE

If your problem is how to get rid of a fireplace you no longer want, remember that the job of removing it calls more for muscle than for skill. The fire surround is fixed by means of screws driven into wall plugs through small lugs on the edge of the fireplace. The exact number and position of these lugs varies from make to make. You cannot see them because they are buried under the plaster, so you have to scrape down to the bare brick all round the surround until they are laid bare. Then you withdraw the screws, and lift the surround clear, bearing in mind that it will be very heavy. The hearth is cemented in place, and needs to be forced up, using a crowbar or stout garden spade as a lever.

The wall can be covered up in many ways. The fire opening can be properly bricked in then re-plastered (a job for a builder, this), or you can use, say, a sheet of asbestos or plywood. Many people, in fact, do not bother about removing an unwanted fireplace, but merely cover it with built-in furniture, a bedhead, for instance.

Whatever you do, you should always leave an unused flue well ventilated. This can be done efficiently by means of a small metal grille. If you block it off completely, damp might get into it and penetrate through to the walls of the room, damaging the decorations.

A NEW FIREPLACE

If you are thinking of having a new fire surround installed, there is a wide range of materials from which to choose – slate, marble, stone (either natural or artificial) and metal, as well as the traditional tiles.

Should you have any problems with solid fuel, get in touch with your local branch of the Solid Fuel Advisory Service. If you cannot find them in the telephone directory, their head office is at the National Coal Board, Hobart House, Grosvenor Place, London, S.W.1.

CENTRAL HEATING

There are two basic types of central heating. One is called the 'wet' system, because it works by means of radiators supplied with hot water; the second, known as the 'dry' system, sends warm air around the house via a layout of ducts. The first is the most popular in Britain, and it is the one you must usually choose if you wish to install central heating in a house that does not have any. The ducts of a warm air system are so big that they have to be incorporated into the structure of the house whilst it is being built. The warm air is circulated through all the rooms by means of a fan.

WET SYSTEMS

Wet central heating systems can be powered by gas, oil or solid fuel. There are also electric boilers, but they have never become popular. All of the three main fuels can be used to power a free-standing boiler, sited in the kitchen or outhouse. The modern open fire in the living room can also have a back boiler of high enough output to supply radiators as well as hot water. So can the room heater, which is the highly efficient stove-like appliance with glass fronted doors.

If you are ordering a central heating system, you must get your installer to tell you at the outset how effective it will be. The usual way of measuring this is to specify the temperature it will provide when the weather outside is at freezing point. The best installers will give you a written temperature guarantee, though how easy this would be to enforce is a matter of speculation. **The ideal temperature** What is the best temperature for a house? This is a highly individual matter, but, in general, 21°C (70°F) would allow you to wander around the house in shirt sleeves, whilst at 18°C (65°F) most people would want to put on a sweater. Anything under 18°C would be merely background heating.

You do not have to have the same temperature in every room. The radiators can be varied so that whilst it is, say, 21°C in the living-room, the bedrooms are at 18°C, and the hall and landing 15°C.

The insistence on better standards of house insulation, following the fuel crises of recent years, has meant that these temperatures are easier to reach with small appliances. And full central heating can be achieved with the better living-room fires.

CHOICE OF FUEL

Which fuel should you choose? This is a very complex question, the answer to which depends on a lot of factors.

If gas is available, it has many advantages. There are no storage or delivery problems, it is a flexible fuel that can be controlled automatically by a programmer, and its installation costs are highly competitive.

Solid fuel systems, too, are comparatively cheap to put in, and to run – especially those based on the living-room fire. Although a coal fire obviously cannot be switched on and off by a programmer, the range of automatic controls of these appliances has been greatly extended over the past few years. You do, however, have to store a fairly large amount of fuel, and you must be sure that your coal merchant will deliver to you regularly. Furthermore solid fuel boilers involve more work because they have to be stoked regularly, and you must clear the ash from them. However, with modern appliances these chores are not so irksome as they used to be, and need not be carried out so often.

The enormous rise in crude oil prices at the end of 1974 made oil for domestic use very expensive. An oil fired system is costly to install, and you have to find room for the storage tank. Moreover, the fuel has to be delivered to you. Nevertheless, it is a flexible fuel, simple to use and capable of being controlled automatically.

All these considerations, however, can be upset by the construction and location of your house. If there is no proper fireplace or flue, then the installation cost of a solid fuel appliance could soar. Your house has to be accessible to the delivery lorries if you are to have oil.

THE SYSTEM IN OPERATION

However, let us see how a wet system of central heating works. As water is heated up in the boiler, two things will happen to it. Some of it will go off round the radiator system, driven by a pump. When the pump is in operation, the water is continually on the move, being warmed up in the boiler, cooling down in the radiators as it warms up the rooms, and coming back to be re-heated.

The rest of the water goes up to the cylinder in the airing cupboard, where the hot water for the kitchen and bathroom taps – the domestic hot water, as it is known – is stored. But it does not go directly into this cylinder, as it would in a system supplying only domestic hot water. Instead, it enters an inner coil – or calorifier – and the heat from this warms up the water in the main cylinder. Thus the heating and the domestic hot water are kept entirely separate. There are two reasons for this. In the first place, you do not want to draw off at the taps dirty water that has swirled all round the radiators. Secondly, you can take a lot of water from the cylinder without cooling down the radiators.

The system has its own cold tank in the loft (the equivalent of the tank that supplies cold water to the rest of the house) to make sure that it is kept topped up with enough water. Both tanks need protection against frost.

Thermostatic controls The system can be controlled thermostatically in three ways. First, the temperature of the water in the boiler can be regulated by a thermostat. In the case of the really flexible fuels – gas and oil – when the required temperature is reached, the main jets will shut off completely, leaving just a pilot light burning. With solid fuel the control is not quite so fine, but the supply of air to the fire is shut down, thus slowing the rate of combustion.

Secondly, a thermostat governing the pump can be positioned on the wall of one of the rooms in the house. When that room reaches the selected temperature, the pump is turned off, and that stops the circulation of hot water, until the room cools, and the thermostat switches on the pump again. It is a rough and ready arrangement, the snag being that a thermostat in one position determines the heat requirement of every room.

There is, however, another possibility, and that is for the radiator in each room to be fitted with a thermostatic valve which closes and cuts off the supply of hot water when the desired temperature is reached. These valves take the place of the wheel valve which you turn by hand when you want to close down the radiator. If you specify them when the system is being installed, then, since you are dispensing with a room thermostat, there will not be much extra cost. You can also have the manual valves on an existing system replaced by thermostatic ones.

Both room and radiator thermostats can be fitted to solid fuel, as well as oil and gas, systems.

The other control is a clock that turns the heating on and off as you wish. It can be set to bring the heat on just before you get up and switch it off as you go to bed, and in addition it can make the system lie idle during the day. Clocks with three on-off operations, for people who come home at midday, are also available.

With oil and gas, the clock will once again turn the main burners on and off as required, as well as shutting down the pump. In the case of solid fuel, it is only the pump that can be time-controlled.

Maintenance All the three fuel authorities offer maintenance arrangements for their heating systems, and you should take advantage of one of them. There are, however, one or two things you can do yourself. For instance, the pump will give less trouble if it is not allowed to lie idle for the whole summer season. So even during hot weather you should run it about once a week for just a few minutes, to give it exercise so to speak. You run the pump by setting the programmer to central heating, instead of to hot water alone.

Another thing you can do is 'bleed' the radiators. A radiator should be so hot when the system is full on that you can hardly bear to touch it with your hand. If it is hot at the bottom, but cold at the top, then air is trapped in it. You let it out by fitting the radiator key (one is supplied when the heating is installed, but they are very cheap to buy) on the square tap inside the air-cock situated at one side of the radiator near the top. As you turn the tap you will hear the air hissing out. Keep an old cup handy to catch the dirty black water that spurts out when the air is released. Then quickly close the tap again.

Sometimes you might get a slight seepage of water near the nuts that hold the radiator valves in place. Try to cure this by tightening up the nut with a spanner. But do not overtighten it or you could make matters worse. Try first turning the nut a quarter of a turn. If that fails to cure the leak, try another quarter turn, then perhaps another. If the water still leaks, you need a plumber.

You will find similar nuts in various parts of the system – on the boiler connections, for instance, and in the middle of some lengths of pipe. Any leaks there should be dealt with in the same way. For leaks elsewhere, you must call in a plumber.

If the system fails Should an oil or gas boiler not be working, check that the time switch is on, that the thermostat is at a high enough setting, that the pilot light is on, and that the electricity supply to the programmer is on. If the boiler does not work after all these checks, then you need professional assistance.

Painting radiators When radiators are supplied, they will usually have been treated with a priming paint. One or two coats of gloss are all that is

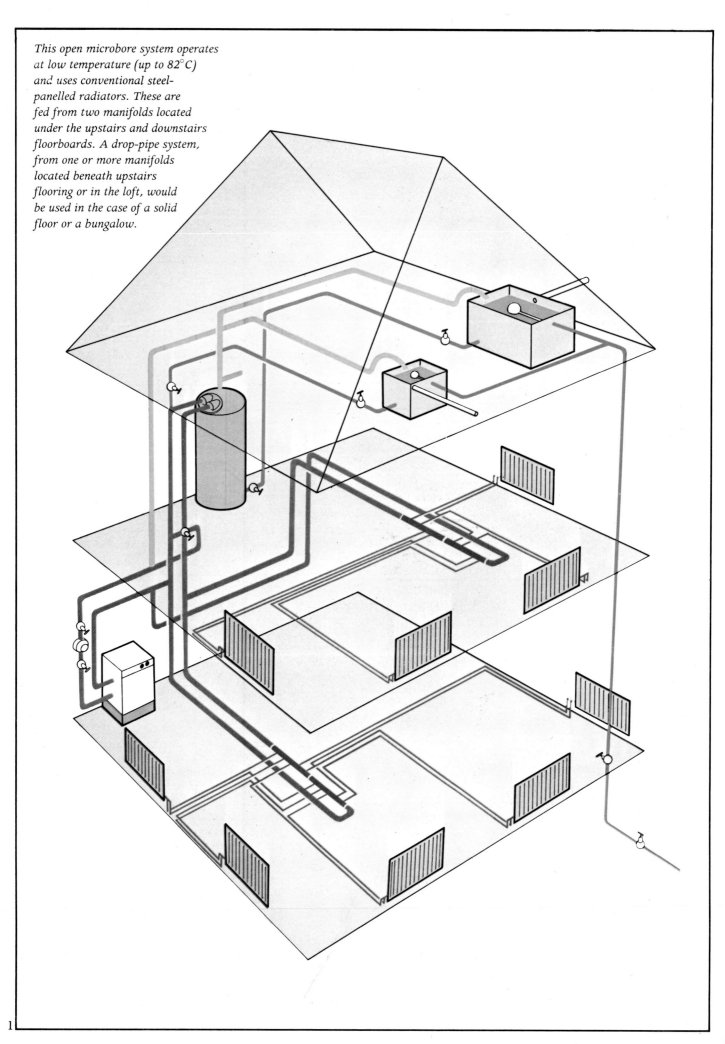

This open microbore system operates at low temperature (up to 82°C) and uses conventional steel-panelled radiators. These are fed from two manifolds located under the upstairs and downstairs floorboards. A drop-pipe system, from one or more manifolds located beneath upstairs flooring or in the loft, would be used in the case of a solid floor or a bungalow.

needed to bring them up to full decorative standard. Do not use a metallic paint, which will impede the emission of heat. Too big a build-up of paint will have the same effect, so when a radiator has been re-painted several times it will be necessary to take off all the old paint with a stripper before you re-decorate again. The best time to paint a radiator is in the spring, to give it the whole summer in which to settle down before it has to withstand heat.

To make it easier to decorate the wall behind a radiator, it is possible to close the wheel valve, slacken off the valve nuts, loosen the radiator from its brackets at the top, and let it roll down to the ground. There is, however, a risk of wrenching the bottom brackets from the wall, or breaking the water-proof joint of the valves. If you are papering the wall, it is safer to push the paper down the back of a panel radiator then push your hands up under the bottom, and pull the paper through. If you are painting, then you just have to stretch the brush as far behind the radiator as you can.

Special radiator brushes are available to help you paint the back of radiators.

'DRY' OR WARM-AIR SYSTEMS

These have many advantages. They are much cheaper to install if they are put in whilst the house is being built, for there are no radiators, and the ducts are made of much cheaper material than the copper pipes that carry hot water around. Less skill is needed in the installation. A grille does not take up as much space as a radiator.

The systems are highly flexible. Heaters can be controlled by thermostats and time clocks, just like 'wet' boilers, but in addition it is possible to close one or more of the grilles to concentrate all the heat in one room when a quick build-up is needed. In summer, they can be run cold to improve ventilation. The main snag, though, is that most of them – though not all – cannot also supply hot water, so you then need an extra appliance for that.

The system at work This is how hot air systems work. They consist of a burner unit, a fan and a heat exchanger – a column of metal fins. The burner heats the fins, and the fan blows air over them, sending it via a series of metal ducts to the various

rooms in the house. There the warmed air will emerge from a grille set low down in the room. There will be a corresponding grille high up in the room, and through this air is drawn back to the exchanger to be heated up. Warm air rises, so that the air released at floor level will quickly find its way to the rest of the room.

This type of system cannot supply domestic water. There is, however, another kind, much less common, in which the heat exchanger is warmed by water heated up in a boiler. With this you can have domestic hot water. Warm air systems are mainly powered by gas or oil, with all the advantages and disadvantages of those fuels. Electric warm air heating is also possible. The Electricaire unit is a king-sized storage heater, the output of which is boosted by a fan, sending warm air along a series of ducts to the rest of the house. This is possibly the easiest warm air system to install in an existing house, but it does not provide such whole-house comfort as the others. There are, too, solid fuel convector

heaters that can disperse the heat to other rooms via ducts.

With warm air systems there is little to go wrong, although the system should be regularly maintained. If the boiler does not work, then follow the procedure outlined in the description of 'wet' boilers.

KEEPING DOWN RUNNING COSTS

Whichever type of heating you have, one of your main concerns will be keeping down the running costs. It is vital, therefore, to have your house well insulated. Even after that, there is a lot you can do to make the bills more reasonable. For instance, try setting the clock to switch on a little later in the morning, and go off a bit sooner at night. You will save only a small amount of fuel each time, but it soon mounts up. Experiment with the setting of the thermostats. You could well reduce them by a few degrees without any of your family feeling uncomfortable. Here again the savings would be significant only over a long period.

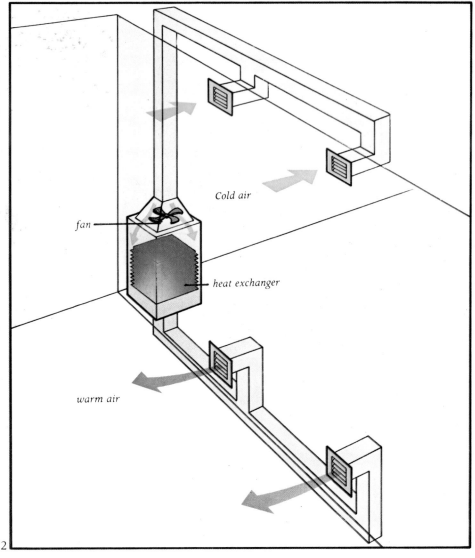

fan

Cold air

heat exchanger

warm air

1. *The microbore system*
2. *Warm air heating system*

2

LIVING WITH GAS

THE GAS BILL

Town or natural gas is piped to the home through a supply tap and a meter similar to the electricity meter except the measurement is in cubic feet. You pay a fixed charge each quarter which is the standing primary or metering charge and a charge for each *therm* of gas used.

To work out from your meter the number of therms you have used you need to know the *calorific value* of the gas used in your area and this is expressed in British Thermal Units. The calorific value of natural gas is between 1017 and 1035 so a quick rough guide is to divide cubic feet by 100 to give you the number of therms. For a more accurate figure, or if you are using town gas, take the number of cubic feet of gas used and multiply by the calorific value figure and divide the total by 100,000. This gives the number of therms. With the coming of metrication gas will be measured in *new therms* based on kilojoules rather than BTUs.

Two-part tariff If you use a lot of gas for central heating and cooking it may save money to ask the Gas Region to put you on one of the tariffs where you pay a higher standing charge but lower cost per therm. The tariffs go under a variety of names, such as 'two part', 'silver star' or 'gold star'.

Alternative tariffs If you use more than 150 therms of gas a year (about 35 therms a quarter) then ask about the alternative tariffs. If you have only a gas cooker it is unlikely you would use more than 100 therms in a year but a gas heater could add another 60 therms and gas water heating 200 therms. Gas central heating in an average sized house will use about 1,000 therms so it is essential, even if you cook by electricity, to be on some sort of bulk discount rate. All Gas Regions have helpful leaflets.

To check your gas bill, take last year's bill for the same quarter and compare the number of therms consumed.

GAS SAFETY

Natural gas is not poisonous because, unlike town gas, it contains no carbon monoxide. It can, however, still be dangerous. It can explode and if gas heaters and gas water heaters are not installed properly nor given the proper ventilation (most need a flue or chimney to the outdoors) then incomplete combustion can create carbon monoxide with dangerous results.

There are strict laws about gas safety (Gas Safety Regulations 1972). You would be committing an offence if you use, or let anyone else use, any gas appliances in a room that is not properly ventilated, or where the products of combustion are not adequately removed, or where the appliance is 'so faulty or maladjusted that it cannot be used without constituting a danger to any person or property'.

In an emergency All the Gas Regions operate a 24 hour emergency service. They have a legal obligation to get to a gas leak within 24 hours, but in practice they will arrive within two or three hours. There is no charge if the leak is their side of the supply tap which is the Gas Region's property but there is normally a charge for mending leaks on your side of the tap. If you find you have a leak then turn off the supply tap before you telephone the emergency service whose telephone number will be in the telephone directory under 'GAS'.

Never try to track down a leak with a naked flame. Rub a little liquid detergent around the suspect joint. If the liquid bubbles there is a leak but take care not to let any detergent get into burner parts or holes.

Gas appliances must always be installed either by the Gas Region or by a firm which shows the registered mark of CORGI (Confederation for the Registration of Gas Installers).

CARE OF GAS APPLIANCES

It is best never to tamper with gas appliances other than simple cleaning and maintenance. Gas central heating boilers should be serviced annually by the Gas Region or a CORGI member. There are three types of maintenance contract: a basic annual clean and adjustment and if anything needs repairing or replacing you pay for the parts and labour. The second type of contract covers the cost of parts; the third parts and labour. A modern system may only need the basic contract but if you have had trouble it may pay you to have the full comprehensive contract.

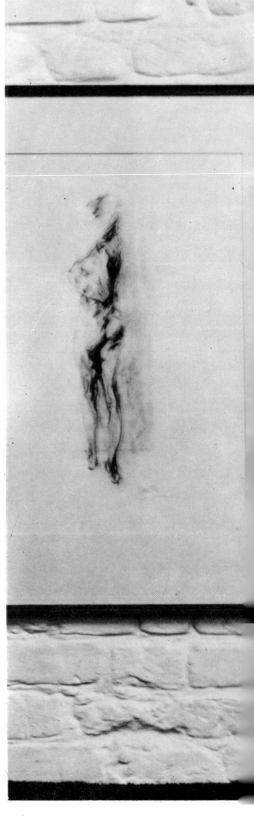

With gas room heaters you may have to replace the clay bars which glow and keep the heat from the burners. There are two types – box and bar – and they fit into slots each side. Replacements are easily obtainable but it is as well to keep spares.

Many fires have automatic ignition from a small battery which will need removing at intervals. Some also have

in electric bulb to give a glow beneath he fuel effect. The bulb is replaced by ifting the fuel effect. Clean the metal discs that create the flame effect at the same time.

Small water heaters can be cleaned and adjusted simply by removing the front panel but follow the maker's instructions. The automatic flame ignition on water heaters and cookers may depend on a pilot jet which can get blocked. It can be cleaned using a specially designed pricker available from Gas Region shops. Do not try to clean it with a hair pin.

GAS CONSUMER COUNCILS
Like the Electricity Boards, the Gas Regions have regional, independent councils to look after the interests of

Gas logs cleverly designed to give the illusion of warmth.

their customers and to handle complaints. The address of the local council is displayed in the Gas Region shops or can be obtained from them, or found in the telephone directory. Do not hesitate to use them if you are not getting proper service.

KNOWING ABOUT ELECTRICITY

ELECTRICITY AND WIRING

There is no need to be frightened of electricity provided it is treated with respect and a few simple rules are followed.

The basic fact about electricity is that it cannot be used until a circuit is completed. An electric current, which is made up of moving electrons, flows rather like water in a pipe, except that it needs a complete circuit through the switch and the appliance and back in order to flow. The two principal wires – 'live' and 'neutral' – connected to an appliance provide this circuit.

Electricity is generated and distributed through a complex distribution system. Every home is supplied from a nearby sub-station which provides electricity at a standard 240 volts. To protect the distribution system one of the supply cables is connected to the earth near the power station and the sub-station. This is the 'neutral' cable, the other cable is the 'live'. A third wire is used in the home in the interests of home safety: this is the 'earth'. Without the 'earth' wire, some types of electrical fault on an appliance could cause a shock if you touched the appliance. For instance, if an uninsulated live wire touches the metal case of an appliance which has no earth connection, there is no safe path to earth for electricity and the fuse may not blow. But if you touched the case of the appliance your body would provide the circuit to earth and you would get an electric shock (see page 243). If the metal case is properly earthed, a complete circuit will be created and a large fault current will flow through this circuit, blowing the fuse and telling you that the appliance or wiring is faulty.

A thick, armoured, two core service cable brings electricity into the home to a fuse unit sealed by the Electricity Board. If this fuse fails call the emergency service of the Electricity Board (it is in the telephone directory but it is a good idea to write the number on the wall close to the meter). Check all the other fuses in the house first as it is rare for this fuse to blow. Check with neighbours that it is not a power cut.

The service cable goes via the electricity meter to the mains switch. In houses thirty or more years old it is still common to find the mains switch in a separate box but in modern homes it is part of the fuse box where the main circuit is split into a number of separate circuits each with its own fuse (1).

Householder's responsibility The electrical equipment and wiring from the meter onwards is the responsibility of the householder. The householder also has to make sure there is an effective earth wiring point to which all the other earth wires in the home are connected. Now that non-metal water pipes are being used, a water pipe can no longer be used as a reliable 'earth' path and an earth connection must be installed by an electrician who usually takes it back to the sheath of the service cable – or, in certain areas, may install a device with an automatic switch called an 'earth leakage circuit breaker'. From the fuse box (sometimes called the consumer's unit), cables form separate circuits, each containing the two supply wires, live and neutral, and the earth wire. In these cables the live is *coloured red and the neutral black* (flexes have different colours). The earth wire is usually a bare conductor but all three are covered with an in-

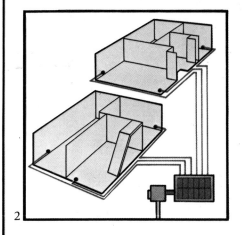

2

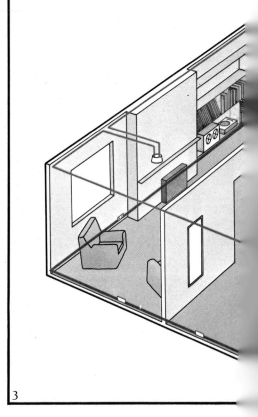

3

2. The old type radial system.
3. The modern circuit system, in which wall sockets are connected by a single continuous loop of cable, one for upstairs and one for downstairs. The cooker, water heating and lighting all have separate circuits and fuses.

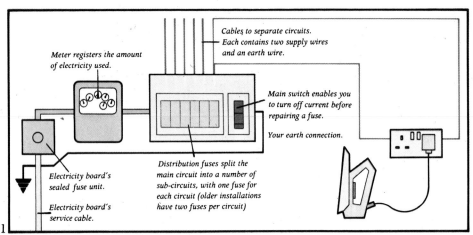

Meter registers the amount of electricity used.

Cables to separate circuits. Each contains two supply wires and an earth wire.

Main switch enables you to turn off current before repairing a fuse.

Your earth connection.

Electricity board's sealed fuse unit.

Electricity board's service cable.

Distribution fuses split the main circuit into a number of sub-circuits, with one fuse for each circuit (older installations have two fuses per circuit)

1

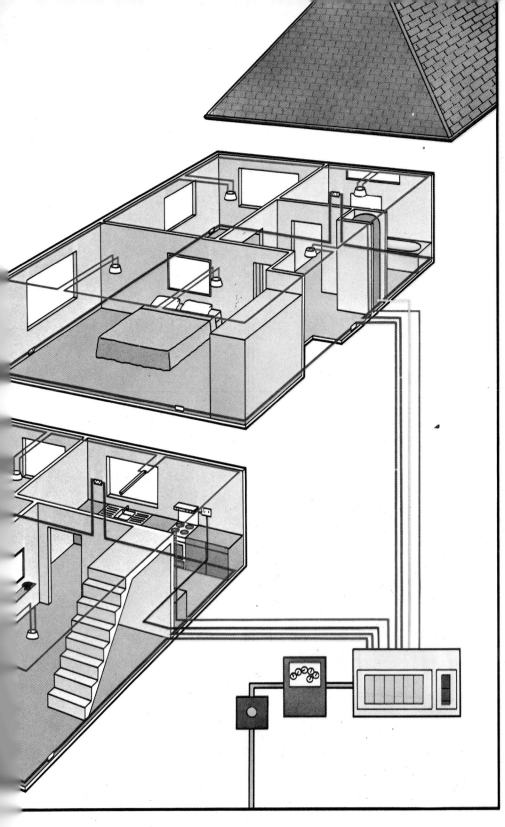

up to 3000 watts rating. This type of socket has safety shutters which automatically close when the plug is withdrawn so children cannot poke anything in to touch the live terminals. A few homes still have 2 amp, 5 amp, or 15 amp sockets. It is advisable to have your wiring modernised if you have only these types. Certainly get rid of two pin sockets as they lack the additional safety provided by the earth wire. Also a three pin plug is not easily reversed and this ensures that the correct pin on the plug connects with the live terminals on the socket. The Electricity Board or a registered electrical contractor will test the wiring installation for safety and quote for repairs or rewiring. The Electricity Board will also check the wiring when you move into a new home after you have completed the forms entitling you to an electricity supply. They should also check all major wiring alterations and only the Electricity Board can connect up their service cable to a fuse box.

FLEX COLOURS AND FLEXES

Three core flexes are all colour coded to a European Standard, *brown for live, blue for neutral and green/yellow for earth* (4); but the flex must be the correct type and amperage to match the appliance. Most appliances come complete with their own flex but if it is not long enough never try to extend it by joining and taping on extra length. Specially made cable connectors in tough plastic are sold, but it is best – and usually cheaper – to buy a complete length of flex and have an electrician fix it to the appliance. The commonly used flexes are: *0·5 mm.*^{2} (3 amp) for up to 700 watts (lamps, radios and blankets), *0·75 mm.*^{2} (6 amp) for up to 1400 watts (irons, refrigerators and small fires) and *1·5 mm.*^{2} (13 amp) for up to 3000 watts (two bar fires and kettles). Do not use twisted unsheathed flex for power appliances.

Double-insulated appliances Always make sure that the earth wire is properly connected. The only exceptions are 'double-insulated' appliances which only have a two-core flex, and shavers which are intended for use with special shaver sockets. The manufacturer will state that an appliance is 'double insulated' on a label or on the equipment itself. Double-insulated appliances should also bear a mark that looks like a box inside a box.

sulating material which is generally grey or off-white. These cables sometimes run in steel, aluminium or plastic tubes but modern practice is to embed the plastic protected cables in the walls. Older homes may have cloth covered and rubber covered cables, black or red. If you find that you have much of this type of wiring, it is best to have it checked by the Electricity Board who only make a small charge for a safety inspection.

Socket outlet circuits There are two types of socket outlet circuit: the

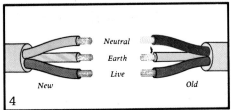

4

radial system (2) and the more modern *ring circuit* system. With the old type there were usually two or more sizes of socket outlets in the home. The ring circuit (3) has only one size – 13 amp sockets. The 13 amp socket, distinguished by its square holes, will supply

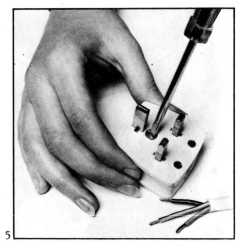

5

WIRING A PLUG

To wire a 13 amp plug (5) begin by cutting away 50 mm. (2 in.) of the outer sheath on the flex but without cutting the insulation around the individual wires. Then take the cover off the plug by undoing the screws and remove the cartridge fuse. Clamp the sheath under the flex clamp provided. Cut the coloured covering off each of the three wires so that there is just enough bare wire to go through the fixing holes, or round the clamping screws (5a). Take care to strip off just enough of the insulation and no more.

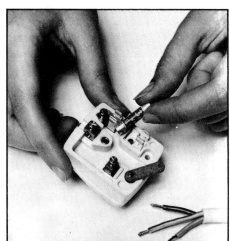

5a

The green or green/yellow wire is the earth lead and goes to the largest of the three pins – marked 'E' (for earth). The brown wire goes to the pin marked 'L' (for live) and the blue wire to the pin marked 'N' (for neutral) (5b).

Clamp the wires firmly in the terminal connections. With some plugs you wind the bared wire clockwise around the pins, in others you fit the bared ends into holes in terminal blocks. In both cases screw down the terminal screws tight (5c).

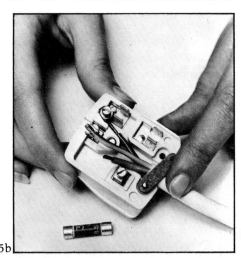

5b

The cartridge fuses for 13 amp plugs are also colour coded. The *3 amp fuse is red* and should be used for table lamps and small appliances rated up to 720 watts. The *13 amp fuse is brown* and is for use with appliances having ratings above 720 watts, up to a maximum of 3000 watts (3 kiloWatts) such as heaters, irons, kettles and toasters. Colour televisions and some appliances which incorporate an electric motor may need a 13 amp fuse even though they may be rated below 720 watts due to the higher starting current required – see the appliance rating plate or the manufacturer's instructions.

Before screwing back the cover on the plug, make sure there are no stray whiskers of bare wire and that the screws holding the wires are hard down – not just finger tight.

Make sure that the outer sheath of flex is firmly gripped under the clamp where the lead enters the plug. This prevents the wires from pulling away from the terminals. There should be no looseness or rattling of any kind when you have finished and all screws or nuts holding the plug together should be firmly tightened.

Do not re-use an old plug which has a cracked plastic base or cover. If either the base or cover is damaged at all, a new plug must be bought.

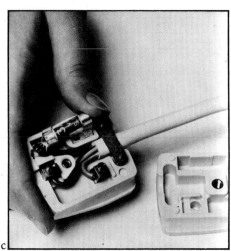

5c

FUSES

The fuse in the 13 amp plug is designed to protect the flex and is a deliberate weak spot in an electrical circuit. If more current flows through a wiring circuit than it is designed to carry, the flex or cable could get dangerously hot. To prevent this, all fuses are made of weaker material than the rest of the circuit, so that it melts or 'blows' when overloading occurs. This stops the flow of electric current and prevents further trouble.

The cable also has its own protective fuse – the most common form being the rewirable fuse. There is usually one for each circuit. The porcelain fuse holders are in the fuse box near the meter, ranged in rows. Each holder carries a fuse wire held in position by brass screws.

Some of the newer systems have *miniature circuit breakers* (6). Looking like ordinary switches or push buttons they automatically flick themselves off if any circuit is overloaded or if a fault in an appliance fails to blow the plug or socket fuse. Instead of the troublesome business of rewiring a porcelain fuse, the circuit can be brought back into use simply by pressing the switch down or

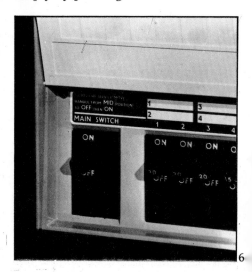

6

pushing the button in.

Some fuse boxes now have *cartridge fuses* (7) which can be replaced as easily as the cartridge fuse in the 13 amp plug (8).

Make the job of fuse finding easier by labelling each fuse in the box beforehand so that it is easy to tell which fuse belongs to which circuit and what rooms or appliances it serves. The fuse carriers on modern fuse units are colour coded: 5 amp is white (for lighting) 15 amp is blue (for immersion heaters and other 3 kW circuits), 20 amp is yellow (for some type of water

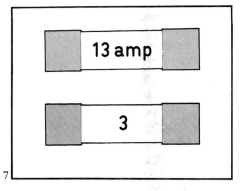

7

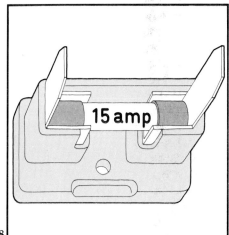

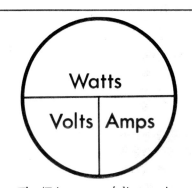

8

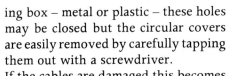

Watts

Volts | Amps

The 'T in a saucer' diagram is a useful way of remembering the formula for calculating voltage, wattage or ampage. For example, if an appliance is rated at 2400 watts and the voltage is 240, then $2400 \div 240 = 10A$, and it will need a 13A fuse to protect it.

heaters), 30 amp is red (ring circuits), 45 amp is green (cookers).

Replacing a rewirable fuse (9) Get a torch. It saves time and trouble to keep one near the fuses all the time. Switch off the main switch. If possible, find out the cause of the fuse blowing, switch off the faulty appliance or lamp and unplug it or remove the bulb, otherwise the new fuse might also blow. Find the blown fuse by taking out and inspecting each fuse in turn. It is usually obvious which one has blown – not only will the fuse wire be broken, but often there will be scorch marks around the fuse carrier. Unscrew the terminal screws on the fuse holder and remove the broken wire. Replace the old wire with a fresh piece of the correct rating (a supply of fuse wire should always be kept near the fuse box). Wind the new wire round one terminal screw (wind clockwise to prevent it from unwinding as screw is tightened) screw wire down, run it across to other terminal post and repeat procedure. Do not stretch or strain the wire when tightening the screws. Replace the fuse carrier, close the box, and then turn on the switch. If the fuse blows again, or there is any doubt, send for an electrician.

REPLACING A SOCKET

More sockets can be added to an existing ring circuit. It is also possible to run a 'spur' from the ring – a single length of cable leading to a new socket taken from the back of an existing socket but this work should be done by a qualified electrician.

When having sockets installed it makes sense to use the switched type, particularly twin switched sockets, which cost very little more than the single type and avoid the use of clumsy adaptors. It is also possible to get sockets with a

red neon indicator which lights up when the appliance is connected and working.

To replace a damaged or broken socket first switch off the electricity at the mains (10). Never attempt any electrical jobs other than wiring a plug without turning off at the mains. Undo the screws holding the socket plate and pry it gently from the wall. Undo the terminal screws and remove wires. If the box on which the socket is mounted is damaged as well, this must be replaced, reinserting the cables through the holes provided. On a new mount-

10

ing box – metal or plastic – these holes may be closed but the circular covers are easily removed by carefully tapping them out with a screwdriver.

If the cables are damaged this becomes a job for an electrician but normally the three sets of wires need only connect to the terminals on the new socket, red to live marked 'L' or mains; black to 'N' and the earth wire to 'E'. Ease the plate onto the mounting box, making sure no wires are trapped and screw tight with the two mounting screws. You may need new screws as the new box will be a metric size.

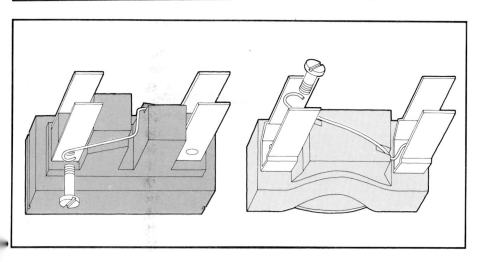

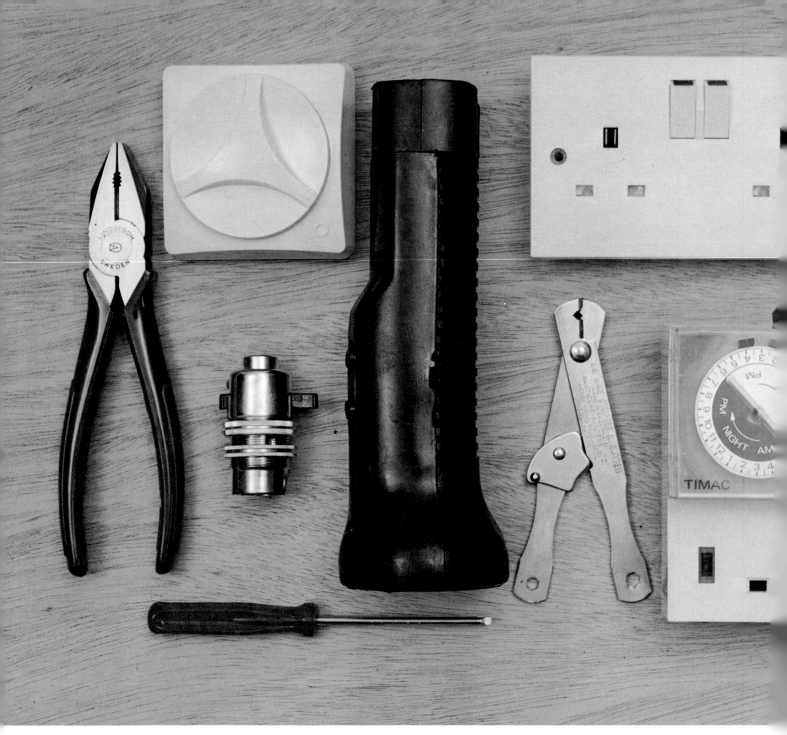

TOOL KIT FOR MINOR REPAIRS

A torch, rubber or plastic covered; an electrician's screwdriver with insulated handle; pliers with insulated handle; a card of fuse wire; spare cartridge fuses (see picture above).

EMERGENCIES AND POWER CUTS

When there is a sudden demand for electricity – as may happen in spells of very cold weather – and it is not always possible to divert supplies from other areas the engineers are obliged to make voltage reductions. This means that lights dim, the television picture gets smaller, electric fires do not burn as brightly and electric cookers cook more slowly. Fluorescent lamps may not light if there is a voltage reduction and should be switched off. Motor operated appliances, like food mixers, should be used only when absolutely necessary as effective working power will be reduced.

There may also be emergencies when the supply is switched off altogether. It may be a temporary power cut due to a severe storm or accident having caused a local breakdown, or a result of industrial action. It is as well to have candles, a torch and possibly a battery or camping lighting and cooking equipment handy somewhere in the house. It is also worthwhile to have some form of portable heating such as a paraffin stove as a power cut will also stop the electric pump motors used in central heating.

Power cuts rarely last more than a few hours but refrigerators should be kept closed as much as possible and make sure the drip tray is in position. The contents of food freezers are not likely to come to any harm for at least ten hours provided the lid or door is not opened, and it is unlikely that a power cut would last that long.

If the house has to be left before power is restored make sure that electric fires and blankets are turned off as there could be an accident if, for instance, something inflammable has been left in front of a radiant fire or draped over a radiant heater.

ELECTRIC SHOCK

If your earth system is effective the risk of a severe shock is very small but it is as well to memorise the following advice. A mild shock produces only a

HOW ELECTRICITY IS MEASURED

The 'flow' of electricity is measured in amperes (amps) written as A. Its 'pressure' is measured in volts (V) and its power (the work it can do) in watts (W). Every appliance has fixed to it a *rating plate* – usually at the rear. This metal rectangle shows the maker's name, the model number (which is quoted for servicing) and the amperage, the voltage, and usually the wattage. Multiplying the amps by the volts, will give the amount of power the appliance uses expressed in watts and this is the guide to the running cost.

1000 watts used continuously for one hour is equivalent to one kilowatt hour (kWh) which is *the unit* by which electricity is measured on the meter.

Dividing the volts into the watts will give the number of amps and this is the guide to fuse and circuit breaker ratings. All fuse wire is marked in amps and it is essential to use the correct fuse wire that matches the amperage of the cable.

READING THE METER

There are basically two kinds of meter: the *digital meter* and the *dial meter*. **Digital meter** This has the number of units of electricity used shown by a simple row of figures. With the special *White Meter* (11), two digital indicators are used: one for lower priced night rate electricity and the other for the day rate. The reading on the digital meter is the total number of units used since the meter was installed so to keep a check on consumption, subtract the previous reading for the new reading.

11

thousands, then tens of thousands, working from right to left and writing them down in that order. Always write down the number the pointer has passed (this is not necessarily the nearest number to the pointer). So if the pointer is anywhere between, say, 3 and 4 write down 3. If the pointer is directly over a figure, say, 7, look at the pointer on the dial immediately to the right. If this pointer is between 9 and 0, write down 6. If it is between 0 and 1, however, write down 7. The illustration shown here gives a reading of 94690.

PAYING THE BILL

Most people get their bills quarterly but arrangements can be made to pay an estimated sum monthly by Banker's Order or GIRO which can help with household budgeting. It is also possible to pay weekly, or in advance, but write to the Electricity Board for details and get their free leaflet which explains payment methods and how the bill is made up, as every Board applies its own tariffs.

Standing charge All electricity bills contain a 'standing charge', so called because the Electricity Boards are entitled to collect this charge whether or not you actually use any electricity, as it covers the cost of making a supply available. Some Electricity Boards spread the amount of the standing charge over the first, say, 100 units in each quarter while the remainder are charged at a lower price. Others make a fixed charge each quarter to cover the standing charge, then charge for the units at a stated price. As charges vary between the different Electricity Boards, it is advisable to get a copy of the free leaflet which explains the

slight tingling sensation but a severe shock makes the muscles contract so that the fingers may tighten and it becomes difficult to let go of a wire or an electrically charged appliance.

Sustained shock can be fatal because of the effect on the respiratory system and heart. Try to break away by pulling hard enough on the flex to jerk out the plug or break it off. Or try to jump with both feet off the ground which breaks the earth connection long enough to let go of the live object you are gripping.

If you discover someone such as a child caught in shock, restrain the instinct to grab him or you, too, could be caught. Switch off the current or pull out the plug. Or throw a tablecloth or coat round the person and pull.

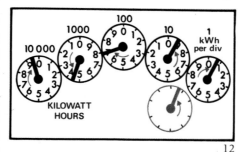

12

Dial meter (12) This has six dials and each pointer goes round in the opposite direction to its neighbour. The dials record units: ten thousands, thousands, hundreds, tens and singles. Ignore any dials registering tenths or hundredths of a unit – usually coloured red.

Start by reading the dial showing single units and write down the figure. Then read the dial showing tens of units, then the one showing hundreds, then 'domestic tariffs' in your area.

Off-peak charges Cheaper electricity is available if it can be used during what are called 'off-peak' periods – normally the night hours. Thermal storage heating systems and electric water heaters are among the high wattage appliances that benefit from the 'off-peak' electricity of the White Meter tariff, although all electric appliances and lighting used during the stated night hours (usually between 2200 hours and 0700 hours) will be able to use the cheap electricity.

Coin meters Those with coin meters should make sure, if the meter is under the landlord's control, that they are not being overcharged. The resale price of electricity is fixed and the Electricity Board will advise on the maximum resale price that can be charged in the area.

RUNNING COSTS

As 1000 watts used for one hour uses one unit of electricity it is easy to work out running costs. Appliances that use electricity in the form of heat have a higher wattage so cost more to run than those using purely motor power.

LIGHT SWITCHES IN THE HOME

These are either rocker or dolly. The rocker needs only a slight pressure from a finger to switch the light on or off, while the older dolly needs a firm, up and down action. Switches look best if they are flush – that is, with the mechanical part recessed into the wall on a metal, plaster-depth box about 28 mm. (1 in.) deep. The surface plate – 73 by 73 mm. ($2\frac{7}{8}$ in. by $2\frac{7}{8}$ in.) – can

MAJOR APPLIANCES	
Cooker	Uses about four units a day cooking for a family of four
Dishwasher	Washes a family's dinner dishes for about 1 unit
Food Freezer	One unit of electricity per week for every 15 litres capacity (2 units for each cu. ft)
Fan Heater	With a loading of 2 kW uses two units an hour
Radiant Heater	With a loading of 2 kW uses two units an hour
Refrigerator	The popular table top height size uses about 1 unit a day
LAUNDRY EQUIPMENT	
Iron (Hand)	Irons for over two hours for 1 unit
Spin Drier	Spins about five weeks laundry for 1 unit
Tumble Drier	Uses about 2 units for one hour
Washing Machine (twin tub)	The weekly wash for a family of four, comprising 140 pieces or 17 kg. (38 lb.) dry weight of laundry will use 11 or 12 units of electricity
Washing Machine (automatic)	The weekly wash for a family of four, comprising 140 pieces or 17 kg. (38 lb.) dry weight of laundry will use around 8 to 9 units of electricity
THE SMALLER APPLIANCES	**FOR 1 UNIT OF ELECTRICITY YOU CAN**
Battery charger	use for 30 hours
Blanket (over)	Keeps the bed warm all night for two or three nights
Blanket (under)	use every night for a week
Blender	make 500 pints of soup
Can Opener	open about 6,250 cans
Carving knife	carve 220 weekend joints
Coffee percolator	make about 75 cups of coffee
Extractor fan	keep it running for 24 hours
Floor polisher	polish for $2\frac{1}{2}$ hours
Food mixer (stand model)	mix 67 cakes
Hair drier	use it for three hours
Hair rollers	have 22 hair treatments
Health lamp (infra red/ ultra violet)	use it for four hours
Juice extractor	collect the juice from over 3,500 oranges
Kettle	boil about 12 pints of water
Light	light a 100W filament lamp or a 5 ft 80W fluorescent tube for ten hours. (The fluorescent tube gives four times as much light as the 100W lamp)
Power drill	have about four hours' drilling
Radio (mains)	listen for 30 hours
Razor	have over 1,800 shaves
Sewing Machine	sew eleven children's dresses
Television (colour)	have three hours' viewing
Television (black/white)	have seven hours' viewing
Tape Recorder/ Record Player	listen for 24 hours
Toaster	make 70 slices of toast
Vacuum cleaner	clean for two hours
Waste disposal unit	grind 1 cwt of rubbish

take up to three rocker switches in line. Up to six rocker switches can be mounted on a double width box. A single switch is called a '1 gang'; two '2 gang' and so on.

Renewing a light switch To renew a light switch follow the same procedure as for renewing a socket outlet except that you must note the position of the wires (in some cases you will find two wires going to one terminal) and follow the same arrangement with the new switch.

Alternative switches It is usually possible to replace a wall mounted switch by a dimmer switch which will not only switch the light on and off, but control the level of illumination. The dimmer must suit the wattage of the lamps it controls. The smallest – 250 watt – will control up to four 60 watt lamps of 100 watt lamps. If candle lamps are used, a dimmer rated at twice the load is required. Fluorescent lamps need special dimmers. There are also dimmers that fit between lamps and holder for table and standard lamps.

The ceiling switch is operated by a shock-proof cord, so the switch and the wiring are out of reach. A pull from almost any angle switches on or off and it can be used not just for lighting but for permanently fixed appliances – particularly heaters. It is the only type of switch permitted in the bathroom. The two-way switch switches lights on and off from two different positions. This type should be installed in bedrooms, on landings and in long halls, on single-flight stairways and in any room with two doors. An extra insu-

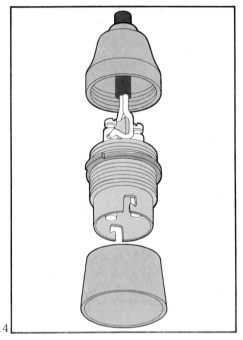

14

lated cable is used – three core and earth instead of two, and the switch has an extra terminal.

REPLACING A CEILING ROSE
Switch off electricity at the main switch and the consumer unit (fuse box). Undo cover of ceiling rose. If this is an old porcelain pattern, or one that has been painted over, it may be necessary to smash it. Undo the flex connections and remove lamp-holding pendant. Loosen terminals gripping the cable ends. If there are more than two connections then be careful not to disturb the cables when withdrawing the ceiling rose base (13).
Unscrew the two fixing screws noting carefully where they are in relation to the cables so that the same fixings can be found when refixing the new rose. Withdraw the ceiling rose base carefully and expose the cable ends. Fit on the new base, and tighten the terminal screws. Insert the fixing screws and refix base to ceiling. Renew flex and, if necessary, lamp holder, using heat

resistant (silicone) 0·5 mm² flex.
Re-insert flex through the ceiling rose cover and refix in terminals on base. Screw on cover. An earth terminal is provided in the ceiling rose to which the earth conductor is connected – if there is one. Older lighting circuits do not have them but they are now installed for metal encased lighting fittings where a three core flex is provided.
Switch on electricity and test – making sure that the bulb is not a dud. The same procedure can be used for replacing a wall switch.

WIRING A LAMP HOLDER
Switch off the electricity at the main switch. It is not enough just to switch off at the light switch. Unscrew cover and then slacken flex from around clamping grooves on centre pillar. Unscrew terminals and remove flex ends. If flex is rubber insulated and cotton braided and has been in use for some time it will almost certainly require replacing with a twin core heat resistant flex. Push each terminal plunger up and down to see if the tension is still good. If not, or if the moulding is damaged, replace with a new lampholder. Thread new cover onto flex. Prepare the ends of the flex by removing a small portion of the covering (14).
Twist the ends neatly if the conductor is made up of more than one wire. Place flex ends into terminals and tighten firmly. Place flex around pillar in grooves provided. Screw down cover, keeping flex slack so as not to affect tension on the lamp contact plungers. Refit lamp.

FLUORESCENTS
A fluorescent lamp gives about four times as much light as a filament bulb of the same wattage, has a long life and is more economical in use. Most ceiling fluorescents come with fitting instructions and installation is similar to replacing a ceiling rose except that the metal case that holds the control gear must be securely fixed to the ceiling using the fitting holes provided.
There are also circular fluorescent fittings, and small miniature tubes from 300 mm. (12 in.) long. For the home ask for a *de luxe* warm white tube which gives a warm colour light similar to the ordinary light bulb. Other suitable tubes are sold under the name of 'Softone' and 'Homelight'.

BELLS AND BATTERIES
Door bells and chimes work from batteries or a small transformer which brings the 240V current down to 8V or 12V. Batteries have a limited life so a small transformer will pay for itself within three years. Thin two-core cable will go to the bell or chime from the terminals on the transformer but connect to the pair marked 8V or the pair marked 12V to suit the voltage marked on the chimes. Connection from the mains side of the transformer is best carried out by an electrician.

DO'S AND DON'TS

DO Switch off at mains when making any repairs or alterations to ring main circuit or lighting.

DO disconnect plug from socket before attempting repairs to electrical appliances; switch off electricity at light switch before changing bulb.

DON'T overload sockets. Total loading at each socket must not exceed 3000 watts – therefore 2- or 3-plug outlet adaptors can only safely be used when the loading of each appliance is known – See ampage chart. Only use fused adaptors fitted with a 13 amp fuse. When fitting new sockets fit double outlets.

DO take care of flexes – have them renewed when they show signs of wear – don't lay them under a carpet or secure them to wall and ceilings – be sure you are using the correct flex for your appliance.

DON'T make joints in flex to repair or lengthen it. Use a specially designed flex connector or, safer still, have a new unbroken length of flex fitted.

DON'T use an extension cable on a reel for high-loading appliances.

DON'T use the light circuit or light sockets for anything other than lighting. Use 13-amp 3-pin socket outlets for all appliances as well as table and standard lamps.

DON'T have any socket outlets or portable appliances in the bathroom. Heaters in the bathroom must be operated by a pull cord switch and fixed out of reach of a person standing in the bath. Have them installed by a registered electrician.

DON'T touch a fire element unless the plug is out and the element is cold.

DON'T handle plugs, switches or sockets with wet hands.

DON'T attempt any electrical job unless you are absolutely certain how to approach it.

KNOWING ABOUT PLUMBING

WATER SUPPLY AND DRAINAGE

The cold water supply from the Water Board enters the house below ground level passing through stop taps, usually one in the garden or in the road, the other normally in the house. At least one domestic tap (almost always in the kitchen) is fed from the rising main to provide drinking water but then the water goes up to a storage tank in the roof space. From the storage tank pipes distribute water to the hot water system, the lavatory cisterns and the cold taps in the house at bath and basin. The waste water from the lavatory, baths and basins is normally fed into a soil pipe connected to the main drains (unless yours is a house with a septic tank). The soil pipe has an extra pipe with an open end at roof level designed to ventilate the system. The system has one or more inspection pits to help in clearing the drains if they should get blocked or need examination.

An important part of every waste system is a water filled trap on every waste outlet. This is the 'U Bend' and its object is to prevent smells from the main drains from finding their way into the house.

It is illegal to tamper with the drains or make alterations to this basic plumbing of the house without informing the Water Board and the local authority. Changing a bath or wash basin, adding a shower fitting, or replacing the W.C. suite needs no permission. An extra bathroom, lavatory or shower needs permission and, strictly speaking, the Water Board should be told if you install an extra tap in the garden or garage. This must, by the way, have a second tap indoors if the connection is from the mains cold supply.

BURST PIPES

Turn the water off at the main and send for a plumber. If you do not know of one, telephone your local Water Board. Some Boards will deal with bursts or recommend someone who will. Alternatively, as long as the burst happens in business hours, you can contact the National Institute of Plumbing at Hornchurch 51236. Better to anticipate the emergency and have the address and telephone number of one of their members in your 'phone book. If it happens at the weekend or at night try the yellow pages in the telephone book under 'Plumbers' and choose one that gives what looks like a home address (some list an emergency number).

If it is the main supply that bursts, turn off the Water Board's stop-cock which is usually in a covered box with the tap about 600 mm. (2 ft or more) below the surface. If it cannot be reached by hand cut a simple deep V in the end of a stout piece of wood, insert it down the hole so the edges of the V grip the arms of the tap: turn slowly clockwise to cut off the supply. The tap will be stiff and a crosspiece bound to the wood will make turning easier.

A burst in the house can be handled by turning off the main supply tap inside the house. If the burst is in a pipe from the tank in the roof turn off the appropriate stop tap found close to the tank or in the cupboard housing the hot tank. If no stop taps have been fitted, try wrapping a cloth round a broom handle and plug the outlet from the tank. This means doing some fishing in the tank although the position of the outlet can be located from the pipe coming out of the tank. Secure the arm of the ball valve using string and a stick if you want to stop water coming in yet still have the kitchen cold tap in use. Turn on the other taps in the house and drain the tank as quickly as possible. This last advice especially applies if it is the tank that has burst. If it is the hot cylinder run the hot taps and remember to switch off the water heating.

If you can get at the burst pipe, make a temporary repair until the arrival of the plumber by wrapping absorbent cloth soaked in a waterproof glue such as Copydex around the pipe. Let the repair get reasonably dry then you can turn on the water again, but if it is a pipe direct from the mains then use only a reduced pressure until the plumber arrives. Hard soap is also an alternative. Rub it into the burst and bind with adhesive tape. Switch off the water heating until the plumber arrives and if you heat your water or your central heating directly from the water supply switch off the boiler or damp down the fire. Most homes with a radiator system have a closed independent water supply to prevent scale. This would not be affected by a burst and can be left on. Check which you have.

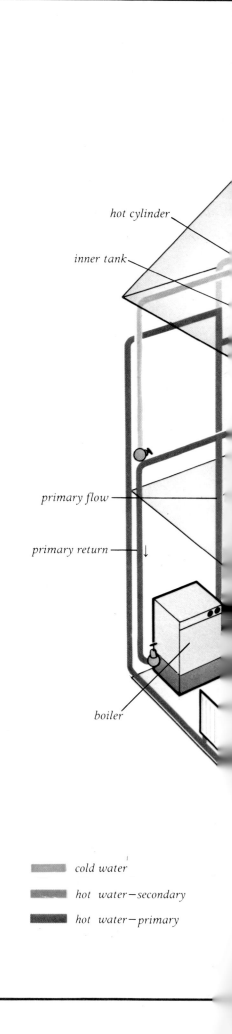

hot cylinder

inner tank

primary flow

primary return

boiler

cold water

hot water—secondary

hot water—primary

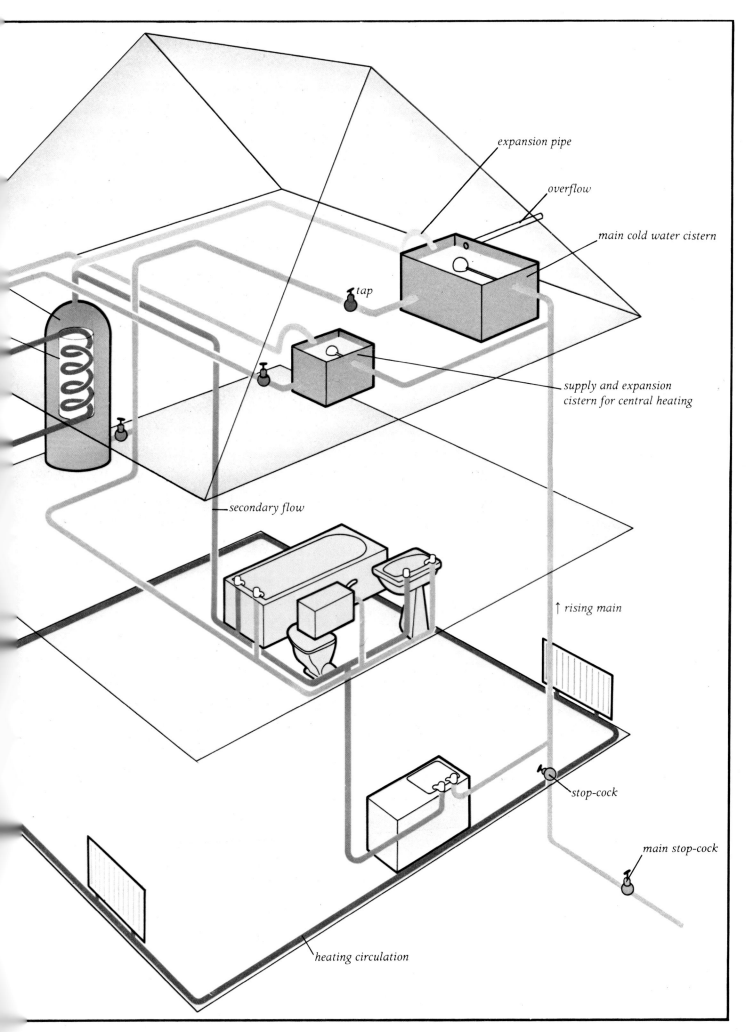

expansion pipe

overflow

main cold water cistern

tap

supply and expansion
cistern for central heating

secondary flow

↑ rising main

stop-cock

main stop-cock

heating circulation

215

WATER PRESSURE AND PURITY

The Water Boards are only obliged to supply water which is drinkable and about half the homes receive water that is 'hard'. Very soft water would have 7 grains of hardness per litre and water with 40 grains would be very hard indeed. Your local Water Board will give you the figure for your road.

Hard water contains calcium and magnesium salts and these cause scale. This is not in itself harmful, indeed these salts are considered to be good for health, but scale or 'fur' reduces the performance of the water heaters and kettles, reduces the efficiency of detergent and soaps, causes unpleasant scum and furs up pipes which can eventually reduce the hot water supply to a trickle.

It is a matter of personal taste whether a water softener is considered worthwhile, but if you live in an area of very hard water ask your local plumber for advice as a softener could save many plumbing problems later on. Small individual softeners are made to fit washing machines and dishwashers or you can buy a softener which will treat all the household water. All these softeners use the same principle: a bed of resin removes the chemicals causing the hardness and the resin is cleaned by inserting a quantity of salt at intervals.

Scale can also be prevented by suspending a small, harmless chemical capsule in the cold water tank. The capsule needs to be renewed twice a year.

The pressure of water from the mains varies throughout the country but you should find out from the Water Board what yours is because some types of washing machines, dishwashers, and water heaters will not work properly if the water pressure is constantly very low.

DEALING WITH BLOCKAGES

The taps Fierce knocking noises in the pipe and air spurting out of taps which cough constantly is a sign of an air lock. Sometimes the water supply may dry up altogether from a tap.

The easiest way to clear the air lock is to force water from the mains supply through the air-locked tap. This pushes the air up and releases it into the tank. A length of hose is taken from the mains supply to the affected tap and secured at both taps with screw-on clips. If you have not got these clips have someone hold the hose or bind

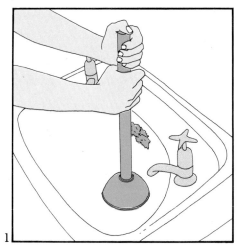

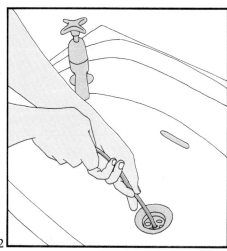

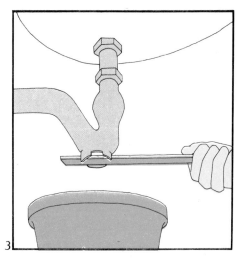

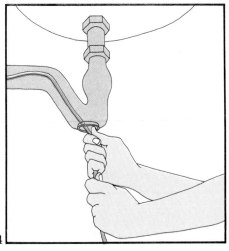

round the taps with a cloth. Turn on both taps for several minutes then turn off the airlocked tap first.

If that does not work try draining the system. Turn off the main supply if the cold taps are affected, or the tap to the hot water cylinder if it is the hot tap. Open all the cold or hot taps until the water ceases to flow. Close each tap starting at the bottom of the house, first by two thirds before turning on the mains supply, then by half. When all the air has been spurted free, reduce the water supply to a trickle, then, in turn, close off each tap again starting at the bottom of the house.

The drains If the outlet from a sink, basin or a bath becomes blocked try using a *plunger* (1) a bell-shaped rubber cup fitted to a wooden handle obtainable from an ironmonger, an item that should be part of standard household equipment. It works by forcing water down the waste-pipe and pushing the blockage away, but the overflow outlet should be closed with a cloth first or the plunger will shoot dirty water out of the overflow. Pump vigorously up and down. Use whenever the waste seems to be running slowly and the plunger will help keep pipes clear and prevent a complete blockage from forming.

A flexible thin wire is another method of clearing a blockage (2) but care is needed with lead or plastic fittings. If the wire is too heavy or too thick it could damage the pipe. Ironmongers sell specially designed flexible clearing cable – either a springy wire on a wooden handle or a length wound on a reel. Best, but messiest, method is to put a bucket or a tray under the U bend and unscrew the brass cleaning trap (3). The cleaning trap has four lugs which undo quite easily using a flat metal bar placed at right angles to the

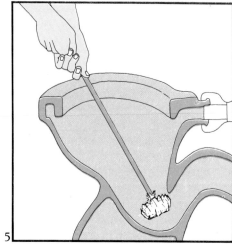

U bend, its edge engaging the lugs. Some traps are made in plastic and the whole U bend unit unscrews. Once the trap or bend is removed it is just a matter of poking out the blockage. Never try to use acids or caustic chemicals (4).

If a lavatory pan is blocked try using a mop with a plastic bag tied tight around it as a plunger – but gently. A flexible rod is an alternative. There is no removable trap in the bend in a lavatory basin (5).

The drains covered with a grid outside the house often become blocked with dead leaves, grit or mud. Some are designed only to drain away surface water, others lead into the main drain. In both cases they should be cleaned out at least twice a year, lifting off the cover and using a small trowel or a ladle to take out sand and grit.

If there is a blockage in the drain, lift the metal cover on the inspection pit in the garden. You will need help with this and probably two hooks to fit the handles. Clear out any loose debris or dirt. If the drain is blocked, the pipe entry into the pit will be empty showing that the blockage is in a pipe between the manhole and the house. Two or more pipes run into the inspection chamber from the house; one carrying drainage water from baths, sinks, washbasins and very likely water from the gutters, and one will be the soil pipe from the lavatory. There is also a pipe up on the side of the chamber fitted at the top with a grid or a flap to keep smells from escaping. If you have no flexible rods you can hire from a local tool hire firm a purpose-designed set of rods which screw together. These need to be pushed up each drainpipe in turn. They have different kinds of screw-heads, brush heads and plunger heads, to break through an obstruction. Flush water down the drain to complete the clearing.

If the inspection chamber is full of dirty water the blockage is probably between it and the sewer. The trap on the outlet side of the chamber has a cleaning hole just above it covered by a stopper. When this stopper is removed the rods can be pushed down and pumping up and down will probably clear the blockage; if not, you need specialist advice. There are specialist firms who offer a 24 hour service on unblocking drains and normally it is better to use them if the blockage is between manhole and sewer. Not only

is it a very dirty and unpleasant job, but also a difficult one.

TAP REPAIRS
Replacement washers should be the same size as the one in the tap. Keep a supply of washers to suit all your taps. The washers on Supataps can be changed without turning off the mains or opening the tap fully. Unscrew the cone shaped shield using a cloth to protect the chrome and an adjustable spanner. Beneath the shield is a large hexagonal nut which is then unscrewed with the spanner. Lift the tap top away from the body. On most taps the washer is mounted on a small loose spindle called a jumper with the washer held on to a circular disc with a small nut. Hold the circular disc with a pair of pliers and unscrew the nut on the washer with a small spanner. Remove the old washer and fit the new one so that the maker's name faces downwards. Replace the jumper and screw the tap back. Turn on the mains and check tap does not drip (6).

Some modern taps have a head which pulls off once a small screw is undone. To get at the screw push a small screwdriver under the button on the top of the tap.

If water leaks out between the spindle on the tap and the cone shaped shield, loosen the shield and tighten up the gland nut and tighten up the nut at the base of the spindle, above the large hexagonal nut. To get at this nut you will have to remove the shield completely by taking off the crosshead which is the part you grip to turn the

tap on and off. It is held to the spindle with a small screw.

If the tap still leaks then turn the mains off and take out the gland nut altogether. Pack the spindle round with three or four turns of string rubbed in Vaseline. Replace the gland and reassemble the tap.

BALL COCKS
The water level in the roof tank and in the lavatory cistern is controlled by a circular, air filled ball fitted to an arm connected to a small valve (7). As the water level rises the ball rises and shuts off the flow. If the ball fails or leaks the water continues to rise and then begins to flow through the overflow outlet. The ball valve screws on and off and a new one can easily be fitted. A temporary repair can be made using sticky tape but first you must empty the water out and find the hole. Or you can empty the water out and tie a plastic bag round it.

Sometimes the ball valve just sticks and flushing will clear the problem. The washer in the ball valve may also fail but as there are several types it usually needs a plumber to replace this.

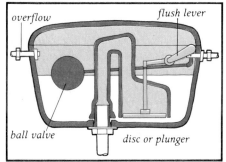

overflow   *flush lever*

ball valve   *disc or plunger*

7

6

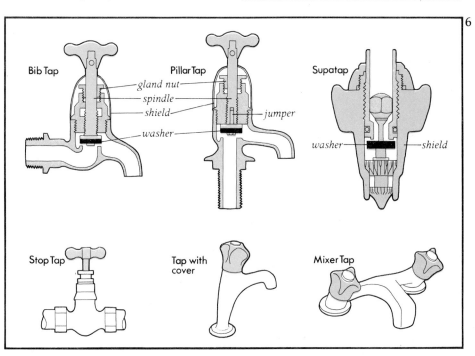

Bib Tap   Pillar Tap   Supatap

gland nut
spindle
shield
jumper
washer
washer   *shield*

Stop Tap   Tap with cover   Mixer Tap

INSULATION

The benefits of good insulation, both in money terms and in comfort, are continuous. The cost of insulating all or part of the house is soon offset by the savings in heating bills. Reduced condensation and a cooler home in summer are further advantages.

In a typical home, 25 per cent of the heat escapes through the roof (more in a bungalow), about 35 per cent through the walls, 10 per cent through the windows, and 15 per cent in draughts, while another 15 per cent is lost into the grounds, so that improving insulation leads to significant reductions in heat requirements.

ROOF INSULATION

A layer of mineral fibre insulation laid between joists in the loft will substantially reduce the 25 per cent of heat loss through the roof (1). The new U.K. standard is met by a 50 mm. (2 in.) thickness but at least 75 mm. (3 in.) is recommended and this is close to the standard adopted by most European countries.

Means of insulation Mineral fibre insulation comes in rolls and works rather like an eiderdown, trapping the air and providing a heat barrier. An alternative is granules of vermiculite spread between the joists but this is not always suitable in windy areas as the granules are very light and have a tendency to pile themselves into drifts away from the prevailing wind, leaving areas of the loft uninsulated.

Other methods of roof insulation include expanded polystyrene, impregnated fibre insulation board, rigid polyurethane and expanded laminated polystyrene/plasterboard fixed to rafters but some of these materials have to be installed by professional tradesmen and only flame retardent or self-extinguishing materials should be used.

Laying insulation Mineral fibre is not only the cheapest but the easiest to install. Fix yourself up with a small kneeling platform of planks which you rest across the joists in the loft. You will also need a temporary light on an extension flex or a torch, and a broom pole to poke the insulation into the eaves and into the corners. Wear a pair

25% of heat is lost through the roof. Heat rises, so the warmer your house, the more heat lost through the roof. Insulation in the loft can substantially reduce this heat loss.

Another 10% of heat is lost through the windows and badly-fitting window frames. Double-glazing is the answer here, with foam strip to stop draughts from badly-fitting windows.

Heat escaping through badly-fitting doors. Draught excluders and metal stripping round the door will solve this problem.

Up to 25% of heat escapes through the walls. Filling cavity walls with insulating material will cut down the heat loss. Solid walls should be lined inside with insulating material such as polystyrene or aluminium foil.

of old gloves and put a pair of elastic bands on your cuffs to hold them to your wrists as the wool fibres can cause skin irritation. It is also advisable to wear a mask to protect your lungs from breathing in not only tiny particles of wool fibre but loft dust and dirt.

Always work from the planks in case you accidentally put your foot through the ceiling. Get rid of any rubbish or piles of shavings left by the builders. Unroll the mineral wool between the joists. Cut it to pass under the pipes and push it into the corners.

Loose fill insulation such as vermiculite granules is simply poured from the bag between the joists and smoothed over with a board cut to give the right depth when resting on the joists. To reach into the corners, nail the board to a broomstick. Most ceiling joists are 100 mm. (4 in.) deep; filling to 1·2 mm. (½ in.) of the top gives a good degree of insulation.

If the roof is not boarded or lined with tarred felt, icy draughts and snow get through the chinks between the tiles. Bad gaps will be clearly seen on a bright day and these should be closed with a ready mix cement. Then line the inside of the rafters with weatherproof, fire-resistant hardboard or roofing felt. Hardboard can be bought for the purpose in narrow widths so it can be taken up through the loft trap. Screw rather than nail the hardboard to the rafters because sustained hammering would dislodge the tiles. Roofing felt comes in rolls and can be tacked with small tacks to the rafters, allowing each length to overlap.

PROTECTING PIPES AND CISTERNS
Water pipes in the roof space should be lagged either by wrapping with mineral wool tied with string, or by using moulded polystyrene pipe laggings. Polystyrene slabs will protect the cold water cistern. Cover the sides of the cistern, cutting slots for the pipes with a sharp knife. Place slab on a plywood sheet to form a removable cover. Do *not* insulate the underside of the cistern as the heat rising from below helps to prevent freezing.

Circular cisterns can be insulated with glass fibre mats.

If there is a fierce cold draught blowing into the top of the cistern from the overflow pipe, get a short extra piece of pipe, taper one end so it can be inserted into the pipe and turn the

other so that it is at right angles with its end just below water level.

WALL INSULATION
The main purpose of cavity walls is to prevent rain from penetrating to the inner leaf or wall. It can, however, be made a lot more effective by filling the cavity between the inner and outer leaf with special insulation materials.

The reason a house loses heat through its walls is straightforward. The heat you put into your house heats the whole structure of the place including the inner leaf of bricks. This, in turn, heats the air, and, through natural convection, the warm air will eventually finish up touching the outer leaf of bricks to which it will transfer the heat. This heat, plus the heat passed from the inside by radiation, gradually escapes so it is the outside air that gets the benefit.

Cavity filling The object of good insulation, therefore, is to hold the air in the cavity stationary and reduce loss of radiation. This is done by pumping into the cavity either a foaming resin (ureaformaldehyde) or mineral fibre. It is a simple matter to do this when the house is being built and quite possible to do in existing houses.

A series of 18 mm. (¾ in.) holes are drilled in the brickwork joints at regular intervals. Either foamed urea-formaldehyde (which sets after a few minutes) or mineral fibre is then injected, forming a low-density insulating infill. The holes are repointed and the brickwork left with little sign of disturbance.

The work of cavity insulation takes about one day and the cost varies according to the size of the house. Choose a reputable firm, for if the quality of the material, or the pressure with which it is pumped in, is wrong, the material may not be waterproof. Rain driving against the outer wall may pass through, cross the bridge provided by the insulation, and soak into the inner skin. Once the inner walls in your home become damp you cannot get into the cavity to take out the defective material and the problem is very difficult to put right.

Insulating solid walls Houses with solid walls can also be insulated but not quite so easily. The most effective method is to line the walls with an insulating material combined with a vapour barrier on the warm side to prevent the penetration of warm, moist air, which could otherwise condense on the inner cooler surface. One way of doing this is to fix slabs of glass fibre between battens which are attached to the wall and held in place by the moisture barrier material. Another method is to stick polyurethane lami-

A front door which has been double-glazed with sliding glass panels for extra warmth.

nated plasterboard to the walls. This is a good method for older properties being converted or modernised, but advice may be needed from a building or insulation specialist as some of the older types of walling may not be suitable.

DRAUGHTPROOFING

Draughts are not just annoying, they also increase heating bills. Just how much can be judged by the fact that an ill-fitting door, front or back, with only a 3 mm. ($\frac{1}{8}$ in.) gap around it is the equivalent to a 174 sq. cm. (27 sq. in.) hole letting in cold air.

Draught excluders – obtainable from most hardware stores – can be fitted to doors and windows very cheaply. Plastic backed foam strips can be easily stuck around window frames and a tougher phosphorbronze strip nailed all the way round the door frame.

Sealing chimneys Unused chimneys should also be sealed to cut down heat loss by blocking up the fireplace openings and fitting a ventilation cap at the top of the stack. A ventilation grille either in the chimney breast or in the material blocking the fireplace will be needed to allow air movement and prevent the build-up of condensation. There is, however, a danger of draughtproofing too efficiently. Houses and people need ventilation and to exclude

all air ingress will lead to condensation problems as well as personal discomfort. Concentrate on draughtproofing doors to the outside, all windows and fireplace openings for simple and significant reductions in heat losses.

FLOOR INSULATION

Insulation for suspended floors is often neglected yet the saving can significantly reduce the 15 per cent of the total heat loss from a house. Sometimes a thick carpet with ample underlay is satisfactory, but for really effective insulation some form of insulating material, such as glass fibre, should be included below the floor surface. With suspended floors where there is a crawl space underneath, much can be done to cut down the heat loss by lining the underside of the floors with rolls of paper-backed glass fibre or expanded polystyrene sandwiched in building paper. Care must be taken not to mask the natural ventilation necessary to prevent dry rot or other damage to woodwork. In a room where a carpet is not completely fitted, excessive draughts and air changes often occur through shrinkage between the skirting board and the floor. This can easily be remedied by nailing a wooden fillet to the floor close up against the skirting. This is one of the easiest do-it-yourself jobs and any timber supplier will sell you wooden fillet or quadrant in lengths of multiples of a metre. It is very easy to cut using a small, fine tooth saw.

HOT WATER TANK

If your hot water cylinder has no lagging, heat is lost unnecessarily and money wasted. Without a lagging jacket enough heat for up to 16 baths a week can be lost. Put another way, this is enough electricity to keep one bar of an electric fire going for 80 hours.

Many electric hot water cylinders are supplied already insulated. If not, a 75 mm. (3 in.) lagging jacket or a box filled with loose insulation should be placed around the cylinder. It is very easy to do. Even a well insulated cylinder will give enough warmth to 'air' the clothes in the airing cupboard. Hot water pipework, too, should be lagged to reduce running costs further. At the same time, lag exposed cold water pipes to prevent freezing.

If the tank has really good lagging you have no need to turn the immersion

heater off when you are out during the day or overnight. (Any saving one might make by switching off would be small and you would lose the convenience of constant hot water on your return.) A time switch may give you further economy but the cost of the switch and installation should be set against fuel saving.

DOUBLE GLAZING

Double glazing can also help to reduce your heating bill although the savings are not as high as with roof and wall insulation. Large windows and those in particularly exposed positions are a big source of heat loss and discomfort, and it can help to provide these with double glazing – certainly with lined curtains to cut down on night-time heat loss. Factory-made double glazing units are produced for new houses or conversions and, as they are also made in most present-day window sizes, it can be just as cheap to reglaze as to fit a system based on using a screw-on inner frame with single glazing. Visually, sealed units are almost indistinguishable from a simple sheet of glass and the air space between the two panes is hermetically sealed to prevent misting.

The savings on the fuel bill of a three-bedroom house with double glazing can amount to something like 5 per cent. The important thing to note about double glazing, whether you choose a factory-made unit, a second applied frame for single glazing, or one of the do-it-yourself systems, is that air from the room must be prevented from entering between the panes. If humid air from the room gets between the panes you will get heavy condensation and pools of water on the frame. Tiny holes drilled at an angle of 45 degrees will carry this water away to the outside and reduce condensation but it is best to ensure a perfect seal in the first place. The air gap between the panes must be at least 3 mm. ($\frac{1}{8}$ in.); anything less gives virtually no heat saving. The ideal gap is between 12 mm. ($\frac{1}{2}$ in.) and 20 mm. ($\frac{3}{4}$ in.). Anything more than this is hardly worthwhile except for improving sound insulation.

The main advantages of double glazing are improved comfort, more floor space for seating purposes and a reduction of external noise. The costs of having double glazing for the whole house installed professionally can be recovered in about 10 years.

CLEANING

GENERAL STRATEGY

Try and plan your home so that it is easy to clean. When buying anything, always ask yourself 'How am I going to keep this clean?' If the answer is not clear, ask the shop assistant, and if the advice given is not satisfactory write to the manufacturer for guidance. Never get landed with furnishings which you do not know how to look after.

Very pale carpets and furnishings will inevitably show the dirt. Remember that patterning, even if the colours are pale, will disguise soiling to some extent. On the other hand, plain dark carpets and upholstery are also tricky to care for, as they show up every bit of fluff, thread and crumb!

The more streamlined your room arrangements, the easier your home will be to keep clean. A wall of fitted wardrobes, for example, is easier to clean than an old fashioned bedroom suite. And a modern built-in kitchen eliminates all those grease-collecting nooks and crannies around a free-standing cooker. On the other hand you may deliberately choose to undertake extra cleaning in order to achieve a particular effect – a beautiful display on open shelving for example.

Installing the same floor surfaces in adjacent rooms and passageways also makes for easy cleaning. If for example you have used the same vinyl from the hall along the passage and into the kitchen, you can clean the whole lot in one operation.

It is amazing how easy it is to forget basic cleaning points when shopping for furnishings – the off-white carpet and cream settee are so beguiling!

Always keep carefully any cleaning instructions that come with your furnishing purchases. A separate file for leaflets, swing tickets, etc., can prove invaluable.

CLEANING EQUIPMENT

You cannot keep your home clean without the right equipment, although exactly what you choose and use will be governed a great deal by personal preferences. Use the following notes, therefore, merely as a general guide.

Try to keep all your cleaning things together in one place. A plastic box with handle is helpful, or even a large plastic carrier bag, so that you can carry everything you need around with you.

Inexpensive basics

Dusters You will need several. You can make very good dusters from cut-up old tee shirts, or men's underwear. Dirty dusters do more harm than good, so wash them out regularly, and make sure they are completely dry before re-storing, or they will go mouldy and smell. Alternatively, you can buy cellular paper cleaning cloths, which you throw away when filthy.

Feather duster Sounds old-fashioned, but if it has got a long handle, it can be very useful for getting cobwebs out of corners.

Dustpan and brush Plastic dustpans are more durable and less noisy in use than metal pans. It is useful to have two brushes: one soft, for brushing up dirt on hard surfaces, the other hard, for dirt on soft surfaces, such as carpets.

Long-handled brush Choose one with medium-hard bristles – very hard bristles are inflexible in use (they are intended for outside), and very soft bristles are annoyingly springy.

Mop Modern mops have a sponge attachment on the end of a long handle which you can squeeze by pressing a lever. In practice, however, the sponge is rather small and tends to disintegrate distressingly quickly, although it is easy to buy replacements. The old-fashioned answer is to use a large thick floor cloth well wrung out in warm water over the end of a broom, and this works very well.

Cleaners, polishes, pastes, etc. It is essential with all cleaning products to read the directions on the pack carefully. Everybody has their own favourites. All-purpose modern aerosols will clean most surfaces, such as mirrors, plastic laminates, tiles, modern furniture and so on. You may, however, prefer a polish for the care of older pieces of furniture, and you can choose a wax, an emulsion or an aerosol (see further notes under 'furniture' below). A liquid household cleaner is preferable to scouring powder, which is too harsh for porcelain or vitreous enamel. You will also need proprietary metal polishes for your metal surfaces for brass, silver and so on. Liquid bleach can be useful; it will remove

Windows should not be cleaned in sunshine.

Leather furniture should be cleaned using the proprietary cleaner recommended by the manufacturer.

stubborn stains from lavatory pans, and you can also use a dilute solution for removing stains from white plastic laminates (always rinse well immediately after use). A small bottle of white spirit can be used for removing heavy grease deposits (see notes under specific cleaning situations, below).

Major equipment A vacuum cleaner certainly makes life easier, but a modern carpet sweeper is an acceptable and efficient substitute until you have saved up the necessary money. If you have large areas of fitted carpet to clean, an upright vacuum cleaner will provide a desirable beating action, as well as sucking up the dirt. These are sold with various attachments to enable you to clean crevices, upholstery, stairs and so on. In practice, these

Curtains should not be washed unless they are pre-shrunk. Lined curtains are always better dry-cleaned.

Painted walls can be washed down occasionally with detergent.

Wood furniture should be regularly dusted and a good wax polish used to maintain the surface.

Vinyl floors are hard-wearing and easily kept clean by sweeping and occasional washing.

attachments can be awkward to fit. A cylinder vacuum cleaner is lighter to handle, and there are types available which can be used on both hard and soft floors. In use, the flexibility of a cylinder cleaner compares most advantageously with the powerful beating action of an upright.

Electric polishers are useful if you have old-fashioned wooden floors. Modern vinyl floors, however, keep their shine with little or no polishing.

A carpet shampooer is useful if you have a lot of synthetic carpets which soil quickly but clean easily. Professional cleaning is recommended for wool or wool/nylon carpets. It is possible to hire electric carpet shampooers for short periods from some hardware shops.

CLEANING SITUATIONS

Here is a list, under alphabetical headings, of the most common cleaning situations which occur in the home, with notes on how to deal with them.

Aluminium Discolouration on the inside of aluminium pans can be removed by simmering rhubarb or any acid fruit in the pan.

Animal fur Often a problem on upholstery. Use the attachment on your vacuum cleaner if you have one; otherwise try a barely damp cloth. A slow, fiddly method, which nevertheless works, is to use lengths of sticky tape: the sticky side of the tape picks up all the fur, which then comes away as you peel off the tape again.

Appliances Follow makers' instruc-

tions for cleaning electrical appliances but in general remember never to clean an appliance without unplugging it first.

Baths It is preferable to use a liquid household cleaner rather than a powdered scouring product, which could damage the surface (see vitreous enamel, below). Stubborn stains under taps in basins and baths may respond to a rubbing with warm vinegar, which should be rinsed off immediately. Very bad brown marks can be treated with one heaped teaspoon of citric acid to a half-cup of washing-up liquid. Apply this to the stain and rub gently with a cloth. Leave for a couple of minutes and rinse. Scratches on plastic baths can be removed with metal polish.

Brass First wash tarnished brass in hot

soapy water, rinse and dry off thoroughly. A piece of lemon dipped in salt may remove tarnishing. Alternatively use Brasso according to directions on the can. Often brass is difficult to clean because it has been lacquered and this finish is now damaged. Remove old lacquer with acetone, and then polish. Respray with lacquer if wished.

Candle grease Deposits on furniture can usually be eased off gently with a knife blade, sponged over with hot water, and buffed dry. Hardened deposits on carpets and upholstery are more tricky. Cover them with blotting paper, and iron gently. The grease will melt and then will be drawn into the paper. Where possible (on a tablecloth, for example), you can sandwich the fabric between two layers of paper. You may still be left with a mark which can be treated with dry cleaning solvent.

Cane furniture Brush regularly or vacuum to remove dirt and dust. When very grimy, wash over with warm, soapy water and a soft scrubbing brush. A cold rinse will stiffen cane, and this kind of furniture is best dried outside in the sunshine.

China Discolouration will often respond to rubbing with a solution of vinegar and salt. Otherwise, soak in a weak solution of household bleach, and rinse thoroughly.

Chrome If in good condition, should only need wiping over with cloth wrung out in warm soapy water. Then polish off with dry cloth. However badly discoloured or pitted finishes can be treated with a proprietary chrome cleaning product available from hardware stores or motor accessory shops.

Copper Use a proprietary cleaning product. Tarnish may also respond to a piece of lemon dipped in salt and vinegar. See also *Verdigris*.

Cork Cork floors should be thoroughly sealed. They then merely require damp mopping for usual cleaning. However, very bad marks and stains can be treated with fine steelwool or fine glasspaper. You should rub gently, otherwise you may damage the cork. It may well be necessary to work right back to the cork, in which case you should renew the sealer finish.

Curtains Follow carefully instructions for type of fabric, as supplied at time of purchase. Remember that many types of fabric are best dry cleaned, and this method is also preferable if shrinkage would be disastrous! Lined or interlined curtains are also best dry-cleaned. Always pull the gathers out of curtain headings before you wash them, so that the heading lies flat; this is the reason why curtain drawstrings should never be cut, but should be wound up neatly and tucked out of sight. Very grimy curtains may respond to an initial soaking of ten minutes in cold water with a little detergent.

Furniture Always read carefully any care labels that come with your furniture. In general, modern furniture finishes require far less care than people think. It is for example a fallacy that furniture should be polished to 'feed' the wood. Most *modern furniture finishes* can be cleaned effectively with a damp cloth and a little household detergent. In particular, avoid using a wax polish on an intentional matt finish. *Finishes on older furniture* which may be based on beeswax or French polish may however become dull from the accumulation of many fine scratches. You can restore the surface of this kind of finish with a good quality wax polish or an emulsion cream. *Teak furniture* may require a light application of oil from time to time, as recommended by the manufacturer. Use a proprietary teak oil and rub in sparingly, having dusted the surface thoroughly first. Do not use raw linseed oil as the surface may remain sticky for some time. *Scratches:* you may be able to disguise these with a wax crayon, or with shoe polish. Or you can buy scratch-removing products from hardware stores. *Ring marks* may respond to a light stroking with fine steel wool dipped in furniture polish; *white heat marks* can sometimes be removed with metal polish. Always wipe immediately with a clean cloth. *Painted furniture* can be cleaned with a solution of warm water and detergent, removing really stubborn marks with white spirit. Rinse well and dry off with a clean dry cloth. *Plastic furniture* can be washed clean with a solution of warm water and liquid household detergent. Scratches can be treated with metal polish. You can finally apply an anti-static plastic furniture polish to cut down further dirt attraction.

Lampshades Remove shades from fittings to clean, having first pulled out plug from socket, or turned off fitting at switch.

Fabric shades If these have been sewn together from washable fabric, you can swish the entire shade in a bowl of warm, soapy water; rinse in clear lukewarm water, and allow to dry naturally, away from any direct heat. Watch out for any trimmings which may run; remove these first if necessary. Very delicate, non-washable fabrics must be professionally dry-cleaned. Do not wash shades that have been merely stuck together; you can only give these a good dusting, removing any marks with a pad moistened with carbon tetrachloride. Alternatively, try a pad of clean cotton wool dipped in oatmeal, rubbed over the shade, and left for ten minutes. Then rub off lightly, using a clean cloth pad. Grubby *lace and silk shades* can sometimes be cleaned with powdered magnesia, applied with a soft brush and rubbed well into the fabric. You should leave the powder for at least an hour, so that it can absorb the grease, then brush it out very gently, making sure your brush is clean. Old-fashioned *parchment shades* can be cleaned with one teaspoon of soapflakes dissolved in a little warm water, with the addition of two teaspoons of methylated spirit. This solution can be sponged over the shade with a clean soft cloth or small sponge. Wipe off any lather. Then follow with application of pure methylated spirit on clean cloth, and allow to dry. Polish off with soft dry cloth. A little olive oil, wiped over the surface with a clean cloth, may finally restore the sheen. *Plastic shades* can be washed with warm water and detergent, but allow a diluted water/detergent solution to dry on the shade as this helps to cut down on dirt attraction.

Lavatory pans Most stains can be shifted with household bleach, left overnight if possible, and then well flushed. Never use bleach and a proprietary lavatory cleaner at the same time, as this can release harmful gases. Stubborn stains on very old pans can be treated with a mixture of one part spirits of salts diluted with six parts water. Rub quickly with old brush or mop, and then immediately flush pan several times.

Leather Use proprietary cleaner for new leather furniture as recommended by manufacturer. Shabby leather on old furniture can be treated with a mixture of one pint of water plus two teaspoons of vinegar and half a teaspoon of household ammonia. Apply with a soft, clean cloth, and then leave to dry. Follow by rubbing with a cloth made moist with castor oil, and when this is dry, finish by polishing with a silicone cream. You may be able to move old stains with eucalyptus oil; as the oil evaporates, the stain should go too.

Matting Take up from time to time, and sweep or vacuum dirt that has fallen through weave. Vacuum or beat the matting itself. Remove any grease stains by scrubbing with a solution of warm water and washing soda. Rush matting can be scrubbed clean with soapy water, rinsed with warm water, and then finally rinsed with cold water to which salt has been added. Make sure all mattings are completely dry before replacing.

Paintwork Wash over with a solution of warm water and detergent, rinse, and rub dry for a smear-free finish. If very dirty, try a household cleaning paste.

Silver Clean with one of the many excellent proprietary preparations on the market, following instructions on the pack.

Sinks To keep your waste pipe clear from grease, pour down a solution of boiling water and washing soda once a week. *Enamel and porcelain* sinks can be cleaned with liquid household cleaners to preserve the finish. These are preferable to scouring powders. On obstinate marks, however, you can use diluted liquid bleach, or a paste cleaner. To protect against surface chipping, use a plastic washing-up bowl and protect draining boards in the same way, by using a plastic drainer. *Stainless steel* sinks do in fact stain rather easily; ideally they should be washed, rinsed, and dried after every use. A proprietary stainless steel cleaner is recommended for removing marks and discolouration, and if you do resort to household bleach, make sure that it is well-diluted, and that you rinse well.

Slate Here is an old-fashioned recipe for restoring the colour to the surface of slate as found in old fireplaces. Mix together equal parts of boiled linseed oil and white spirit. Rub on this mixture with a soft cloth, and then polish up with soft dry cloth.

Stone Remember that any soap, or scouring powders may affect the colour of the stone. The simplest remedy is a scrubbing with a wire brush dipped in water. However there are also proprietary products for cleaning soot from stone fireplaces, and products for removing oil and grease stains from stone are sometimes sold by motor accessory shops (who sell them for cleaning stone garage floors).

Upholstery Follow carefully any instructions supplied by manufacturer. Clean fixed upholstery regularly, using the attachment on your vacuum cleaner supplied for the purpose. A gentle beating with a ruler will bring dust to the surface. If you do not possess a vacuum cleaner, use a brush instead; you can buy special upholstery brushes. On no account should you vacuum down-filled cushions, which should be merely brushed, and lightly shaken. Odd spots and stains can be treated with a sponging of weak solution of detergent and warm water. If stain lingers, try a proprietary dry cleaning product, testing out the cleaner first on an inconspicuous area, in case it causes a colour change. You can buy an upholstery cleaning kit containing small brush and shampoo for all-over soiling. *Plastic coverings*, including polyurethanes and p.v.c. It is wisest to avoid any form of cleaner or polisher. Simply wipe clean with damp cloth or sponge, and dry off with soft cloth.

Verdigris is the greenish staining you sometimes find on copper. A rub with vinegar and salt will remove slight deposits. If marks are stubborn, use French chalk mixed with methylated spirit applied with a soft cloth, rubbing with fine steel wool if necessary. Finish with a suitable metal polish.

Vinyl floors, tile and sheet All floors of this kind should be swept regularly, or vacuumed if you have a cleaner of the cylinder type. To preserve built-in sheen, simply mop over with cloth wrung out well in warm water; avoid strong solutions of detergent which can cause yellowing on some floors. If you feel it necessary to polish, use a proprietary liquid emulsion according to directions on pack; it will dry to a soft shine. On very stubborn marks, you can use a scouring pad, with a little white spirit if necessary, but be careful not to damage the floor finish, and be sure to wash off all traces of spirit. Sometimes old polishes have been allowed to build up into an ugly thick deposit; this can be removed with a solution of ammonia and detergent and warm water; rinse well, allow to dry, and then apply a liquid emulsion polish.

Vinyl wallcoverings can be washed with a detergent solution; they can even be scrubbed if necessary. You should work upwards from floor level, and try to avoid scrubbing across the joins. Stains should respond to a gentle, sparing application of white spirit, and very stubborn marks can be rubbed with scouring powder, but do not use these treatments on the new vinyls which have a metallic finish.

Vitreous enamel is in fact glass bonded onto metal, and harsh cleaners should be avoided to preserve the finish. Suitable cleaners in the shops are marked with the seal of approval of the Vitreous Enamel Development Council.

Wallpaper Papers described as '*washable*' are usually only spongeable so avoid flooding them with water. Work from the bottom of the wall upwards, cleaning with a sponge merely dampened in a solution of detergent and warm water. Avoid using solvents such as white spirit, which could damage the finish. *Non-washable papers* can sometimes be cleaned with wedges of fresh bread; use plenty and keep reforming the bread to present a fresh surface. It should absorb quite a lot of dirt.

Walls To wash painted walls, equip yourself with a large sponge and a bucket of warm water and detergent solution. Work in strips of about three feet at a time, or whatever you find comfortable. Change the water frequently, and work from the skirting board upwards. Then rinse off, working from the top downwards.

Windows Best cleaned on a warm dull day. There are many satisfactory cleaning products on sale in the shops, including aerosols and creams. Use one cloth for applying them, and keep a fresh cloth for polishing off. However it is possible to clean windows quite adequately with a sponge and a solution of warm water and detergent, finishing off with plenty of newspaper, rubbing well until all smears vanish. Stubborn fly marks can be removed by an application of methylated spirits.

Wood You can sometimes shift marks made on wood floors with turpentine, but if they persist, also rub lightly with steel wool. *Wooden draining boards* can be scrubbed with cold salt water and a hard scrubbing brush. Marks on *varnished wood* can often be shifted with white spirit, but you may also have to use steel wool, after which you will have to re-colour and polish.

REMOVING STAINS

Most of us have at least one garment which has been spoiled by a stain that cannot be removed. Either the stain has set in the fabric or we have forgotten what it was and are therefore uncertain how to remove it. The best way to deal successfully with stains is to act immediately. If you delay, certain stains cannot be removed from synthetic fabrics and ones with drip-dry finishes. Worse, some stains damage the fibres: notably iron mould which rots viscose rayon and acetates such as Dicel or Tricel. At best, a neglected stain needs harsher removal methods than one which is tackled before it has been thoroughly absorbed. Drastic measures can harm delicate fibres and affect dyes. To avoid turning an accident into a major catastrophe, test stain removal agents before using them where possible damage may show, such as the inside of the hem or on a seam allowance. Never rub at a stain however much you may feel compelled to do so. Pinch it with a clean cotton cloth, a piece of cotton wool or a paper tissue. When you apply the removal agent work from the outside of the stain to the centre. This will prevent the stain from spreading too far.

CLEANING AGENTS
Obviously you cannot provide imimmediate treatment without a battery of chemicals. Some are poisonous if inhaled or swallowed, others are inflammable. They should be labelled and kept out of harm's way in a locked box. It should contain:

 Amyl acetate
 Benzine
 Carbon tetrachloride
 Cotton wool, paper tissues, white
 cotton fabric such as sheeting
 Glycerine
 Household ammonia
 Household bleach
 Hydrogen peroxide
 Methylated spirit
 Photographic hypo
 Oxalic acid crystals
 Turpentine
 White spirit
 White vinegar

COMMON STAINS
Here is a list of common stains with instructions for their removal.

Beetroot, blackcurrant and other fruit juices, cocoa, coffee, ice lollies, ice creams, milk pickles, soft drinks, sauces, soup, sugary foods, wines, spirits, washable ink
If **fresh**, soak in cold detergent solution. Then wash normally. If **dried** on, soak in a mixture of one part glycerine to two parts water and leave for ten minutes before following instructions for fresh stains.

Chocolate, cream, egg, jam, mud, nappy stains, syrup, tomato ketchup
Scrape off build-up. Follow treatment above for fresh or dried on stains.

Blood, meat juice
Soak in cold water before following instructions above for fresh or dried on stains. After being laundered faded stains may remain; treat as for iron mould.

Any stains in this group that remain on white fabric that can be bleached may be soaked in one part of 20 vol. hydrogen peroxide to nine parts water for one hour before being laundered once more.

Two pad method This is a useful method of removing stains which can apply to many of the stains listed below.

Ballpoint ink
Hold pad of cotton wool above stain. Dab underside of stain with pad of cotton wool moistened in methylated spirit or – if fabric is Dicel or Tricel – in benzine. When ink has soaked through onto top pad replace pad. Follow by laundering in the usual way.

Bicycle oil, light machine oil
Follow two pad method described above using Carbon tetrachloride.

Chalks and washable crayons
Brush off loose powder. Dab with strong detergent solution. Launder as usual.

Chalks and indelible crayons
Use two pad method with methylated spirit

Chewing or bubble gum
Try two pad method using methylated spirit or benzine in the case of Dicel and Tricel. If the build-up is prohibitive harden by rubbing with an ice cube. Pick off gum by hand, finish with two pad treatment followed by usual laundering.

Cooking fat, cod liver oil, heavy grease
Follow two pad treatment using carbon tetrachloride, then launder.

Contact adhesives such as Copydex and Evostick
Follow two pad method using amyl acetate, then launder.

Felt pen ink
Follow the two pad method using methylated spirit (benzine for Dicel or Tricel), then launder as usual.

Grass stains
Follow the two pad method using methylated spirit (benzine for Dicel or Tricel) then launder as usual.

Greasy make-up
Follow two pad method using carbon tetrachloride, then launder as usual.

Hair lacquer
Follow two pad method using amyl acetate, then launder as usual.

Home dyes
Articles can be stripped back to their original colour or paler with Dygon, although the original colour may be affected. Accidental splashes of colour can also be removed from nylon, cotton, velvet, linen, viscose and acetate rayons such as Dicel and Tricel but *not* from polyester fabrics such as Terylene, Crimplene, Dacron, Tergel or Terlenka or from acrylics such as Acrilan, Orlon or Courtelle or from fabrics with special finishes. Dygon will not remove colour from fabric fast-dyed by manufacturers.

Iodine
Soak in solution made up of one teaspoon of photographic hypo crystals dissolved in one pint of warm water. Watch closely and as soon as stain disappears rinse thoroughly in plain water, then launder as usual.

Iron mould on white cotton and white linen
Isolate stained area by bunching up and tying tightly with cotton. Immerse isolated area in solution made up of half a teaspoonful of oxalic acid crystals in half a pint of hot water. Leave two or three minutes. Rinse thoroughly and launder as usual.

Iron mould on wool, synthetics and delicate fabrics
Dab stain with lemon juice. Leave for ten minutes, place under a damp cloth and press with iron at temperature suitable to the fabric. Repeat whole process again if necessary then launder as usual.

Lipstick, cream eye shadow, eye pencil
Follow two pad method using carbon tetrachloride then launder as usual.

Marking ink

Use marking ink eradicator according to the instructions.

Metal polish
Follow two pad method using carbon tetrachloride then launder as usual

Mildew on white cottons and linens without special finishes
Soak in one part household bleach to one hundred parts of water containing one tablespoonful of vinegar. Rinse thoroughly then launder as usual.

Mildew on coloured articles
Stains will fade if soaked regularly before being laundered in strong detergent solution.

Mildew on white drip-dry fabrics
Soak in solution made up with one part of 20 vol. hydrogen peroxide to nine parts of water. When stain has disappeared rinse thoroughly and launder as usual.

Nail varnish
Follow two pad method using amyl acetate – except on Dicel or Tricel – then launder as usual.

Permanent ink on white cotton and linen
Isolate stained area by bunching up and tying with cotton. Immerse isolated area in solution made up of half a teaspoonful of oxalic acid crystals dissolved in half a pint of hot water. Leave two or three minutes. Rinse thoroughly and launder as usual.

Paint (emulsion)
Remove immediately by sponging with cold water. Dried-on stains cannot be removed.

Paint (oil)
Follow two pad method using white spirit, then launder as usual.

Paint (cellulose)
Follow two pad method using amyl acetate, then launder as usual.

Perspiration
If fresh damp with water then hold over an open bottle of ammonia. If dried on, sponge with white vinegar, rinse thoroughly then launder as usual.

Plasticine
Pick off build-up by hand. Follow two pad method using carbon tetrachloride, then launder as usual.

Scorch marks
Soak in cold detergent solution and launder as usual. If this is ineffective, damp area with water, dab marks with glycerine then launder as usual. Remaining traces may disappear if soaked in solution made up with one part 20 vol. hydrogen peroxide to nine parts of water. Article must then be rinsed thoroughly and laundered as usual.

Heavy scorch marks cannot be removed.

Shoe Polish
Soak stain with glycerine then follow two pad method using Carbon Tetrachloride. Launder as usual.

Sun tan oil
Follow two pad method using carbon tetrachloride then launder as usual.

Tar
Scrape off build-up. Follow two pad method using carbon tetrachloride then launder as usual.

HOUSEHOLD EQUIPMENT
Stains on covers and curtains can be removed by the above methods. Stains on equipment are different, however. The following table includes remedies to solve the more common problems in the absence of a proprietary solution.

Bath (enamelled)
Brown stains caused by dripping taps can be removed by scrubbing with spirits of salts. Wear gloves when handling this very dangerous acid.

Bath (acrylic)
Light scratches can be removed by rubbing with metal polish.

Carpets and rugs
Before they are dry, puddles made by untrained puppies can be neutralised if soaked for thirty minutes with water containing a little soda. Rinse with plain water and towel dry.

Cooker
Burned-on stains on the enamelled top can be removed with spray-on oven cleaner. Repeat application if necessary and wipe off with cloth moistened in hot water.

Decanters
Wine stains can be removed by half filling decanter with water and adding a handful of shot or rice. Holding stopper securely swirl and shake the mixture. When clean, rinse empty decanter in hot water.

Marble
Badly stained polished marble cannot be cleaned without removing the shine. Fume stains from cigarettes, logs or coal may be removed by rubbing with a cloth soaked in vinegar. Rinse. Bad stains on unpolished marble can be removed by applying a poultice made up of one part by weight of soft soap, two parts by weight of whiting mixed to a paste with a quarter part by weight of caustic soda, dissolved in a small amount of water. Taking care not to burn yourself with the caustic soda, apply the mixture with a brush. Leave

for a day. Brush off with plenty of water and repeat whole process if necessary.

Mirrors
Hair lacquer can be removed with methylated spirit.

Piano keys
Ivory keys that have yellowed may be whitened if they are rubbed with a cloth moistened with lemon juice.

Polished wood (waxed)
Stains that have been absorbed by the wood can only be removed by rubbing off the polish with white spirit and sanding off the surface of the wood until the stain has gone. The wood must then be re-waxed. White water marks can be removed by rubbing away with methylated spirit, rubbing with linseed oil then re-waxing. Oil stains on *bare* wood may be removed by poulticing with a mixture of water, whiting and trisodium phosphate in equal portions.

Polished wood (french polished)
Spirit or heat will dissolve the polish and stains that have reached the wood underneath cannot be removed without stripping the polish, sanding the wood and re-polishing. Superficial blemishes to the polish can be removed by rubbing the spot with brass polish applied speedily and sparingly on a lint-free cloth. Allow it to dry thoroughly between coats and do not reapply on same cloth.

Skirtings
Stains made by orange polish should be poulticed with a generous application of colourless shoe polish. Leave 12 hours and remove. Stains made by clean-and-polish products must be washed off with a strong detergent.

Stone floors
Red polish may be removed by rubbing with white spirit then scrubbing with a strong detergent solution.

Vases
Glass stained by hard water can be cleaned if rubbed with mild scouring paste, or pumice powder. If you cannot get your hand far enough inside, use a stick with a cloth wrapped round the end. Dip it in pumice powder and rub on the stain. Rinse and dry, then polish with jeweller's rouge.

Wallpaper
Greasemarks should be covered with blotting paper which will absorb the oil when pressed with a medium hot iron. Adhesive left by cellulose tape is removed if rubbed with a clean cloth soaked in petrol lighter fuel.

227

LOOKING FOR TROUBLE

HOUSEHOLD PESTS

However well built a house may be and however well it is maintained it is always liable to be invaded by various unwanted insects or rodents.

Many of these creatures are casual wanderers from the garden and only a few are harmful to man or the building but it helps to know which is which.

Improved standards of hygiene have greatly reduced infestations by fleas, bedbugs and many flies. On the other hand, modern central heating, fitted carpets and the increased use of untreated softwood timbers tend to encourage carpet beetles, clothes moths and woodworm. Mice have developed a resistance to certain pest control chemicals and there are legal restrictions on alternatives.

You should be able to recognise insect or rodent damage and be able to decide what types of control measures, if any, are necessary to get rid of them safely.

Under the Prevention of Damage by Pests Act 1949, property owners are bound to take steps to prevent infestations or to report infestations to the Public Health Department.

To deal with most household pests it is usually necessary to use some form of chemical. This may be a powder, an oil-based spray, a lacquer, a puffer pack, a bait or an insecticidal smoke. Fumigation may occasionally be needed, but this can be undertaken only by specialist contractors.

Pest control precautions Before using any insecticide or rodenticide in the home, read the instructions on the label and follow them exactly.

Do not leave any chemicals in unlabelled jars or tins. Store all pest control chemicals where children cannot possibly reach them.

Pest control liquids should not be placed in cups or glasses or bottles which might be reached by children. Splashes of liquid on your skin should be washed off and after pesticides have been used hands should be washed before food is prepared or eaten. Before using an aerosol make sure the hole in the release button is pointing in the right direction.

Avoid inhaling vapour or fumes from sprays and do not allow domestic animals to have access to baits, liquids or powders. Do not spray near naked flames and do not smoke while applying them. This applies particularly to wood preservatives. Open windows and doors to improve ventilation.

Residues should be carefully disposed of by washing them down an outside drain with plenty of water. In the case of aerosols, never throw them on a fire or puncture the can but place the empty unit in a dustbin.

Burn or bury deeply the bodies of rats or mice killed by rodenticides.

Never apply insecticidal chemicals directly to the fur of cats or dogs unless they are specified for the purpose. Proprietary brands of flea powder or insecticide for veterinary use are available.

Where food is prepared or stored take care not to spray utensils, working surfaces or the food itself. Pyrethrum formulations are the safest to use near food. Some other chemicals have an aromatic odour which can taint food. Formulations sold for household purposes are safe when *used as directed in accordance with the manufacturer's instructions.*

When extra help is needed The range of domestic pesticides available to you is necessarily limited and in the case of large infestations of any pest, or where insects seem difficult to kill, it is often wise to call on the services of a professional pest control servicing company.

INSECT AND RODENT PESTS

Ants In the larder these are a common nuisance. Any food rich in sugar or protein is intensely attractive to them and the workers from a nest soon cluster all over it. They can be easily controlled if all their nests are found but these are often inaccessible.

Black garden ants which invade the house should if possible be traced to their nest outside. Boiling water can then be poured into the entrance hole as a quick 'first aid' measure. A spray or dust containing lindane or carbaryl is more effective and more permanent, but these substances should not be used near food. A jelly bait containing chlordecone, marketed in tubes, is very effective and the workers destroy the whole colony by feeding it to the queens and young in the nest. Effective protection is also given by painting insecticidal lacquer on to the thresholds, pipe runs, skirting, etc., along which the insects run.

Bedbugs Modern hygiene has almost reduced bedbugs to a rarity but they still exist.

They are wingless, round, flat, brown insects, found behind peeling wallpaper, in cracked plaster or woodwork or in bed frames and mattresses.

At one time, bedbugs were dealt with by fumigation but persistent insecticides are now more widely used in infested premises. Upholstered furniture, however, may well need fumigating and this can be carried out by a fumigation contractor.

Beetles (various) A lindane or diazinon aerosol or a puffer pack of carbaryl insect powder accompanied by the thorough removal of all infested food residues will dispose of the beetles at all stages of their life cycle. Some, like the bread beetle and the spider beetle, are found in stored food. Others may wander in from the garden.

Carpet beetles (1) Housewives are often perturbed or puzzled to find small golden-brown 'woolly bear' grubs in an airing cupboard, at the edges of carpets or in a piece of stored carpet felt. These are the larvae of one of the species of carpet beetles which thrive in warm, dry conditions.

The adult beetles are small, oval in shape, not unlike a small brown-and-yellow ladybird.

The damage caused by carpet beetles usually consists of well-defined round holes often along the seams of fabric where the grubs bite through.

If carpet beetles are found, try to trace their origin. Search the loft and eaves for birds' nests or the dead bodies of birds or rodents and remove them. Check pipe lagging and vacuum clean shelves, floorboards, cupboards, carpets and upholstery.

Spray affected carpets or furnishings with a mothproofing aerosol which contains lindane. A persistent contact insecticide of this type is necessary because the 'woolly bear' larvae often survive exposure to a short-life insecticide. Dust between floorboards, under carpet felts and crevices with an insect powder based on carbaryl.

Clean carpets regularly and every six months spray the double thickness at the edges of fitted carpets and areas under heavy furniture with a residual insecticide. Spray both surfaces at the edge of a carpet and into cracks be-

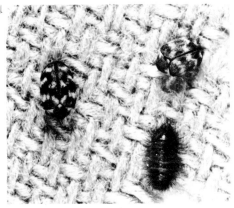

tween floorboards, and the seams of upholstery.

Clothes moth (6) The common clothes moth and the brown house moth are the commonest moths affecting stored clothing. These moths do not eat any material and in fact are incapable of feeding. All the feeding, and therefore the damage, is done by the larvae and stops as soon as they pupate.

Clothes moths and house moths cannot develop in clean wool and fur.

Preventative measures are the best answer. Keep your clothes scrupulously clean and store woollens in sealed polythene bags or closely wrapped in paper, in tightly closed drawers or cupboards, preferably in a cool room. Before putting woollens away, fold in one or two discs or tablets based on paradichlorobenzene or napthalene. Hang moth repellents in wardrobes and cupboards.

Cockroaches (5) The cockroach may still be found in older houses and flats, usually appearing in bathrooms and kitchens where they can cluster in warm, moist, favourable sites around pipes, stoves and sinks.

They are nocturnal in habit, emerging at night from the narrowest cracks to forage for any of a wide variety of human food. They contaminate more than they consume, polluting everything with a foul 'roachy' odour which is very persistent.

The basis of effective cockroach control is to place insecticide where the insect hides, although it often needs specialist equipment to deal with cockroaches in their inaccessible harbourages. Use Rentokil Insectrol, sprayed liberally from its aerosol container into infested floor cavities, pipe runs, areas behind sinks, pipes and stoves to control cockroaches. For tiled surfaces an oil-based spray or an insectical lacquer will provide long-lasting protection – best applied by a servicing company.

Earwigs These are often brought into homes on cut flowers and are frequent intruders from the garden, usually in search of suitable crevices as hiding places. They normally emerge only at night and cause no real damage in houses. Dust lindane or carbaryl in the humid areas where earwigs are found and remove creepers and herbage from around the walls of the home.

Flies Although the most commonly tolerated pests, they are among the most loathsome.

Control houseflies in two ways – by scrupulous hygiene and prompt disposal of all food residues, empty tins and bottles to deprive them of possible breeding sites. Every disposal bin or refuse bag should have a close fitting lid and be thoroughly emptied at regular intervals. It is a good idea to spray or dust the inside of the dustbin with an insecticide during the summer. Wrap kitchen refuse before putting it in the bin. Adult flies indoors are best dealt with by an aerosol containing pyrethrins.

Impregnated strips of plastic giving off vapours of the organophosphorus insecticide dichlorous are sold for fly control.

Mice (2) The house mouse, and sometimes the long-tailed field mouse, seek the warmth and shelter of buildings for nesting sites and food. Traces of the small, grey house mice first noticed by the householder are the presence of dark-coloured droppings or damage to stored foods, packaging or wood.

In common with all rodents they have a compulsive need to gnaw in order to keep their incisor teeth worn down to a constant length. Electric cables, water pipes and gas pipes, packaging and woodwork may all be seriously

damaged by mice and several instances of electrical fires and floods have been recorded as a result of mouse activity. They contaminate far more food than they consume and are capable of carrying many diseases particularly *Salmonella* food poisoning.

Mice are erratic, sporadic feeders, nibbling at many sources of food rather than taking repeated meals from any one item. They do not need free water to drink as they normally obtain sufficient moisture from their food.

Because of these habits, traditional baiting techniques and trapping are often unsatisfactory and a combination of rodenticides may be necessary as well as mouseproofing their entry.

Until recently the most widely used and effective rodenticide has been warfarin. Only a very small proportion of the chemical is mixed with the bait, usually oatmeal, so there is no danger of humans or pets consuming a lethal dose accidentally.

In probably half the area of Britain, however, mice have now become resistant to warfarin and a different type of mouse killer based on the drug alphachloralose has been developed and is marketed as Alphakil. It is quick, humane and safe to use indoors as directed on the instructions.

Mites Not true insects, they often escape detection by the householder until their numbers build up to a serious infestation.

Treatment consists of disposing of affected food, ventilating and drying the larder, or, in the case of the furniture mite, heating the room to a high temperature for 24 hours.

Gooseberry Red Spider Mites occasionally invade from the garden. A spray of malathion or lindane around doors and windows will usually control these mites and it may be necessary to cut back vegetation for about 1 m. (3 ft) from the walls of the house.

Mosquitoes An aerosol of pyrethrins gives the required knock-down against mosquitoes and if larvae are found in situations such as water-butts a drop of paraffin or light oil on the surface will stop them developing.

Plaster beetle In a new house, or where damp plaster occurs in old property, very small dark-coloured beetles may be encountered, only about 2 mm. long. These insects and their larvae feed on the moulds and mildews which grow on damp walls. If the rooms are heated and thoroughly ventilated the moulds will die and so will the beetles.

Rats The rat has plagued man for thousands of years.

Like mice, they need to gnaw to keep their constantly-growing incisor teeth worn down and they damage woodwork, pipes and wiring cables by their gnawing. They are capable of spreading many diseases from their filthy surroundings.

Where rats are found, one of the proprietary ready-mixed warfarin baits such as Rodine should be used. These can be obtained as handy sachets which can be placed unopened near signs of infestation. Keep replacing the baits until no more are taken.

For serious or persistent rat infestations call a pest control servicing company or your local Public Health Dept.

Silverfish This primitive, wingless insect often appears in baths or other damp situations. It is silvery grey with a 12 mm. ($\frac{1}{2}$ in.) long cigar-shaped body and darts about very quickly when disturbed.

It does very little harm, feeding on moulds that grow on carbohydrate substances such as wallpaper paste. A carbaryl spray or dust will control silverfish and for a large number you can use an Insectrol aerosol or puffer pack of insect powder.

Spiders Although they cause no harm, most people regard them with feelings of revulsion. They feed on other insects and are, therefore, beneficial. Spiders, having eight legs, are not insects but arachnids. Three species are common in houses and are responsible for the household cobwebs. If you must get rid of them, use an aerosol such as Insectrol.

Wasps These invade kitchens in late summer. They generally cause more anxiety than harm but their sting is painful. The best relief comes from an anti-histamine cream after making sure that none of the sting mechanism is left in the skin.

Household aerosols or insecticidal sprays will knock down adult wasps and a nest in a bank or wall can be dealt with by puffing Rentokil Wasp Nest Killer into the entrance. Treat nests at dusk when the wasps are safely inside, wear gloves as a precaution and leave the vicinity of the nest quickly.

Woodlice Harmless grey segmented creatures, they are not insects but crustaceans. One species rolls up into a characteristic tight ball when disturbed. Usually associated with damp conditions in corners of bathrooms, kitchens or under doormats. Any good household insecticidal powder or spray will kill them, but remedy the cause of dampness to prevent recurrence.

CARE OF WOOD OUTDOORS

In the garden, sheds, gates, seats and rustic work will all last longer if protected from decay and for such items an organic solvent type of wood preservative should be painted on in two liberal coats or sprayed at a coverage of about 4·5 l. (1 gal.) to 28 sq. m. (300 sq. ft) of surface area. If dipping is convenient, small timbers should be dipped for 3–5 minutes and large timbers for 10 minutes. Wooden post ends to be sunk into the ground should be steeped for at least an hour or, better still, overnight in a good proprietary wood preservative.

Organic solvent wood preservatives are available in clear brown, or green, the green being specially made for wood that may come into contact with plants.

It is also possible to buy a cedarwood water-repellent finish which is ideal for maintaining the rich colour of western red cedar – or for giving cedar colour to other outdoor timbers. This stabilises the wood and prevents cracking as well as discolouration by weathering. It stops wood going grey, preserves it, and cannot peel, flake, crack or blister. Maintenance is simple, just wash off surface dirt and apply another coat. A clear water-repellent finish is also available. These are ideal for treating cladding, room extensions or sheds and fencing.

Garden furniture may be of celcurised softwood which needs no further pre-

1. The yellow fruiting body of the fungus that causes dry rot in woodwork. It thrives in damp, badly-ventilated conditions.

1

4

serving, but the traditional garden seats, benches and stools are in elm, teak or oak and all these will benefit from an occasional coat of teak oil to restore some of the natural lustre that exposure to the weather will remove. Exterior joinery of houses built to NHBC standards in the past six years should have been treated with a preservative primer. Where wet rot has occurred in older window frames and sills, be sure to treat replacement wood with a clear preservative before painting.

FIRE PRECAUTIONS

Fire in the home is a terrifying experience and even a small outbreak can leave a legacy of smoke smell and water damage long after it has been put out.

Apart from the obvious need to safeguard exposed coal, gas or electric fires, paraffin stoves and other heaters, it is sensible to check up on other pos-

2. Dry rot which has affected
the joists under the floor-boards.
3. A window-frame attacked
by wet rot.

sible causes of fire. Are the electrical wiring circuits in good order? Mice gnawing insulation can cause short circuits for instance. Are the thermostats on electrical appliances working as they should? Immersion heaters that overheat can be disastrous.

Many of the safety precautions against fire can be learned so that they become habits. Never go out leaving anything cooking on the stove. You may be de-

layed getting back. Unplug the TV set and switch off all unused power points at night or when going away. Shut doors to confine any possible outbreak to one room.

Many kitchen fires are caused by hot fat or especially cooking oil igniting in the pan. Do not try to carry it outside and do *not* use water on it. Snuff it out with the lid of the pan, or best of all with a Sentinel fire blanket. Made of woven glass fibres, the fire blanket is quickly released from its pack, will smother the fire and can be re-used. Consider, also, installing a domestic fire extinguisher.

Surfaces of combustible materials such as wood panelling, hardboard and insulating board can be flameproofed by the Albi range of intumescent flame retardant surface coatings. These should be applied by a contractor.

DAMP, MOULD, CONDENSATION AND INSULATION

It is a curious fact that as standards of amenity and comfort in our homes rise, so do complaints about mould growing on plaster, paint and wallpaper in houses. A common cause is condensation, itself caused by inadequate ventilation.

Dealing with mould It is possible to eliminate mould by depriving it of water. First wipe down affected surfaces with antiseptic or a fungicidal solution to remove existing growth. A solution of household bleach, rinsed

off afterwards may be sufficient to clear it off.

If we can eliminate water from the surfaces of our homes, mould spores will not germinate and we can prevent further trouble.

Moisture on or within walls may come from rising damp in old property, moisture of construction in new homes not fully dried out, faulty plumbing or exterior drainage systems, or most probably, from condensation.

First check for broken guttering, overflows, bad pointing in brickwork or leaking plumbing if there is a severe localised damp problem. Make sure the damp-proof course is not bridged by a flower bed or path against the wall.

Today the cure of rising damp in walls is far easier than it was twenty years ago. Insertion of damp proof membrane by the Discovac system or installation of an electro-osmotic damp-proofing system that carries a proper 20 year guarantee involves little of the mess and inconvenience of older traditional methods. You will just need patience while the wall dries out after the installation, before you can redecorate. In a new house, fungicidal paints, plenty of ventilation and adequate heating should cure any dampness as the water of construction evaporates, although local damp patches such as those caused by a cold concrete lintel over a window may need further attention. Keep gutters, downpipes and brickwork in good condition.

WOODWORM

The increasing use of softwood building timber with a high proportion of vulnerable sapwood (over 50% on average) means that the woodworm problem in structural timbers is likely to increase. Modern rafters 10 by 5 cm. (4 by 2 in.) will not suffer a sustained woodworm attack without being weakened. As far as furniture is concerned, Cuban mahogany is immune from woodworm attack, as are the popular modern teak furniture suites. Beech is thought to become susceptible after about forty years and oak after about 60 years so all second-hand or old furniture should be inspected carefully for holes. Often apparently solid furniture is only veneered pine or has a cheap plywood backing that may be attacked. Teak and afromosia, incidentally, will benefit from a wipe over with a special teak oil to keep their appearance and natural lustre.

The adult furniture beetle is a small brown insect about 6 mm. ($\frac{1}{4}$ in.) long which can fly strongly. It may fly into a house and set up home in the loft or it may be introduced in old packing cases, wicker baskets or furniture.

Fresh woodworm holes show clean white wood inside and a little wood powder or 'frass' may drop out.

Old-fashioned remedies such as wiping furniture with turpentine do *not* give lasting protection and there are on the market effective woodworm killing fluids, which consist of a special insecticide in a light and penetrating solvent. These will deal permanently with all stages of the woodworm life cycle in one thorough treatment. However, it is not sufficient only to treat areas where holes are seen, as grubs may be tunnelling anywhere in an infested item.

All surfaces should be thoroughly coated by brush or spray, including inside drawers, backing, undersides and feet. In addition, extra penetration in hardwood may be obtained by using a special injector with a patent nozzle to squirt some of the woodworm killer into the holes about every four inches. Woodworm in furniture should never be neglected. It may spread to the rafters and the floor unless they are of vacuum-pressure pretreated timber.

Woodworm in structural timbers is often spotted by a surveyor when a house changes hands and might well reduce the value of the house.

Building societies may withhold part of a mortgage on a house if woodworm is present when it changes hands and they may insist on expert treatment covered by a guarantee. It is now possible to insure against woodworm by paying an annual premium. If woodworm subsequently occurs while you are covered by the policy, the company will treat it free of charge.

TREATING WOODWORM YOURSELF

If you are prepared to take the trouble to do it correctly, woodworm can be effectively eradicated by the average handywoman.

Use an inspection lamp or powerful hand lamp to check rafters, joists, floorboards, panelling, picture rail, skirtings and the cupboard under the stairs. In order to check flooring you need to take up a few floorboards to inspect the undersides and joists.

Before you start For working in a roof wear a thick cap or light helmet, old overalls and when spraying use old gloves, a light smog mask and goggles. If you have a sensitive skin apply a barrier cream. Never smoke while spraying or afterwards when there is still vapour in a confined space. Cover the cold water storage tank to avoid contaminating it with spray and paint any exposed rubber covered cables with a wood sealer before spraying. Avoid spraying expanded polystyrene insulation as woodworm fluid tends to dissolve it. Make sure before you start that any electrical wiring in the area is sound and well insulated.

A board cut to fit across several joists, with battens to prevent it slipping, will enable you to move about a roof without putting a foot through the ceiling.

Tackling the work Clean down all the timbers with a stiff brush and use a vacuum cleaner to remove the debris from between joists so that the woodworm fluid makes good contact with the wood. Take out any old bird's nests or pieces of loose wood.

Modern woodworm fluids will kill all stages of the life cycle so treatment can be carried out at any time of the year provided all surfaces are thoroughly wetted by the fluid.

Use a gallon sprayer that can be pumped up to maintain a good pressure and use a spray lance with a fairly coarse nozzle that gives a fan spray pattern. Reach well into the apex and eaves and if floorboards are involved take up every fourth or fifth board so that you can reach the undersides and joists. Replace boards and spray the top surface. Floors will take a week to dry out thoroughly but if you wish to replace furnishings quickly, cover the treated surface with a sheet of polythene.

WHAT IS ROT?

Rot in the timber of a house can often be dealt with successfully by the handywoman but only provided the treatment is really thorough.

Dry rot This is serious because it is caused by a fungus which has the ability to spread throughout a building, breaking down structural, joinery and flooring timbers. It does not, however, occur spontaneously in a well-maintained house. It is usually a symptom of neglect, or the consequence of faulty design or construction, because it thrives only in dampness and poor ventilation. If the defects causing these conditions are put right, the dry rot can be eradicated by thorough treatment.

Wet rot This is caused by one or more different types of fungus which do not normally spread from the original site of attack. Again, dampness and lack of ventilation enable wet rot to take hold and its presence is sometimes an indication that dry rot may be near by.

Recognising dry rot True dry rot is the name given to a particular decay of timber brought about by the activity of one particular species of fungus, *Merulius lacrymans*. The word 'dry' is descriptive of the dry and friable condition of the rotten wood.

Rust-red 'dust' caused by spores from a pancake-shaped fruiting body indicates an advanced attack of some duration. The spores only accumulate in still, unventilated conditions but will germinate on damp timber.

A covering of matted fungal strands over the timber occurs as thin sheets of silvery grey or mouse-grey appearance, tinged here and there with lilac or occasionally yellow patches. This sheet of combined hyphae is known as the mycelium.

In very humid conditions the covering of matted fungus over the timber, known as the mycelium, grows rapidly and is snowy white, rather like cotton wool, and the specific name, *lacrymans*, refers to a characteristic which the fungus shows in damp conditions when globules of water are formed like teardrops – *lacrymans* means 'weeping'.

Wood decayed by the fungus shows deep cracks, the wood breaks up into cubes and becomes dark in colour but light in weight owing to the breaking down of the cellulose.

A very important characteristic of dry rot is the ability of the fungus to produce water-carrying strands or 'rhizomorphs'. The importance of the rhizomorph is that it conveys the water from damper wood which has been decayed to drier wood elsewhere, the strands passing over brickwork, stone, or metal.

Wet rot indications Outbreaks of wet rot are almost twice as frequent as those of dry rot, but are seldom so serious. The wood-decaying fungus most often causing wet rot is the cellular fungus, *Coniophora cerebella*.

The fungal strands are never so thick as those of dry rot, seldom exceeding the diameter of thin string or twine. These strands are brownish or black and when growing on the surface of wood, or over damp plaster, often develop a dark fern-like shape.

The fruiting body and spores are rarely found indoors in any accumulation, but the spores are so light that they are present almost everywhere in the air, consequently any timber with a sufficiently high moisture content is likely to be attacked.

Causes of rot Dry rot cannot develop in wood containing less than about 25 per cent moisture, and the optimum moisture content for its growth is probably between 30 and 40 per cent. Poor ventilation and a high atmospheric humidity cause its rapid spread throughout buildings, and in such premises its familiar mushroom-like odour can be detected. The optimum temperature for growth is about 23°C (75°F), but the fungus is sensitive to higher temperatures, the maximum for survival being 26°C (79°F). A temperature of 40°C (104°F) will destroy the fungus in 15 minutes.

Wet rot requires more moist conditions than dry rot and the optimum water content for growth in the wood is said to be between 50 and 60 per cent – hence its name. It is correspondingly sensitive to drying.

The wet rot fungus attacks both hardwoods and softwoods, although the latter are probably more readily attacked.

In the decay caused by wet rot the damage very often remains hidden by a superficial layer or veneer of practically sound wood which reveals the decay beneath only when it is broken or penetrated by a sharp tool. When wood is severely decayed it becomes brittle and crumbles to powder between the fingers.

A piece of timber such as a floor joist or wall plate that is sufficiently damp to support a growth of wet rot, may also be attacked by dry rot in its less moist part. Similarly, timbers that have dried out enough to kill any wet rot attack may still support the dry-rot fungus so, when remedying the effects of either fungus, drastic measures are usually called for.

The first signs of dry rot may be buckling of the wood, or the appearance of cotton-wool-like growth on the wooden surfaces. This may be behind a skirting board, in a cupboard, or beneath panelling. Often, however, an attack starts on the underside of floorboards or joists where it will not be detected until it is in an advanced stage.

Treatment of dry rot Any outbreak of dry rot needs prompt, thorough treatment. Defective plumbing, faulty damp-proof courses and blocked air bricks or similar faults must first be put right. Cracked paintwork around window frames often allows driving rain to penetrate to the wood, setting up the conditions in which rot starts. Once the moisture is in the wood, it cannot evaporate because of the paint film.

In checking a building for dry rot, start from the outside. Examine the roof, downpipes, hopper heads, gutters; the condition of pointing, rendering, brickwork, or masonry; the level of the soil in relation to damp courses and air bricks. All should be checked to find where any water is getting into the building. Make sure that gutters and air bricks are not blocked. If the house has been flooded, or burst pipes have soaked timbers, be sure to check that the wood has been thoroughly dried out.

After inspecting the outside, make a systematic examination inside the house, even though the site of the outbreak may seem obvious.

If the outbreak of dry rot is easily accessible and obviously very limited in extent, *cut out and burn* the affected timber and cut out apparently sound wood for two feet beyond the last visible sign of decay. Soak the surrounding wood and masonry with Dry Rot Fluid and use it on replacement timber.

Unless the outbreak is very small and obviously easily treated, call in a specialist wood preservation firm to survey and make recommendations. Dealing with serious dry rot is no job for the amateur.

Clear any air bricks that have become blocked, to ensure adequate ventilation. Check the damp-proof course and carry out any necessary work to prevent rising damp. This work is best entrusted to an expert.

Treating wet rot The treatment of wet rot is less drastic than that required for dry rot, and as long as the cause of dampness is removed and the timber allowed to dry out, no further growth of the fungus will take place.

Test all timbers in the area of fungal attack with a strong, pointed instrument to determine the extent of subsurface breakdown. Cut out and burn all timber which has suffered surface or subsurface breakdown due to fungal attack, together with all dust, dirt and debris.

Select thoroughly dry, well-seasoned timber for replacement, cut to size and give two liberal coats of a good dry-rot fluid or wood preservative over all the surfaces of those replacement timbers and also over the adjacent surfaces of existing timbers and brick, block and concrete areas before placing the replacement timbers in position and fixing.

Timber adjacent to the exposed area should be thoroughly treated with a suitable fungicide by surface application. Ends of joists should also be painted with bituminous paint or covered by bituminous felt.

Treatment with a good proprietary fungicide by applying it liberally to the surface and immersing the cut end-grains in the fluid provides effective protection. This pre-treatment of new timber is a vitally important part of any remedial work and must be carried out after the timbers have been cut to size. Cut end-grains should be immersed for at least five minutes in the preservative to ensure good penetration. Remember that many specialist timber treatment companies make a good living out of dealing with outbreaks of dry rot that have been inadequately treated by amateurs.

The moral is, seek expert advice. It need cost nothing as most reputable specialists give free surveys with no strings attached.

EXTERNAL UPKEEP

EXTERIOR CHECK LIST

For most of these jobs, you will need professional help. In particular, the inexperienced should avoid working at a height. You will find the following notes handy for briefing and supervising your builder. Make sure all work is done as specified. Builders often skimp on roofs in particular as they know you cannot see what is going on!

The roof Loose or missing tiles or slates must be repaired or replaced. If possible examine your roof from the inside; climb up into the loft, and if your roof is unlined, turn off the light. Chinks of light will show up where tiles are cracked, missing or slipped. If your roof is lined, keep the light on and look for water stains which will indicate leaks (1).

Chimneys Crumbling brickwork should be re-built: it could be very dangerous. Crumbling mortar between bricks should be raked out and replaced. If in poor repair, the concrete 'flaunching' at the top of the stack into which the chimney pots are set could be causing damp (2). Chimneys no longer in use can be sealed off.

Roof flashings 'Flashings' seal the gaps where your roof meets another surface. You will find them around chimney stacks, dormer windows, skylights, over bay windows, around vent pipes and so on. Your flashings may be made of felt, mortar, lead, zinc, or of an asbestos/bitumen compound. If torn or cracked they will be letting in the damp, and should be repaired (3). Simple repairs may be possible with waterproof tape, or with several coats of a proprietary bituminous emulsion. Crumbling mortar fillets should be hacked off and renewed.

Gutters All gutters should be flushed through with a hose to clean, with a bowl placed at base of downpipe to catch debris. Check for small leaks occurring at joints between sections, or through cracking (4). A waterproof repair tape or a non-hardening mastic can be used for repairs. Damaged lengths should be replaced completely or repaired in part with glass fibre repair kit. The slope of gutters should

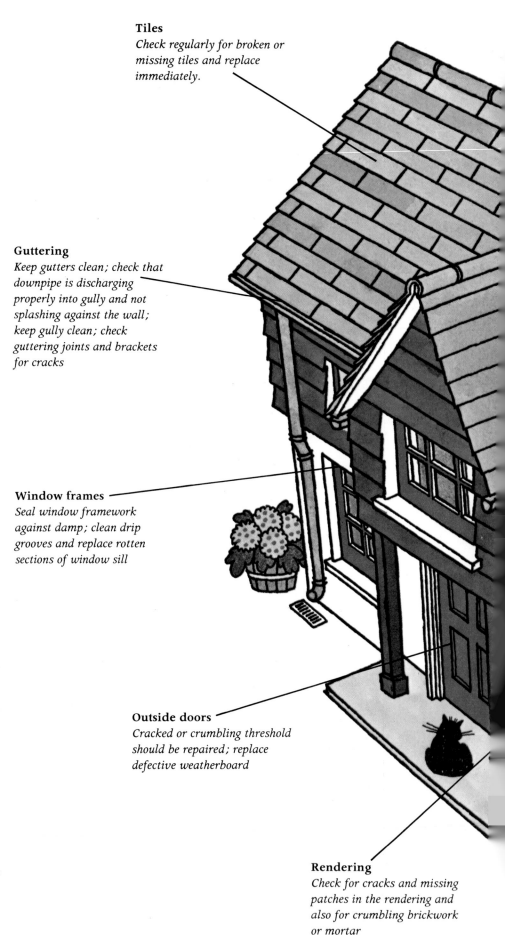

Tiles
Check regularly for broken or missing tiles and replace immediately.

Guttering
Keep gutters clean; check that downpipe is discharging properly into gully and not splashing against the wall; keep gully clean; check guttering joints and brackets for cracks

Window frames
Seal window framework against damp; clean drip grooves and replace rotten sections of window sill

Outside doors
Cracked or crumbling threshold should be repaired; replace defective weatherboard

Rendering
Check for cracks and missing patches in the rendering and also for crumbling brickwork or mortar

234

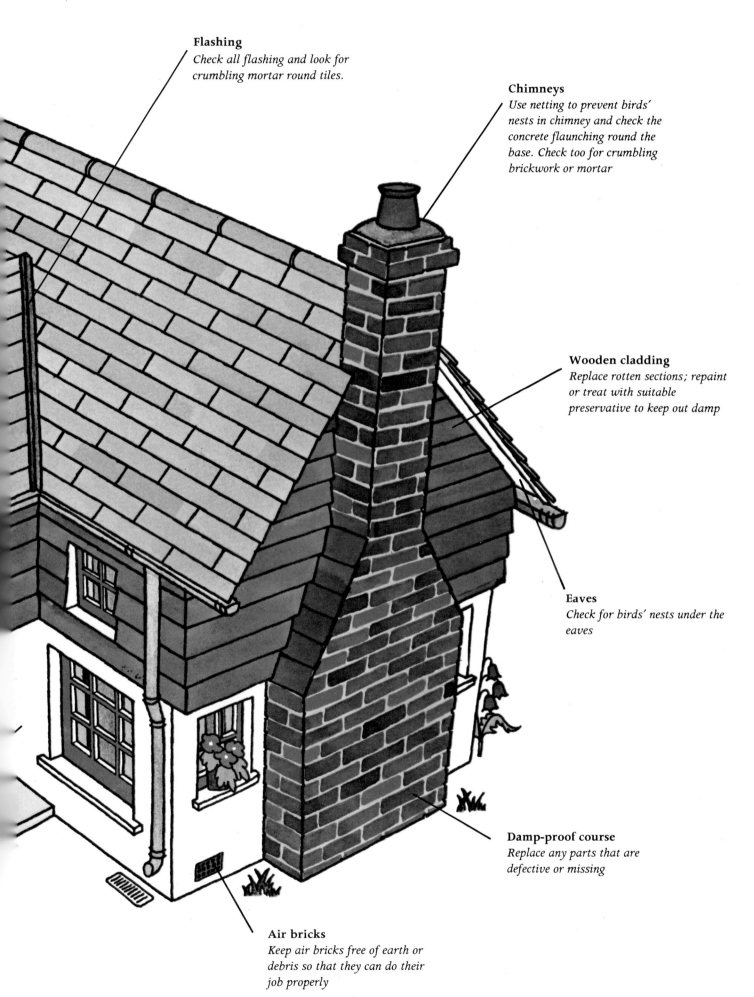

Flashing
Check all flashing and look for crumbling mortar round tiles.

Chimneys
Use netting to prevent birds' nests in chimney and check the concrete flaunching round the base. Check too for crumbling brickwork or mortar

Wooden cladding
Replace rotten sections; repaint or treat with suitable preservative to keep out damp

Eaves
Check for birds' nests under the eaves

Damp-proof course
Replace any parts that are defective or missing

Air bricks
Keep air bricks free of earth or debris so that they can do their job properly

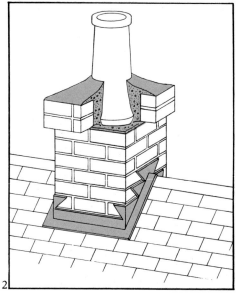

be adjusted if necessary, so that all water drains away. Check bracket fixings and have any parts of rotten fascia boards replaced. Cast-iron guttering can be replaced with a plastic system which needs little maintenance and no decoration.

Downpipes Check that each downpipe connects satisfactorily at its top with the gutter. Check downpipe brackets for firm fixings. Check that water can run freely down the pipe: blockages must be cleared if necessary. Make sure downpipes discharge into gullies at the bottom and not onto the ground or the wall (it may be necessary to replace their end sections) (5).

Gullies Old-fashioned gratings can be cleaned by scrubbing with hot water and soda, or placing in a fire for a few minutes. Blocked gullies should be cleared of debris and flushed through with water. A brick kerb can be built around a gully and fitted with a removable plywood cover to prevent

further blockages (6).

Pointing Pointing is the mortar between the bricks which crumbles after a while. All loose pointing should be raked out to a depth of at least 12 mm. ($\frac{1}{2}$ in.) and the crevices brushed out with a stiff brush. Re-pointing should be finished with a weather joint: the face of the mortar is cut back by about 12 mm. ($\frac{1}{2}$ in.) at the top of the crevice to prevent rainwater collecting (7).

Brickwork Porous walls allowing damp to reach the inside can be treated with a clear silicone water repellent. This should be applied to the exterior surface during a fine spell. It will also protect brickwork from frost.

Rendering and pebbledash Cracks and missing patches must be replaced speedily, as water can collect behind the rendering and cause damp patches on the inside walls (8). Really big cracks and holes must be cut back until sound rendering is reached. The holes can then be filled with mortar, which

should be applied in two layers. For pebbledash, pebbles can be mixed with the second layer. Larger cracks can be filled with a proprietary exterior filler. Hairline cracks can be disguised by a stone or masonry paint containing small particles of crushed rock. You will have to paint the whole area to avoid unsightly patches. Any mould or algae must be scraped before painting. Wash down the whole area with a solution of one part ordinary domestic bleach to 4 parts water. Repeat 24 hours later. Allow to dry for 2 days, and then rinse with clear water.

Wall tiles Wall tiles for cladding are nailed to battens which are nailed to the wall. Loose tiles can allow damp to enter. Each tile should be given a sharp tug to make sure it is firmly fixed. Loose tiles may be caused by corroded nails or rotten battens. Tiling should be stripped back until the defective tile is reached; this should be re-fixed, replacing rotten battening if necessary.

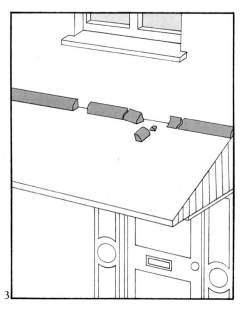

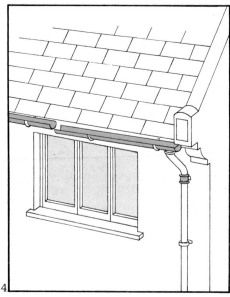

The rest of the tiles should then be re-fixed with new nails.

Wood cladding Rotten sections should be replaced. Old paint should be stripped off with scraper and paint stripper. New painting should consist of primer, undercoat and a minimum of two top coats. Old varnish can be removed with scraper or chemical paint stripper, and then the surface should be scrubbed with wire wool and water containing a little ammonia. A proprietary wood restorer can be used to restore the original colour, before re-varnishing.

Windows and doors All gaps between frameworks and walls should be sealed against damp. Non-hardening mastic can be used for narrow gaps, but crevices should be first cleaned out with a stiff brush. It is possible to paint over this type of filler, which is usually an ugly grey. Wide gaps will need an initial plugging with rope or rolled up rags, finished off with mastic. Renew all cracked areas of putty on window frames, using metal casement putty or dual purpose putty for metal frames (ordinary linseed oil putty is only suitable for wooden frames). All new putty should be painted within seven days, and the paint line should be carried onto the glass by about 3 mm. ($\frac{1}{8}$ in.). Rotten sections of window sills should be replaced. Drip grooves (narrow channels cut into the underside of your sill parallel with its edge) should be cleared. Bare timber sills and threshold should be oiled; cracked stone sills should be repaired and painted. Rotten weatherboards at base of exterior doors should be replaced (9).

Airbricks Airbricks provide ventilation for suspended floors, and prevent dampness from condensation. You will find them set low down in an outside wall, looking like an ordinary brick with small round holes, or a small grating. They should be cleared of clogged-up soil, leaves or rubbish.

Rising damp Houses built since the 1870's will have a damp-proof course (d.p.c.) set into the brickwork on the ground floor. Its purpose is to prevent water from the soil rising up the walls. Your d.p.c. will appear as a thick black line or an extra thick band of mortar running through the brickwork two or three courses above the ground. The d.p.c. can become bridged, thus allowing damp to enter the house. To ensure that your d.p.c. is clear, and able to perform its function, you should dig away any soil to at least 15 cm. (6 in.) below the d.p.c. (10).

The level of concrete paths and adjoining outbuildings should also be adjusted to below 15 cm. (6 in.) of the d.p.c. (10a & b) Any concrete rendering covering the d.p.c. should be hacked away (10c). If your d.p.c. appears defective even when cleared, you should enlist the services of a specialist company, who will also be able to advise on older houses.

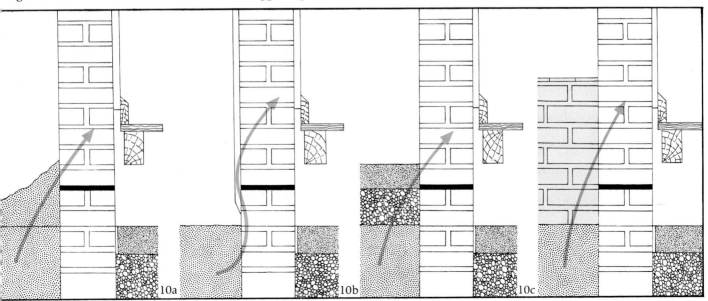

RUNNING YOUR HOME

Running a home efficiently is similar to running a small business, and to a lesser degree failure to run a home on sound business lines can cause trouble. Efficient management takes the anxiety out of budgeting and paying the bills and generally contributes to peace of mind.

FILING AND STORAGE

One of the most certain deterrents to running your home in a businesslike fashion is the lack of organised storage for the few necessary files and notebooks. These are usually so few that only about 85 cubic cm. (3 cu. ft) are required, but this space is well worth reserving. Bills and documents are dreary enough in their right place without having to ransack your whole living area to find them. Your make-up drawer, handbag and the breadbin are not suitable resting places for documents.

Desk area If you have no room for a desk in a living room, a small area of the kitchen is probably the best place. You will need a home file with folders for each category of document, a diary, writing paper, envelopes and stamps, pencils and pen (and you should publicly announce that they are yours and not to be borrowed), a reel of sellotape, a pair of scissors, a cash analysis book, an indexed telephone book with emergency telephone numbers easily available, a note pad and that is about all.

A small typewriter is by no means a luxury and carbon paper makes the keeping of copies of correspondence very easy. Anything of real negotiable value such as insurance policies and share certificates should be deposited in the bank. Above all, make a point of filing everything you may need later immediately the matter in hand has been dealt with.

One file should contain recipes. Some people collect them all the time. Space for cooking and reference books is also a great help.

MONEY

Looking after your money requires a little organisation and Mr. Micawber's

dictum still applies. Spend more than you earn, or of your housekeeping allowance, and troubles loom ahead. So budgeting must take priority. To many this is a dirty word and symbolizes an act which takes the pleasure out of spending but it involves a discipline which ensures that you know where you stand.

Planning ahead Even if you live alone, a cash analysis book is well worth keeping. It helps you to know *where* your money is going. There is a rhythm about most household expenditure that enables you to know when to expect the big horror bills – for heat, light, rent, mortgage, rates, etc. A good tip is to use your analysis book to budget ahead, making your entries in pencil and then to enter the actual amounts in ink as the bills are paid. The pencil figures will tell you roughly what to expect, the inked-in figures that the situation is better, or worse, than you expected. Budgeting ahead provides a good early warning system of financial trouble on the way. Banks provide detailed statements which should be filed, after reconciling their figures with your cheque stubs – mistakes have been known to creep into the system. National Giro, too, provide comprehensive statements whenever your account has operated.

Standing orders All banks, including National Giro, provide standing order facilities which are extremely useful for regular outgoings such as rent and H.P. commitments. They save money on postage. Local authorities allow payment of rates by monthly standing order, as do the public utilities – electricity, gas and central heating companies, a facility which reduces the sting of a huge half yearly or quarterly bill. Always file the bills to keep a check on consumption or an error in the bill.

Borrowing money Borrowing money costs money, but is a perfectly sound method of acquiring large items. Few of us would own houses or flats without building society or local authority loans. Bank overdrafts are convenient in emergencies but cost more than building society loans. It is a good idea to keep in close touch with your bank. Your manager can be a good friend and it is well worth meeting him. He can advise on all sorts of matters like insurance, making a will, savings and so on.

An account with a building society has much to commend it. If you are a regular saver the society will be much more inclined to allow you a mortgage. There is the added advantage that your money is earning interest free of tax and is easy to withdraw when required. All the details of your dealings are contained in one small pass book.

EMPLOYING PROFESSIONALS

Solicitor He is a professional friend you will certainly need if you are buying a property or signing a lease. It is not worth your while (unless you have more time on your hands than most) trying to unravel the complexities of conveyancing or the small print of any sort of legal document you may have to sign. Most solicitors are friendly and, like your bank manager, sources of all sorts of information you may think you will never need. He will rate a folder in your home file.

His fees are generally based on a scale which depends on the price of the house, or the amount of the rent. If the work is particularly complex, he will charge what is 'fair and reasonable'. If his charges seem unreasonable to you, apply to the Law Society for a decision.

Architect He is a professional who should enter your life if you are building a house or undertaking anything but the simplest home alterations or conversions. He can save you money by acting as a trained go-between in dealing with builders, plumbers and other suppliers of labour and services. He knows, too, about the structure of your home and should prevent you from carrying out alterations that might endanger the building.

Builders, plumbers and decorators Handle with care. Always ask for estimates in writing, several if possible for comparison, and ask for addresses of local people who have used their services recently if your job is of any magnitude, and check up on the quality of their work before engaging them. (See note about your friendly neighbourhood architect).

Public and other authorities You are never completely alone. The welfare and other people supply all sorts of services that can be of use to you. They range from the Citizens Advice Bureau through Marriage Guidance Councils, Alcoholics Anonymous, the Department of Health and Social Security to the Omsbudsman. When in doubt, the Citizens Advice Bureau will tell you whom to contact.

Insurance It is a comforting feeling to be hedged about by insurance. It is vital to insure your home, its contents, especially any valuables you may possess, and your car. Home insurance should cover any sort of accidental damage including Acts of God. Beyond these essential insurances, insurance by means of endowment and other policies are excellent ways to save. Your bank manager or your solicitor can guide you as to the type best suited to your needs, or insurance companies will supply quotations. Good, impartial judgment is sometimes needed, in which case you may need to consult an insurance broker. He should know which company is offering the best terms at any particular time.

Doctor Not much office work required beyond keeping your medical card in your files and the doctor's number and address and details of the local hospital on display in the kitchen (for many accidents happen at home and it is handy for your rescuer to know your doctor's name). Your doctor's folder in your file may be useful for notes on drugs you have been prescribed in the past, any to which you may be allergic, and other relevant health information.

CHILDREN

If you have children, keep a file of all their statistics – birth certificates, inoculation particulars, as well as school reports. Even their garment sizes are well worth recording. You should enter all significant dates in your diary. Beginning and end of term dates, parties and P.T.A. meetings should all be recorded. Keeping a diary provides an interesting record of their progress. Even details of their illnesses are invaluable to them in later life.

Modern aids to painless record-keeping are simple and often decorative. To use them effectively all you need is to train yourself to use them all the time – and the sooner you do this the better.

MORTGAGES

Building societies, insurance companies and local authorities lend money for house-buying, under certain conditions. Although the title deeds of the property will be transferred to the mortgagee (lender) as a security until the loan is repaid, the mortgagor (borrower) is, for all practical purposes, the owner.

Building societies: monthly repayments of a mortgage from a building society vary according to rate of interest and period of repayment. A householder qualifies for tax relief on his loan, though if he does not pay income tax at the standard rate he may benefit from the option mortgage scheme. If a building society is sure of the borrower's ability to repay the loan, it will normally lend about 80 per cent of what its surveyor thinks the house is worth (which may be less than the purchase price). The costs of the building society's solicitor and surveyor are paid by the borrower. Most societies have schemes for combining house-purchase with life assurance.

Insurance companies: these generally lend up to 75 per cent of their surveyor's valuation of the property (70 per cent if the borrower needs more than £7,000). This applies to freehold property and usually to leasehold property with at least another 35 years to run after the end of the loan period. In certain cases a company may advance up to 80 per cent of the valuation. To repay the loan, the borrower takes out an endowment life assurance policy with the insurance company.

Local authorities: all local authorities have power to lend money for house purchase. Usually the house must be in the area administered by the authority and be freehold or at least a 30 year leasehold. Some authorities will lend the full purchase price, but the normal loan is about 85 per cent. The interest rate is $\frac{1}{4}$ per cent above the rate at which the authority itself borrows the money from the Public Works Loan Board. Banks do not normally lend money for house purchase, but they may be prepared to give a customer what is called a bridging loan if he has to pay for a new house before receiving the money from the sale of his present one.

FENCES, WALLS AND HEDGES
The title deeds of a house, especially if it is part of a housing estate, may show who owns and should maintain the boundary fences, walls and hedges. Otherwise, there are certain legal 'presumptions'. For instance, each neighbour is presumed to own half a dividing hedge. If, however, it has a ditch alongside it, both hedge and ditch are presumed to belong to the person on the hedge side. Again,

fences and walls are presumed to belong to the person on whose ground any supporting posts or buttresses stand. The owner of a boundary is not legally obliged to repair it, unless his title deeds state that he must.

Shared fences, walls and hedges are regarded in law as being cut vertically between their joint owners unless repairs are covered by a covenant. Neither party can be forced to pay for repairs to be done, although neither must do anything to his half which would endanger the other half. In Scotland many fences and walls are under common ownership, which has the advantage that the owners share the cost of repairs.

FIXTURES AND FITTINGS
When a house is being sold, the question of what fixtures and fittings are included in the sale often arises. The general rule is that anything permanently attached to the land or house which cannot be removed without causing substantial damage is included, anything less firmly fixed – for example, a greenhouse standing on bricks or a free-standing kitchen range – is not.

To avoid any disputes, the purchaser should insist that a list of fixtures is prepared and included in the contract. Garden produce such as fruit and flowers (but not whole trees or shrubs) may be removed by the seller if it matures before the sale is complete.

Tenants are entitled to take with them any fixtures to whose removal the landlord has agreed and any ornamental and domestic fixtures which can be removed without substantial damage to the property.

Surveyor No one should buy a house without first having a survey done. (Building societies usually do their own.) This is particularly important if you are buying an old house, which might well have hidden disasters of all kinds, such as dry rot, woodworm, rising damp etc. His fees will range from £10.50 to £26.25 depending on the size of the property and the time taken to carry out the survey.

HOME IMPROVEMENT GRANTS
The kind and amount of grant you can claim depends on the classification of your area, which is decided by the local authority.

Housing Action Areas which covers slums, dilapidated city centres etc.,

have many types of grant available.
General Improvement Areas also qualify for a high level of help.
Other Areas are still entitled to some degree of help.

If you want to do a conversion or even just put in another lavatory, contact your local Town Hall and ask to speak to the Housing Officer. He will advise on the classification of your area and types of grant and provide the relevant application forms.

TYPES OF GRANT
Improvement Grant for general improvements to housing in disrepair or property conversion. This is available in all areas.

Conversion Grant covers the conversion of a property of three or more storeys (including basement) into separate units – also available in all areas.

Intermediate Grant allows the supply of missing standard amenities (bath, lavatory, hot and cold water supply etc.) This again is available in all areas.

Special Grant to supply missing standard amenities (bath, lavatory etc.) in multiple occupation dwellings.

Repairs Grant helps the needy to finance general repairs. Only available in Housing Action Areas or General Improvement Areas.

Environmental Works Grant to bring external appearances and grounds up to standard. This is only available in Housing Action Areas.

Qualifying Conditions

(1) Normally, no work must have been started before an application for a grant is made. (Local authority can waive this condition in special circumstances.

(2) An applicant must hold the freehold, or at least 5 years of the lease must remain.

(3) Owner occupiers must undertake that the house will remain their only or main dwelling for five years, occupied exclusively by themselves and members of their household. (This condition does not apply to Special Grants.)

(4) Landlords must undertake that the property will be available for letting for five years (seven years in Housing Action Areas and General Improvement Areas) as a residence to persons other than a member of the applicant's family.

Also, the rateable value of the property must not exceed £300 in Greater London or £175 elsewhere, and the building must not be later than 1961.

FIRST AID

Accidents will happen, in spite of measures taken to prevent them. When they do, you can make them less serious by knowing sufficient first aid to treat them properly. To learn the subject, it is possible to attend courses, including an emergency two hour crash course, run by the St. John's Ambulance Brigade. There are also a number of books on the subject.

THE FIRST AID KIT
Keep a first aid kit handy. There is no necessity to have an actual box, though it is advisable, but proper supplies can be kept in a clean box or drawer. Keep them readily available, but out of the reach of children.

What you will need Lint, gauze, cotton wool, a 25 mm. (1 in.), and a 50 mm. (2 in.) roll of bandage (remember it is better to have wider bandages than narrow ones, simply because you can always split a wide one down the middle), adhesive plasters, in varying shapes and sizes; mixed sterile dressings; triangular bandages for slings, or to secure fractured limbs; safety pins; a packet of needles; antihistamine cream; surgical spirit; bicarbonate of soda.

It is interesting to note that antiseptics are no longer considered a must, except to wash your hands in, to sterilise them before you help the injured person. First aid has been greatly simplified over the years, for practical reasons – complicated instructions cause panic at a time when calm is of the utmost importance. Also if the injury is serious, it is safer not to do more than the minimum yourself. *Ring for help.*

General procedure following an accident The first thing to do is keep calm. Your fear can spread to the patient, cause panic, or in severe cases even death. It is important to calm and reassure the patient, making him comfortable before you treat the injury. If the situation is confusing or gets out of hand, ring for help. Dial 999 for an ambulance rather than ringing your doctor. When the emergency service answers, give your name and address, and clear instructions as to where the ambulance is required. This may sound simple but it is surprising how often premature death can be caused by panic and the consequent inability to think of the simplest remedies. Write the call for help instructions in the lid of your first aid box, or drawer. If you tell yourself what to do, it is easier to follow.

FIRST AID FOR SOME COMMON ACCIDENTS
Burns Note first that you need not carry anything in your first aid kit for burns. This is because all you should do is to immerse the burnt part of the body in cold water and wait for the pain to subside. This can take up to 10 or 15 minutes. Dry gently and put on a dressing to keep the wound clean. If serious, ring for help. Do not try to remove clothing. Lay casualty down, and cover with a blanket.

Resuscitation This is the way to cope when someone has actually stopped breathing and is asphyxiated. It can be caused by an electric shock, gassing (i.e., a suicide) an obstruction in the throat, choking, or an overdose. So please keep all pills away from children, who can easily mistake them for sweets and suffer disastrous effects. If breathing has stopped, it is essential to get air into the lungs to inflate them, and quickly. Lay the person on his back. Tip the head back. Pinch the nostrils together. Seal his mouth with yours. Blow gently, watching for the casualty's chest to rise. Take your mouth away and watch the chest deflate. What you are doing is breathing for him until he can start to breathe naturally again. Other remedies, such as cardiac massage, must be left to the expert.
Always make sure that the tongue is in the right position, and does not block the throat. It can fall back and block the air passage.

Bleeding and dealing with wounds Whenever the skin is broken, a certain amount of bleeding will occur. This bleeding must be controlled and infection prevented. If the wound is minor (i.e. a cut or a graze), gently wash with water, washing away from the wound, and cover with dry, sterile dressings, remembering that damp wounds should not be covered with adhesive plaster, because it will not stick.

When the bleeding is severe, it is imperative to control the flow of blood, otherwise the patient can die of shock from the rapid loss of blood. Apply direct pressure with the fingers to the bleeding point, over a dressing if available. If a large wound, press sides of the wound firmly but gently together. Squeeze the end of the tube if possible, and try to make the blood flow uphill. This means lifting the limb or part of the body affected, if possible, although not if you can see it is broken as well. The flow of blood is lessened. Keep the pressure on the wound, apply a pad, and bandage firmly. If the patient has cut an artery, you need to be very swift in your actions. When serious, ring for help. If blood soaks through bandage, apply further dressings and pads on top of the original dressing and bandage more firmly.

An excessive loss of blood causes shock, which may be fatal. So reassure the patient, lay him down, cover him with a blanket, but do *not* give him a hot water bottle, or extra heat; and do not give him anything to drink.

The unconscious patient Any unconscious patient should be laid on his side, with the topmost leg up, in a bent position (i.e. at right angles to the body) (1). This stops the tongue from falling down the back of the throat and obstructing the airway. It is worth noting that a large number of people die not from their injuries, but because they are left lying on their backs, and the tongue chokes them. It takes precisely four minutes to stop breathing, so you must act calmly and swiftly. By turning the patient onto his side, the tongue will automatically fall out from the back of the throat.

Bruises Use a cold compress.

Poisons There are two types of poisons.

1. *Corrosive:* such as a household bleach. This will be painful in the mouth, throat and possibly the stomach, and there may be signs of burns around the mouth and in it.
Treatment: Do not try to make him vomit. If he is conscious, give him as much water, milk or barley water as possible, to dilute the poison. SEND FOR HELP. Remove urgently to hospital.

2. *Narcotics:* this means drugs, an overdose, or a child swallowing pills. There is no sign of burns to lips and mouth.
Treatment: If he is conscious, remove casualty to hospital quickly by car or ambulance. Do not try and make him vomit, or give him anything by mouth. If the patient is unconscious lay him on

his side in the recovery position described earlier. Check that the mouth and throat are free from obstruction. If there are signs of vomiting, ensure that the airways are clear (so that he cannot asphyxiate). Send for help. Remove the casualty to hospital quickly by ambulance.

Fainting If you think someone is about to faint sit him down immediately. Put his head between his knees.

If the patient has fainted, lay him on the floor, turn his head to one side, raise his legs on cushions. On recovery, sips of water may be given. It is not usually serious, and you probably know the cause, but if in any doubt, ring for help.

Electric shocks This may bring about a burn and unconsciousness. Treatment: switch off the current. If necessary give artificial respiration. Treat the burn (see earlier instructions).

Nose bleeds Sit the patient down in a current of fresh air if possible. Make him lean forward, and pinch the nose just below the hard part (the blood vessels are sited here at the bottom). Apply a cold compress to the nose. Send for a doctor if bleeding persists. Note that ice on the back of the neck, and keys down the back are old wives' tales. They do not do any good.

Broken bones Really all you need to know is if they are broken, in which case you ring for help. Normally the injury swells up, and the patient is totally unable to move. Make him as comfortable as possible, and cover with blanket until help arrives.

Sprains Apply a cold compress, then bandage firmly and call for your doctor. But if there is any doubt, treat as for broken bones.

Foreign bodies Pins and other small objects, such as coins and buttons, are often swallowed by young children. If you know what has been swallowed, then remember that as long as the objects are small, smooth or round, they need not necessarily be a cause for alarm. Eventually they will pass through the body. However, if in doubt, start by being calm yourself, then calm the patient. Talk gently. If the object is sharp dial 999. Do not try to give anything via the mouth, such as juices, tea or water Hospitals need an empty stomach when they delve down to extract the object, and a child who has drunk something is usually sick (cotton-wool sandwiches are out).

Choking This is now appallingly common, and needs quick action. If the sufferer an adult, thump sharply between the shoulder blades. If a young child, place across the knee, face downwards, and strike gently as above.

If a baby, hold securely by the feet, upside down, and strike lightly between shoulder blades.

Objects stuck in nose and ears Make NO attempt to remove them. Get the patient to hospital as soon as possible. If you try to do anything else (such as trying to get the objects out) you will only succeed in pushing them further into the ear or nose, causing more pain and anxiety, and the hospital is there with all the right equipment to deal with them immediately.

Foreign bodies in eyes Pull down the lower lid, and if you can see the object, remove with the corner of a clean hanky. If this does not work, take the patient to a doctor or hospital.

Stings If the sting is present, then remove it, first having calmed the patient. Use forceps or tweezers or the point of a needle which has been sterilised by passing it through a flame. Then apply antihistamine cream immediately, or surgical spirit, or a weak solution of ammonia, or a solution of bi-carbonate of soda.

If the sting is in the mouth, give a mouth wash comprising one teaspoon bi-carbonate of soda to a tumbler of water. If there is much swelling there, or any difficulty in breathing, place the patient in a recovery position and give him ice to suck. This is to avoid blocking the throat and causing suffocation. SEEK MEDICAL ADVICE IMMEDIATELY.

Mosquito bites These are very common and such a nuisance. The best remedy is to apply vinegar to the bite as it is immediately soothing and stops the swelling.

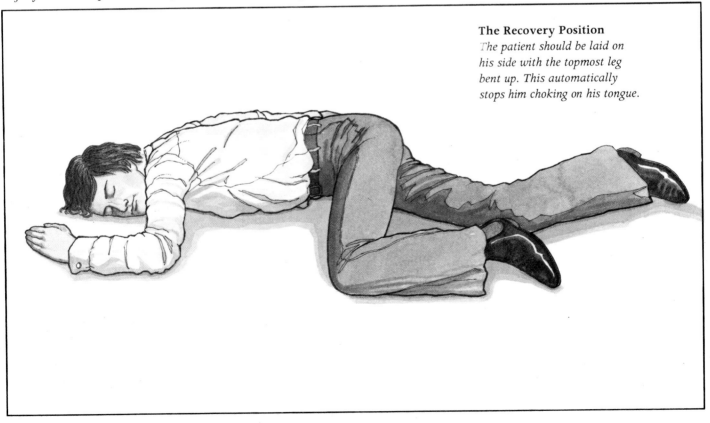

The Recovery Position
The patient should be laid on his side with the topmost leg bent up. This automatically stops him choking on his tongue.

GLOSSARY

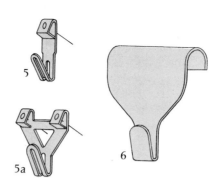

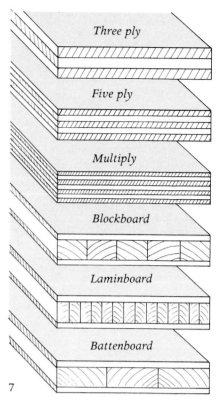

Three ply

Five ply

Multiply

Blockboard

Laminboard

Battenboard

7

USEFUL HARDWARE FITTINGS

Round cup-hooks in brass or coloured plastic can be used for a multitude of hanging purposes. They can be screwed into a vertical surface (e.g. edge of shelf) or into a horizontal surface (e.g. underside of shelf).

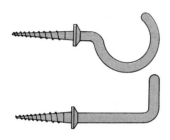

Square dresser hooks are easier to use for objects with thicker handles, such as mugs and kitchen utensils.
Rod sockets are handy for fitting hanging rails (1).

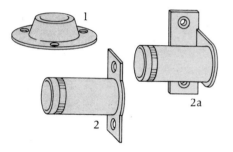

Curtain rod brackets come in two versions: *straight* for fitting against a return wall (2), or *cranked* for flush mounting (2a).
Small hooks and eyes can be used with expanded curtain wire for a curtain that is quick and easy to make – simply run the wire through a top hem (3).

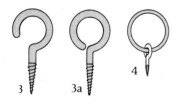

Screw rings are useful for hanging pictures (4).
Picture hangers come in a single or a double version; the latter is for heavier pictures (5 and 5a).

Moulding hooks can be used to hang pictures from old-fashioned picture rails (6).
Mirror plates can be used to fix small cupboards to the wall (two versions).
Cabin hooks are useful for providing a lock on sliding doors.

Repair and corner plates Various types can be used to repair old furniture or to strengthen your own structures.

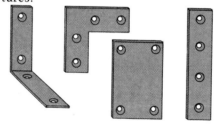

BASIC SIZES OF SAWN SOFTWOOD

Half the secret of successful d-i-y is getting to know the materials in your local d-i-y or timber shop, so that you can exploit their properties and standard sizes to your best advantage.
Chipboard is made from wood particles firmly bonded together; it is less strong than solid wood but much cheaper. The cheapest grades have a slightly pitted surface, but you can stain or paint them satisfactorily. You can buy chipboard 1·25 cm. or 2 cm. ($\frac{1}{2}$ in. or $\frac{3}{4}$ in.) thick, and the standard sheet size is 244 cm. by 122 cm. (7 ft by 4 ft). The board can be used for shelving etc., and standard widths are available, including 23 cm. (9 in.) and 30·5 cm. (12 in.). These boards usually have a decorative facing, in plain white melamine, or a real or imitation wood veneer. For lightweight objects, chipboard shelving should be supported at least every 92 cm. (3 ft), but shelves for heavy books will need supports every 46–51 cm. (18–20 in.).
Hardboard is a brown sheet material commonly 3·2 mm. ($\frac{1}{8}$ in.) thick, with a smooth side and a rough side. Although it is not very strong on its own, it can be used very satisfactorily if glued and pinned to a frame of softwood battens. You must position the framing right at the edge of the hardboard sheet, and the board must be supported along its length every 41 cm. (16 in.), plus cross supports every 122 cm. (4 ft). The standard sheet size is the same as for chipboard (see above) but lots of smaller sizes are also available.
Tempered hardboard has improved strength and water-resistant qualities.
Enamelled hardboard can be used for lining walls and ceilings in bathrooms and kitchens, and for splashbacks.
Moulded hardboard is available for pelmets and other fittings.
Perforated hardboard, often called peg board, can be used in conjunction with special clips for hanging kitchen utensils, etc.
Laminated boards Numerous types are available (7) including plywood, blockboard and laminboard. Although expensive, these boards are very strong, and easy to work with. Consult your supplier for the best board for the job you have in mind.

Countersunk head. For general carpentry and joinery.

Roundhead. For fixing sheet material too thin to be countersunk.

Raised countersunk head. For use with ironmongery and screwcups.

Dome head. For fixing mirrors and plastic panels.

Other drive methods. Phillips and Pozidriv heads.

Generally preferred screw sizes

Length in	mm	Diameter 0	1	2	3	4	5	6	7	8	9	10	12	14	16	18	20 guage mm
		1·6	1·8	2·0	2·3	2·6	2·9	3·3	3·7	4·1	4·5	4·9	5·6	6·3	7·0	7·7	8·4
¼	6·4	○	○	○	○	●											
⅜	9·5	○	○	○	●	●	●	●		○							
½	12·7			○	○	●	●	●	●	●	○	○					
⅝	15·9				○	○	●	●	●	●	●	○	○				
¾	19·1				○	○	●	●	●	●	●	●	○				
⅞	22·2					●	●	●	●	●							
1	25·4				○	●	●	●	○	●	●	●	●	○			
1¼	31·8					○		●	●	●	●	●	○	○			
1½	38·1					○	○	●	●	●	●	●	●	●	○	○	○
1¾	44·5					○		○	●	●	●	●	○	○	○		
2	50·8					○		○	●	●	●	●	○	○	○	○	
2¼	57·2							○	○	●	○	●	●	○			
2½	63·5							○	○	●	●	●	○	○			
2¾	69·9								○		●		○				
3	76·2								○	●	●	●	●	○	○		
3¼	82·6											○	○	○			
3½	88·9									○		○	○	●	○	○	
4	101·6									○		○	○	○	○	○	○
4½	114·3												○	○	○		○
5	127·0												○	○	○	○	○
6	152·4													○	○	○	○

● Slotted and recessed head   ○ Slotted head

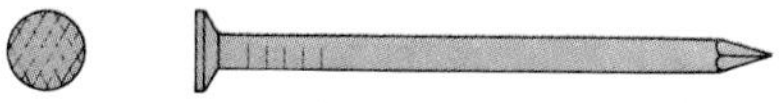

French or round wire nail. General carpentry, case making. Strong fixing.

Oval wire nail (oval lost or brad head). Joinery, unlikely to split wood if section follows grain.

Round lost head. Joinery. Head can be punched below surface leaving only a small hole.

Cut floor brad. All-purpose carpentry nail.

Cut clasp. General-purpose carpentry. Grips strongly.

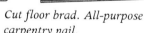
Panel pin for light joinery and cabinet work. Fine gauge.

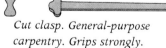
Veneer pin. Very fine shank and head for small mouldings.

Hardboard (deep-drive or diamond-point) pin. Head is self-countersinking.

Screw nail. For securing sheets of ply, hardboard or metal to timber, e.g. floors.

Helical threaded nail. For roofing, especially corrugated sheets.

Plaster-board nail. Has jagged sides to assist holding; 30 mm., 40 mm. (1¼ and 1½ in.).

Clout nail (slate nail). Roofing slating, fencing.

Extra-large head clout (felt nail). Roofing felt and external fabric.

Pipe (chisel-point) nail. Fixing drain pipes and gutters direct into masonry.

Masonry nail. Hardened steel to penetrate masonry and concrete.

Chair nail. Decorative upholstery work.

Cut tack. Upholstery, carpets, canvas and other heavy fabrics.

Sprig. Headless tack for holding glass into wooden frames.

Staple for fixing wire to wood. Made mostly from galvanised wire. Tenterhook has longer point on one side for easy fixing.

SOME SIMPLE WAYS OF JOINING WOOD AND BOARD

Choose nails which are around three times longer than the thickness of the timber they must hold, and always nail your lighter work to your heavier.

To make strong nailed joints, drive nails in from opposite directions and bend the points into the wood; this is called clench nailing. Where joints meet at right angles, they should be skew-nailed. The sections can be simply butt-jointed, but a housing joint will be stronger, as shown in the drawing below.

Dovetail nailing, where the nails are fanned slightly inwards, provides the best grip when nailing into end grain. The diagram shows a simple joint for man-made boards, using proprietary plastic blocks.

Corrugated fasteners (Wiggle nails) can be used for battens to make simple frameworks.

MAKING A FIXING INTO A WALL

It is not possible to screw directly into a wall. It is necessary first to drill a hole, then to fill the hole with a suitable 'plug' into which the screw can be fixed. The plug then holds the screw securely in the hole.

For fixings into brick, stone, breeze block and similar materials, first carefully mark the position of the necessary fixings. Then make a hole in the wall using an electric drill or hand drill fitted with a masonry bit; or you can use an inexpensive tool called a Rawldrill, which you tap gently with a hammer, turn, and then tap again, tapping a bit harder when you are through the plaster. Your screw will need to be long enough to penetrate through the plaster and about 2–2·5 cm. ($\frac{3}{4}$–1 in.) into the masonry.

When you have made your hole deep enough (you can mark your drill bit with adhesive tape as a guide), insert the tip of your screw into a plug – nylon plugs are well-suited for amateurs, though fibre plugs make firmer fixings. Give the screw a couple of turns, and push both screw and plug home into the hole. Then remove the screw and re-insert it into the hole through whatever you are fixing – e.g. a bracket, or a pre-drilled timber batten.

It is very important that screw, plug and hole are all the same size, therefore make sure that you buy screws and plugs of the same number. Number 8 screws and plugs, for example, are suitable for fixing shelves, and you can buy a Rawldrill, and a selection of screws and plugs, all number 8's, in a handy pack. Masonry drill bits are also numbered accordingly.

Various spring toggle fixings are available for making fixings into cavity walls, partitions and hollow doors etc.

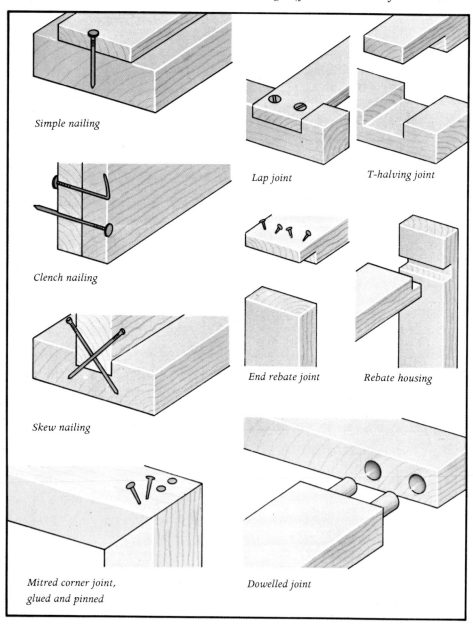

Simple nailing

Clench nailing

Skew nailing

Mitred corner joint, glued and pinned

Lap joint

T-halving joint

End rebate joint

Rebate housing

Dowelled joint

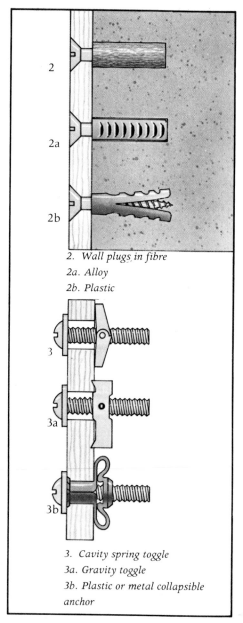

2. Wall plugs in fibre
2a. Alloy
2b. Plastic

3. Cavity spring toggle
3a. Gravity toggle
3b. Plastic or metal collapsible anchor

When tackling d-i-y jobs, the first major hurdle for the uninitiated is all the unfamiliar words and phrases used in leaflets, instructions, catalogues, shops and so on. Here is an alphabetical guide to some of them; the explanations to other puzzling terms are made clear within the relevant sections. To start with, we suggest you have a quiet read through the list below – it is the kind of information that could come in handy at any time. The words and phrases come from all aspects of home maintenance, including decorating, electricity, building, plumbing, carpentry and so on. You may not even need to know their meaning for the type of work you tackle yourself, but these terms could crop up when discussing work with a tradesman, and our list will make sure everyone is talking the same language.

AC This stands for alternating current, as opposed to direct current (DC). Alternating current reverses its flow at a regular rate, rather like the pattern of waves in the sea. With mains electricity in this country, the complete cycle occurs 50 times a second, and this is known as the *frequency* of the supply. DC current is now supplied only to very few districts in this country, and is the type of current produced by batteries. Inside a house, AC current can be transformed to very low voltages – for example, for use in bells and buzzers.

Aggregate This is a collective term for the mineral particles which are mixed with cement to form concrete. There are various grades. For example, *heavy* aggregate is made from sand, gravel, crushed stone or brick, and is used in concrete. *Fine* aggregate, usually made from sand, can be used in plaster, or in final rendering (q.v.).

Airbrick This looks like an ordinary brick, but contains small round holes, or a small grating. It will be set low down in an outside wall, and its purpose is to ventilate wooden ground floors, and prevent dampness caused by condensation.

Amps Short for amperes. A unit of measurement for electric current named after a French scientist. Amps are used to measure the volume of the flow of an electrical current – you could compare them with the number of gallons or litres flowing in a water pipe. See also *Volts* and *Watts*.

Arris This is the sharp corner or edge where two surfaces meet; you may come across this term in brickwork or masonry, where the corners of bricks and stones are known as *arrises*.

Asphalt This is made by adding sand or gravel to bitumen (q.v.), to produce a black, hard-wearing, waterproof material used for roofing, paving, flooring, and various kinds of waterproofing. It is applied hot, when it is soft and easy to work with. It hardens on cooling.

Balusters These are the upright sections that support the hand-rail on a staircase.

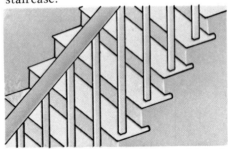

Batten A length of timber which is small in cross-section. Battens are used for the supporting frame of structures such as cupboards, window-seats and so on, e.g. 5 cm. × 2·5 cm. (2 in. × 1 in.). Or for supporting wall-fixed shelves and cupboards, e.g. 16 mm. × 2·5 cm. ($\frac{5}{8}$ in. × 1 in.) or 16 mm. × 5 cm. ($\frac{5}{8}$ in. × 2 in.).

Beading is a small strip of moulding, made of timber or plastic, often used to finish off work, either to conceal a join, or for decoration.

Bearer Bearers provide *horizontal* support; this term is often used for small timber sections supporting shelves, sinks, cupboards and so on.

Bevel An angled or sloping edge, as for example in a bevelled mirror, which has a decorative sloping edge.

Bitumen A tar-like waterproof material which is used for making asphalt,

roofing felts, and damp-courses. Bituminous coatings are often applied to exterior pipes and gutters to seal and protect them. Before painting, you must seal with an aluminium sealer, otherwise the paint top-coat will become discoloured.

Bleeding through The technical term for discolouration of a top coat of paint, caused by colouring coming through from the surface underneath. It can usually be cured by the correct primer.

Blockboard See previous reference section on materials.

Bolster Bricklayer's chisel.

Breeze blocks Large building blocks of precast clinker concrete.

Brick Standard metric size is now 215 by 102·5 by 65 mm. ($8\frac{1}{2}$ in. × 4 in. × $2\frac{1}{2}$ in.), slightly smaller than the old imperial brick. New metric bricks can be used with existing brickwork by very slightly increasing the mortar joint. *Commons* are general building bricks; *facings* are bricks which are decorative, as well as being durable and weather-resistant; *engineering* bricks are practically impervious to moisture and are very hard with a high load-bearing capacity; *stocks* are clay bricks made in various districts, the colour varying accordingly, e.g. Kentish stocks are usually yellow.

Brushing out Painter's language for spreading or brushing paint out to form an even coating over a surface.

Burning-off A method of removing paint by using a blowlamp to soften and blister the paint covering, which can then be scraped away.

Butt-joining Joining two surfaces together without any overlap; it is the kind of join you make when hanging wallpaper.

Cavity wall A wall made in a double layer, with a gap in the middle, tie-irons or cavity ties hold the two walls together at intervals.

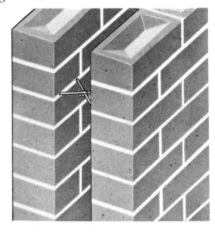

Cement is made from chalk or limestone and clay, with a small amount of gypsum. It is used for making mortar (q.v.) and for concrete (q.v.). Small quantities for minor repairs are available from DIY shops.

Centres Carpentry or fixing instructions will often tell you to fix things 'at x centres'. This means make your fixings at intervals of whatever x is.

Chamfer This is a carpentry term, describing where two surfaces meet at right angles, and the edge is shaved away to form an angled corner.

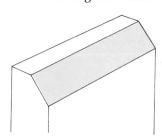

Channel This simply means a groove, either cut into a material or fixed onto it as a 'U' shaped section.

Chase or chasing A channel or groove cut out to receive a pipe or wiring, for example.

Chipboard See previous reference section on materials.

Circuit breakers are fitted to fuse boxes in some houses, instead of fuses, as a protection against overloading.

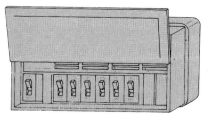

Cisterns are tanks for water, either for storage or for flushing.

Cladding Any material used to face a building or structure.

Concrete is made from a mixture of cement, sand, water and aggregate (q.v.), which sets hard and is used for a variety of building purposes.

Conduit The protective casing for electric cables.

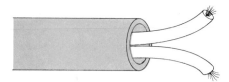

Coping is the brick or stone used to finish off the top of a wall.

Course A horizontal layer of bricks.

Cove A moulding which fits into the angle between the top of the wall and

the ceiling – useful for concealing cracks, or the edges of ceiling tiles.

Cramps An alternative for *clamp*.

Cross-lining Hanging lining paper lengthways (horizontally) so that the joins in the lining will not occur at the same places as the vertical joins in the top covering.

Curtain wall This is a term you may meet in modern architecture for a non-loadbearing (non-structural) wall.

Cutting-in is a term for painting right up to an edge, e.g. on window frames. It is best to use a special brush with an angled edge.

Dado The lower part of an inside wall, with a different decorative finish from the rest. Dados can vary in height from about 76 cm. (2 ft 6 in.) to 1·37 m. (4 ft 6 in.).

Damp-proof course (d.p.c.) The layer at a bottom of a wall that stops the progress of damp. It can commonly be made of slate, lead, bitumen, copper or zinc. Electro-osmosis, and injected silicone are ways of installing a d.p.c. in an old building.

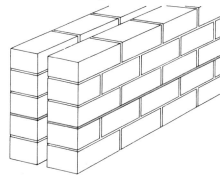

Damp-proof membrane A damp-proof layer applied to floors to check the penetration of damp.

Distemper A type of paint which is virtually obsolete. It was made from finely ground chalk (whiting), colouring, and size (q.v.).

Dovetails are found in 'dove-tail' joints. Two pieces of timber to be joined at right angles are cut into a series of fan shapes which fit into each other exactly: very strong and decorative.

Dowel A small piece of wood (or sometimes metal) shaped like a cylinder, and used for fixing two pieces of material firmly together.

Drop pattern A term used for wall-coverings, where the pattern does not repeat in a horizontal line from edge to edge of paper, but 'drops' at each joint.

Drying-out The process by which new plaster and brickwork loses the large quantities of water used in the building process. During this period, no paint or wallpaper should be applied.

Dry rot Wood decay caused by fungus.

Earthed When an appliance is earthed, it is in effect connected for safety reasons to the mass of the earth. The earth wire in a flex is coloured yellow and green, the live is coloured brown (previously red) and the neutral is coloured blue (previously black).

Eaves The lowest overhanging part of a sloping roof.

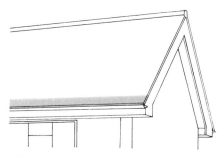

Efflorescence Technical term for white crystalline substances that sometimes appear on new brickwork or fresh plaster; deposits should be cleaned off with dry coarse cloth, or brushed away. Then apply two or three coats of a neutralising liquid.

Eggshell Used to describe the level of shine in a paint finish, about halfway between matt and gloss.

Elbows are pipe fittings for connecting two lengths of pipe to each other at various angles, e.g. 90°, 135°

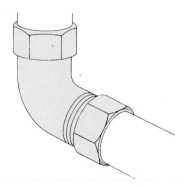

Elevation Term used by architects and designers for drawings to scale of the vertical (or upright) parts of a building, i.e. each wall of the building seen straight on from the front; usually drawn in conjunction with a plan, which illustrates the design of the building as seen in horizontal section.

Embossed papers have a raised pattern,

and are also known as relief papers.

Female fitting Plumbing term for a pipe fitting which has a socket, plain or threaded, into which a tube or 'male' fitting can be inserted.

Figure Used when talking about timber to describe the character of the graining patterns.

Fillers The wide range of preparations available for filling holes, dents, cracks, chips, etc. There are different types according to the material(s) to be filled.

Fillet A term used in joinery for a small, thin strip of wood.

Flat A 'flat' finish is a matt finish.

Flock paper and vinyls have a raised pile design, with a velvety texture.

Flush To finish off flush is to finish off level or flat.

Fuses Cartridge fuses are small tubes sealed at both ends with metal caps. They contain a deliberately weak link of thin wire which protects an electrical circuit from overloading, as a safety measure.

Gauge A standard of measure for the thickness of items such as sheet metal, wire, and screws.

Galvanized When steel is galvanized, it has been coated with zinc to prevent rust.

Gland A sealing ring around the stem of a tap, valve or fitting. Glands prevent leaking and are generally adjustable.

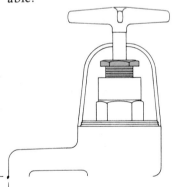

Glasspaper is the correct term for sandpaper available in coarse, medium and fine grades for different applications.

Glazing beads are strips of timber used with putty to hold glass within a frame.

Grain This describes the way the fibres of wood run.

Ground The term used for a plain background colour, of say, a wallpaper or carpet.

Grout or grouting is a waterproof cement-based paste used for filling in gaps between ceramic tiles; conveniently available ready-mixed.

Gully Gullies at ground level outside a house carry waste fluids (e.g. from sinks and baths) down into the drains.

Hardboard See previous reference section.

Hardcore Broken brick, stone or rubble used as a base for floors, pavings and roads.

Hardwood Simply means timber from any deciduous tree, and even includes balsa wood.

Hips The line where two sloping edges of a roof meet.

Housing A channel (or groove) usually cut across the grain to 'house' or hold fittings such as shelves.

Immersion heater A metal-sheathed electric element inserted into a hot water tank or cylinder to heat the water.

Inspection chamber Commonly called a manhole. A way of getting down to an underground drainage system.

Jamb The vertical face inside a door or window opening.

Jelly paint – see thixotropic.

Joist Timber or steel beam supporting a floor or ceiling. An r.s.j. (rolled steel joist) is used to support a ceiling when a structural wall has been removed.

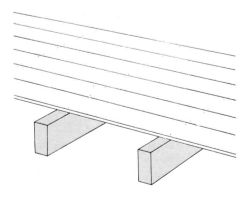

Jubilee clips Handy bands of metal which can be tightened by means of a metal screw to fit rubber hose or piping firmly onto taps.

Kerf The cut made by a saw.

Key To key a surface is to roughen it so that another material can adhere properly, in painting, for example.

Kilowatt A unit of electricity equal to 1,000 watts.

Kilowatt hour The amount of electricity used by an appliance is measured in kWh; this is 1,000W used for one hour.

Knots are the round marks left in timber by branches. 'Live' knots must be sealed with 'knotting', a proprietary compound made from shellac and methylated spirits, before painting, otherwise sticky resinous substances may start to bleed through (q.v.) after a while. 'Dead' knots, usually black around the edge, will come out easily; they should be removed, and the gap filled.

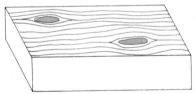

Lagging The insulating material which is wrapped around pipes and tanks to prevent them from freezing. Hot water tanks should also be lagged as an economy measure.

Lap joint Wallpaper joint with a slight overlap (c.f. butt joint).

Laying-off A term used in painting for the final brush strokes, which should leave the surface absolutely smooth. As a general rule, you should 'lay off' on wood in the direction of the grain.

Lintel The stone, timber or reinforced concrete beam spanning an opening such as a door or window.

Load-bearing wall A wall which is carrying the weight of the structure above it, which could be another storey, or the roof.

Making good Getting rid of surface defects before painting or papering.

Masking out Covering up a surface (e.g. with adhesive tape) to prevent paint from adhering.

Mitre A 45° diagonal join between two right-angled surfaces. Usually cut with the aid of a mitre block.

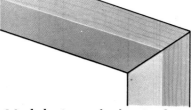

Module A standard unit of size.

Mortar A mixture of lime or cement with sand and water for joining and bedding bricks, stones etc.

Mortise A hole, usually rectangular in shape, which has been cut out of a piece of wood to take a fitting. In the case of joints, the *mortise* is cut to take the *tenon*, which is the shaped end of the piece of wood to be joined, cut exactly to fit the mortise hole.

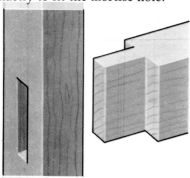

Mullion A vertical division between windows; it can be stone, metal or wood.

Newel The main supporting post for stairs and bannisters.

Nipple A small valve which when opened with a key allows air to escape from a system.

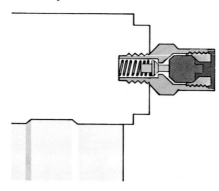

Nosing The overhanging part of a stair tread.

Offering up Fixing instructions will sometimes tell you to 'offer up' the fixture to the wall; this means hold it in the right position, so that you can mark the correct position for the fixings.

Oilstone A fine-grained stone used with a lubricant for sharpening tools.

P.a.r. An old-fashioned term standing for 'planed all round'. Prepared, or planed timber, will be slightly smaller, say 3 mm. ($\frac{1}{8}$ in.), than its stated size.

Pebble dash is a wall surface made from fine gravel thrown onto soft mortar.

Pilot hole A hole drilled to make passage easier for the subsequent screw.

Plug To plug a wall is to fill a pre-drilled hole with a material (e.g. wood, fibre, or nylon) which will take a screw.

Plumb simply means vertical or true.

Pointing The mortar joints between brickwork; re-pointing involves raking out the old, soft mortar and re-filling the joints with mortar mix.

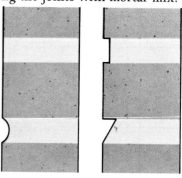

Primers (There are many different types suitable for different surfaces). They are a vital part of the painting processes, ensuring that the paint can adhere to the surface; on some surfaces primers prevent staining; on metals they guard against corrosion; they are also used to seal porous surfaces.

Quarry tiles Durable clay floor tiles, of a reddish colour.

Quoin The external corner of a wall.

Rails Horizontal parts of a frame, e.g. for a door or a table.

Rebate A rectangular recess or step cut along an edge of a piece of wood.

Rendering A layer of cement mortar applied as a protective coating to outside brickwork.

Reveal The side of a window or door opening.

Ring main An electrical circuit arranged in the form of a ring.

Riser The vertical part of a step.

Rubbing down The process of making a surface level, e.g. before painting, by using an abrasive (q.v.).

Screed A thin layer of plaster on a wall, or a thin layer of concrete applied to level a floor.

Scribing Marking a cutting line, usually with a knife or some other sharp instrument. Scribing strips or pieces are cut from thin timber or hardboard to fill uneven gaps between walls and fitments such as sink units, or built-in wardrobes.

Seasoning Allowing timber to dry out before it is used.

Section The shape of an object (e.g. a moulding) as you would see it if the whole thing was cut through at right angles to its face. Sectional drawings used to illustrate instructions can seem very confusing, but once you learn to understand them, they are extremely helpful.

Shake A fault in a piece of timber, usually a split or a crack.

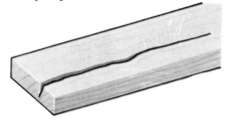

Size Thin liquid glue used to seal a porous wall before hanging paper; do not size emulsion-painted walls.

Slip The ease with which a pasted length of wallpaper or vinyl can be moved when first applied to the wall (to allow correct positioning).

Soaking means leaving a length of pasted wallpaper folded to become pliable before hanging. Different papers need different soaking times.

Soffit This describes the *underside* of an architectural feature. The soffit board, for example, is the horizontal board fixed to the underside of overhanging rafters.

Softwood simply means timber from cone-bearing trees, not necessarily particularly soft.

Solvent Liquid which will dissolve or soften other substances.

Spreading capacity The average area covered by paint, varnish etc., expressed in sq. m. per litre. Will vary according to porosity of surface.

Spur An electrical term, meaning a branch cable from a ring circuit.

Stetcher A brick laid with its long sides in line with the face of the wall.

Stile The upright at the edge of wooden framing.

Stop cock The valve on a pipe which allows you to turn off the water supply.

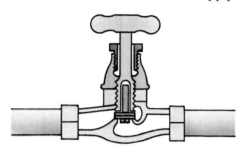

Stopped If a channel (q.v.) or rebate (q.v.) is stopped, it means that it does not run the whole length of the piece of timber.

Stopping Trade term for filling gaps and cracks before painting.

Stoved (as in stoved enamel), A paint coating which has been dried and hardened in an oven.

String The timber side of a staircase which supports the steps.

Strippers Various proprietary mixtures of chemical solvents which can be applied to remove old paintwork. always follow directions on the bottle carefully. *Stripping* is also the term used for removing old wallcoverings.

Stucco A coat of fine plaster on a wall or ceiling.

Studs These are the uprights in a partition. A stud partition is constructed on a timber framework or skeleton.

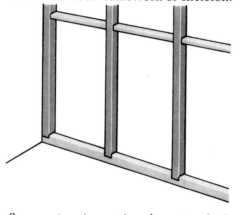

Sugar soap A caustic substance which is dissolved in water and used for washing down dirty paintwork before repainting.

Template A wood or metal pattern used as a guide for marking out a shape before cutting.

Thermal capacity The amount of heat a substance will absorb and store.

Thermostat A device for maintaining a constant temperature.

Thinners are liquids which are mixed with paint to make it more workable.

Thixotropic describes specially-constituted jelly paints which cover in one coat, will not run, and do not need stirring.

Throat A narrowing in a chimney flue.

Tolerance The agreed amounts by which sizes may differ from standard sizes, to allow for imperfections in cutting etc.

Traps Sinks, WCs and gullies all have traps to seal off smells coming from the drains. The trap is a section of the pipe shaped so that water always remains in it to act as the seal – e.g. the S bend.

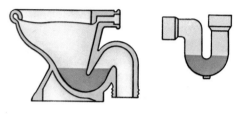

Turpentine substitute is white spirit.

Two-pack Describes products (e.g. adhesives and paints) which must be mixed together to react before use.

Unit The charge for electricity is based on the number of units used. A unit is 1,000 watts (1kW) of electricity used for one hour. See also *Kilowatt*.

Veneer Very thin sheets of decorative timber, used as a surfacing material.

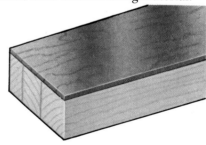

Volts (V) The unit for measuring the pressure or force which causes an electric current to flow in a circuit.

Water hammer Knocking sound occurring when a pipe is turned off quickly.

Watts The pressure of an electric current is measured in volts. The size of the current is measured in amps. The resulting power is measured in watts. The wattage and voltage of an appliance are usually marked on it.

Wet-and-dry-paper Waterproof abrasive papers that can be used wet for rubbing down paintwork, the water acting as a lubricant.

INDEX